THE TUDOR AGE

JASPER RIDLEY

THE TUDOR AGE

The Overlook Press
Woodstock · New York

First published in 1990 by
The Overlook Press
Lewis Hollow Road
Woodstock, New York 12498

Library of Congress Cataloging-in-Publication Data

Ridley, Jasper Godwin.
    The Tudor Age / Jasper Ridley.
        p.   cm.
    Includes bibliographical references.
    1. Great Britain—History—Tudors, 1485–1603.   2. Tudor, House of.
1. Title.
DA315.R53   1990
942.05—dc20
ISBN: 0-87951-405-1

Printed in Hong Kong

The emblem on the half-title page represents the Union of the Red and White Roses, symbolised in a late fifteenth-century tapestry, of which fragments remain in Winchester College. *Photograph by Derrick Witty.*

The frontispiece reproduces a portrait of Sir Walter Raleigh with his son, painted by an unknown artist in 1602. Soldier, sailor, explorer of the Americas, courtier, poet and historian, Raleigh epitomized the adventurous and accomplished gentleman of the Tudor Age. He was finally imprisoned in the Tower by James I, and beheaded in 1618.

TO MY SON JOHN

By the same author

NICHOLAS RIDLEY
THOMAS CRANMER
JOHN KNOX
LORD PALMERSTON
GARIBALDI
THE ROUNDHEADS
NAPOLEON III AND EUGÉNIE
THE STATESMAN AND THE FANATIC
HENRY VIII
ELIZABETH I

CONTENTS

COLOUR PLATES

ACKNOWLEDGEMENTS

I wish to thank Roy Armstrong, Agathe Lewin, Dr Michael Smith, and Mr E.C. Till for their advice and assistance on various aspects of this book; John and Jennifer Arnold and Tony Mercer for their hospitality on my travels while I was researching; the staff of the London Library for their help at all times; the Gloucestershire County Archivist; the staff of the British Library, the Kent County Library at Tunbridge Wells, and the Worcestershire County Library at Evesham; and my wife Vera and my son John for their painstaking work in correcting the proofs.

Jasper Ridley
Tunbridge Wells
12 July, 1988

CHRONOLOGY

1485	Aug.	Henry Tudor defeats and kills Richard III at Bosworth and becomes King Henry VII.
	Sept.	Sweating sickness appears in London.
1486–7		Revolt of Lambert Simnel and the Earl of Lincoln suppressed by Henry VII.
1489		Henry VII refuses to finance Columbus's voyage across the Atlantic.
1490–1510		Extensive building in brick, with new building methods.
1492		Henry VII's expedition to Boulogne. Treaty of Etaples.
1494		Syphilis first appears in Naples.
1495		Execution of Sir William Stanley.
1495–7		Perkin Warbeck's invasions of England.
1496		Statute of Labourers regulates wages and hours of work.
1497		John Cabot sails to Newfoundland. Building of Canterbury Cathedral tower completed.
1498		Sheen Palace burned; rebuilt as Richmond Palace.
1499		Execution of Perkin Warbeck and the Earl of Warwick.
1501		Marriage of Arthur, Prince of Wales, to Catherine of Aragon.
1502		Death of Arthur, Prince of Wales.
1509		Death of Henry VII. Accession of Henry VIII, who marries Catherine of Aragon.
1510		New Sumptuary Law regulates the dress to be worn by the different classes.
1512		Wolsey becomes Henry VIII's chief minister. Expedition to Fuentarrabia; English troops mutiny because of lack of beer. College of Physicians founded.
1513		Henry VIII invades France; the Earl of Surrey defeats and kills James IV of Scotland at Flodden.
1514		Marriage of Henry VIII's sister Mary to Louis XII of France. Wolsey begins to build Hampton Court and York Place (later Whitehall).
1515		Henry VIII's sister Mary marries the Duke of Suffolk.
1516		Sir Thomas More's book *Utopia* published. Birth of Henry VIII's daughter Mary.
1517–18		Virulent outbreak of the sweating sickness in England.
1519–21		Magellan's expedition from Spain sails round the world.
1520		Henry VIII meets Francis I of France at the Field of Cloth-of-gold.
1521		Execution of the Duke of Buckingham.
1525		William Tyndale translates the New Testament into English; it is illegally smuggled into England from the Netherlands.
1525–30		Anne Boleyn introduces the fashion of the French hood for women.
1527		Henry VIII begins divorce proceedings against Catherine of Aragon.
1528		Renewed outbreak of sweating sickness.
1529		Fall of Wolsey. The Reformation Parliament meets.
(1529 ?)		Morality play, *Everyman*, performed.
1530		Intensification of the suppression of the English Bible. New severe legislation against vagabonds. Death of Wolsey, while being brought as a prisoner to London.
1530–40		Bishop Vesey builds houses for labourers in Sutton Coldfield.

1531		Henry VIII separates from Catherine of Aragon, and Anne Boleyn lives with him as his mistress.
1533		Henry VIII marries Anne Boleyn, who becomes Queen. Repudiation of Papal supremacy over the Church of England. Birth of Henry VIII's daughter, the future Elizabeth I. Thomas Cromwell becomes Henry VIII's chief minister.
1535		Execution of Bishop Fisher, Sir Thomas More, and the Carthusian monks. Henry VIII cuts his hair short and grows a beard. Nicholas Udall's play, *Ralph Roister Doister*, performed.
1536		Execution of Anne Boleyn. Henry VIII marries Jane Seymour.
1536–9		Suppression of monasteries.
1536–7		Revolt of the Pilgrimage of Grace in Lincolnshire and Yorkshire.
1536–44		Housing legislation deals with slum property.
1537		Birth of Edward VI. Death of Jane Seymour. Henry VIII permits the publication of the English translation of the Bible.
1538		Execution of Cardinal Pole's family.
1538–46		Henry VIII builds Nonesuch Palace.
1539		Act of the Six Articles against the Protestants.
1540		Henry VIII marries and divorces Anne of Cleves. Fall and execution of Thomas Cromwell, and intensified persecution of Protestants. Henry VIII marries Katherine Howard. Foundation of the College of Surgeons. The hottest summer within living memory.
1540–50		Beards and short hair become general. Hose gives way to trunk hose in men's dress.
1541		Execution of the Countess of Salisbury. Henry VIII's journey to York. Katherine Howard arrested for adultery; execution of her lovers.
1542		Execution of Katherine Howard.
1543		Severe restrictions on reading of the English Bible. Renewed persecution of Protestants; the Windsor heretics burned. Henry VIII marries Katherine Parr.
1544		English troops burn Edinburgh. Henry VIII captures Boulogne.
1545		French threaten to invade England; *Mary Rose* sunk. Henry VIII suppresses London hospitals. Henry Brinkelow illegally publishes *The Complaint of Roderick Mors*. The Spanish farthingale first worn by ladies at the English court.
1545–56		Inflation; prices rise by 100 per cent in ten years.
1545–70		Gentlemen wear increasingly large ruffs.
1546	July	Burning of Anne Askew and other Protestants.
	Dec.	Henry VIII suppresses the Catholic faction in his Council.
1547	Jan.	Death of Henry VIII; accession of Edward VI, with the Duke of Somerset as Lord Protector.
	Feb.	Somerset and Archbishop Cranmer take the first steps to make England a Protestant nation. Statute making vagabonds slaves (repealed in 1550).
1549		First Book of Common Prayer suppresses the Catholic Mass. Catholic revolt in Devon and Cornwall suppressed. Kett's agrarian revolt in Norfolk suppressed.
	Oct.	The Earl of Warwick (later Duke of Northumberland) overthrows Somerset.
1550		Act against unlawful assemblies. Workhouses for vagabonds introduced.
1550–3		Consumer protection legislation increases.
1551		Last great visitation of the sweating sickness.
1552		Execution of Somerset. The Second Book of Common Prayer introduces a more extreme form of Protestantism. The play *Gammer Gurton's Needle* produced.
1553	May	Willoughby and Chancellor sail from London to find the North-east Passage.

1553	July	Death of Edward VI; Jane Grey proclaimed Queen; Mary Tudor defeats Jane Grey, and becomes Queen.
	Aug.	Execution of Northumberland; Protestant leaders arrested.
	Dec.	The Catholic Mass restored.
1554	Jan.	Sir Thomas Wyatt leads a Protestant revolt in Kent.
	Feb.	Suppression of Wyatt's revolt; Jane Grey executed; Elizabeth sent to the Tower.
	Apr.	Chancellor received in Moscow by Ivan the Terrible.
	July	Mary marries Philip of Spain, who becomes King of England.
	Nov.	Cardinal Pole returns from exile and reunites England to Rome.
1555	Feb.	Burning of Protestants begins; Rogers and Hooper burned.
	June	False report that Mary is pregnant.
	Oct.	Ridley and Latimer burned at Oxford.
1555–8		280 Protestants burned.
1555–87		Sir William Cecil (later Lord Burghley) rebuilds Burghley House at Stamford.
1556		Cranmer burned at Oxford.
1558	Jan.	The French capture Calais. John Knox publishes four books in Geneva which justify Protestant revolutions against Catholic rulers.
	Nov. 17	Death of Mary; accession of Elizabeth I, with Cecil as Secretary of State.
1559		Elizabeth I repudiates Papal supremacy and makes England once again a Protestant nation; Third Book of Common Prayer published.
	May	Protestant revolution in Scotland.
	Dec.	Elizabeth I sends William Winter and a fleet to the Firth of Forth to help the Scottish revolutionaries.
1560	July 6	Treaty of Edinburgh ends French control of Scotland and makes Scotland a Protestant nation.
	Sept.	Death of Amy Robsart; Lord Robert Dudley suspected of her murder.
1560–75		Trunk hose, in men's clothes, give way to breeches ('Venetians').
1561		Mary, Queen of Scots, returns from France to Scotland.
1561–4		Anthony Jenkinson's voyage to Russia, Khiva and Persia.
1562		John Hawkins and Francis Drake go on their first slave-trading voyage to Guinea. Sackville and Norton's play *Gorbaduc* produced.
1562–3		Elizabeth I intervenes disastrously in the French civil war.
1563		A new Statute of Labourers fixes wages and hours of work.
1563–4		17,000 die of plague in London.
1563–75		Cecil builds another house, Theolbands, near Cheshunt.
1566		Outbreak of Protestant revolt in the Netherlands against the rule of Philip II of Spain.
1567		Murder of Darnley; Mary Queen of Scots deposed and imprisoned in Scotland. Sir John Thynne begins building his house at Longleat.
1568		Severe repression of Protestants in the Netherlands by the Duke of Alva. Hawkins and Drake attacked by Spaniards in the West Indies.
	Dec.	Elizabeth I seizes Alva's treasure-ships; Alva seizes English property in the Netherlands.
1568–9		Thomas Randolph's mission as ambassador to Moscow.
1569–72		Hostility and economic sanctions between England and Spain.
1569		Catholic rising in the North suppressed by Elizabeth I.
1570		Pope Pius V's Bull excommunicating and deposing Elizabeth I.
1572		Massacre of St Bartholomew of Protestants by Catholics in Paris. New outbreak of Protestant revolt in the Netherlands.
1574		The Earl of Leicester authorises his players to act before the public in the London inns.
1575		Sir Humphrey Stafford builds Kirby Hall in Northamptonshire.
1576		First compulsory contribution imposed for alms for the impotent poor.

1576–8		Martin Frobisher's voyages to find the North-west Passage.
1577		James Burbage opens The Theatre in Finsbury Fields.
1577–80		Drake sails round the world.
1579–81		Revolt in Munster, Ireland, suppressed.
1580		Massacre of Spanish prisoners at Smerwick in Ireland. Men begin to wear their cloaks 'Collywestonwise'. The French farthingale replaces the Spanish farthingale in women's dress.
1584		Elizabeth I expels the Spanish ambassador. Assassination of William the Silent by a Catholic agent in the Netherlands.
1585		Treaty of Nonesuch between Elizabeth I and the Dutch Protestants. Leicester leads an army of English troops to help the Protestants in the Netherlands. Very large ruffs begin to come into fashion.
1585–6		Drake's expedition to the West Indies; he loots and burns Cartagena.
1585–7		John Davis's expeditions to find the North-west Passage.
1585–97		Elizabeth Hardwick, Countess of Shrewsbury, rebuilds Hardwick Hall in Derbyshire.
1586		The Babington plot; trial of Mary, Queen of Scots.
1586–8		Thomas Cavendish sails round the world.
1587		Execution of Mary, Queen of Scots. Drake attacks the Spanish Armada in Cadiz harbour. Marlowe's play, *Tamburlaine*, produced in London.
1588		Defeat of the Spanish Armada and Philip II's plan to invade England. Sir Francis Willoughby, the coalowner, completes the building of Wollaton Hall near Nottingham.
1589		Failure of the English expedition to liberate Portugal from the Spaniards. Assassination of Henry III of France by a monk; Henry of Navarre's right to succeed to the throne as Henry IV challenged by the Catholics because he is a Protestant. Elizabeth sends troops to help Henry IV in France. Thomas Kyd's play, *The Spanish Tragedy*, produced in London. Richard Hakluyt's book, *The Principal Navigations of the English Nation*, published.
1589–97		Legislation to provide housing for agricultural labourers.
1591		Sir Richard Grenville killed in sea-battle with Spaniards off the Azores. The Earl of Essex leads English troops to help Henry IV against the Spaniards and Catholics in France.
1592		Shakespeare's first play, *Henry VI, Part III*, performed in Southwark.
1592–1602		Twenty-four of Shakespeare's plays performed in Southwark.
1593		Henry IV of France becomes a Catholic.
1594–7		Four wet summers in England cause bad harvests and inflation. Food prices rise by 10 per cent per annum every year.
1594–1603		Hugh O'Neill, Earl of Tyrone's, rebellion in Ireland.
1595		Sir Walter Raleigh's expedition to the River Orinoco in South America. Tobacco smoking becomes very popular in England.
1595–6		Hawkins and Drake both die of disease while leading an expedition to the West Indies.
1596		An English expedition, under Essex, captures and burns Cadiz.
1597		New Poor Law legislation extends relief to the impotent poor (re-enacted in 1601).
1598		Ben Jonson's play, *Every man in his humour*, produced in Southwark with Shakespeare acting the part of old Knowell.
1599		Essex's unsuccessful expedition to Ireland; fall of Essex.
1601		Essex's rebellion; his supporters perform Shakespeare's *Richard II*; defeat and execution of Essex.
1602		Spanish expedition to Ireland defeated at Kinsale.
1603	Mar. 24	Death of Elizabeth I; accession of James VI of Scotland as James I of England. Lord Howard de Walden (later Earl of Suffolk) begins building Audley Hall in Essex. 38,000 die of plague in London.

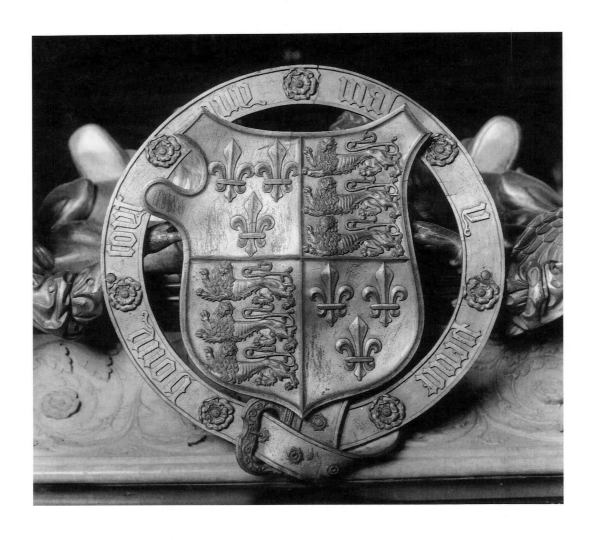

A gilt cast-bronze Gartered shield of the Tudor Royal Arms at the foot of Piero Torrigiani's tomb to King Henry VII and Queen Elizabeth of York, Westminster Abbey. *Photograph by Theo Cockerell.*

THE TUDOR FAMILY

THE Tudor Age began on 7 August 1485, when Henry Tudor, Earl of Richmond, landed at Milford Haven at the head of an army of 2,000 soldiers, intending to overthrow Richard III and make himself King of England in Richard's place.

Henry Tudor's claim to the throne was very dubious. His grandfather, Owain ap Meredith ap Tewdwr, was a Welsh gentleman who had enlisted in Henry V's army and fought in the great victory of Agincourt. Like all Welshmen, Owain had only patronymics, and no surname; but in England they treated his grandfather's name, Tewdwr, as if it were Owain's surname, and called him Owen Tudor. When Henry V died in 1422, and his nine-month-old son became King Henry VI, Owen became an officer in the baby King's bodyguard.

The Queen Mother was the French Princess whom Henry V had married after his conquest of France – Shakespeare's 'fair Katherine of France'. She was only twenty when she became a widow, and within a few years she had noticed Owen Tudor. According to a story which was current at the time, or shortly afterwards, she first heard about him when she was told that he was trying to seduce one of her ladies-in-waiting, and had made an assignation to meet the lady in a gallery in the palace. The indignant Queen Mother decided to teach Owen a lesson by disguising herself as the lady-in-waiting and administering him a sharp rebuff. Instead, she fell in love with him. Whatever the truth of this story, there is no doubt that she became his mistress, and they were probably secretly married.

The Duke of Gloucester, who was Lord Protector for the infant King, was very angry that Owen had presumed to marry the Queen Dowager without his consent. Owen was eventually clapped into prison, and Katherine was forced to retire to a convent, where she died at an early age; but before this, they had had three sons and one daughter. When Henry VI became old enough to exercise the royal power himself he released Owen from prison. Henry maintained very friendly relations with his Tudor half-brothers, and created Edmund Tudor, the eldest son of Owen and Katherine, Earl of Richmond.

The children of the Queen Mother by a subsequent marriage to a commoner had of course no claim at all to the throne; but Edmund Tudor married Lady Margaret Beaufort, who was the great-granddaughter of Kind Edward III's son, John of Gaunt, Duke of Lancaster, by John of Gaunt's mistress, Katherine Swynford. John of Gaunt married Katherine Swynford, after the death of his first wife, and a special Act of Parliament was passed which legitimized their bastard children; but there was a provision in the Act that although the children were to be regarded as legitimate, they were not entitled to succeed to the crown of England.

Margaret Beaufort was only twelve when she married Edmund Tudor, and in January 1457, when she was thirteen, she gave birth to her son, Henry Tudor. By this time, Henry VI's right to the throne had been challenged by Richard Duke of York. Henry VI was descended from John of Gaunt, who was Edward III's fourth son, by John of Gaunt's first wife. The Duke of York was descended on his father's side from Edward III's fifth son, but on his mother's side from Edward's third son, so in law his claim to the throne was better than Henry VI's. This led to civil war between the Yorkists and the Lancastrians. Today we call this civil war the Wars of the Roses, because the Yorkists adopted a white rose, and the Lancastrians a red rose, as their emblems. The chroniclers who wrote about the war in the sixteenth century called it 'the Wars between the Royal Houses of York and Lancaster'; but, contrary to what has sometimes been stated, the phrase 'the wars between the Roses' was occasionally used in the Tudor Age.

By 1471 the Yorkists had won the Wars of the Roses, and their leader, Edward Duke of York, had become King Edward IV. He imprisoned and murdered Henry VI; and Henry VI's son, Edward Prince of Wales, was killed in battle. The only surviving Lancastrian who had any claim to the throne was Henry Tudor, Earl of Richmond. He escaped abroad, and became a refugee in Brittany, which for a few more years, until 1491, remained a sovereign state independent of France.

Before long, the victorious Yorkists were quarrelling among themselves. When Edward IV died, his brother, Richard Duke of Gloucester, alleged that Edward's infant children were bastards, and made himself King Richard III. He had several of the leading Yorkist nobles beheaded, and based his support chiefly on the gentlemen of Yorkshire, which he had governed for Edward IV. It was widely believed at the time, both in England and abroad, that he murdered Edward IV's two children in the Tower of London; and he never disproved this by parading the children through the streets of London, which everyone would have expected him to do if they had still been alive.

After Henry Tudor became King Henry VII, it was officially announced that

Henry VII in middle-age, holding a rose. Painted by an unknown artist, this is one of a group of early Tudor portraits, all painted on panels cut from the same tree, 1515–21.

19

Richard III by an unknown artist, c.1490. *By Gracious Permission of Her Majesty The Queen.*

Richard III had murdered the children, and this has been generally believed for five hundred years; but a few writers in the seventeenth, eighteenth and nineteenth centuries thought that Richard was innocent, and that the children were murdered after his death by Henry VII. Since 1950, this theory has been put forward more vigorously than ever before; but most historians who have examined the question in depth believe that Richard was guilty. The case against Richard is much stronger than the case against anyone else. There is not a shred of evidence that Henry VII murdered the children, and he was never accused of it by any of his enemies during his lifetime.

The Yorkist nobility in the south of England, after fighting in the Wars of the Roses, were not easily shocked by crimes and atrocities; but they were shocked that Richard III had murdered his nephews, and were perhaps even more shocked by the prospect that they themselves might be murdered by Richard and their lands given to his northern supporters. Some of them plotted to overthrow Richard and place Henry Tudor, Earl of Richmond, on the throne; and to strengthen Henry's claim and win Yorkist support, they planned that he should marry Edward IV's daughter, Elizabeth of York, who was being held by Richard, virtually as a prisoner, at the castle of Sheriffhutton in Yorkshire.

On Christmas Day 1483, Henry Tudor took an oath in Rennes Cathedral in Brittany that if he became King of England he would marry Elizabeth of York. Richard persuaded the Duke of Brittany to extradite Henry Tudor; but Henry escaped to France, and by the summer of 1485 he had assembled, with the help of the King of France, an army of 2,000 men. Apart from a few Lancastrian supporters who were refugees in France, his force consisted of Breton, French and Scottish mercenaries, under the command of the Breton general, Philibert de Chaudée. Although he set out to win the crown of England with this army composed almost entirely of French and Scots, the hated national enemies of the English, he was relying on the support of Englishmen, both Yorkists and Lancastrians, whom he hoped would join him because they hated Richard III.

He sailed from Harfleur, and after a six-day voyage landed at Milford Haven on Sunday 7 August 1485. His original plan was to march as quickly as possible towards London to encourage the people to rise in his support; but he heard at Milford Haven that Sir Walter Herbert, who supported Richard, was at Carmarthen with an army, barring his road to England and preparing to advance on Milford Haven. He did not wish to fight a battle until more supporters had joined him, so he marched north, along the shores of Cardigan Bay, till he reached Machynlleth. Despite his Welsh origin, very few Welshmen joined him.

It was said, at the time, that near Machynlleth he met the local bard, David Llwyd ap Llewellyn, and asked him to foretell whether his expedition would end in victory or defeat. David said that he could not give an immediate answer, but would think about it during the night, and tell Henry before he marched on next morning. David discussed the problem with his wife. She told him to tell Henry that he would be victorious, because if he foretold this, and Henry did in fact win, Henry would reward him for his prophecy; but that if Henry lost, he would not survive to reproach David for his error. David followed her advice. Whether this story is true or not, there is no doubt that David was made a gentleman of Henry's bodyguard soon after the victory.

From Machynlleth, Henry marched due east through Wales. His army moved quickly, and eight days after their landing at Milford Haven had reached Shrewsbury, having marched 115 miles in eight days. Henry was very worried, for he had completely failed to rally support; but at Shrewsbury his luck changed, and as he moved more slowly, by Newport, Stafford and Lichfield, to Tamworth, his English supporters came to him. By the time he reached Atherstone in Warwickshire on 21 August, his army had increased to 5,000 men. Richard III, who had advanced from Nottingham to meet him, was seven miles away in the village of Sutton Cheney in Leicestershire. He had an army of 18,000 men, but 8,000 of them were the followers of Lord Stanley, who had married Margaret Beaufort after Edmund Tudor's death. Stanley had a secret meeting with Henry Tudor at Atherstone, but had not yet definitely made up his mind on which side he and his men would fight.

On the morning of Monday 22 August, the armies of Richard and Henry fought a battle which was named the Battle of Bosworth from the nearby village of Market Bosworth. There has recently been some dispute over the site of the battle, but it was almost certainly at the foot of Ambion Hill, about half a mile west of Sutton Cheney. As Richard's men charged down the hill, Henry's brave and seasoned soldiers had difficulty in holding their ground against a force about twice their size. But Lord Stanley's brother William and his 8,000 men were watching the battle from a position on the north of the battlefield, and were apparently remaining neutral. In desperation, Henry, escorted by a small bodyguard, galloped over to Stanley's position to tell Stanley that it was now or never, and to urge him to join in the battle at once on his side. Richard, at the top of Ambion Hill, saw what Henry was doing, and charged down on him at the head of his men. At that moment, Sir William Stanley attacked Richard on his flank. His intervention decided the issue. Richard cut his way through to within a few yards of Henry, but there he was killed. In those two or three minutes, the course of English history was settled.

After his victory, Henry sent men to fetch Elizabeth of York from Sheriffhutton, while he marched to London. There he summoned a Parliament, which immediately passed an Act declaring that he was the rightful King of England. This had become the usual practice whenever a new King had succeeded in wresting the throne of

The Battle of Bosworth: a fanciful illustration in the first edition of Holinshed's *Chronicles of England*

England from the former King; but Henry's claim to the throne was so questionable that neither he nor Parliament, nor any of his spokesmen and supporters, ever stated the grounds on which he based his title. His wife Elizabeth, the Yorkist heiress, was in law the rightful sovereign; but Henry did not wish to become King by right of his Yorkist wife, and made a point of postponing his marriage to her until after he had been crowned King and had exercised the royal power for five months as an unmarried man. It was not easy for him to argue that he was the lawful heir through his mother's descent from John of Gaunt and Katherine Swynford, since the Act of Parliament which legitimized their children had expressly stated that they and their descendants could not succeed to the crown; and even if they could, what right had Henry to be King while his mother was still alive? He seems to have thought at one time of claiming the throne by right of conquest; but the Act of Parliament merely stated that he was undoubtedly the rightful King, and that the truth of his claim had been proved by the fact that God had given him victory on the field of battle.

But his throne was not yet secure. He was threatened by several revolts of supporters of pretenders to the throne who claimed that they were Yorkist Princes; the most formidable was Perkin Warbeck, who passed himself off as Richard, Duke of York, the murdered son of Edward IV. But Henry eventually succeeded in defeating all his opponents, and when Perkin was captured in 1497 and executed two years later, the Wars of the Roses were over at last.

A characteristic clash of bowmen, pikes and cavalry during the late stages of the War of the Roses recorded in a Flemish miniature in *Chronique d'Angleterre* by Jean de Waurin.

There is little doubt that the people of England were shocked by the Wars of the Roses, though it may well be that, like other traumatic historical events, they seemed more terrible in retrospect to the next two or three generations than they had done to those living and taking part in them at the time. If we reckon them as beginning with the first battle at St Albans in 1455 and not ending until Perkin Warbeck was finally defeated in 1497, they lasted for forty-two years, although there were long periods of peace between the campaigns, and fighting was not going on for more than eighteen months of these forty-two years. All the battles took place in only a dozen of the forty counties of England, for apart from the battles in Northumberland in 1464 and Perkin Warbeck's defeat at Exeter, the wars were fought entirely in the Midlands, in the area between Hertfordshire and South Yorkshire; but the nobles who took part in them called up many of their tenants to join the armies. The losses among the combatants were heavy, as both sides usually murdered their prisoners, particularly their aristocratic prisoners, after their victories; and if the contemporary reports are accurate, no less than seventy-five thousand men were killed, which is as high a proportion of the population as the casualties suffered in the First World War.

The constantly recurring civil wars between members of the royal family, who murdered their cousins and stuck up their severed heads, arms and legs over the gates of various English towns, did not seem right to the people; and the Tudors had good reason to remind their subjects of the horrors of the wars, and of the evils which would return if their royal dictatorship was relaxed, and the realm relapsed again into anarchy. When Eustace Chapuys, the ambassador in England of the Holy Roman Emperor, Charles V, was trying in 1533 to prevent Henry VIII from divorcing his wife, Catherine of Aragon, and marrying Anne Boleyn, he warned Henry's Privy Council that this policy could lead to civil war in England, and 'that heretofore the Roses had troubled the kingdom, but now it seemed they desired to sharpen the thorns of the Roses'.

Sixty years after Chapuys, Shakespeare, in his play *The Third Part of King Henry VI*, showed the horror of the Wars of the Roses, in which a soldier discovered that the enemy whom he had just killed was his own father, while another soldier similarly discovered that he had just killed his son; in the scene, the 'Son that hath killed his Father' and the 'Father that hath killed his Son' exchange condolences. This would have been quite possible if the fathers and sons had joined the households of different lords, for in battle they would have worn helmets with visors which concealed all their faces except for the eyes.

Perhaps the most important result of the Wars of the Roses was their psychological effect on the Englishmen of the Tudor Age. The subjects of Henry VIII and Elizabeth I believed that such evils could only be prevented by absolute obedience to royal autocracy, and that the execution of a few traitors every year or so was a small price to pay to prevent another civil war.

Henry VII succeeded in defeating all the revolts against him, and in ruling over an increasingly prosperous England. He was one of the shrewdest and wisest of English kings. He was remarkably merciful to his enemies. He occasionally put to death some more or less innocent person whom he regarded as a dangerous rival. He had no more compunction about ordering the execution of the young Earl of Warwick, who as the son of Edward IV's brother, the Duke of Clarence, was a possible claimant of the crown, than in beheading his stepfather's brother, Sir William Stanley, whose intervention had saved him at Bosworth, when he suspected that Stanley was plotting against him. But although he was confronted with three serious revolts, as well as with several conspiracies, he only put to death a handful of the defeated rebels and traitors. This is an extraordinary contrast to the wholesale killing of prisoners during the Wars of the Roses and the hundreds of rebels and traitors who were executed by his son Henry VIII and his granddaughter Elizabeth I, each of whom faced only one serious revolt during their reigns.

Henry VII's foreign policy was cautious, pacific and successful. He was involved in only two wars during his twenty-four-year reign. One was against France in support of his ally, the Duke of Brittany, which he ended within a few months on favourable terms. The second was against the Scots, who ravaged Northumberland in support of Perkin Warbeck. Henry made peace with the Scots, and married his daughter Margaret to King James IV of Scotland. He made an alliance with King Ferdinand and Queen Isabella of Spain, who had united the kingdoms of Castile and Aragon and conquered the Moorish kingdom of Granada to create Spain as a new nation; and he married his son Arthur, Prince of Wales, to Ferdinand and Isabella's daughter, Catherine of Aragon. England's traditional ally, the Habsburg Holy Roman Emperor who governed the Netherlands, had supported the Yorkist cause, and at first encouraged the revolts of the Yorkist pretenders against Henry; but Henry eventually persuaded the Emperor to revive the old alliance with England and to extradite his rebels.

Despite his successes at home and abroad, Henry became very unpopular towards the end of his reign. His nobles and knights were dissatisfied with his pacific foreign policy, and were disgusted when he led them to the siege of Boulogne and then brought them home without fighting a battle or suffering more than a handful of casualties, even though he induced the French to sign a peace by which they paid him an annual tribute in money and the cost of his military operations. The people of all classes grumbled at the heavy taxes which he imposed. More than a hundred years later, when Francis Bacon wrote his *History of the Reign of King Henry VII*, people remembered the taxes extorted by Henry's Lord Chancellor and Archbishop of Canterbury, Cardinal Morton. 'Morton's Fork' was the trick by which landowners were assessed for tax according to their annual expenditure. If they lived lavishly they were told that this showed that they were wealthy and could afford to pay large amounts in tax; if they lived frugally, this showed that they did not need a great deal of money, and could therefore similarly afford to pay high taxes. But in fact, Morton never operated such a system; and if there was any basis at all for the story of 'Morton's Fork', it was in an idea that was envisaged at one time by another of Henry VII's ministers, Richard Foxe, Bishop of Winchester.

Because of the large amounts which Henry VII collected in taxes, he was – or at least made people think that he was – immensely rich. The foreign ambassadors at his court wrote that he was by far the richest king in Christendom, and stories about his great wealth were always circulating. Modern historians today deny this, and say that, far from being the richest, he was one of the poorest kings. They do not explain why, if he was not in fact rich, all his contemporaries believed he was, and were

One of the vault pendants of King Henry VII's Chapel in Westminster Abbey, described by Leland after their completion as 'the wonder of the world'. In the words of a modern architectural critic, John Harvey: 'They seem to float in the air, sustained by Virtue's gossamer traceries'. An engraving by S. Sparrow, after a drawing by E. Mackenzie, 1807.

always borrowing money from him and from his son, Henry VIII, when he inherited his father's throne and wealth. The explanation is probably that when Henry VII's contemporaries said that he was rich, they meant that he had a great hoard of gold, whereas the modern historians are thinking in terms of economic resources.

But it is wrong to think of Henry VII as a miser, or as a shabby, unimpressive king who was too mean to live in a grand style. He dressed in splendid and costly garments, and put on a suitable display of wealth at court; and, being deeply religious, he spent a great deal of money in building a new chapel in Westminster Abbey as well as a new palace at Richmond. He was devoted to his wife, Elizabeth of York, whose placid beauty was so greatly admired by those who saw her; and as far as we know, he was never unfaithful to her. When their eldest son, Arthur, died at the age of fifteen, Henry and Elizabeth were heartbroken, and drew even closer to each other in their grief. Elizabeth's death two years later was another blow to Henry. His health soon gave way, and after surviving a series of critical illnesses, he died, five years after his wife, on 21 April 1509, at the age of fifty-two.

All the children of Henry VII and Elizabeth of York who survived their infancy were vigorous and powerful characters. Arthur died too young for us to know what he was like, and, only four months after his marriage to Catherine of Aragon. Twenty-five years later, the great issue in the divorce proceedings between Henry VIII and Catherine of Aragon was whether Catherine's marriage to Arthur had been consummated. Catherine always strongly denied it, and most historians have believed her; but she was quite capable of lying in the interests of her dynasty and the foreign policy of her nephew, the Emperor Charles V, and there is some evidence that her fifteen-year-old husband, Arthur, had indeed consummated the marriage with youthful gusto.

Henry VII's two daughters, Margaret and Mary, were strong-minded women. Margaret married King James IV of Scotland. She was twenty-four when her husband was killed at Flodden while waging war on her brother, Henry VIII. She became the regent for her one-year-old son, James V, but was forced to flee to England after antagonizing the Scottish nobles by marrying Archibald Douglas, Earl of Angus, less than a year after the death of James IV. Soon afterwards she fell in love with a handsome young nobleman, Henry Stewart, Lord Methven, and became involved in a matrimonial quarrel and protracted divorce proceedings with her pro-English husband, Angus, which not only sparked off a new civil war in Scotland but completely disrupted Henry VIII's foreign policy. Margaret paid no heed at all when Henry, forgetting all about his own matrimonial difficulties, severely reprimanded her for being unfaithful to her husband.

Henry's other daughter, Mary, was only eighteen when Henry VIII married her to the aged and decrepit King Louis XII of France under a clause in the peace treaty

Elizabeth of York, Queen of Henry VII, by an unknown artist, probably a pair to the portrait of the King reproduced on page 19.

The Tudor Succession, by
Lucas de Heere, c.1560,
painted in Elizabeth's reign.
Elizabeth is prominent on
the right of the painting,
followed by the goddess
Flora and the fruits of peace.
Between Elizabeth and
Henry is Edward VI. On the
left of the picture are Mary
and her husband, Philip of
Spain, followed by Mars, the
god of war. From Sudeley
Castle, home of the Seymour
family.

MARKE OF HER PEOPLES AND HER OWNE CONTENT.

31

Henry VIII, a painting after Hans Holbein the Younger, c.1536. An almost indistinguishable replica of the famous painting in the Thyssen-Bornemisza Collection, but painted on copper.

which ended his first war against the French. But King Louis died three months after the marriage, and Mary, without asking Henry VIII's consent, married Charles Brandon, Duke of Suffolk, the English ambassador in France, with whom she had been in love for some time. Henry was incensed, and for a time it seemed as if Suffolk might be severely punished; but he was soon persuaded to forgive Suffolk and allow the marriage to Mary, chiefly because of the skilful way in which Mary handled the situation with just the right mixture of courage, defiance and submission. She lived very happily with Suffolk for eighteen years, at court and at his house of Westhorpe in Suffolk, until she died at the age of thirty-seven.

Both his personality and his position made Henry VII's second son, Henry VIII, the most formidable of his children. When his brother Arthur died, Henry became the heir to the throne, and he succeeded Henry VII as King two months before his eighteenth birthday. His accession was welcomed with great enthusiasm by his people, particularly by intellectuals like Lord Mountjoy and Thomas More; and he increased his popularity by executing his father's hated ministers, Richard Empson and Edmund Dudley, who were considered responsible for the oppressive taxation of Henry VII's reign.

Henry VIII was 6 foot 4 inches tall, and broad-shouldered, with very fair skin, as soft as a woman's, red hair, and a thin, high-pitched voice. He hunted every day, except when prevented by the weather, and sometimes chased stags for thirty miles without alighting from his horses. He was a fine archer, and could compete at the butts with the best bowmen of his guard; and he excelled at jousting in tournaments. He nevertheless found time to attend Mass five times a day. In the evenings, he attended masques and balls, and often sat up late into the night gambling at cards and dice. His appetite for food and drink was enormous.

He was an intellectual as well as an athlete. He wrote books on theology, and was very musical, playing the lute and composing love-songs and church music. He patronized intellectuals like Colet and More, and by bringing the eminent foreign writers Erasmus and Vives, and the artist Hans Holbein the younger, to England, he was partly responsible for introducing the Renaissance into his kingdom.

Throughout his reign, he had a succession of able ministers – Cardinal Wolsey, Thomas Cromwell and Stephen Gardiner – and this has led to a controversy among historians as to how far Henry himself was responsible for his domestic and foreign policy, and how far it was his ministers who decided everything in his name. It is difficult for us today to be certain about this. His ministers acted in his name; his enemies, hesitating to attack the King himself, always blamed his ministers whenever Henry adopted measures which they did not like; and Henry from time to time sacrificed them as the scapegoats for policies which he had ordered, or allowed, them to pursue, and which had become unpopular.

Sir Thomas More, after Holbein, 1527. One of the 'intellectuals' whom Henry VIII patronized.

There is no doubt that Henry did not play an active part in the day-to-day administration of government. He rarely attended meetings of his Privy Council, and left his counsellors to carry on the work of government while he went out hunting; but he took the important decisions himself. His secretaries often found it difficult to persuade him to attend to business; but he usually spent two hours with them in the evening dealing with correspondence before or after supper. He often discussed international affairs with the foreign ambassadors at his court, who by accepted diplomatic practice were entitled to demand an audience with him; and he handled these interviews with courtesy and skill in his excellent French or Latin.

The traditional picture of him which has been handed down to us today is of a handsome, well-meaning young man who turned into a fat tyrant with syphilis, who could always be persuaded to change his policy and execute his favourite ministers, in an outburst of rage, by scheming courtiers helped by beautiful women who were offered to him as a new wife. This is almost certainly a wrong picture of Henry, and it was not how his contemporaries saw him. He did not have syphilis. He certainly

Hans Holbein the Younger, aged forty-five: a self-portrait. He was one of several artists and writers brought over from the Continent by Henry VIII.

became very fat, for we know from his suit of armour in the Tower of London that in his last years he was fifty-four inches round the waist; but he was almost as much of a tyrant when he was young as when he was old. Even in the early years of his reign he executed more people than his father did in his whole life. There is very little contemporary evidence that he ever flew into a violent rage, and everything suggests that he calmly planned his changes of policy, and the executions which always accompanied them, as acts of cold, calculating policy. He could be charming and courteous, not only to the ladies at his court, and to the common people whom he met on his travels through his realm, but also to the ministers whom he had marked for destruction and to foreign ambassadors immediately before declaring war. Geoffrey Baskerville in 1937 rightly described him as *faux bonhomme* and Pollard in 1902 just as accurately as 'Machiavelli's Prince in action'.

He strongly opposed all Lutheran and Protestant sects, which he thought were

Anne Boleyn, by an unknown artist. She wears the French hood, which she brought into fashion after 1525.

seditious and a threat to the power of princes, until he decided to obtain a divorce from Catherine of Aragon, who had been unable to give him a male heir, and to marry Anne Boleyn, with whom he had fallen in love. He tried for six years to persuade the Pope to grant him his divorce, but finally decided that he had no alternative but to repudiate Papal supremacy and proclaim himself Supreme Head of the Church of England. This policy led him to encourage the Protestants; and Protestant divines, who a few years earlier had been in danger of being burned as heretics, were now appointed to official positions in the Church, and in some cases made bishops. The Protestant arguments gave him an excuse to suppress the monasteries, which were officially denounced as places of immorality, and to seize their valuable property; but he never liked the Protestants, and, realizing that his pro-Protestant line was unpopular with many of his subjects, he began a fierce persecution of Protestants in 1539 which continued nearly till the end of his reign.

He never allowed his policy to be influenced by his wives, or by any woman. He

Jane Seymour, after Holbein, an almost exact copy, at Woburn Abbey, of the painting by Holbein in the Kunsthistorisches Museum in Vienna. Tests have proved that this panel dates from three or four years after Holbein's death. She wears the gable hood with turned-up lappets.

was very much in love with Anne Boleyn, but he began divorce proceedings against Catherine of Aragon chiefly because he believed that she could not give him the male heir which he and his country required; and not all his passion for Anne Boleyn could persuade him for six years to break with Rome until events made it politically necessary for him to do so. He had Anne Boleyn beheaded because she had not given him a son, and because he wished to marry Jane Seymour; but although Jane sympathized with the Catholic faction at court, who had put her forward in the hopes that she would induce Henry to adopt a pro-Catholic policy, he surprised everyone by being more Protestant than ever after he had married her. He divorced his fourth wife, Anne of Cleves, whom he found repulsive, when he executed Thomas Cromwell, who had favoured his marriage to her; but he had already initiated the Catholic backlash, which followed the fall of Cromwell, a year before his marriage to Anne of Cleves. Katherine Howard was supported by the Catholic faction; but when

37

Katharine Parr, a painting attributed to William Scrots, c.1545.

the Protestants denounced her to him as an adulteress, and he had her beheaded, he intensified his persecution of the Protestants, though he had just married his sixth wife, Katherine Parr, who was a secret supporter of the Protestants.

Although Henry simultaneously executed Catholic supporters of the Pope and Protestant heretics, he only persecuted unpopular minorities; and all the evidence indicates that he was popular with the majority of his subjects, particularly with the influential sections of the middle class, the country gentlemen and the merchants and burghers of the cities and towns, some of whom benefited from his seizure of the monasteries by buying the monastic property from him at comparatively low prices. The majority of the population did not like the domination of a foreign Pope, and did not like the Protestant innovators who attacked their traditional Catholic beliefs; and they approved of a king who imprisoned and executed both these elements. Henry's ministers received reports nearly every week of men who had spoken against the

King and his counsellors in inns, in churchyards after Mass, in the nearby town on market day, or on the road going there. This shows how his political opponents hated him, and how savagely he suppressed them; but it also shows how many of his loyal subjects were prepared to act as unpaid informers, and denounce these seditious rumourmongers to the authorities.

One reason for Henry's popularity with his subjects was his success in his wars. Soon after he became King he reasserted the traditional claim of the Kings of England to the French throne, and declared war on France. His campaign of 1513, when he was twenty-four, was very successful, for he invaded France, won a victory over the French, and captured two of their towns, while at the same time his armies at home, led by the Earl of Surrey, defeated and killed James IV of Scotland, who had invaded England in support of his French ally, at the battle of Flodden.

For the rest of his reign, Henry's policy towards France alternated between friendship, cold war and open warfare. After his victorious campaign of 1513, he made peace with France and married his sister Mary to the French King, Louis XII; but when Louis died, and was succeeded by the twenty-year-old Francis I, Henry became alarmed at Francis's victories in Italy. For four years Henry financed the wars which the Holy Roman Emperor, the Swiss, and the Italian states were waging against France, but then signed a new treaty of friendship with Francis I. It was during the ensuing interval of friendly relations that Henry and Francis met in June 1520 on the frontier between France and the English territories at Calais. The place where the meeting took place, between Guisnes and Ardres, was called the Field of Cloth-of-gold, because cloth-of-gold material was used to decorate many of the temporary buildings and tents erected for the fortnight's meeting. But within two years Henry had again gone to war against Francis, and sent his armies to devastate the North of France in a savage campaign in which the French civilian population were the chief sufferers.

Henry allied himself with Francis I, and made use of him, when his divorce of Catherine of Aragon and his repudiation of Papal supremacy brought him into conflict with the Emperor Charles V; but he made a new alliance with Charles V, and went to war with France for the third time, in 1544, when he took the field and commanded his armies at the siege of Boulogne. Although the capture of Boulogne was followed by a threat of a French invasion of England, the invasion did not take place, and the war ended with a peace which left Henry in possession of Boulogne. During this last war, Henry's armies ravaged Scotland, devastating the Border districts and burning every house in Edinburgh except the Castle.

Henry's subjects were delighted at his victories over the French and Scottish enemy, and after his death remembered him with pride as a great King and conqueror. 'How did King Henry VIII scourge them!' wrote Bishop Aylmer, twelve years after Henry died, 'In his youth won Therouanne and Tournai, and in his age Boulogne, Blackness, Newhaven [Ambleteuse], The Old Man, and all that country'.[1] In 1575 the poet Ulpian Fulwell praised him as

> A second Alexander he . . .
> A Solomon for godly wit,
> A Solon for his constant mind,
> A Samson when he list to hit
> The fury of his foes unkind . . .
> And many years to rule and reign
> To England's joy, to Scotland's pain.

When he died on the night of 27 January 1547 at the age of fifty-five, he was succeeded by his nine-year-old son Edward VI. A few months before his death he had made another shift in policy and had destroyed the power of the Catholic party in the Council; and he appointed more Protestants than Catholics to be the guardians of his infant son. The young King's uncle, Edward Seymour, Duke of Somerset, became Lord Protector, and he and Archbishop Cranmer introduced Protestant doctrines and practices into the Church of England, abolishing the Mass and substituting the Protestant services of their new Book of Common Prayer. This led to a serious Catholic revolt in Devon and Cornwall in 1549, and at the same time an agrarian insurrection broke out in Norfolk against land enclosures and the oppressive conduct of the landowners. The revolts were suppressed, but caused the downfall of Somerset, who was thought by the nobles and landowners to be too sympathetic to the labourers. John Dudley, Earl of Warwick (later Duke of Northumberland) succeeded Somerset as the King's chief minister, and in due course Somerset was beheaded.

Edward VI was a brilliant boy, with a great aptitude for learning and a strong will of his own. If he had lived longer, he might have been one of the greatest of English kings; but he died of consumption at the age of fifteen. He had been brought up to be a devout Protestant, and was shocked that his eldest sister, Mary (the daughter of Henry VIII and Catherine of Aragon), was a Catholic who refused to abandon her Catholic Mass and accept the new Protestant doctrines. When he knew that he was dying, Edward decided to prevent her from succeeding him as Queen by making a will in which he bequeathed the crown to Lady Jane Grey, the granddaughter of Henry VIII's sister Mary, Duchess of Suffolk. Jane Grey had recently married Northumberland's son, Lord Guilford Dudley, and Northumberland was generally

---

[1] Blackness, Newhaven and The Old Man were names given by the English to forts near Boulogne.

Edward VI granting the Foundation Charter to Christ's Hospital in June 1553. Governors of the Hospital are shown on either side of the Throne, recognizable as such since they carry the green staves, a custom that survives to this day on ceremonial occasions. On the King's left stands the Lord Mayor of London, and on the King's right is, presumably, the Bishop of London, Nicholas Ridley. Boys and girls of the Foundation kneel in the foreground.

ANNO DNI   1544

LADI MARI   DOVGHTER TO
THE MOST   VERTVOVS PRINCE
KING HENRI   THE EIGHT

THE AGE OF   XXVII YERES

Queen Mary I, painting by Master John, 1544.

supposed to have instigated this attempt to make her Queen. He probably suggested it to Edward in the first place; but it was the dying fifteen-year-old boy who, receiving the members of his Privy Council alone, one by one, on his deathbed, commanded them, and badgered them into agreeing reluctantly, to support his devise of the crown to Jane Grey and the exclusion of Mary.

When Edward died on 6 July 1553, Jane Grey was proclaimed Queen by Northumberland and the Council in London; but Mary, taking refuge in the castle of Framlingham in Suffolk, called on the people to rise in support of her, their lawful Queen, against the usurper Jane Grey. Within a fortnight, Jane's cause had collapsed, and the members of her Privy Council, hurriedly changing sides, had proclaimed Mary as Queen in London, amid great demonstrations of support from the people. At first, Mary contented herself with executing Northumberland and two of his supporters; but six months later another revolt broke out in Kent under the leadership of Sir Thomas Wyatt, and this persuaded her that it was necessary to take severe measures, so Jane Grey and several other rebels were executed.

Mary was a woman of strong character, firm principles, and a strong psychological reluctance to compromise. She was seventeen when her father Henry VIII divorced her mother Catherine of Aragon and she herself was deprived of her title of Princess and proclaimed a bastard. She took her mother's side, and for three years refused to submit and acknowledge that her parents' marriage was void and that she was illegitimate. Eventually, after being imprisoned under house arrest, bullied, and humiliated by her father, she gave way when he threatened to put her to death if she continued her defiance. She acknowledged her bastardy and the King's supremacy over the Church; but she remained a devoted Catholic, and after Henry VIII's death, under the more lenient régime of Edward VI, she defied the government and refused to abandon her Mass. She showed great courage during her rising against Jane Grey, and during the Wyatt rebellion, when she went to the Guildhall and called on the Lord Mayor and the citizens of London to stand firm in her support against Wyatt and his rebels who were advancing on the city.

Although she had a religious horror of sex, she agreed to marry Prince Philip of Spain, the son of the Emperor Charles V, because she knew that it was her duty to cement the alliance with the Habsburg Empire by the marriage, and to produce an heir to the throne. Philip landed at Southampton and married Mary in Winchester Cathedral in July 1554, and Philip and Mary reigned as King and Queen of England. In November Mary reunited England to Rome, when Cardinal Pole, returning from twenty years of exile, arrived as Papal Legate to absolve the realm of England from its sin of schism. Mary then persuaded Parliament to pass the necessary legislation to authorize a savage persecution of Protestants, and nearly three hundred of them were burned during the remaining four years of her reign.

Philip II of Spain, painting
by an unknown artist,
c.1580. Philip was Queen
Mary's consort, and later
Queen Elizabeth's adversary.

In her private life, Mary was very kind, doing much charitable work and winning the love of her ladies-in-waiting; but she was pitiless towards those whom she considered to be God's enemies, and was undoubtedly more responsible than anyone else for the religious persecution of her reign. Her last years were unhappy. Soon after her marriage she believed that she was pregnant, but it was a hallucination, and to her disappointment no child was born. She was very sad when, having gone to war

The 'Phoenix' portrait of Queen Elizabeth, attributed to Nicholas Hilliard, c.1575. The jewel suspended from her necklace depicting a phoenix is an emblem of hereditary royalty.

against France in alliance with Spain and the Empire, the French captured Calais, which the English had held for more than two hundred years; and she feared that the worst would happen after her death, when she would be succeeded by her sister Elizabeth, who she knew was a Protestant at heart.

These fears were realized when Mary died of cancer at the age of forty-two on 17 November 1558. Elizabeth, the daughter of Henry VIII and Anne Boleyn, had been brought up as a Protestant, but converted to Catholicism to save her life in Mary's reign, when she was sent as a prisoner to the Tower, and was in great danger of execution for her suspected involvement in Wyatt's revolt. Within a year of becoming Queen she had repudiated Papal supremacy, suppressed the Mass, and made England once again a Protestant state.

She was a sincere Protestant, but not as extreme as many of her supporters. She came into conflict with the Puritans in the House of Commons, and with many of her

Robert Devereux, 2nd Earl of Essex (1566–1601), painting after Marcus Gheeraerts the Younger.

ministers in her Privy Council who sympathized with them. Her belief in royal absolutism made her very hostile to Protestants in foreign countries who rebelled against their Catholic rulers; but the interests of her foreign policy, the need to have allies against the hostility of Catholic Europe, and the pressure of her ministers and Protestant supporters persuaded her reluctantly to give them aid, and her support was decisive in ensuring the victory of the Protestant cause in Scotland and the Netherlands.

Her Protestant policy alienated the sympathies of her sister Mary's husband, Philip

Robert Dudley, Earl of
Leicester (1532–88), painting
by an unknown artist,
c.1576.

II of Spain, and caused her to pursue what would today be called a neutralist policy
between the two great contending European powers, Spain and France. Although
she wished to avoid war with Spain, she was eventually drawn into it after thirty years
of hostility chiefly because her seamen, sailing all around the world, challenged
Spain's monopoly of the slave trade and naval supremacy on the 'Spanish Main' (the
Western Atlantic and the Caribbean). It was not until the English and Spaniards had
been fighting each other for some years in Ireland, Holland and Central America that
open war was declared. Elizabeth had always inspired the devotion of the great
majority of her subjects; and the defeat of the Spanish Armada, and of Philip's plan
for the invasion and conquest of England firmly established her reputation as the
saviour of her country, in the minds not only of her subjects in her lifetime but also of
the English people for four hundred years. The victory over the Armada did not

however end the war with Spain, which continued with a series of successes and setbacks for the rest of Elizabeth's life.

She never married, and has been remembered in history as the Virgin Queen, despite the fact that it was very important for her to give birth to an heir, because until she did, the heir to the throne of England was the Catholic Mary Queen of Scots. This gave the Catholics a great incentive to assassinate Elizabeth so that she would be succeeded by a Queen who would restore the Catholic religion in England. In the first years of her reign she was very much in love with Robert Dudley, whom she later created Earl of Leicester; but it was politically impossible for her to marry him after he was suspected of murdering his wife, Amy Robsart, who died when she fell downstairs at her house at Cumnor Hall near Abingdon in Berkshire. In later years, Elizabeth considered several possible marriages, and was once on the point of agreeing to marry the French King's brother, the Duke of Anjou and Alençon; but at the last moment she refused to marry him.

Her hesitations about her marriage may have been chiefly due to her inability to make up her mind, which she carried to extraordinary lengths, and which contrasts so sharply with the rapid decisions of her father Henry VIII. When, at the age of twenty-six and just over a year after becoming Queen, she took the daring decision – one of the most important of her life – to send her navy to help the Scottish Protestant revolutionaries expel the French from Scotland and make Scotland a Protestant state, she changed her mind three times in a fortnight before finally deciding to intervene; and when in 1587 she authorized Drake to attack Cadiz and destroy the Armada which was gathering to invade England, she sent him four contradictory instructions within a few days, as to whether he was or was not to commit this act of war against Spain. Her chronic reluctance to take decisions, and her inability to adhere to them when she had taken them, was partly due to some inherent facet of her character, and partly to her contradictory position as an ardent believer in royal absolutism and as the champion of Protestant rebels in Europe.

The disastrous consequences of her indecision were very largely, but not entirely, prevented by the very able ministers whom she appointed to advise her, of whom William Cecil, Lord Burghley, was the greatest. But under the system of government in the sixteenth century, her ministers never considered themselves to be anything more than her advisers, and all important decisions were made, in the last resort, by Elizabeth. She deserves the credit for these decisions, and for the triumphs which resulted from them, even if she showed such lamentable and costly indecision before reaching them.

She also deserves the credit for the relative toleration and mildness of her régime. It may seem tyrannical when compared with nineteenth or twentieth-century democracy, but it was much less oppressive than the governments of Henry VIII and

Mary. She sometimes raged at her ministers and courtiers, and especially at any of her ladies-in-waiting who dared to say that they wished to marry; but none of them went in fear of their lives and liberty unless they openly rebelled against her authority, or, in the case of her ladies-in-waiting, if they disgraced her court by engaging in illicit love affairs. In contrast to the endless succession of counsellors and favourites whom Henry VIII sent to die on the scaffold or at the stake – often only a few months after they had sat as judges on the court which had condemned their predecessors to death – Elizabeth only executed her nobles and counsellors if they had engaged in open rebellion, like the Earls of Northumberland and Essex, or had plotted against her, like the Duke of Norfolk, who had planned to depose her and place Mary Queen of Scots on the throne. She imprisoned her Secretary of State, Sir William Davison, in the Tower because he had sent off her warrant for the execution of Mary Queen of Scots, although he knew that she did not wish him to do so; but her counsellors did not fear her. In their private letters to each other, they were never afraid to criticize her for her indecision, which none of Henry VIII's ministers would have dared to do.

Elizabeth I reigned for forty-four years. When she died at the age of sixty-nine on 24 March 1603, the Tudor Age ended, 118 years after it began at Bosworth. Henry VIII's line became extinct, for none of his three legitimate children – Edward VI, Mary and Elizabeth I – had any children.[2] All the descendants of the Tudors who are living in 1988 are descended from one or other of the two daughters of Henry VII – from Mary, Queen of France and Duchess of Suffolk, or from Margaret, Queen of Scots. Margaret's direct descendant, in the fifteenth generation, is our present Queen, Elizabeth II.

[2] Henry VIII's only known illegitimate child, Henry Fitzroy, Duke of Richmond, also died childless, at the age of seventeen, in 1536.

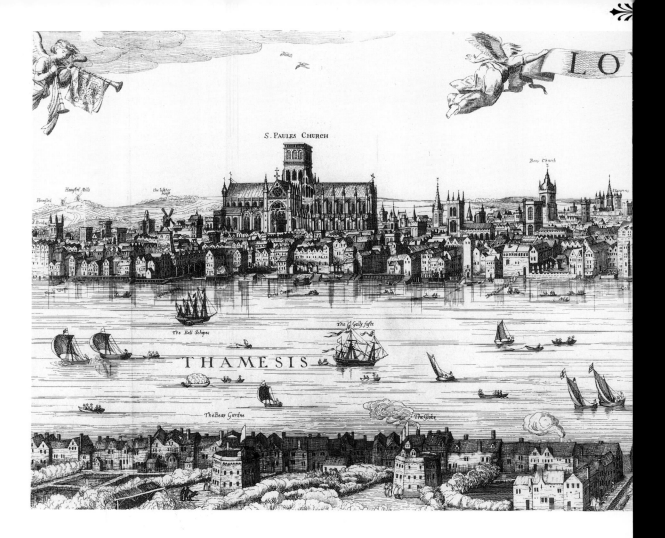

HENRY VII ruled over a country with less than three million inhabitants. In the absence of any official census figures, historians can only estimate the size of the population by examining tax returns and the call-up for military service, which are not always a reliable guide, and experts therefore disagree to some extent about the figures. But recent research indicates that the total population of England, having risen from approximately 2,000,000 in 1066 to nearly 4,000,000 in 1340, fell again, as a result of the Black Death and other plagues, to 2,100,000 in 1400, then rose during the fifteenth century to 2,600,000 in 1500 and to 4,000,000 by the end of the Tudor Age in 1600.

There were probably about 50,000 inhabitants of London in 1500. London could not compare in size with Naples and Paris, each with over 200,000 inhabitants but it was nevertheless one of the largest cities in Europe, and much bigger than any other town in England. Its population increased fourfold during the Tudor Age, rising to

FLUVIUS

South Warke

100,000 by 1560 and to 200,000 by 1600. The second largest city in England was probably Norwich, with about 13,000 inhabitants in 1500, followed by Bristol and Newcastle with 10,000 and Salisbury, York and Exeter with 8,000. There were some

Above: a section of Visscher's panorama of the Thames. It is taken from the South Bank, with Southwark near the centre of the portion reproduced here. Allowing for artist's licence, and distortion of perspective owing to the curve of the river's course, this is substantially the landscape and riverscape which Shakespeare would have seen on his arrival in London from Stratford-on-Avon in 1586. Though the engraving was not published in London until 1616, the artist, Nicholas John Visscher, probably engraved it in Amsterdam on the basis of maps and perspective drawings done several years earlier.

The pre-Wren St Paul's dominates the landscape on the left of the engraving, as does London Bridge on the right. The wooden steeple on St Paul's had been burnt down in 1561, and was never rebuilt. On the North Bank skyline, to the East of St Paul's, are marked Bow Church, with its ornate lantern, the Guild Hall, the prominent spire of St Laurence Poultney, and the oriental tower of the Royal Exchange. Close to the far end of London Bridge are the steps leading down to the river.

51

thirty other towns, most of which are today the county towns of England, with a population of about 5,000 each. Most of the 760 market towns had less than 2,000 inhabitants. The rest of the people lived in the countryside, in the villages and hamlets which still exist today, in nearly every case with a very similar name.

Most of the towns were still surrounded by their medieval walls, which remained until nearly a hundred years after the end of the Tudor Age. The gates in the walls were closed at nightfall, making it impossible for anyone to enter or leave the town at night without giving a good reason to the officers at the gatehouse. London was surrounded by its old walls to the east, north and west, with the south side protected by the River Thames. The whole length of the walls, from the Tower of London in the south-east to Blackfriars in the south-west, was nearly two and a half miles.

The walls of London looked rather untidy and patched-up. There was nearly always some part of the wall which was in a bad state of repair, even if it had not completely fallen down. Then one of the city livery companies, or a monastery, or some wealthy merchant living nearby, would repair their portion of the wall at their own expense, so that this part of the wall would then look much newer and more secure than the adjacent parts. The wall had originally been surrounded on the outer side by a great ditch; but though parts of the ditch still remained, elsewhere it had been filled in.

There were ten gates through which people could enter and leave London by land. On the eastern side, there was the postern gate at the Tower and the great gate at Aldgate; on the northern side, the great gate at Bishopsgate, the postern gates at Moorgate and Cripplegate, and the great gate at Aldersgate; and on the western side, the great gates of Newgate and Ludgate, beyond which was the Fleet river running south from Holborn into the Thames. On the southern side there was the Bridge Gate on London Bridge, apart from the public and private watergates at which it was possible to land from barges. Another postern gate was built in the north wall in 1553, after the old monastery of the Greyfriars had become Christ's Hospital.

London Bridge was the only bridge over the Thames between the sea and the bridge at Kingston, twenty miles up river. The older, wooden London Bridge had been replaced three hundred years earlier by a stone bridge which had taken thirty-three years to build, between 1176 and 1209. The Londoners were proud of London Bridge, and remembered the construction of the bridge in the popular song

London Bridge is falling down.
How shall we build it up again?
Build it up with silver and gold?
Silver and gold will be stolen away.
Build it up with iron and steel?

Iron and steel will bend and bow.
Build it up with wood and clay?
Wood and clay will wash away.
Build it up with stone so strong,
Then 'twill last for ages long.

A woodcut from the *Chronycle of Englonde*, published by Caxton's successor, Wynken de Worde, in 1497. It is a somewhat fanciful image of the Tower of London.

John Norden's view of London Bridge, looking from the East to the West, c.1593. In his address to the Lord Mayor, printed below the map, Norden explained that this map, though published some twenty years later, was drawn in Queen Elizabeth's reign. He described the bridge as 'the most famous in the world . . . adorned with sumptuous buildings, & statlie and beautiful Houses on either side, inhabited by wealthy Citizens, and furnished with all manner Trades.'

It was to last for 623 years, until 1832, and then it did not fall down, but was demolished because its twenty arches, sixty feet high and thirty feet wide, with only twenty feet between each arch, did not allow enough room for the bigger ships of the early nineteenth century to pass. But not all the bridge was of stone. A short part of it, near the southern end, was a wooden drawbridge, which could be raised by the guards at the Bridge Gate to prevent an enemy force from crossing the bridge.

There was a tower and a gate at both ends, and houses on both sides of the bridge. The people living in the houses in 1485 had had some frightening experiences in recent years. In 1450 the rebels under Jack Cade had tried to cross the bridge into London, and had been driven back after a sharp fight on the bridge. In 1471, a Lancastrian force attacked Yorkist London, and burned all thirteen houses at the side of the drawbridge. In 1481, one of the houses fell into the river, and five people in the house died. But most of the inhabitants of London Bridge survived, and went on living on the bridge as London entered the Tudor Age.

There were several other bridges leading out of London. There were three stone bridges across the Fleet Dike. Fleet Bridge was at the bottom of Ludgate Hill outside Ludgate, at what is today Ludgate Circus at the end of Fleet Street. Holborn Bridge, a quarter of a mile to the north of Fleet Bridge, crossed Fleet Dike near the present

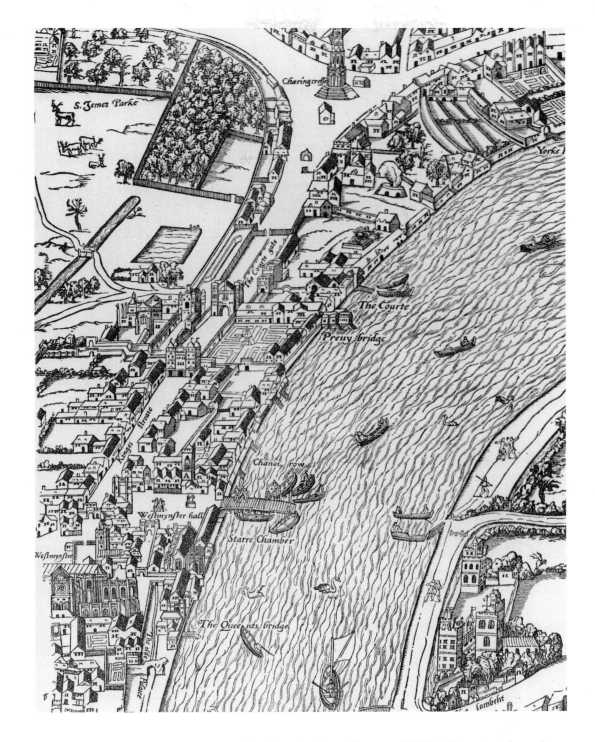

A leaf from the Ralph Agas map (1560) showing what is now known as Whitehall running down from 'Charingcrosse' towards Westminster. At the foot of 'Kinge's Streate', on the left, is Westminster Hall, backing on to the 'Starre Chamber'. Beyond that is Westminster Abbey.

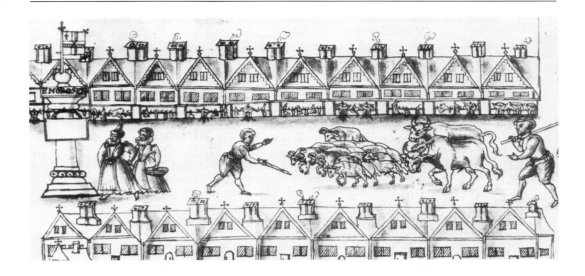

Livestock being driven to market in Eastcheap. An engraving from *A Caveat to the City of London*, by Hugh Alley, 1598.

Holborn Viaduct, and was the road taken by travellers who left London by Newgate for the north and west. About 150 yards north of Holborn Bridge, a wooden bridge named Cow Bridge also crossed the Fleet Dike by the Bishop of Ely's town house, Ely Place, just north of the village of Holborn, near the place where today Gray's Inn Road crosses Clerkenwell Road and Theobalds Road. There were also other bridges across the Town Ditch, which were crossed by travellers immediately after they passed through the gates to the north and east of London.

By the beginning of the Tudor Age, the boundaries of the city of London had spread beyond the walls and ditch at every point. To the east, the houses stretched for more than a mile along the northern bank of the Thames to Ratcliff, from where the road continued into the country down an avenue of elm trees to Lime Hurst, which by the end of the Tudor Age was more often called Limehouse. To the east of Aldgate, the houses went as far as the White Chapel and half a mile beyond it. The houses near Limehouse were often inhabited by sailors. On the north side, the houses stretched even further beyond the wall, from Bishopsgate to Shoreditch and from Moorgate to the village of Finsbury. Travellers who left London through Newgate and went north came first to the open space at Smithfield, where heretics were burned, before reaching the houses around Clerkenwell Priory. Just south of the priory the road forked. The right-hand fork carried on to the east of the priory along the road to the village of Islington. The left-hand fork went west across Cow Bridge to Tyburn, which is now called Marble Arch, and to Kensington and Hammersmith.

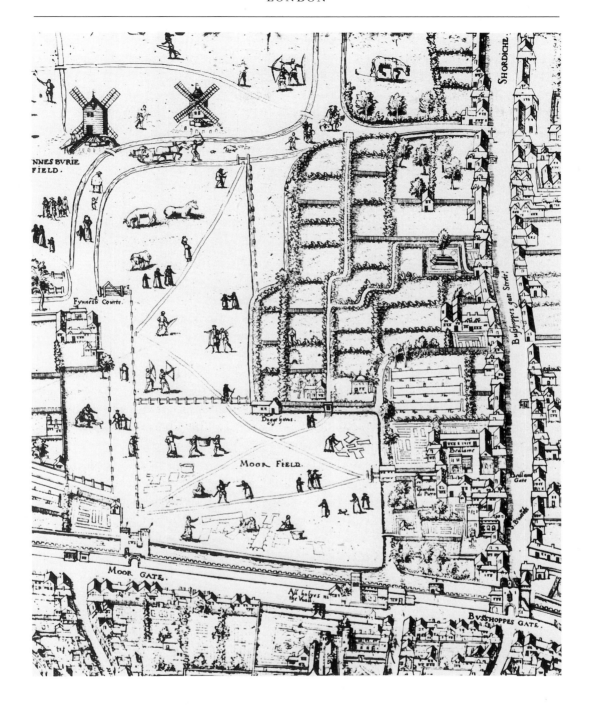

Another leaf from the Agas map, showing Moor Gate and 'Byshoppes Gate', with Moor Fields in the centre, looking much more like a moor than they do today.

The built-up area extended furthest to the west. The road through Ludgate went down Ludgate Hill, past the Fleet prison, across Fleet Bridge and up the hill between Fleet Market and the Temple, which had ceased to be a monastery nearly 200 years before and had become the site of two of the Inns of Court where the common lawyers lived and worked. On passing Temple Bar and leaving the limits of the City of London, the traveller immediately entered the City of Westminster, which by the beginning of the Tudor Age was rivalling London in importance. On its northern limits, in Drury Lane, which nearly touched Holborn, there were houses of important courtiers; by the middle of the sixteenth century these included Cecil House, the town house of William Cecil, Lord Burghley. There were also houses of important people all along the Strand on the north bank of the Thames as far as Charing Cross; these included Somerset Place, the house of Edward Seymour, Duke of Somerset, and Durham Place, the Bishop of Durham's town residence.

The traveller who turned left at Charing Cross, following the bend in the river, soon came to the large mansion on the waterfront which Cardinal Wolsey, Henry VIII's Lord Chancellor and Archbishop of York, had finished building by 1525. This splendid residence of the Cardinal of York was known as York Place. After Wolsey's fall from power in 1529, he was persuaded to give it to the King in a futile attempt to regain the royal favour. It then became known as Whitehall, and was the chief residence in Westminster of Henry VIII and his three children, Edward VI, Mary and Elizabeth I. Like all the large houses on the river in London and Westminster, it had its private stairs leading down to the water, and a landing place where the residents in the palace could leave and arrive by barge.

About half a mile south of Whitehall was Westminster Hall and Westminster Abbey. Westminster Hall was the chief public building in the realm, where all the most important official meetings were held. It was here that the King addressed Parliament, and that the House of Lords sat, though the House of Commons met in the adjacent building, St Stephen's Chapel. The King's common law court, the Court of King's Bench, sat in Westminster Hall; the great state trials of traitors were held

Opposite: The earliest painting of London. A miniature in the Flemish style painted in England *circa* 1500, as a frontispiece to a volume of poems composed by Charles, Duke of Orleans, who was the Commander of the French forces at Agincourt and was taken prisoner and brought to London. The Duke is shown looking from an upper window of the White Tower of London. He is also shown sitting in the White Tower and writing a letter to France just before his release in 1440, and, yet again, riding with his ransomer through the Byward Tower on the left. These historical scenes are shown against a background of London buildings as they looked some sixty years later. In the distance are Tower Bridge and St Paul's. The impressive colonnaded building in the background, to the right, is either the Customs House or Billingsgate.

Lambeth Palace, still the London home of the Archbishop of Canterbury, with a distant view across the Thames towards Westminster and the Strand. The brick gatehouse tower was completed in 1484. Each of the great palaces of the Strand had a similar gatehouse. The large oil painting of which a detail is reproduced above was done by an imitator of Leonard Knyff in the 1680s.

here; and it was used for the coronation banquet after the new King had been crowned in the Abbey.

At the beginning of the Tudor Age, Westminster Abbey was one of the most important of the 513 monasteries in England. With its twenty-five monks it was only the seventeenth in size, but it was the richest of all; its annual income was £2,409, whereas the priory of Christchurch in Canterbury, which was the largest monastery in the country with seventy monks, had an annual income of £2,374. Westminster Abbey was on the very edge of the built-up area of Westminster and London. The open country began with Tothill Fields, at the Abbey gates, where Tothill Street and St James's Underground Station stand today. The fields and woodlands continued to the north of Tothill Fields, surrounding the new royal palace of St James's which Henry VIII built at the end of his reign, and linking up with Hyde Park. To the south and west of Tothill Fields, the open country continued up river to the village of Chelsea, two miles away.

By the beginning of the sixteenth century there was a substantial built-up area on the south bank of the river across London Bridge in the borough of Southwark. By 1600 there were continuous buildings and little alleyways on both sides of the main street, Long Southwark, which ran south from London Bridge for a mile to the New Town (or Newington), where the open country began. There were continuous buildings for a mile along the south bank to the west of London Bridge, which reached nearly to the village of Lambeth, where the Archbishop of Canterbury's palace was situated; while the buildings extended the other way along the south bank to the east of London Bridge, along St Olaf's Street, for half a mile to the village of Rotherhithe.

The river was the boundary between the counties of Middlesex and Surrey and the dioceses of London and Winchester; but the jurisdiction of the Lord Mayor and corporation of London had been extended to apply to Southwark. There were important houses and buildings in Southwark. The Bishop of Winchester had his town residence there, on the fringe of his diocese. In the reign of Henry VIII, the King's great favourite and brother-in-law, Charles Brandon, Duke of Suffolk, built a mansion in Southwark. The Marshalsea prison was on the east side of Long Southwark, about half a mile from London Bridge. It afterwards became famous, in the nineteenth century, as a debtors' prison; but in Tudor times Ludgate was the debtors' prison, and the Marshalsea, along with the Counter, the King's Bench prison and the Clink in Southwark, the Fleet prison and Newgate across the river, and the Gatehouse in Westminster, was used as a prison for various kinds of offenders, including political suspects charged with sedition, whose offences were thought not to be sufficiently serious to merit imprisonment in the Tower and a charge of high treason. Many prominent politicians and propagandists, after

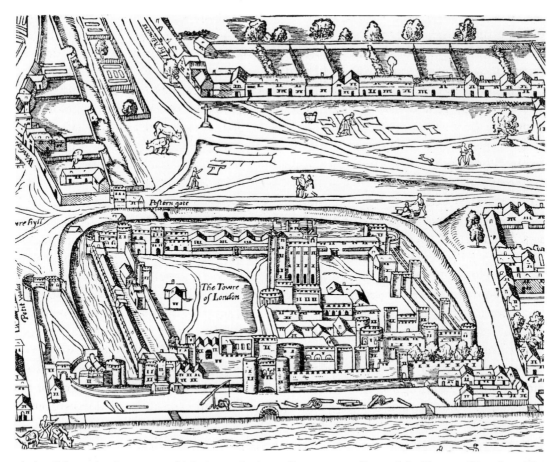

A detail from the Agas map which shows the immediate surroundings of the Tower of London. The watergate, seen in the middle of the frontage to the Thames, was where those about to be imprisoned were landed from barges, to avoid demonstrations. Tower Hill is in the top left-hand corner of this map, near the Postern Gate.

experiencing the shock of being arrested for sedition, were relieved to find that they were being sent to the Fleet or the Marshalsea and not to the Tower.

The city was dominated by the great Tower of London, at the south-east edge of the city on the north bank of the Thames. Nearly everybody in England, including Shakespeare, believed that the building of the Tower had been started by Julius Caesar; but a few historians and antiquaries knew that this was untrue, and that it had first been built by William the Conqueror in 1078. It covered an area of 400 yards square, and had eighteen towers and other buildings. By 1597 the tower on the riverside was being called 'the Bloody Tower' because of the mysterious suicide or murder there of the Earl of Northumberland in 1585, but in the Tudor Age it was usually called 'the tower by the watergate'. People who left or arrived at the Tower by barge embarked and landed at the watergate. Important prisoners who were arrested on a charge of high treason were often brought to the Tower by barge, including Henry VIII's second Queen, Anne Boleyn, and her daughter, the future Elizabeth I, when she was the Lady Elizabeth in the reign of her sister Queen Mary. It was more difficult for the prisoners to escape from the barge than if they were taken by land through the streets of London, and it avoided the risk of demonstrations of sympathy for the prisoners from the Londoners. So the watergate afterwards became known as 'Traitors' Gate'; but the name was not used during the sixteenth century.

The Tower was a royal residence and an arsenal as well as a prison. The King's apartments were in the White Tower. Most of his cannon, and a large quantity of other weapons, such as pikes and armour, were ordinarily stored in the Tower. In times of rebellion hundreds of prisoners were sometimes herded into the Tower; but usually only the most serious offenders were imprisoned there. Some of the prisoners were kept in strict confinement in their prison cells, in complete isolation from the other prisoners; but the social conventions of the age made it impossible to deprive a nobleman or a gentleman, however heinous a traitor or heretic he might be, from being attended by his personal servant; nor could a noble lady or a gentlewoman be prevented from being attended by her lady's maid. These servants were sometimes able to smuggle messages in and out of the Tower; but the authorities were of course aware of this danger, and the servants were very carefully watched. They hardly ever succeeded in arranging for their imprisoned master or mistress to escape, and only the Jesuit, Father Gerard, and his friend John Arden in 1597 succeeded in escaping from the Tower during the Tudor Age.

If a prisoner's offence was not considered to be outstandingly serious, he was allowed 'the liberty of the Tower', which meant that he could walk freely in the garden and anywhere he wished within the walls of the Tower. Prisoners in strict confinement, and their families and friends, petitioned the King and the Council to be allowed the liberty of the Tower; and if the favour was granted to a prisoner after he had been confined in his cell for some weeks or months, it was usually a sign that the authorities were going to take a lenient view of his offence, and perhaps that his release might be imminent.

The King had other royal palaces in London besides the Tower, for he sometimes stayed at Baynards Castle and Bridewell; and by the sixteenth century it had become the custom that the King resided in the Tower for the first few weeks after he came to the throne, until his coronation, and never stayed there again, unless he was threatened with great danger. Henry VII sent his wife and children to stay in the Tower when the Cornish rebels marched on London and reached Blackheath in 1497; but none of the succeeding Tudor sovereigns ever lived there after their coronation, no doubt because they believed that if it were known that they had taken up their

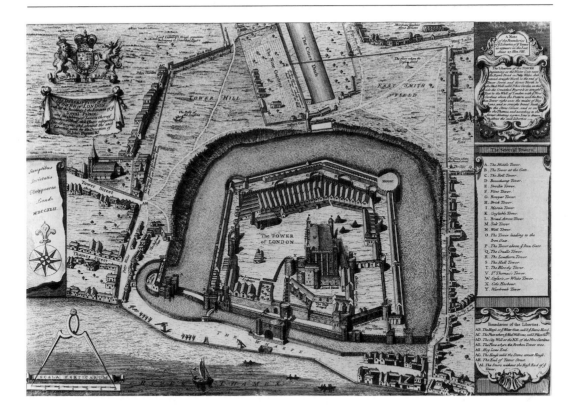

'A True and Exact Draught of the Tower Liberties, survey'd in the Year 1597 by Gulielmus Haiward and J. Gascoyne.' Tower Hill is towards the top left-hand corner of the engraving. 'The Citie's Ditch' is top centre. The 'Liberties' of the Tower were the areas in which favoured prisoners, or those about to be released, were allowed to take exercise or meet their friends.

residence there, this would start a rumour that they were threatened by a dangerous revolt.

The coronation of the new King, with the religious ceremony and its link with the ancient biblical concept of anointment, had made such an impression on the people that in earlier times the idea had spread unofficially that a King did not obtain his authority to reign, and his right to demand allegiance from his subjects, until after he had been crowned. For this reason, the coronation was always held almost immediately after the new sovereign's accession. This idea had been firmly dispelled by the beginning of the Tudor Age, but it was still thought desirable for him to be crowned as soon as possible.

In the nineteenth and twentieth centuries it became the practice to postpone the coronation for more than a year after the accession; but every Tudor sovereign was crowned within three months of coming to the throne. Henry VII, after defeating Richard III at Bosworth on 22 August 1485 and being proclaimed King on the battlefield, had wished to be crowned at Westminster as soon as he reached London; but the outbreak of the terrible sweating sickness forced him to postpone the coronation until 30 October 1485. When Henry died at Richmond on 21 April 1509, the new King, Henry VIII, who had been at his father's bedside at Richmond, moved within a few days to the Tower of London, and fixed the date of his coronation on 24 June, Midsummer Day and the Feast of St John the Baptist.

On the day before the coronation, Henry VIII went on the traditional procession through the streets of London on his way from the Tower to Westminster. He always loved ceremony and show, and his coronation procession was more splendid than any of his predecessors'. The streets were decorated with cloth-of-gold; the Lord Mayor and aldermen, and the masters of the livery companies, were in the streets to salute the King as he passed; so were virgins dressed in white, and priests who censed him and his Queen as they passed. Henry, who was dressed in crimson velvet lined with ermine and a coat with gold, diamonds, rubies and emeralds, rode on a

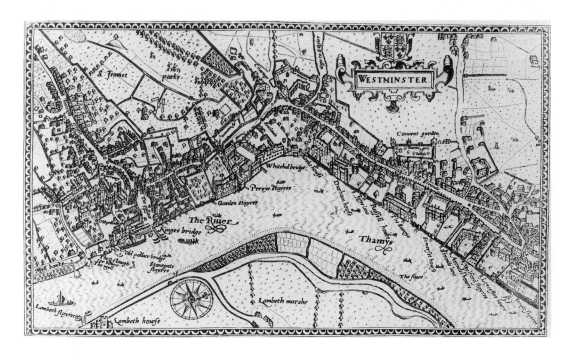

A page from the *Speculum Britanniae* of John Norden, published in 1593.

65

Westminster Abbey, the north aisle of Henry VII's chapel. An engraving by S. Sparrow, from a drawing by J.C. Smith, published in 1808.

66

splendidly accoutred horse, surrounded by his bodyguard, along Bread Street, Gracechurch Street, Cheapside and Cornhill; and his Queen, Catherine of Aragon, whom he had married twelve days before, followed a little way behind him in a litter escorted by her ladies and attendants. On leaving London and entering Westminster at Temple Bar, the King and the procession went along the Strand to Charing Cross and then continued to Westminster Abbey, where Henry and Catherine slept that night as guests of the monks, while the great crowds who had lined the streets went home filled with admiration for their handsome young King.

Next day the coronation took place in the great church of the Abbey. After the coronation, the King and Queen and the notables went across the road for the traditional coronation banquet in Westminster Hall. During the meal, the King's Champion rode into the hall on horseback and offered to fight any traitor who denied the King's right to the throne. The office of King's Champion, which was hereditary, was held by Sir Robert Dimock. He had performed this duty as King's Champion at the coronation of Richard III in 1483. Just over two years after he had challenged any traitor who denied that Richard was the lawful King, Dimock performed the ceremony again at the coronation of Henry VII, who had proclaimed Richard a usurper and killed him. Twenty-four years later, Dimock, performed the ceremony for the third time at the coronation of Henry VIII.

Edward VI, who was nine when he became King at Henry VIII's death on 28 January 1547, was crowned within a month, on 20 February. Again there was a procession from the Tower to Westminster on the eve of the coronation, with the city dignitaries, the cheering crowds, pageants and acrobats. The national pride had been aroused by the capture of Boulogne and the burning of Edinburgh in the last years of Henry VIII's reign, and the people looked forward to the day when their new boy King would grow up and emulate and extend his father's victories, and rule over England, Ireland, Scotland and France. As he passed through the streets of London in the coronation procession, the people sang a new song that someone had composed for the occasion:

> He hath gotten already Boulogne, that godly town,
> And biddeth sing speedily up, up, and not down.
> When he waxeth might and to manhood doth spring
> He shall be straight then of four realms the King.
> Sing up, heart, sing up, heart, and sing no more down,
> But joy in King Edward that weareth the crown.

After Edward died on 6 July 1553, Mary defeated Jane Grey's supporters and was proclaimed Queen in London on 19 July. She arrived there after her march from

Norfolk on 3 August, and was crowned on 1 October. Her coronation procession through London was a little more subdued than those of Henry VIII and Edward VI, perhaps because she was too preoccupied with the religious changes which she was contemplating to encourage a great popular demonstration in her own honour. Although she was an accomplished horsewoman, and had ridden into London through Aldgate on horseback two months before, she rode in a coach in the coronation procession. Next, in a coach immediately behind the Queen, came those two well-known Protestant ladies, the Lady Elizabeth and her stepmother the Lady Anne of Cleves, who were both about to become Catholics, under duress.

Elizabeth I became Queen on Mary's death on 17 November 1558, and was crowned on 15 January 1559. Her coronation procession through London on the previous day was not merely, as always, a festive occasion, but was also a great Protestant demonstration by her supporters. She had already made it clear that she intended to restore the Protestant religion in England; she had stopped the burning of heretics, and had walked out of her chapel royal when the priest elevated the Host during Mass. The savage persecution of Protestants in Mary's reign had increased their support in London; it was probably the only part of the country, except for Kent, where they were already a majority of the population.

The five pageants along the route of the coronation procession, in Gracechurch Street, Cornhill, at the Great Conduit in Cheapside, in Paul's Churchyard, and at the conduit in Fleet Street, were all Protestant propaganda. There were pictures, and actors representing, not only the Queen's father Henry VIII, who had overthrown the power of the Pope, but also her Protestant mother, Anne Boleyn, who had never been officially rehabilitated after her execution for adultery and high treason, but was still regarded as an innocent victim by the Protestant extremists. There were pictures of 'Deborah the judge and restorer of the house of Israel', and several slogans comparing Elizabeth with this Old Testament heroine who, though a woman, had been chosen by God to save His people. At the conduit in Cheap, the Queen was handed a Protestant English Bible; she held it to her breast, and promised that she would always read it and adhere to its teaching.

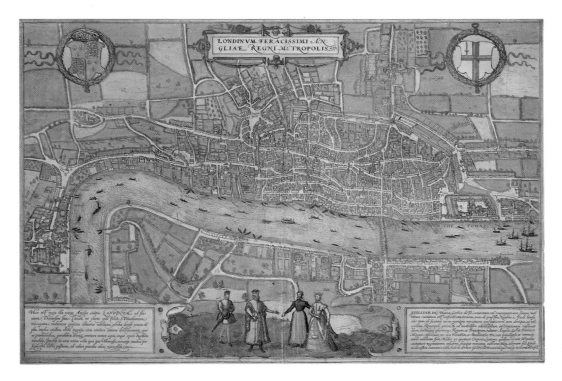

Above: Braun and Hogenberg's copper engraving of London was published in a German edition in 1572. The edition reproduced above is of 1574 and is assumed to show a view of London c.1558.

Below: A tin-glazed earthenware dish with an inscription in praise of Queen Elizabeth. It is dated 1600 and is believed to be unique. The buildings in the background are assumed to be the Tower of London.

On the eve of his Coronation in 1547 the young Edward VI went in procession from the Tower of London to Westminster. Here he is seen, on a white horse caparisoned in crimson, under a canopy held by four outriders, passing along Cheapside. These Coronation processions began in the reign of Richard II and continued until the reign of James II. The illustration above is reproduced from a

watercolour copy made in 1785 by S.H. Grimm for the Society of Antiquaries of a picture painted c.1547, which was at Cowdray until it was destroyed by fire in 1793. Along the route here illustrated are the church of St Mary-le-bow, with its conspicuous clock, the great cross in Cheapside, the spire of St Paul's, Ludgate and Charing Cross. In the distance are the woodlands of Southwark.

71

Clemens et Regni moderatrix iusta Britâni
Hac forma insigni conspicienda nitet.

Tristia dum gentes circùm omnes bella fatigant,
Cæciq; errores toto grassantur in orbe.
An. Dni. pace beas longa, vera et pietate Britannos: 1 5 7 9
Iusticia moderans miti sapienter habenas.
Chara domi, celebrisq; foris, longæuaq; regni
Hic teneas, regno tandem fruitura perenni.

THE KING'S HIGHWAY

T HE countryside in the sixteenth century had a different appearance from the
countryside today, though the removal of so many hedgerows in the last
forty years has made the England of 1988 look a little more like Tudor
England than did the England of 1950. The low-lying and fertile parts of the country
consisted of large fields unbroken by hedges, and only occasionally by stone
boundary-walls. Only Devonshire and parts of Kent were divided into small fields by
hedges, and probably looked very like the counties that we know.

The countryside was interspersed by roads, the King's highway, which was
sometimes straight and sometimes winding, and linked the market towns. No roads
bypassed the towns, for their chief use was to enable the people to get to market;
where there were no towns, there were no highways, only rough tracks leading to the
farms and villages.

Most of the people travelling along the roads were going to, or returning from,
market. Most walked on foot, though some of them rode on horseback. Many were
driving herds of animals along the roads. There were carts carrying various
commodities, including some kinds of food, such as fruit and vegetables; but as there
was no way of preserving the food for very long, it was seldom taken further than the
nearest town. It was very unusual for meat to be carried along the roads in carts; the
butchers in the towns normally arranged for cows, sheep and pigs to be driven to the

Opposite: The frontispiece to Christopher Saxton's *Atlas of England and Wales*, 1579. The engraving is
attributed to the geographical draughtsman Hogenberg. Queen Elizabeth, enthroned in robes of
state, and bearing the crown and sceptre, is flanked by figures representing Astronomy and
Geography. In a medallion above her head Peace and Justice embrace one another. Below, on the left,
a cartographer is drawing a map of England, whilst in the right-hand corner an astronomer examines
through a cross-staff the progress of a comet.

town from some farm in the country on their four feet and then kept alive, wandering in their gardens or in the streets outside their shops, until they were ready for slaughter.

At the beginning of the Tudor Age, the animals were usually slaughtered by the butcher on his premises in the town; but many of his neighbours found this objectionable. In London, the people who lived in the parishes of St Faith's and St Gregory's near St Paul's Cathedral objected to the slaughtering of animals and the scalding of swine that was carried on at the butchery of St Nicholas Fleshamless. After the canons of St Paul's had been complaining about the butchery for sixteen years, they and the parishioners presented a petition to Henry VII. They told him that the air in the district was polluted by 'blood and other fouler things unto your most noble Grace not to be named', which flowed through the streets from the slaughterhouse. The stench pervaded to that part of the palace adjoining St Paul's where the King waited before entering the cathedral when he came there on state occasions; and this may have helped to persuade Parliament to pass an Act in 1489 which prohibited the slaughter of animals, not only within the city of London, but also within the confines of any walled town in England, except Berwick and Carlisle. The ban remained in force for forty-three years; but it was repealed in 1533 after the butchers at the slaughterhouse of St Nicholas had built underground sewers to take the blood and filth, so that the butchery was no longer a nuisance to the local inhabitants.

People who were ill, or very old and incapacitated, sometimes travelled in litters carried by servants on foot or drawn by horses; but there were no carriages or coaches at the beginning of the Tudor Age. The first coaches to be seen in England appeared in the streets of London in the 1550s. Walter Rippon, a Dutchman living in London, built a coach for the Earl of Rutland in 1555; in 1564 he built a coach for Elizabeth I, for whom he built another coach twenty years later. But even at the end of the Tudor Age there were only a few coaches in England; they did not become common until the seventeenth century.

Some people on the road in 1500 were travelling further than the nearest market town. Pilgrims went to the famous shrines to pray beside the corpses or bones of the saints. They came from all over England, and from many parts of Western Europe, to the most famous of them all, the shrine of Our Lady of Walsingham in Norfolk and the tomb of St Thomas of Canterbury – Archbishop Thomas Becket – in the cathedral where he had been assassinated by order of King Henry II in 1170. Scholars travelled to the universities of Oxford and Cambridge from all parts of England, and learned foreign doctors came there from the universities of Europe. English and foreign merchants travelled far to attend the great national and international fairs in London and the Stourbridge Fair in Cambridge. They came from Antwerp,

Ruins of the Priory Church, Walsingham, one of the two great places of pilgrimage in the sixteenth century. Engraved by S. Rawle, after a drawing by Joseph Gandy, for John Britton's *Architectural Beauties of Great Britain*, 1835.

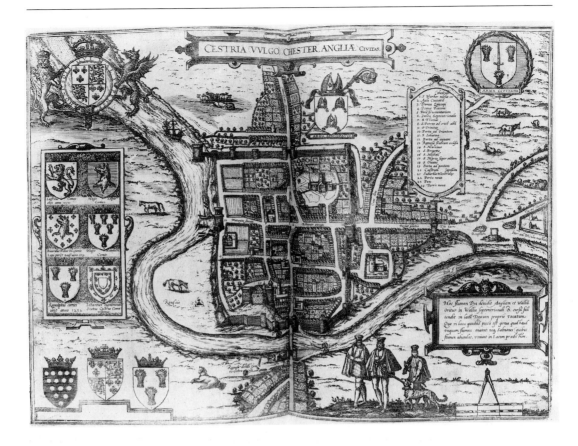

Chester. The town plan edited by Georg Braun and engraved by Frans Hogenberg in *Civitates Orbis Terrarum*, published in Cologne between 1572 and 1618.

Scandinavia and the Hansa towns of North Germany to Harwich or Ipswich by sea and on from there to Cambridge along the Essex and Suffolk roads.

Many Englishmen, and an even larger number of Englishwomen, never in their lives left the parish in which they were born, lived and died; but others, more adventurous, travelled to London or elsewhere to seek their fortune, or just to visit friends, though they risked arrest and a flogging if they left their parish without a licence from the authorities, and could give no satisfactory explanation of their reason for travelling. There were also the officials travelling on government business, and the couriers taking letters, reports and instructions from the Privy Council and royal officials in Westminster to the local administrators in the country, and returning with the administrators' reports to the Council. Foreign ambassadors regularly sent long letters to their Kings containing reports on the situation in England; at times of crisis, they might write several times a week. Their couriers were constantly riding along the roads of England and Western Europe, in all weathers and at all seasons of the year, with these letters in their pouches.

If the common man wished to travel a great distance across England, he usually walked. As the old song put it:

> Which is the way to London town?
> One foot up, the other foot down,
> That is the way to London town.

If a man was not wealthy enough to own a horse, he could hire one for his journey; but this was expensive, for it cost one shilling – three days' wages for the agricultural labourer – to hire a horse for the thirty miles from Southwark to Rochester.

The traveller on foot could not hope to go much more than twenty miles a day at the most, and the ordinary horseman went only a little further. It was unusual for a traveller to ride more than thirty miles a day; and in bad weather, on the muddy roads, or in hilly country, progress could be restricted to two miles an hour, or some fifteen miles a day. The roads had been deteriorating for over a thousand years, ever since the days of the Romans. A minimum of road repairs was carried out by forced labour. An Act passed by Queen Mary's Parliament in 1555 required every cottager and householder to work for eight hours a day on four days in the year repairing the roads in his parish, or to find someone else to do his stint for him. Every landowner holding land which was worth £50 a year or more was required to provide two men to work on the roads for this length of time. In 1563, an Act of Elizabeth I's Parliament increased the labour to eight hours a day for six days in the year.

Greater efforts were made to improve the streets in some of the towns and the busy approach roads to London. In 1534 the inhabitants of Holborn petitioned Henry VIII to take action about the state of the road leading out of London from Holborn Bridge to the bars at the west end of the street, for 'not alonely your subjects and inhabitants within the said street of Holborn' but also the carriers and other travellers 'repairing weekly and monthly to your city of London' along the street (which was 'the common passage for all carryings carried from the west and north-west parts of the realm') were in danger of their lives from the risk of falling into the holes in the road. An Act was therefore passed which required every landowner whose property had a frontage on the road to pave his side of the road. This principle was extended by an Act of 1543 to many streets in London and Westminster, from Tothill Street and Petty France along the Strand and as far as Moorgate and Smithfield. A statute of 1571 ordered that the roads between Aldgate and Whitechapel, and between the Tower and Ratcliff, should be paved by the landowners, because travellers 'on horseback and on foot are become so mired and foul in the winter time as hard it is to have any passage for the same through the said ways'.

Between 1544 and 1549 the streets of Cambridge, Chester and Calais were paved, for Parliament did not know that Calais would be captured by the French nine years later and would never again be an English town. Acts of Mary's Parliament in 1553 required the roads from Shaftesbury to Sherborne and from Gloucester to Bristol to be paved by the inhabitants of the parishes all along the roads. Elizabeth I's Parliaments in 1576, 1581, 1597 and 1601 ordered the paving of the streets of Chichester and of all the roads within five miles of Oxford, and the repair of the bridges at Rochester, Chepstow, Newport, Caerleon and Wye, and the two bridges over the River Eden near Carlisle; but nothing was done to repair the dangerous wooden bridge across the Tweed at Berwick until the reign of James I. James had been very frightened when he crossed the bridge at his first entry into his new realm of England in 1603, and he ordered that the bridge should be demolished and replaced by a new stone bridge which, under the name of the Old Bridge, still stands.

The roads in the Weald of Sussex, Surrey and Kent were a special problem, because the carts in which the ironmasters carried coal to their foundries, and their iron products from the foundries to their destination, caused a great deal of damage to the roads. After various other remedies had failed, an Act of 1597 required every ironmaster in the Weald who carried three loads of coal or one ton of iron for more than one mile along the roads between 12 October and 1 May, or thirty loads of coal or ten tons of iron in the summer, to contribute to the cost of repairing the road with cinders, gravel, stone or chalk.

There were four great long-distance roads in England which were kept in a relatively good state of repair and were used by many important travellers. There was the Great North Road from London to Berwick and on across the Border into Scotland; the Watling Street from London to Chester, which was used by travellers to Ireland; the Dover Road, which travellers used to go from London to Dover for the crossing to Calais; and the great road from London to the West, to Exeter and on to Plymouth. The King's messengers used the relays of fresh horses which were awaiting them at the 'staging posts' along these roads; the staging posts were usually inns about twenty or thirty miles apart. Riders travelling 'in post' could cover much greater distances in a day than the ordinary traveller.

The Great North Road left London through Bishopsgate, and passed through Islington, Enfield, Hoddesdon, Ware, Royston, Huntingdon, Stamford, Grantham and Doncaster on the way to York. North of York, the traveller entered a very sparsely populated area, but the Great North Road continued through Thirsk and Northallerton to Darneton (Darlington), which was an important military post and the rear headquarters of the military administrative staff during campaigns against the Scots; then on through Durham, Newcastle and Alnwick to the frontier town of

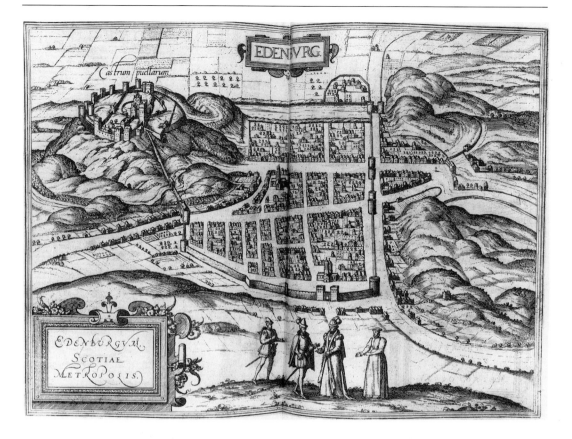

Edinburgh. The town plan edited by Georg Braun and engraved by Frans Hogenberg in *Civitates Orbis Terrarum*, published in Cologne between 1572 and 1618.

Berwick-upon-Tweed, the important bridgehead across the Tweed which the English had captured in 1296 and recaptured in 1482, and which they regarded as the counterpart of their other bridgehead, Calais, on the French side of the Channel. The Great North Road continued into Scotland for another sixty miles along the coast by Dunbar and Haddington to Edinburgh.

The Great North Road was one of only six roads which existed in England north of York. Another was the road into Scotland from Newcastle by Otterburn across the Cheviot Hills to Jedburgh and Kelso, which was the shortest way to Edinburgh, but much more dangerous for travellers than the Great North Road, because of the 'moss-troopers', the bandits who robbed and killed travellers on both sides of the Border. The King's Street ran north from Lancaster to Penrith and Carlisle. Two roads went from east to west, the road from York by Catterick Bridge to Penrith and the road running from Newcastle to Carlisle by Hexham and Haltwhistle along the north bank of the Tyne. The sixth road north of York was the road from York to the port of Scarborough, from where a busy trade was carried on with Scandinavia.

The journey from London to Edinburgh took the normal traveller a fortnight at his rate of thirty miles a day; but messengers in post could do it in five days. The record for the journey was set up in March 1603, when the news of Elizabeth I's death was carried to her heir, King James VI of Scotland, by Sir Robert Carey, a gentleman of Northumberland, who earlier had won a wager of £2,000 by walking the 340 miles from London to Berwick in twelve days. Elizabeth died at Richmond in Surrey at about two o'clock in the morning of Thursday 24 March 1603. Carey left Richmond at once and, after waiting for a few hours in Westminster, rode that day to Doncaster, a distance of 155 miles. Next day he rode 140 miles to Widrington in Northumberland, and on the Saturday went on for 100 miles to Edinburgh, reaching James's palace of Holyroodhouse just as the King was sitting down to supper at 6 p.m., having covered the distance from London in less than sixty hours. His achievement was not equalled till it was surpassed by a stage-coach which brought the news from London to Glasgow of the passing of the Reform Bill in 1832; and soon after this, the building of the railways made it possible for any traveller to do the journey from London to Edinburgh in ten hours.

The Dover Road ran across London Bridge and along the south bank of the Thames to Gravesend, though wealthy travellers usually covered the first lap of the journey by barge down the river. From Gravesend they proceeded overland to Rochester, Sittingbourne, Faversham and Canterbury, and across Barham Down to Dover. The seventy-mile journey could just be done in two days by the ordinary traveller; but there were good posthorses on the road, and a fit and strong rider travelling in post could do the whole journey in one long day's hard riding.

A third great road ran along the route of the old Roman road, the Watling Street, from London by Dunstable, Stony Stratford, and Tamworth to Shrewsbury, and on to Chester, which was the chief port of embarkation for the Tudor sovereigns' second realm of Ireland. The fourth road went west from London to Exeter and Plymouth; but travellers who went further west into Cornwall had to go by tracks and byways.

The 215-mile journey from London to Plymouth took the ordinary traveller a week; but by Elizabeth's reign posthorses were available at eighteen staging posts along the road, and government officials and messengers travelling in post regularly covered the distance, by Basingstoke, Andover, Salisbury, Shaftesbury, Sherborne, Honiton, Exeter and Ashburton, in thirty-six hours. In 1595 a letter from a local official to the Secretary of State, Sir Robert Cecil, at Windsor, left Plymouth at 9.30 a.m. on 23 September, was at Exeter by 4.30 p.m., at Sherborne by midnight, at Andover by 6.30 a.m., and was received at Staines at 5 p.m. on 24 September.

Cardinal Wolsey made a famous rapid journey along the Dover Road when he was

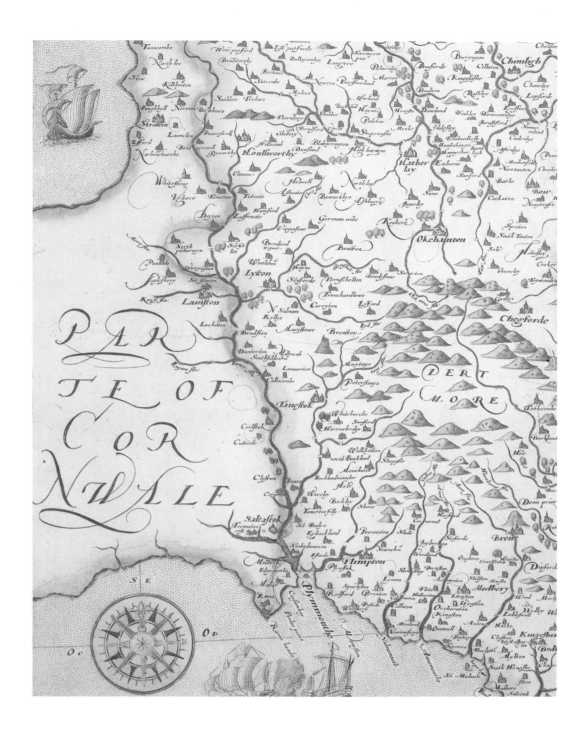

A section of Saxton's *Atlas of England* showing the environs of Plymouth and the coast off which the Spanish Armada was first sighted.

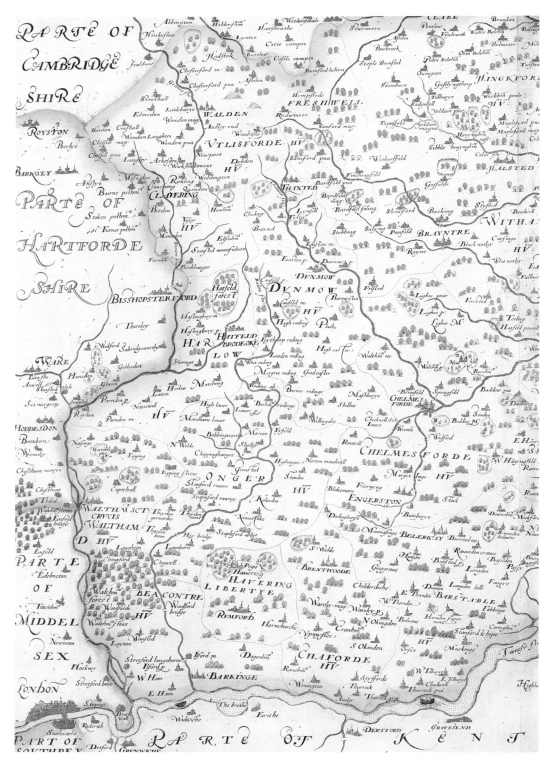

A section of Saxton's *Atlas of England and Wales*, 1579, including the south-west part of Essex.

a rising junior official in Henry VII's service. The King, who was at his palace at Richmond, ordered Wolsey to go on a diplomatic mission to the court of the Holy Roman Emperor, Maximilian, which was probably at or near Gravelines in the Netherlands; and Henry impressed on Wolsey the urgency of the business. Wolsey left Richmond at noon, and rode to London, where he took a barge to Gravesend. He arrived at Gravesend after a three-hour journey, and rode through the night in post to Dover. He reached Dover early in the morning, and, as the wind was favourable, he crossed to Calais in three hours and rode to Gravelines, reaching the Emperor's court there on the evening of the second day. Next morning he had an audience with the Emperor, and left by noon with Maximilian's reply to Henry's message. He was in Calais by nightfall, and, crossing the Channel on the morning of the fourth day, was in Dover by 10 a.m. and at court at Richmond that night. When the King saw Wolsey next morning, ninety-six hours after he had ordered him to go on his journey, he reprimanded him for not having left already; but he was amazed, and very favourably impressed, when Wolsey explained that he had already been and returned.

But if ambitious young men travelled quickly, established dignitaries travelled slowly. Today it is considered smart to travel fast, but in the Tudor Age the smart thing was to travel slowly. In 1518, when Henry VIII sent the Earl of Worcester on a diplomatic mission to Paris, Worcester took ten days to travel from Boulogne to St Denis, and waited for two days at Senlis, because, as he explained to Henry, a nobleman could not fittingly travel on 'Our Lady's Day' (8 December) though a gentleman of lower rank might have done so. When Wolsey, thirteen years after his quick journey to Flanders, went from Calais to Bruges on a diplomatic mission to the Emperor Charles V, he insisted on travelling at a pace which was consistent with his rank as Archbishop of York, Lord Chancellor of England, and a Papal Legate; and though the Emperor was waiting impatiently for him, and urging him to hurry, he took three days over the sixty-mile journey.

When kings and queens travelled, they went even more slowly. Apart from the question of dignity, they were slowed down by the numerous bodyguards, servants and carts which accompanied them, and by the official receptions, with speeches and toasts in wine, at the county and parish boundaries. When Henry VIII and Elizabeth I went on a 'progress' through their realm, they did not usually travel more than ten miles a day.

On four occasions during his reign, Henry VIII visited 'his town of Calais' – on two occasions when he was at war with France, and twice to meet the French King at a friendly interview. On the first two occasions, in 1513 and 1520, he went from Greenwich to Gravesend by water, and then overland to Dover, taking five days over the journey, and staying overnight at Rochester, Sittingbourne, Faversham and

Canterbury. On his last two visits, in 1532 and 1544, he went from Gravesend to Faversham by sea to avoid the plague which was raging at Rochester, and called on the way at the house of the Lord Warden of the Five Ports, Sir Thomas Cheyney, in the Isle of Sheppey.

During the Middle Ages, the Kings of England often travelled all over their kindgom, showing themselves to their people. Henry VII continued this tradition, going to Newcastle and Exeter, and on several occasions to York and Lincoln; but Henry VIII hardly ever left south-east England. Apart from his four visits to Calais, he went twice in his life north of the Trent, once to Nottingham and once to Lincoln and York; but for thirty years he never went north of Grafton Regis in Northamptonshire or west of Bristol, though his contemporary sovereigns, the Holy Roman Emperor Charles V and Francis I of France, travelled almost continuously throughout their dominions. Henry VIII's son, Edward VI, only once left the neighbourhood of London during his short life; and Henry's daughter Mary, after she became Queen, never travelled further from London than Winchester. Elizabeth I often travelled throughout south-east England, but never went north of Worcester or west of Bristol.

This reluctance of the Tudor sovereigns to leave south-east England was only partly due to the bad state of the roads. A more important factor was probably their fear of what would happen if they went too far from London. In 1553, during the nine-day reign of Jane Grey, the Duke of Northumberland marched from London to Cambridge at the head of an army to suppress the rising in favour of Mary. His colleagues on the Privy Council carried out a *coup d'état* as soon as he had left London which put Mary on the throne and led to the execution of Jane Grey and Northumberland.

In 1541 Henry VIII at last decided to make his long-promised visit to Lincolnshire and Yorkshire, where a serious revolt, the Pilgrimage of Grace, had broken out five years before. In view of the possible danger to his life among his formerly rebellious subjects, he was escorted by 7,000 soldiers, who slept in tents while Henry and his councillors and courtiers stayed in the King's hunting lodges and in the houses of the noblemen and gentlemen in the counties who had been ordered to receive and entertain him.

Henry left Whitehall on 30 June, and planned to take three weeks over the journey to Lincoln. He spent the first night at Enfield, the second at St Albans, the third at Dunstable, and the fourth at Ampthill. So far he was up to schedule, but at Ampthill he heard that a hundred miles to the north the roads had been flooded by the heavy rains of a very wet summer. He decided to wait at Ampthill until the floods had subsided, and stayed there for three weeks. He then moved north to Langley, to Grafton Regis and Pipewell in Northamptonshire, to Liddington in Rutlandshire, to

Collyweston, to the Duke of Suffolk's house at Grimsthorp near Bourne, and to Sleaford, and entered Lincoln in state on 9 August. He then went on to Gainsborough, to Scrooby in Nottinghamshire, and, after entering Yorkshire, to Hatfield Close, Cawood, Wressel in 'Howdenshire', and to Leconfield and Hull in the East Riding, before entering York on 18 September, having taken eighty-one days to travel there from Whitehall. After staying in York for nine days, he travelled home more quickly, taking only thirty-two days to go from York, by Hull, to Thornton Abbey across the Humber in Lincolnshire, to Ingoldsby, Sleaford, Collyweston, Fotheringhay, Higham Ferrers, Ampthill and Windsor to Hampton Court, where he arrived on 29 October.

Kings and queens stayed in the houses of the nobility and gentry, who had the delicate task of impressing the king by the lavishness of their hospitality without arousing his anger and resentment by being too lavish and thus showing that they were presumptuous enough to seek to live above their social station. Ordinary travellers had to stay in inns along the road. There were many inns offering reasonably comfortable accommodation and hospitality, where the traveller would find plenty of food and ale. Shakespeare, and many people in his audiences, knew what the First Murderer in *Macbeth* was talking about when he said:

> The west yet glimmers with some streaks of day.
> Now spurs the lated traveller apace
> To gain the timely inn.

Travel was dangerous as well as arduous, because there were robbers and 'footpads' on the King's highway. The roads were not as dangerous in the Tudor Age as they would become a hundred years later, after 1650, when the country had been thrown into the chaos of another civil war, and after the expansion of trade, the development of banking, and increased national wealth caused many more valuable consignments to be carried for long distances overland than in the sixteenth century. But robberies and murders did take place on the highway in the Tudor Age. There was a spate of them in the autumn of 1577, when four yeomen of Kent were robbed of £200 by eleven 'lewd persons' on the highway between the important city of Coventry and the little town of Birmingham. A month later, the Privy Council gave orders to the sheriffs to suppress rogues and vagabonds who were committing offences on the highways in Middlesex, Kent, Essex, Hertfordshire, Buckinghamshire, Berkshire and Surrey. Shakespeare was thinking of more recent incidents than the activities of Sir John Falstaff in 1403 when he included a scene in his *First Part of King Henry IV* of a robbery of travellers on the Dover Road at that dangerous spot, Gadshill, just south of Blackheath.

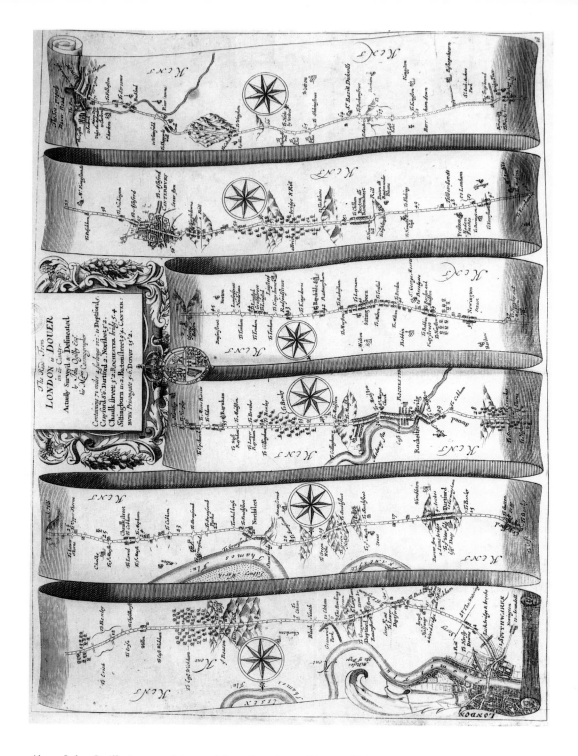

Above: John Ogilby's map of the road from London to Dover. Although published in his collection of road maps, *Brittania*, in 1675, the roads were surveyed by him much earlier and this map represents, in its individual pictorial style, the route as it existed through most of the sixteenth century.

86

Although the highway was cluttered up with so many cattle and pedestrians, as well as with the smaller number of horsemen, the comparative shortage of roads meant that travellers could be reasonably sure of meeting, and not missing, other travellers coming from the destination to which they were going. They were particularly unlikely to miss travellers who were important people accompanied by a large escort. It was always possible, however, for fugitives from justice, and others who did not wish to be seen, to avoid meeting other travellers by leaving the road and riding across country by the byways or the fields.

In the summer of 1527 Wolsey was awaiting the arrival in England of an ambassador from the ruler of Hungary, the Vayvode John Zapolya. Charles V's brother-in-law, King Ladislaus II, who reigned over Bohemia and Hungary, had been killed by the Turks in the battle of Mohács in August 1526, and Hungary was overrun by the Turks, who set up Zapolya, a Hungarian nobleman, as their puppet ruler. Henry VIII and Wolsey had recently quarrelled with their ally, Charles V, and were in the process of making an alliance with Francis I of France against Charles; so they wished to encourage Zapolya to make trouble for Charles in his rear. It was not easy to establish contact with Hungary across Charles's intervening territories, but Zapolya managed to send an ambassador, Jerome à Lasco, to England by way of Italy and France.

Wolsey would have liked to receive the ambassador, but then decided to go to France to meet Francis I. It was more important to meet the French King than the Hungarian ambassador, so Wolsey left before à Lasco arrived; but they met on the Dover Road. They had no difficulty in recognizing each other, for Wolsey travelled accompanied by several officials and gentlemen and an escort of nine hundred horsemen; and à Lasco, though he had a far smaller retinue, was suitably escorted. They met on the road between Sittingbourne and Faversham, and discussed the situation in Eastern Europe before proceeding on their journeys.

Another important political meeting on the road took place in July 1553. When Edward VI was dying, his Protestant councillors were preparing to proclaim Jane Grey as Queen. Their first action was to try to arrest Mary so as to prevent her from causing trouble; as she was at her house at Kenninghall in Norfolk, they summoned her to come to court at Greenwich. She set out on the journey, but one of her wellwishers decided to warn her of her danger. Knowing that she would be travelling to London, he set out to intercept her. He met her on the Great North Road at Hoddesdon, and warned her that if she went on to Greenwich, she would be arrested. She turned her horse's head and rode back to Cambridgeshire and Norfolk, where she called on her supporters to join her at Framlingham Castle and to fight for her as their rightful Queen. Within a few days, Jane's supporters had capitulated, and Mary had triumphed. The meeting at Hoddesdon had changed the course of history.

In the autumn of 1565 a Protestant revolt broke out in Scotland in an attempt to prevent their Queen, Mary Stuart, from marrying a Catholic, Lord Darnley. It was led by Mary's illegitimate half-brother, the Earl of Moray. Elizabeth I was persuaded by her Council to encourage the rebels, but gave them no effective support; and when they were driven across the Border and took refuge at Newcastle, she was eager to dissociate herself from them. She sent a messenger to Newcastle with a letter to Moray and his colleagues, ordering them not to come to her presence. But Moray, leaving the others at Newcastle, had already set out for London, travelling quickly in post along the Great North Road. He had already reached Hertfordshire when the messenger met him on the road between Ware and Royston. The messenger gave him the Queen's letter, but Moray decided to risk her anger by continuing his journey, as he had already gone so far, and was admitted to her presence at Whitehall. She strongly reprimanded him in the presence of the French ambassador, but allowed him and the other rebels to stay at Newcastle, and refused to extradite them to Scotland to stand trial for high treason.

THE ESTATES OF THE REALM

Tudor society was based on clearly recognized distinctions of class and rank. Under the King was the nobility, who sat in the upper House of Parliament, the House of Lords. Compared with the eight or nine hundred peers of the nineteenth and twentieth centuries, there were very few nobles. In the middle of the fifteenth century, before the outbreak of the Wars of the Roses, there were sixty-four peers in England; but nearly half of them died without heirs during the Wars of the Roses, and when Henry VII became King in 1485 there were only thirty-eight. But it is an over-simplification to say that the Wars of the Roses eliminated the nobility. It was not unusual for nobles to be killed in battle at an early age before they had produced an heir, apart from the cases of early deaths from natural causes. The new factor was that Henry VII did not replenish the nobility by creating new peers as earlier kings had done.

This was probably because of his reluctance to create a powerful class of nobles who could challenge his authority and renew the civil wars. He carried this policy to the lengths of not appointing noblemen to the great offices of state – the Lord Deputy of Ireland, and the Wardens of the Marches who guarded the northern frontier against the Scots. Instead he held these offices himself, or granted them to his infant children, leaving the real work of the offices to be performed by Deputy Wardens, for the deputies would not normally be noblemen, but merely knights and gentlemen. He created very few new peerages, though he made his uncle, Jasper Tudor, Duke of Bedford, his stepfather, Lord Stanley, Earl of Derby, and his Breton general at Bosworth, Philibert de Chaudée, Earl of Bath. Henry VIII reversed his father's policy, and created a number of new peers early in his reign, and new peerages were created by Edward VI, Mary and Elizabeth I. The result was that in the sixteenth century nearly all the nobility were new *parvenus*.

Sir John Howard was created Duke of Norfolk in 1483; but his title was forfeited after he had been killed fighting for Richard III at Bosworth, and was only restored

Charles Brandon, 1st Duke of Suffolk, in middle age, by an unknown artist.

to the Howard family in 1514. The Stafford family's title of Duke of Buckingham was forfeited when the second Duke was beheaded in 1483 for supporting Henry Tudor against Richard III; and after Henry VII had restored the title to his son, it was finally lost for ever to the Stafford family when Henry VIII executed the third Duke as a traitor in 1521. Four years later, Henry created his illegitimate son Duke of

Richmond; but the boy died a natural death, without heirs, in 1536. That left two dukes, Norfolk, and Henry VIII's boon companion and brother-in-law, Charles Brandon, Duke of Suffolk. But these two ducal titles duly disappeared. After Suffolk died without sons, his title was granted to his son-in-law, Henry Grey; but this Duke of Suffolk was beheaded for supporting the plan to place his daughter, Jane Grey, on the throne, and his title forfeited. The third Duke of Norfolk was condemned to death as a traitor in 1547 and his title forfeited; and though his life was saved when Henry VIII died before he could sign the death warrant, and his title was restored to him by Queen Mary, it was lost again when the fourth Duke was beheaded as a traitor by Elizabeth I in 1572. In Edward VI's reign, his uncle and Lord Protector, Edward Seymour, was created Duke of Somerset; but he was executed as a traitor and his title forfeited by his former colleague, John Dudley, who was created Duke of Northumberland, but in his turn was executed as a traitor and his title forfeited when Mary became Queen. After Norfolk's execution in 1572, there were no dukes in England for the last thirty years of the Tudor Age.

At the beginning of the sixteenth century, there was one Marquess in England. Thomas Grey, Marquess of Dorset, whose title had been forfeited during the reign of Richard III, was restored by Henry VII; but the title was merged in the dukedom of Suffolk when Thomas's grandson was made a duke, and was forfeited along with the Suffolk title at his execution. In 1526 Henry VIII created Henry Courtenay Marquess of Exeter; but twelve years later he was executed as a traitor, and his title forfeited. When Anne Boleyn became Henry VIII's mistress, he created her Marquess of Pembroke in her own right; but she ceased to use the title after he married her and she became Queen of England, and it was forfeited after her execution. William Parr, the brother of Henry VIII's last Queen, was created Marquess of Northampton under Edward VI. He was convicted of high treason, and his title forfeited, in Mary's reign; but his life was spared, and his title was restored to him by Elizabeth I. That shrewd and conscientious civil servant, William Paulet, who remained a member of the Privy Council under Henry VIII, Edward VI, Mary and Elizabeth I, was created Marquess of Winchester, and retained the title until his death in 1572; his contemporaries said of him that he was like the willow, not the oak, who would bend to every wind, but never break. Of all the dukes and marquesses in Tudor England, he was the only one, apart from Henry VIII's brother-in-law and illegitimate son, who was never attainted as a traitor.

At the beginning of the Tudor Age, the lords spiritual seemed to be much more secure than the lords temporal. The bishops and abbots, who sat in the House of Lords, exceeded the number of nobles, with two archbishops, nineteen bishops, twenty-eight abbots and two priors against the forty-one temporal peers – three dukes, one marquess, ten earls, and twenty-seven barons. Most of the bishops had

William Paulet, Marquess of Winchester, the only one of Henry VIII's Privy Council who retained his title – and his head – until his death in 1572.

larger dioceses than in later times. The Archbishop of Canterbury had one of the smallest dioceses, dividing Kent with the Bishop of Rochester. The Bishop of London's diocese was Middlesex, Hertfordshire and Essex; the Bishop of Chichester's, Sussex; the Bishop of Winchester's, Hampshire and Surrey; the Bishop of Salisbury's, Wiltshire and Dorset; the Bishop of Bath and Wells's, Somerset; the Bishop of Exeter's, Devon and Cornwall; the Bishop of Hereford's, Herefordshire and Monmouth; the Bishop of Worcester's, Worcestershire and Gloucestershire; the Bishop of Coventry and Lichfield's, Staffordshire, Shropshire and Cheshire; the Bishop of Norwich's, Norfolk and Suffolk; the Bishop of Ely's, Cambridgeshire and Huntingdonshire. The largest diocese in the province of Canterbury, south of the Trent, was Lincoln, which extended in a broad diagonal from the south bank of the Humber, right across the Midlands, to Oxford and Berkshire. Wales was divided between the Bishops of Llandaff and St David's in the south, and St Asaph and Bangor in the north.

North of the Trent there were three dioceses in the province of York. The Archbishop of York's diocese included all Yorkshire and Lancashire, and Derbyshire and Nottinghamshire north of the Trent. The Bishop of Durham's diocese was Durham and Northumberland, and the Bishop of Carlisle's Cumberland and Westmorland.[1]

In 1540 Henry VIII created six new bishoprics – Peterborough, Westminster, Bristol, Gloucester, Oxford and Chester – with dioceses carved out of the older dioceses of Ely, London, Bath and Wells, Worcester, Lincoln, and Coventry and Lichfield respectively. One of his reasons for doing this was to be able to reward those abbots, who had collaborated in the suppression of their abbeys, by appointing them as the new bishops.

But at the beginning of the Tudor Age, the 513 monasteries and 130 nunneries in England and Wales did not seem to be in any danger of suppression. There were fewer monks in the monasteries than there had been in the great monasteries of the early Middle Ages. By 1500 the largest house was the Priory of Christchurch in Canterbury, with seventy monks. Next came Gloucester with fifty-six, York with fifty, and Bury St Edmunds with forty-four. Four hundred and seventy-three monasteries had less than twenty monks. But the monks formed only a minority of the inmates of a monastery. There were also the laymen working in the monastery, the servants, the agricultural labourers in the fields, and the guests who were nearly always staying in the monastery; for the monasteries provided hospitality for

---

[1] Although the geographical areas of the dioceses were approximately those of the various counties, several of them included small pockets in the middle of other dioceses.

travellers, from the King and his escort to the humblest pedlar walking to the nearest market town or the pilgrim making a longer journey to a distant shrine of a saint.

There was a monastery in every county in England. Westmorland and Rutland had only one, Durham had two, and Huntingdonshire, Berkshire and Cornwall each had six, whereas Norfolk had thirty-three, Lincolnshire fifty-one, and Yorkshire the largest number with sixty-four. Some were in the centre of the most important towns, in London, Canterbury, Oxford and Cambridge; some were in the smaller boroughs, some on the roads in the open country, and some in the heart of the northern moors.

The first duty of the monks was prayer. Often they had the special obligation to pray for the souls of dead benefactors who had given money to the monastery on this condition, for the Church taught (and the great majority of the people in 1500 believed) that the souls of the dead who were not eternally damned to suffer in Hell stayed for a shorter or longer period in Purgatory; there they suffered punishment until they were purged of their sins and allowed into Heaven, and the length of their stay in Purgatory could be shortened by the prayers of the monks.

The monks in the monasteries were among the very few people in England who actually did what all Christians were in theory supposed to do, and attended Mass eight times a day. They rose in the middle of the night to attend Matins at midnight. They then attended Lauds at dawn, Prime at 6 a.m., Tierce at 9 a.m., Sext at noon, Nones at 3 p.m., Vespers at sunset, and Compline at 9 p.m. before going to bed for the night. They spent the rest of the time in study, in administering the affairs of the monastery, supervising the work of the servants and the labourers in the fields, or gossiping with each other in the refectory or monastery garden. Some of the brothers might be sent out to ride around the district inspecting the monastery's property and collecting the rents from its tenants. On such occasions, and on many others, the monks engaged in these duties would be granted dispensations from attending Mass at the eight canonical hours. This property-inspection and rent-collecting could involve a great deal of travelling, for many of the monasteries had acquired land far away from the site of the house. The very wealthy priory of Lewes in Sussex owned lands in fourteen counties from Devon to Yorkshire. Some of the monks spent their time in study, and the more learned of them were often given a dispensation to leave their monasteries to study and teach at the universities of Oxford and Cambridge.

By the beginning of the Tudor Age, the monks had acquired a bad reputation. Most people in England believed that they were immoral, or at least that their behaviour fell far short of the high standard which they were supposed to attain. The ordinary Englishman joked about the vices of the monks and nuns, but their jokes showed that they disapproved, and expected better behaviour from them. It is difficult to know how true these allegations were, and how general were the instances

William Warham, Archbishop of Canterbury from 1504 to 1532 and Lord Chancellor from 1504 to 1515. He was Chancellor of Oxford University from 1506 to 1532, in which year he died. A drawing by Hans Holbein (1504) in the Royal Library at Windsor.

of immorality which were reported. The stories told in humorous ballads may be exaggerated. When, in 1535, Henry VIII sent commissioners to investigate the state of the monasteries, they reported many cases of the most shocking immorality; but they knew that they were expected to find such cases, and that the King wished to use their report as an excuse to suppress the monasteries and seize their wealth. But there were too many stories told, in the first part of the sixteenth century, before the idea of suppressing the monasteries had ever been thought of, about abbesses having illegitimate children and whores being smuggled into monasteries, to leave any doubt that the morals of many monks and nuns were very lax.

The monks were unpopular with their tenants. They were accused of being harsh and greedy landlords, and they also had a bad reputation as a result of enclosing common land and depriving the local inhabitants of their old-established common rights. The figures for Leicestershire may not be typical of the country as a whole; but they show that the King was responsible for two per cent of the land enclosed, the nobility for twelve per cent, the monasteries for eighteen per cent, and the local gentry for sixty-eight per cent. But the criticism of the monasteries, as far as the majority of the people were concerned, seems to have been only on the surface. However unpopular the monks may have been, the people expected and wanted the monasteries to continue to be there, partly because they provided employment for the local inhabitants and hospitality for travellers, and probably partly because, despite everything, their religious significance still meant something to the people. In 1525, Cardinal Wolsey, acting as Papal Legate with the full authority of the Pope, dissolved twenty-two monasteries so that he could seize their property and use the proceeds to endow a new college at Oxford, but his suppression of Bayham Abbey in Sussex provoked a riot among the local inhabitants; and when Henry VIII, eleven years later, ordered the far wider dissolution of all the smaller monasteries, the first outbreak of the great revolt in the North, the Pilgrimage of Grace, was the popular resistance to the dissolution of Hexham Abbey in Northumberland.

The reputation of the priests was as low as the reputation of the monks. It had been a law of the Church for four hundred years that priests were not allowed to marry; but many of the parish priests lived more or less openly with a concubine, and this was winked at by the Church authorities. The priests spent a great deal of time dealing with non-religious business. They were indeed usually called 'the secular clergy' to distinguish them from 'the religious', the monks and nuns; and the word 'religion' was often used to refer exclusively to monasteries.

The Church offered a promising career to intelligent and ambitious young men. In 1500, as at most other times in human history, influence and family connections helped a man's career. Some critics were dissatisfied that so many of the important positions in the Church, like so many of the headships of the wealthiest abbeys and nunneries, were in the hands of the sons and daughters of noblemen; but at the beginning of the Tudor Age it was still possible, as it had been during earlier centuries, for men of the lowest social origin to rise to positions of power in the Church, and through the Church to the highest rank in the State and in society.

But no ambitious young man who hoped to rise to these heights through the Church became an ordinary parish priest. He began by going from school to one of the two universities, Oxford or Cambridge, usually at the age of fourteen. There he studied divinity and the canon law of the Church. After taking his degree as a Bachelor of Divinity or Doctor of Divinity, he would try to obtain an introduction to some bishop or nobleman who would appoint him to be his chaplain or secretary. If he made a good impression, the nobleman or bishop would appoint him as rector or vicar in some parish which they controlled; but he would not be expected to reside in his parish, or ever to visit it. He would be given a dispensation not to reside there, and would sometimes be given another dispensation allowing him to be appointed as the parish priest in two or more parishes at the same time, with leave to absent himself from both. This made it possible for him to live on the revenues of his benefices while carrying on his duties as secretary in the household of the nobleman or bishop; and the duties of the priest of the parish were undertaken by a curate to whom he paid a small annuity to do the work.

If the young priest was successful and lucky, he would soon move on from the household of the bishop or nobleman to the King's service. He might then be appointed an archdeacon, or given some more benefices, again with a dispensation to be absent, as he performed more and more important duties in the King's government. In due course, if he made his way to the top, he would be appointed a bishop, almost always before he reached the age of forty. This meant that he was one of the hundred most important persons in the State, as well as one of the leaders of the Church. He might become a member of the King's Privy Council, which was the supreme governing body in the realm under the King, and in many ways the equivalent of the Prime Minister's Cabinet today. He would often be sent as an ambassador to a foreign sovereign, and perhaps ordered to stay there for some years as resident ambassador at the foreign court, accompanying the King to whom he was accredited on his journeys through his realm. From now on, his chief anxiety was that he would suddenly fall from favour, and would be imprisoned or executed as a traitor.

Just as a priest could obtain a dispensation to hold several benefices, so a bishop could be permitted to hold several bishoprics simultaneously with leave of absence from all of them. Cardinal Wolsey was at the same time Archbishop of York and Bishop of Durham, without ever visiting either diocese, as well as Abbot of St Albans, Lord Chancellor of England, and Papal Legate. Later he was Archbishop of York and Bishop of Winchester while also obtaining the revenues of the bishoprics of Durham and of Badajoz in Spain, as well as several other Spanish benefices. At the end of the fifteenth century, it became the custom that two bishops, one of whom was usually the Bishop of Worcester, should be two Italian cardinals who lived in Rome and represented English interests at the Papal court. They never visited their English dioceses, but were expected, in return for receiving their revenues, to use their influence in Rome to persuade the Pope to grant the King of England the favours and dispensations for which he asked, and to pursue a pro-English and anti-French foreign policy.

Very few bishops had ever carried out the duties of a parish priest. Very few of them celebrated Mass or officiated as a priest, except sometimes on great state occasions, though they attended Mass every day with their chaplain as the celebrant. Before 1530, it was unusual for a bishop to preach a sermon, for until then, sermons played a very small part in the church services. But after Henry VIII repudiated the

Papal authority and introduced some of the religious changes which the Protestant reformers advocated, sermons were used as a means of government propaganda. The bishops spent nearly all their time in carrying out administrative, diplomatic and judicial duties.

The result of this system was that the bishops and other nationally prominent churchmen were usually canon lawyers, or 'canonists'. They were often also 'civilians' – experts in the civil law, or Roman law, which prevailed in continental Europe and was used in negotiating international treaties, though the English common law, which was applied in the ordinary courts in England, was administered by the common lawyers in the four Inns of Court in London. The domination of the canon lawyers is very evident if we study the reports of the arguments about religious doctrine in the heresy trials, at synods of the clergy, and in the books in which the Catholics and the Protestants, the conservatives and the reformers, put forth their conflicting views. The participants were of course learned in divinity, but their method of argument and of thought was completely legalistic, based on precedents and interpretations of biblical texts and on the 'patristic' writings of the early fathers of the Church, who lived in the first four centuries after Christ.

The Protestants, who believed in the necessity of Bible-reading and who relied on the authority of the Bible against the authority of the Church, criticized this domination of the canonists, and believed that a bishop should be first of all a pastor, and a student of the Bible and theology, rather than of the canon law. This was why Thomas Cranmer made his famous proposal, which first brought him to the attention of Henry VIII, that the universities should be consulted about the King's divorce from Catherine of Aragon. The history books nearly always record merely that Cranmer advised that the universities should be asked to give their opinion about the divorce. But according to Cranmer's secretary, Ralph Morice – from whom the martyrologist John Foxe heard about the incident and who is the only

Opposite: Henry VIII at the opening of Parliament, 1523. A watercolour drawing done by, or for, Sir Thomas Wriothesley, who was Garter King of Arms from 1505 to 1534. *From the Royal Library at Windsor, reproduced by Gracious Permission of Her Majesty The Queen.* The drawing shows the King, crowned and carrying the dove sceptre, with the royal arms and garter above him, and his feet upon a cushion. Seated on the King's right, and distinguished by their arms, are Warham, Archbishop of Canterbury, and Cardinal Wolsey.

Behind the back of the bench on which they are sitting is Tunstall, Bishop of London, holding the roll of the opening speech which on this occasion he read on behalf of the Archbishop of York, who, as Chancellor, had moved over to the right. On the carpet decorated with lilies are the cap of maintenance (the King himself is wearing his crown) and the sword of state, both borne by earls. At the top of the front 'temporal' bench, before the King, sit two Dukes, Norfolk holding his baton as Earl Marshal, and Suffolk. The dukes alone wear coronets; all the other peers are in hats. On the 'spiritual' side the front bench is occupied by nine bishops and the back bench by seventeen black abbots.

99

THOMAS . CRANMER , BIS
. MARTIR .

Thomas Cranmer, Archbishop of Canterbury, a painting by an unknown artist in Lambeth Palace, reproduced by courtesy of the present Archbishop. When the more familiar portrait of Cranmer was painted by Flicke in 1545, he was clean-shaven, but after the death of Henry VIII he grew a beard to show his grief.

original source for all we know about it – Cranmer's suggestion was that the King should consult the theologians instead of the canonists, and approach the theological faculty in the universities rather than the canonists, in and out of the universities, who had been consulted hitherto. But despite the Protestants' emphasis on the importance of divinity as opposed to the canon law, their foremost champions, like Nicholas Ridley and Cranmer himself, continued until the 1550s to argue like canonists in their theological disputes with the Catholics.

Preaching became more common, and played a very important part in the religious and political struggles, after Henry VIII repudiated Papal supremacy in 1533. It had always been the law that no one was allowed to preach without a licence, because the authorities remembered how the revolutionary priest, John Ball, preaching on village greens and before parish churches throughout Kent, had incited the peasants to rise in a formidable revolt in 1381; and unauthorized sermons by unorthodox preachers were obviously a source of danger to an authoritarian government. A number of rebellious spirits defied the law and preached illegally. One of the most incorrigible was John Harridaunce, a bricklayer who lived on the eastern outskirts of London at Whitechapel. He used to climb on to a tub in his garden and preach to the passers-by who were walking along the road, and they often stopped to listen to him. He was summoned before the Archbishop of Canterbury on more than one occasion and detained for some weeks in prison for his offence.

After the break with Rome, the controls on preaching were tightened, for several priests who held preaching licences from their bishops were opposed to the King's policy, and ventured to criticize it by subtle means in their sermons. On the other side, the Protestants, who were eager to press further ahead with the Reformation than Henry VIII wished to go, obtained preaching licences from those bishops who were sympathetic to Protestantism, and preached sermons which the Catholics denounced as heresy. So in 1534 Henry issued an order rescinding all preaching licences and forbidding anyone to preach without a new licence; and precise instructions were issued as to what they were permitted to say in their sermons.

The most important sermons in England were those at Paul's Cross in London. The famous cross was a pulpit which stood in the churchyard of St Paul's on the north-east side of the cathedral. The pulpit was covered, but was open at the sides, and the congregation had to stand in the open air, which they did every Sunday morning in all weathers throughout the year. Usually several thousand people assembled to hear the sermon.

The King and the Privy Council chose the preacher who was to preach at Paul's Cross, and the choice of preacher was often seen, rightly, as an indication of the King's religious policy. When, in the 1530s, a Protestant reformer who had hitherto been out of favour, or had even been persecuted as a heretic, was suddenly chosen to

A preacher at Paul's Cross; woodcut from Foxe's *Book of Martyrs*, 1563.

preach at Paul's Cross, it was seen as a sign that Henry VIII had decided to introduce Protestant innovations into the Church of England; when a conservative Catholic preacher was selected, this indicated that the King was reverting to a more Catholic policy.

It was unusual for a bishop to preach at Paul's Cross. The preachers were usually prominent churchmen just a little below episcopal rank. But in May 1521 John Fisher, the Bishop of Rochester, preached against Luther at Paul's Cross, when Luther's books were publicly burned. In February 1536, when Henry VIII decided to launch a great propaganda campaign against Papal supremacy, he ordered a bishop to preach at Paul's Cross on seven successive Sundays. Cranmer preached on the

Stephen Gardiner, Bishop of Winchester, 1531–1550 and 1553–55, by an unknown artist, in the collection at Hardwick Hall.

STEEVEN   GARDNER

Sunday after Candlemas; next week the Bishop of Rochester preached; on the third Sunday, the Bishop of London; on the fourth Sunday, the Bishop of Durham; on the fifth, the Bishop of Salisbury; on the sixth, the Bishop of Worcester (Latimer); and on the seventh, the Bishop of Bangor.

The political significance of the sermons at Paul's Cross aroused much comment in Lent 1540. Robert Barnes, the Prior of the great Barnwell Priory in Cambridge, had become a Lutheran and had been accused of heresy in 1525; he only escaped being burned because he recanted his Lutheran doctrines in a sermon at Paul's Cross. After the repudiation of Papal supremacy, he came into Henry VIII's favour, and was employed on important diplomatic missions, as well as serving on many commissions dealing with ecclesiastical affairs. But in 1539 Henry switched his religious policy, and ordered Parliament to pass the Act of the Six Articles, which initiated a persecution of Protestants. Thomas Cromwell, the Lord Privy Seal, was sympathetic to Protestantism and, while officially supporting the King's anti-Protestant policy, he still hoped to persuade Henry to abandon it; while Stephen Gardiner, the Bishop

John Fisher, Bishop of
Rochester. Drawing by Hans
Holbein in the Royal Library
at Windsor, c.1528.

of Winchester, who was the leader of the conservative and Catholic faction in the King's Council, was encouraging the King to suppress the Protestants.

In March 1540, Gardiner was appointed to preach the sermon at Paul's Cross on the first Sunday in Lent. He criticized some Protestant doctrines as heretical. A fortnight later, Barnes preached at Paul's Cross and attacked Gardiner's sermon. This was an unprecedented situation – one officially appointed preacher at Paul's Cross criticizing the sermon of another officially appointed preacher. It obviously

104

could not continue, and could have occurred only because a power struggle was going on within the Council. The King ordered Barnes to preach again and recant his criticisms of Gardiner, and Barnes did so. All the observers rightly concluded that Gardiner had won an important political victory over Cromwell. A few months later, Cromwell was arrested as a traitor and executed, and Barnes was burned as a heretic.

But Gardiner was in a difficult position in the reign of Edward VI, when Somerset and Cranmer were making England a Protestant state. He had always enforced absolute obedience to the King's religious policy; but he was strongly opposed to the Protestant innovations of Somerset and Cranmer. He therefore wrote to Somerset and the Council, arguing that the supreme power over the Church held by an adult King should not be exercised by a regent during the infancy of an infant King, and that Somerset and Cranmer should not introduce any religious changes until Edward reached the age when he could rule himself. Gardiner was arrested and sent to the Fleet prison, and afterwards to the Tower, where he remained for more than five years until Edward VI's death and Mary's accession to the throne. He was also deprived of his bishopric of Winchester.

Bonner, the Bishop of London, had been an active persecutor of Protestants in the last years of Henry VIII's reign. After Edward VI became King, he adopted the same position as Gardiner, and argued that a Lord Protector should not alter religion during the King's infancy. Somerset and the Council thereupon ordered Bonner to preach a sermon at Paul's Cross in which he was to tell the people that the power of an infant King, acting through his Lord Protector, was as absolute in religion and in political matters as the power of an adult King ruling in person. Bonner preached the sermon as required, but managed to evade the issue of the powers of an infant King. Somerset and the Council saw this as an act of defiance of the royal authority. Bonner was deprived of his bishopric of London and imprisoned in the Marshalsea by order of the Council: he remained a prisoner there until Mary became Queen.

During the nine-day reign of Jane Grey, when Mary was assembling her forces at Framlingham, the Council ordered Nicholas Ridley, the Bishop of London, to preach a sermon at Paul's Cross, telling the people that Jane was the lawful Queen and that Mary was a bastard. But there was great sympathy for Mary, even in London, which was the main centre of Protestantism. Ridley was heckled and shouted down, and the uproar was so great that he had to abandon his sermon. This demonstration of support for Mary encouraged her partisans, and was one of the reasons why, three days later, the majority of the Lords of the Privy Council went over to her side and proclaimed her as Queen in London, to the great joy of the people.

Mary immediately took steps to restore the Catholic doctrines to the Church of England as a preliminary step to restoring Papal supremacy. She released Gardiner

Edward Seymour, 1st Duke of Somerset, uncle of the nine-year-old Prince Edward, who became Lord Protector on Henry VIII's death. This portrait, by an unknown artist, has never been fully authenticated, but in comparison with others, in groups, it appears to be a good likeness.

from the Tower and Bonner from the Marshalsea, and restored them as Bishops of Winchester and London; and she appointed Gardiner to be Lord Chancellor. Ten days after she entered London in triumph, Bonner's chaplain, Dr Bourn, preached at Paul's Cross. When he criticized Protestant doctrines, some Protestants in the audience interrupted and heckled him, and one of them threw a dagger at him, which missed him. Two prominent Protestant divines, Rogers and Bradford, who were in the audience, succeeded in quieting the Protestants, and escorted Bourn to a place of safety; but the incident was used as an excuse by the Queen to begin arresting leading Protestants throughout England, including Rogers and Bradford. When they pointed out that they had saved Bourn, they were told that the fact that they had been able to appease the Protestants in the crowd showed that they were their leaders, and had secretly incited the riot against Bourn.

106

By the autumn of 1554, Mary was ready to restore Papal supremacy and to begin the burning of Protestants. In preparation for this, Gardiner himself preached at Paul's Cross on 30 September 1554, in favour of Papal supremacy, though, as head of the government and in charge of foreign policy, he no longer concerned himself normally with religious issues.

Four years later, after nearly three hundred Protestant martyrs had been burned, Mary was dying of cancer, and everyone was waiting for Elizabeth to become Queen. It was well known that Elizabeth had formerly been a Protestant, though she had gone to Mass and become a Catholic to save her life in Mary's reign. Both Catholics and Protestants, in England and abroad, were speculating as to whether she would make England Protestant again when she came to the throne.

They did not have to wait long for the first sign of her intentions. Mary died at 7 a.m. on Thursday 17 November 1558; on the following Sunday, Dr Bill preached at Paul's Cross. In Mary's reign, he had been ejected from his office as Master of Trinity College, Cambridge, because he was regarded as a Protestant, though he escaped arrest and was allowed to live quietly in the country. The fact that the new Queen had chosen him to preach at Paul's Cross within three days of her accession was very significant. In his sermon, Bill made a few cautious Protestant remarks. Next week Christopherson, Mary's Catholic Bishop of Chichester, preached at Paul's Cross; Elizabeth had chosen him to preach there, but had told him not to enter into controversy. In his sermon, Christopherson said that Bill had preached heresy on the previous Sunday. Elizabeth ordered that Christopherson should be confined under house arrest in his palace for having disobeyed her orders to be non-controversial. All the Catholics and the Protestants and the foreign ambassadors interpreted these events correctly. Within six months, Parliament had passed the necessary legislation to repudiate Papal supremacy and make England once again a Protestant realm.

HERETICS AND TRAITORS

THE great majority of Englishmen in the sixteenth century accepted the fact that one of the duties of a king was to decide what religion his subjects should adopt and issue orders from time to time telling them exactly what they should believe about religion, and exactly how they should worship. If the King told them to worship the wrong religion, this was something for which he would have to account to God, but the duty of all subjects was to obey the King in religion as in all other matters.

The accepted doctrine was that it was the duty of the subject to obey the King, not only from fear of punishment in this world if he did not, but also because failure to do so would be sinful, against the law of God, and would lead to eternal damnation. This doctrine was taught assiduously by the Church to the people, particularly under Henry VIII. It was a very convenient doctrine for all the bishops, noblemen, country gentlemen, mayors and justices of the peace who were expected to enforce the King's religious policy. When there was a Catholic sovereign, they could supervise the burning of Protestant martyrs; then, when the King changed his policy, or was succeeded by a new King who made England Protestant and suppressed the Pope's supporters, the mayors and JPs could arrest and torture the Papists, and revert once again to burning Protestants if a Catholic sovereign came to the throne. They could do it with a perfectly clear conscience, for on each occasion they did their duty to God by obeying the King.

Nearly everyone believed this. Even among the minority of Protestants and Catholics who decided to disobey the King and submit to martyrdom, there was very little criticism of the government officials who were the King's instruments in carrying out the persecution. When John Knox, in his books in 1558, reminded his readers that God, in the Old Testament, had not merely punished Pharaoh himself for persecuting Moses and the children of Israel, but had also drowned Pharaoh's soldiers in the Red Sea to punish them for their sin in obeying Pharaoh's wicked

Lady Jane Dudley
(née Grey).
Proclaimed Queen
in 1553
and executed
the following year.

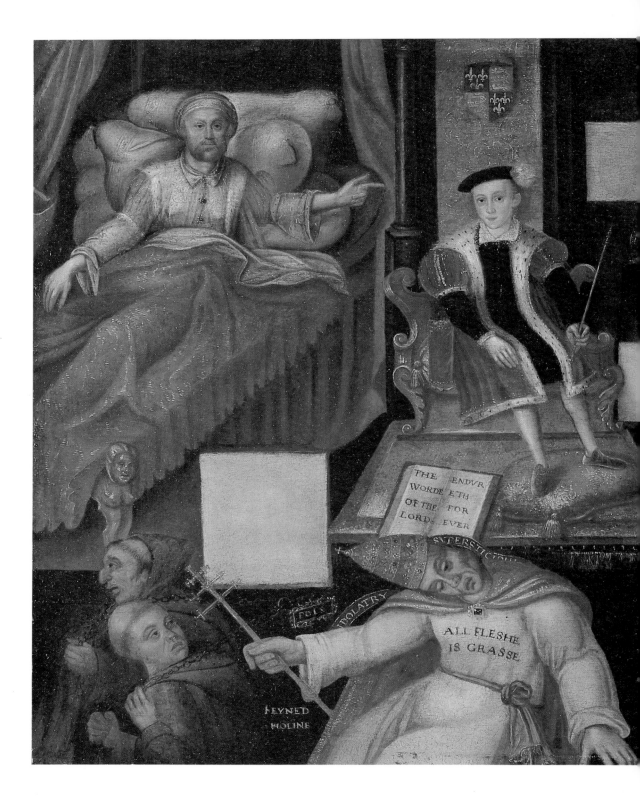

Edward and the Pope, an anti-papal allegorical painting by an unknown artist, c.1548–49. Henry VIII is depicted on his deathbed giving directions to his son on confounding the Pope. In the background are Edward Seymour, the Protector, and members of the Council of Regency, including John Dudley, Cranmer and John Russell. The Pope is shown being crushed by the Prayer Book. Through the windows soldiers can be seen destroying religious statues in obedience to the Protector's orders.

Queen Mary. Painting by Hans Eworth, 1554. This painting was presented to the National Portrait Gallery by Richard Burton and Elizabeth Taylor.

orders, he was putting forward a new and revolutionary doctrine which, even by the end of the Tudor Age, had been accepted by only a small section of the people of England.

At the beginning of the sixteenth century, the service of the Mass was governed by one of five prayer books. Over most of the country the church service followed the rules of the Sarum Use, which had been first adopted in the diocese of Salisbury; but in other areas, the York Use, the Lincoln Use, the Hereford Use and the Bangor Use were followed. There were only small differences in the form of service prescribed in these five Uses; but as religion became more and more regimented under Henry VIII, the King and the authorities decided that even this very small degree of differentiation and regional independence was dangerous, and in 1543 Henry abolished the other four Uses and ordered that only the Sarum Use should be adopted throughout the realm.

When Somerset and Cranmer introduced Protestantism in the reign of Edward VI, the Sarum Use was replaced by the Book of Common Prayer of 1549, which prescribed in every detail the service to be used in 'the Supper of the Lord and the Holy Communion, commonly called the Mass', reducing the number of times when the priest crossed himself from twenty-seven to two, and abolishing the elevation of the Host. Three years later, the Second Book of Common Prayer of 1552 expressed the more radical and Protestant doctrines which had in the meantime been accepted by the government. Under Mary, the Book of Common Prayer was abolished, and the Sarum Use restored; but within a year of Elizabeth's accession, the Third Book of Common Prayer had been issued. It was less radical than the 1552 Book.

A small minority of the people did not believe that the subject must always accept the King's religious doctrines, and thought that the duty to obey the King was qualified by the overriding duty to obey God. The King should be obeyed except when he ordered the subject to offend against the law of God; in that case, it was the subject's duty to refuse to obey the King, and to offer himself for martyrdom.

By 1525 the numbers and activity of the Protestants in England had increased, after the country felt the repercussions of Luther's defiance of the Papal authority in Germany and the popular fervour which it produced there; but the Protestants continued to be a small minority of the people. They were strongest in south-east England – in Norfolk, Essex and Sussex, and particularly in Kent and London. There were hardly any in the west and the north. Of the 280 Protestant martyrs who were burned in Mary's reign, only one was burned north of the Trent (in Chester); one was burned in the diocese of Exeter (in the city); and three in Wales (Cardiff, Carmarthen and Haverfordwest); while 48 were burned in London (including Westminster and Southwark), 47 in Kent, 43 in Essex, 23 in Sussex, 18 in Suffolk and 14 in Norfolk.

Even at the time of Elizabeth I's accession in 1558, after thirty years of religious turmoil and persecution, the majority of the English people were Catholics; but the situation changed after forty years of official Protestant propaganda during her reign. Devon and Cornwall had been staunchly Catholic at the time of the rebellion there against the introduction of the Protestant Book of Common Prayer in 1549; but these counties provided most of Elizabeth I's sailors who fought so valiantly for the Protestant cause against Philip of Spain and his Armada.

The Protestants and their martyrs came from every social class and age group, but chiefly from the young artisans of south-east England and from the intellectuals, especially from the divinity students of Cambridge University. Protestant doctrines became increasingly attractive to the younger generation; at the height of the persecution in Mary's reign, the Venetian ambassador reported that hardly anyone under thirty-five was a Catholic at heart.

The Protestants attached great importance to reading the Bible, appealing from the authority of the Church to the authority of the Word of God. The Protestant William Tyndale, who in 1525 translated the Bible into English, stated that his aim was to make every ploughboy as knowledgeable in Scripture as the most learned clerk; but to the Catholic Church this was encouraging the common people to question the doctrines of the Church, to argue about theology, to rebel against their superiors, and was seditious. A royal proclamation of 1530 made it a criminal offence to possess or read the English Bible, and every copy was to be publicly burned; but those who were found with the English Bible risked more than this, for it was often held to be sufficient proof of heresy to send them to the stake.

Tyndale and his supporters printed an English translation of the Bible illegally in the Netherlands and smuggled copies into England hidden under bales of straw. Several of the Protestants who secretly distributed them were caught and burned. Thomas Hitton had bad luck. He was walking through the fields near Gravesend on his way to take ship for the Netherlands after a successful mission in England when he was stopped by some local people who suspected him of stealing some clothes. When they searched him, they did not find the clothes, but they found copies of the English Bible. He was burned at Maidstone in 1530 at the instigation of Sir Thomas More, who described him as 'the Devil's stinking martyr'.

In 1537 Cromwell and Cranmer persuaded Henry VIII to permit the publication of an English translation of the Bible; but after the fall of Cromwell and the Catholic reaction in 1540, new measures were taken against the English Bible. An Act of 1543 made it an offence for anyone to read it aloud to another person, and for anyone under the rank of a gentleman to read it privately to himself.

The reading of the English Bible was permitted under Edward VI, and after being forbidden under Mary, was again allowed and encouraged by Elizabeth. By this time, many Englishmen and women were reading the English translation of the Bible which John Knox and his colleagues had written, and which was published in Geneva in 1560. It contained footnotes, which were as long as the text of the Bible itself, which were printed at the top and bottom and the sides of every page, in which Knox's revolutionary interpretation of Scripture was set forth.

The Protestants challenged the dogmas of the Catholic Church on many issues, and in every case the Protestant doctrine had the effect of weakening the position of the priest and minimizing his part in the relationship between the individual layman and God. But in England throughout the whole of the Tudor Age the main issue between the Catholics and the Protestants was belief in transubstantiation and the Real Presence of Christ in the sacramental bread and wine after they had been consecrated by the priest at Mass. Nearly all the Protestants who were burned were condemned for denying the Real Presence, even if they were sometimes also accused of other heresies.

The arguments between the theologians in the sixteenth century about the Real Presence can only be understood by someone who has been educated in the principles of Aristotle's philosophy, which distinguished between the true reality of an object and its 'accidents', such as its shape, its smell, its appearance, and so on. It seems extraordinary to us today that people could condemn their opponents to be burned, and be prepared to suffer death in the fire, because of their differing views about this question. Even if the Protestant divines, who understood the theological arguments involved, were prepared to die for their beliefs, how could it happen that uneducated labourers felt so strongly about this? But in the Tudor Age, religion was the arena in which the revolutionary youth and the conservative Establishment fought out the political and psychological struggle between them which takes place in every century in one form or other. The young artisan might not understand Aristotelian philosophy; but once he had been told that there were learned divines who taught that the consecrated Host, which officialdom ordered him to venerate as the Body of Christ, was in fact only a piece of bread, and that it was idolatry to worship it, he was eager to defy authority by desecrating the Host, with a complete disregard both of the religious feelings of the majority of his neighbours and of the terrible punishments which would be inflicted on him for his conduct.

When a suspect was accused of heresy, he was arrested and brought before the court of his diocesan bishop, where he was tried and examined, either by the bishop himself or by the bishop's Ordinary – a judicial officer who was a skilled canon lawyer. After Henry VIII repudiated Papal supremacy, the bishops' jurisdiction in heresy cases was abolished; but as Henry was determined to suppress any Protestants who advocated doctrines which he had not yet authorized, he appointed commissioners to try cases of suspected heresy. The defendants would normally be tried by a number of commissioners, some of whom were bishops and divines, and others lawyers who were laymen.

In the last years of Henry's reign, most heresy trials took place in London and Westminster. Under Edward VI, the Protestant government in general discontinued the practice of burning heretics; but two Protestant extremists who denied the doctrine of the Trinity were burned in London after being tried by commissioners. In Mary's reign, the bishops' jurisdiction to try cases of heresy was restored, and heresy trials took place all over south-east England. Four Protestant extremists, who were denounced as Arians or Anabaptists, were burned in the reign of Elizabeth I.

When an ignorant, uneducated labourer was accused of heresy, he usually merely asserted his beliefs and stated that he would not recant because he knew that his doctrine was God's truth. His judges pointed out to him that he was uneducated and unlearned, and that it was presumptuous of him to challenge the doctrines which learned divines had shown were the true doctrines of the Church. But when the suspected heretic was himself a learned doctor of divinity, he and the judges engaged in lengthy arguments about the nature of Christ's Presence in the bread and wine, exchanging quotations from Scripture and from the works of Chrysostom, Origen and other early fathers of the third and fourth centuries. The judges would accuse the learned heretic, not of presumption in challenging the opinions of men more learned than himself, but of prostituting the great gifts of intelligence and learning with which God had endowed him, by using them to argue against, and not in favour of, the doctrine of Christ's Church.

These arguments at heresy trials were conducted according to the strict rules of medieval disputations, with a major and minor proposition, an answer, an explication, and the ensuing discussion. But the detached academic atmosphere of the university divinity schools was not always maintained. When, at the beginning of Mary's reign, Cranmer, Ridley and Latimer were brought as prisoners to Oxford to take part in a great propaganda disputation with Catholic divines in the presence of a thousand spectators, they were constantly interrupted by the insults of the indignant Catholics in the audience who had come to show their detestation of the heretics. As they all knew, the disputation was the first step in the proceedings which ultimately led to the burning of Ridley, Latimer and Cranmer for their heresy.

The defendant at a heresy trial was given every opportunity to recant his heresies. If he did, he was not burned, but was sentenced to some lesser punishment, such as a few months' imprisonment, or incarceration in a monastery, where he was subjected to a strict régime of penance and hardship. He was sometimes also required, after his release from prison, or the monastery, to wear a badge of a faggot on his arm for the rest of his life, as a mark of shame. If he was a prominent figure, such as a learned divine, he was usually required to preach a sermon at Paul's Cross expressing his

'The Burnyng of Cranmer'. An illustration in John Foxe's *Ecclesiastical History, contayning the Actes and Monuments of thinges past in every Kinges time in this Realm*, subsequently known as Foxe's *Book of Martyrs*, the second volume, 1570. This records the Archbishop's stretching his hand into the flame and saying 'Lord receive my spirite'.

repentance and denouncing his past heresies. He arrived at the ceremony with a faggot on his shoulder, as a reminder that he deserved to be burned for his heresy; and the heretic who was sentenced to take part in these proceedings was said, in popular parlance, to have 'carried his faggot'.

A heretic who recanted, and was released after carrying his faggot, was not spared if he was guilty of heresy a second time. He was then condemned as a relapsed heretic, and this time he was sentenced to be burned even if he again recanted. A new precedent was established in 1556 when Cranmer, who had never previously been condemned as a heretic, was burned, despite the fact that he recanted. This marked a new stage in the intensification of the persecution.

If a heretic refused to recant, he was excommunicated by the judges who heard his case. By an Act of Parliament of 1401, a heretic who had been excommunicated by the ecclesiastical court could be burned without any further legal process under a writ issued by the King, though the King was entitled to pardon the offender. At this stage, further efforts were sometimes made to induce the heretic to recant; but if he remained obdurate, the writ for his burning was issued, and sent by the King's Council to the sheriff of the county.

The sheriff and his subordinate officers – or in London the Lord Mayor and the city corporation – had to make the arrangements for the burning. They fixed the time and place, arranged for a supply of the necessary faggots to be available, and saw to it that the timber-merchants supplying the faggots did not overcharge the King for them. They ensured that men-at-arms were available to keep order at the execution, and prevent an escape or rescue; but Englishmen in Tudor England had a deep respect for law and the duty of obedience to the royal authority, and there is not a single recorded case in England of an attempted escape, or of an attempt to rescue a condemned heretic from the stake, such as occurred on several occasions at the burning of heretics in the sixteenth century in Scotland and the Netherlands.

Heretics were always burned in public. The burning of a heretic was an unusual, but not a very rare, occurrence. Twenty-four heretics were burned in the twenty-four years of Henry VII's reign; eighty-one during the thirty-eight years of Henry VIII; two in the six years of Edward VI; 280 in Mary's five-year reign – all within the space of three and three-quarter years – and four in Elizabeth I's forty-four years. The last heretics to be burned in England died at the stake seven years after the end of the Tudor Age in 1610. In the years between 1485 and 1589, when the last heretic of Elizabeth I's reign suffered, burnings took place in more than sixty towns, most of them south-east England. Many people in this part of the country had an opportunity to watch the burning of a heretic, and thousands of them must have done so.

In London, where more heretics were burned than in any other single town, the burnings usually took place at Smithfield, just outside the wall at the north-west corner of the city, beyond Newgate. In the provincial towns, they were normally held on some waste land very near the town, and often on market day, when the largest number of persons would be in town to witness this salutary punishment of heresy. When Christopher Wade, a linen-weaver of Dartford, was burned there in July 1555, the execution took place at ten o'clock in the morning in a gravel pit about a quarter of a mile outside the town, where felons were usually hanged. The people from the surrounding villages came in large numbers to see it, and the local fruiterers, realizing that there would be many onlookers there, brought horse-loads of cherries to sell to the people while they waited for the burning to begin. It was not only idle curiosity which made people come to see a heretic burned. His family, friends and sympathizers usually made a point of coming to give him moral support. Towards the end of Mary's reign, there were sometimes open demonstrations in favour of the heretic, and in the summer of 1558 the Queen issued an order that anyone who showed sympathy for a heretic at an execution was to be arrested and would be flogged.

When the heretic had been brought to the place of execution, the proceedings began with a sermon preached by some suitable preacher selected by the government. When Catherine of Aragon's former confessor, Friar Forest, was burned as a heretic in 1538 – he was the only Catholic during the whole of the Tudor Age to be burned as a heretic for supporting the old Catholic doctrines – the sermon was preached by the Bishop of Worcester, Latimer, who seventeen years later was himself burned as a Protestant heretic in Mary's reign; but it was unusual for a bishop to be appointed to preach the sermon at a burning, and this duty was usually performed by a rising churchman of a slightly inferior rank. After the sermon, the heretic said goodbye to his friends, and often gave them his gown or some other parting gift. Sometimes he drank a last cup of wine. He could choose whether he preferred to be burned in his outer garments, or to remove them and be burned in his underclothes. He was then fastened to the stake and surrounded by the faggots; and at a sign from the sheriff, the faggots were lit.

How long the heretic suffered in the fire varied in every case. In England, the burnings were carried out more mercifully than in some countries, such as France and the Netherlands, where additional tortures were sometimes inflicted as a further punishment on a heretic who refused to recant or who defied the authorities at the stake. In England, the heretic's friends were allowed to supply him with some gunpowder to hang around his neck, so that the gunpowder would explode when the flames reached it and cause the heretic to die instantaneously. Even without the gunpowder, the heretic might die very quickly by being suffocated almost immediately by the smoke. But the burning could be horribly prolonged. The gunpowder sometimes failed to explode because it was damp or defective; and sometimes the fire burned slowly, especially if the faggots were green or damp. There were some slow burnings of heretics in the summer of 1556, after the very rainy winter and spring had made the wood wet.

When Latimer and Ridley were burned at Oxford in October 1555, Latimer died almost immediately in the smoke; but Ridley suffered terribly from slow-burning faggots. His brother-in-law rushed forward and piled on more wood, in the hopes of ending Ridley's sufferings; but the effect was to dampen down the flames and to prolong the agony. When Hooper, the Protestant Bishop of Gloucester and Worcester, was burned at Gloucester in February 1555, he took three-quarters of an hour to die. All the Catholics and Protestants who watched the heretics burn considered that whether death was quick or prolonged was a manifestation of the will of God.

Occasionally a cruel executioner deliberately tried to prolong the heretic's sufferings. When John Lambert was burned at Smithfield in 1538, the men-at-arms who carried out the burning hoisted his burning body on to the point of a pike and lifted him out of the reach of the flames, before bringing him back into them again, in order to prolong the execution.

Heresy was not the only crime which was punishable by burning alive. It was also inflicted on women who were guilty of high treason, or who committed petty treason by murdering their husbands or their employers; but witches, who were burned in Scotland and in most other countries, were hanged in England, where the fear of witches and the drive against them did not really get under way until the seventeenth century, after James I, who had acquired a great dread of witches in Scotland, became King of England.

Male traitors who committed high treason against their highest overlord, the King, or petty treason against their immediate overlord by murdering their masters, were sentenced to be hanged, drawn and quartered; but in the case of noblemen it was always commuted to beheading, and sometimes this mercy was extended to gentlemen and men of lower rank. High treason was regulated by the Act of 1351, which is still in force in 1988, and which enacted that it should be high treason to attempt to kill the King, to take part in a revolt against the King, or to aid the King's foreign enemies in wartime. Later Acts of Parliament were passed, particularly in the sixteenth century, which made other offences high treason. One of them enacted that it was high treason to deny any of the King's titles, and this Act was used to execute several Catholic supporters, including Bishop Fisher and Sir Thomas More, who denied that the King was the Supreme Head of the Church of England. Another Act made it high treason to pretend to foretell the date of the King's death. This was directed against those who prophesied that the King would die within a few months, hoping that this prophecy would encourage the people to rebel. One result of this Act was that when Henry VIII was dying, his doctors, who realized that he had only a few hours to live, did not dare to tell him this, in case they were accused of high treason for foretelling the time of the King's death. Sir Anthony Denny, who was one of Henry's most intimate attendants, was prepared to take the risk, and warned the King to prepare for death.

When a man was found guilty of high treason, the sentence of the court was that he should be hanged by the neck, but cut down while still alive, castrated, and, being yet living, should be disembowelled and his bowels burned before his eyes, before he was beheaded and his body cut into quarters. His head and four quarters were then fixed on a pole on London Bridge, or on the gates of London, York and other cities.

The execution of traitors, like the burning of heretics, took place in public. Men were hanged, drawn and quartered at Tyburn, about three miles west of London on

Nicholas Ridley (?1500–55), Bishop of London, probably the most able theologian of the Protestant bishops, who supported the claims to the throne of Lady Jane Grey, and advocated them in a sermon at Paul's Cross in July 1553. Condemned as a heretic, he was burnt in 1555. This portrait is by an unknown painter.

Hugh Latimer (?1485–1555), Bishop of Worcester, painted by an unknown artist in the year of his death by burning, in company with Ridley.

122

the northern edge of Hyde Park, where Marble Arch is today. The traitors were brought to Tyburn from Newgate, or some other prison where they had been confined, tied face downwards on a hurdle drawn by horses. As with a burning, how much and how long they suffered varied in every case. The traitor or his family usually paid money to the executioner to allow the traitor, contrary to the sentence of the court, to hang until he was dead, or to dispatch him quickly with a stroke of the knife as soon as he was cut down, and before his bowels were cut out. If the executioner was not paid enough, or was vindictive towards the condemned man, he might deliberately prolong the execution.

As the international ideological struggle between Catholics and Protestants became increasingly bitter during the sixteenth century, a demand arose for more savage punishments of the traitors. In 1584 the murderer of the Protestant leader, William the Silent, in the Netherlands was executed by prolonged torture, and after this had been widely publicized in London, the loyal English Protestants wished to inflict similar punishments on Catholics who plotted to assassinate Queen Elizabeth. When Anthony Babington and his colleagues were convicted in 1586 of a conspiracy to murder Elizabeth with the approval of Mary Queen of Scots, Elizabeth wished the judges to sentence the convicted traitors to be executed by such means as the Privy Council should determine, so that they could be made to suffer a more painful death than hanging, drawing and quartering. She abandoned her demand when Lord Burghley convinced her that such a sentence would be illegal, and that if the sentence of hanging, drawing and quartering was properly carried out, it would be very painful and prolonged. She soon changed her mind, as she so often did, and after she had been told of the agony which Babington and three of the other traitors had suffered during their hanging, drawing and quartering, she ordered that the remaining traitors who were executed next day should be allowed to hang until they were dead.

Noblemen, and other traitors who were allowed to be beheaded, were executed on Tower Hill, just outside the walls of the Tower on the western side. They had usually been imprisoned before their execution in the Tower, and were allowed to walk the few yards to Tower Hill instead of being drawn there on a hurdle. The condemned traitor made a short speech to the crowd of spectators before he was beheaded. He was expected, in this speech, to praise the King who had ordered his execution, to urge the people to be loyal subjects, and to acknowledge his guilt; and the great majority of condemned men made the speech that was expected of them. Most of them behaved with courage and dignity on the scaffold. They usually gave a small gift to the executioner, to encourage him to do his job well and quickly. Sometimes the victim died at the first stroke of the axe, but sometimes two or three strokes were necessary.

The burning of Latimer and Ridley at Oxford in October 1555. Latimer died almost immediately; but Ridley suffered horribly from the slow burning of the faggots. The preacher at this morbid ceremony was Dr Smyth. This graphic and detailed illustration occupied a full page in the 1570 edition of Foxe's *Book of Martyrs*.

Very occasionally, a condemned traitor was not beheaded on Tower Hill, but on the Tower Green within the Tower, in the presence of only a few selected officials, and not of the general public. This privilege was extended to Henry VIII's two Queens, Anne Boleyn and Katherine Howard. Anne Boleyn was not beheaded by the public executioner with an axe, but with a stroke of a sword by an executioner who had been specially brought from St Omer because he had experience of beheading with a sword. The old Countess of Salisbury, whose chief crime was to be the mother of Henry VIII's great enemy, the exiled Cardinal Pole, was beheaded on Tower Green in 1541, and so were Lady Jane Grey in 1554 and the Earl of Essex in 1601.

The crimes of murder and theft, and other felonies, were punished by death by hanging, the convicted criminal being hanged on a gallows and left to hang until he was dead; but after a rebellion, rebels were sometimes hanged in chains, being hung on a gibbet by chains under their armpits and left hanging there until they died of

Prisoners in close confinement in Lollards Tower. An illustration in the second volume of Foxe's *Book of Martyrs*.

hunger. Other crimes were punished by imprisonment in Newgate, the Fleet, the Counter and the Marshalsea in London and Southwark, and in the various county jails. Short terms of imprisonment were often imposed, but it was very unusual for anyone to be sentenced to a fixed term of imprisonment of longer than a year. Political offenders were usually sentenced to imprisonment during the King's pleasure, and could then be held in the Tower, the Fleet or the Marshalsea indefinitely, or be released when it pleased the King and the Council.

Another common form of punishment was a whipping. Offenders were sometimes sentenced to be whipped through the streets when tied behind a slow-moving cart –'whipped at the cartarse'* – usually on market days, when there would

* The nineteenth-century historians bowdlerized this expression, and changed it to 'whipped at the cart-tail'.

be more people in the town to witness the punishment. Offenders were also placed in the stocks, where they were forced to sit fastened by the legs, or to stand in the pillory fastened by the arms. In the stocks or the pillory, they were surrounded by crowds who pelted them with eggs, stones and offal, while they sat or stood there, a fixed and defenceless target.

Sentences of mutilation were also imposed. The criminal was sentenced to have an ear nailed to the pillory, or to have the ear cut off. This was usually carried out in the market town on market day. Sometimes, as an aggravated punishment, the criminal was sentenced to have both ears cut off, often losing the second ear a week or a month after the other, on the next market day, so as to prolong and renew the pain of the punishment.

Various Acts of Parliament were passed, providing that certain offences were to be punished by cutting off the offender's hand. In order to prevent any violence at court, which might endanger the King's person, an Act provided that anyone who shed blood within the area of the court should lose his hand. In 1541, two gentlemen of the King's household quarrelled during a game of tennis in the tennis court at Hampton Court, and one of them, Sir Edmund Knyvett, drew his sword and wounded the other in his anger. He was sentenced to have his hand cut off, as usual in public. But at the last moment, when the King's master cook was there with the knife, the Sergeant of the Scullery with the mallet, and the King's master surgeon with the searing iron and the bandages, word arrived that the King had pardoned the offender.

There was no pardon for the Puritan propagandist, John Stubbs, when he wrote a book in 1579 denouncing the project for Elizabeth I to marry the King of France's brother, the Duke of Anjou. Elizabeth was very angry, for she considered it seditious for one of her subjects to meddle with the question of her marriage or her foreign policy. Stubbs was convicted under an Act which had been passed in Mary's reign in 1555, which provided that anyone who published a writing which vilified the Queen should have his hand cut off. The sentence was carried out before a disapproving crowd in Palace Yard in Westminster. After losing his right hand, Stubbs took off his hat with his left hand and cried 'God save the Queen!' before he fainted. He was also sentenced to be imprisoned during the Queen's pleasure, and was held for more than a year in the Tower before he was released.

The Privy Council itself dealt with political offenders, and exercised judicial as well as executive powers. People suspected of sedition were summoned to appear before the Council. Occasionally the suspect was arrested and brought to the Council by men-at-arms, but much more often he was merely ordered to appear on a fixed day, and came freely of his own accord, out of the respect for the royal authority which was so deeply ingrained in the ordinary Englishman during the Tudor Age;

though in sixteenth-century Scotland a person summoned to appear before the 'Secret Council' (Privy Council) of the King of Scots would almost certainly have refused to come, and would have taken refuge in the territory of some powerful lord where the government would not venture to pursue him.

The Privy Council never imposed the death penalty; if the King wished the offender to be put to death, he had to be tried and convicted by a special commission, or by a jury in the King's common law courts. But the Council, after hearing what the accused person had to say, could sentence him to lose an ear in the pillory, or to imprisonment during the King's pleasure. Sometimes he was sentenced to be held under house arrest, either in his own house or in the house of some member of the Council, or of some politically reliable member of his own family. In the reign of Edward VI, the Catholic bishops, who refused to submit and accept the Protestant doctrines and Church services prescribed by the Book of Common Prayer, were sometimes ordered to be confined as prisoners in the household of one of the Protestant bishops, who would argue with the recalcitrant bishop during his sojourn there and put him under moral pressure to submit. Sometimes the suspect, after the hearing before the Council, was bound over to be of good behaviour in some very large sum of money – £10,000, or an amount equal to most of his property – which he would forfeit to the King if he broke the conditions of his bond and offended against the royal authority.

An important part in the judicial system was the use of torture to elicit information from a suspected prisoner. Torture was more widely practised in England during the Tudor Age than in any other period before or since. It was not used in the ordinary criminal procedure of the English common law; for although painful punishments, such as hanging, drawing and quartering and mutilation, were imposed by the common law judges, there was no place for the torture of suspects in the English system of trial by witnesses and verdicts by juries, unlike the procedure under the civil law of continental Europe and Scotland, with the inquisitorial system of direct questioning of the defendant. The English common lawyers always frowned on the use of torture, though probably more from their professional dislike of the Roman law than for humanitarian reasons.

But the canonists of the Church and the 'civilians' in the King's government, with their training in the Roman civil law of the Continent and the canon law of the Church, considered torture to be a proper legal procedure in certain circumstances. Torture came into use in cases of high treason and sedition about the middle of the fifteenth century, and became much more common under Henry VIII, Mary and Elizabeth I. It ceased to be used in England early in the seventeenth century, and was declared illegal by Parliament in 1640, though it continued in Scotland until 1708.

Unlike those countries in the twentieth century where torture is used in

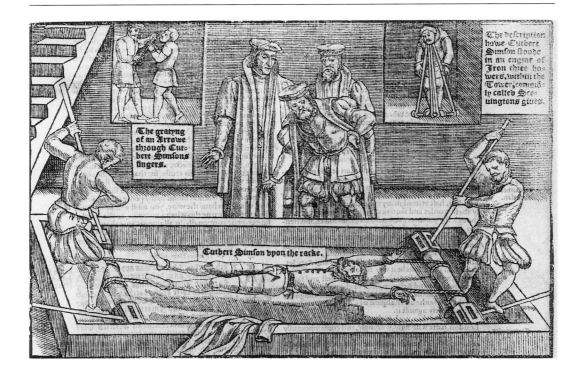

The racking of Cuthbert Simson 'in an engine of iron' for three hours in the Tower. An illustration to the second volume of Foxe's *Book of Martyrs*. A refinement of the punishment was 'the gratyng of an Arrowe through Cuthbert Simson's fingers'.

interrogation by the police, torture in the Tudor Age was openly acknowledged and legal, and the circumstances in which it could be used were strictly prescribed. It could only be inflicted under a warrant signed by the King or the Privy Council. The practice was only to torture a prisoner as a last resort. Although other forms of torture were occasionally used, by far the most common was the rack; the prisoner was fastened to a rack, which was extended by pulleys so that his arms and legs were painfully extended and dislocated, often inflicting substantial physical injury. The theory behind the use of torture was that if the prisoner was innocent, God would give him the strength to endure the pain, but that if he were guilty, it would force him to confess and speak the truth which he was obstinately refusing to reveal.

The practice was to question the prisoner several times without 'the pains'. If he refused to disclose important matters which he was suspected of concealing, he was taken to the torture chamber and 'shown a sight of the instruments' of torture, and then again questioned without 'the pains'. If he still remained obdurate, the King or the Privy Council signed a warrant authorizing the application of torture, and he was questioned 'under the pains', usually in the presence of a member of the Privy Council.

Noblemen and noble ladies, and the members of the royal family, had the privilege of being exempt from interrogation under torture; but gentlemen and their wives were sometimes tortured. When Mary Queen of Scots was imprisoned in England, she was suspected of being involved in the plot of the Italian banker, Ridolfi, to assassinate Elizabeth I. Mary's representative in London, the Bishop of Ross, to whom she had accorded the rank of her ambassador, was arrested by Elizabeth's government and accused of complicity in the plot. As he refused to reveal the information which the government required, he was examined by the Privy Council and threatened with interrogation under torture. He claimed that, as Mary's ambassador, he had diplomatic immunity from torture; but Lord Burghley and the Privy Councillors denied that he was a properly accredited ambassador, or that he had immunity from being questioned under the pains. The matter was not put to the test, because the Bishop of Ross ultimately gave the information which was required of him without being tortured.

The severity of the criminal law was considerably modified by the doctrines of sanctuary and benefit of clergy, which had been established during the Middle Ages, when the Church was at the height of its power. A fugitive from justice who succeeded in entering a church or monastery was safe from arrest as long as he stayed there, for the authorities were not permitted to enter the church to seize him; and although there were a few notorious cases in which the right of sanctuary was violated by the pursuers, it was nearly always respected. Some important abbeys and cathedral churches were given additional privileges of sanctuary; at Beverley and Hexham, the area of the sanctuary was extended for one mile from the abbey in every direction, and the limits of the sanctuary were marked by boundary stones.

A criminal who had reached the safety of sanctuary was allowed to remain there for forty days. He was then compelled to leave the sanctuary and go before a JP and confess his offence; but he was given a specified number of days in which to go unmolested to the nearest port and leave the kingdom, after he had promised not to return to England without the King's permission.

Banishing criminals from England proved to be unsatisfactory. They were not welcome abroad, and foreign governments adopted the same policy which the English Privy Council did with regard to gipsies and foreign criminals who came to England, ordering them to leave the realm within a given number of weeks on pain of death. English criminals who had gone abroad from sanctuary had no choice but to break their oaths and return secretly to England without the King's leave, landing at some unguarded place on the coast and continuing their life of crime. So the law was changed; instead of banishing the fugitives who were in sanctuary, they were allowed to remain there permanently under the supervision of a 'Governor of the Sanctuary'.

Benefit of clergy was a privilege won by the Church in the thirteenth century which established that members of the clergy who committed a felony should not be hanged, but suffer some lesser punishment; it was extended to deacons and any person remotely connected with the Church, and to anyone who could read; but it did not apply to women, not even to nuns, as women could not be clerks in holy orders. When literacy became more widespread in the sixteenth century after the introduction of printing, many laymen were able to take advantage of benefit of clergy. After the Bible in English had been printed and widely circulated in Elizabeth I's reign, the courts adopted the practice of inviting a convicted felon to read the first verse of the 51st Psalm: 'Have mercy upon me, O God, according to thy loving kindness; according unto the multitude of thy tender mercies, blot out my transgressions'. This became known as the 'neck verse', because any convicted felon who could read it, or who had been given the useful tip to learn it by heart and could therefore pretend to read it, was able to save his neck and avoid being hanged by claiming benefit of clergy.

The right of sanctuary and benefit of clergy were repeatedly modified during the Tudor Age, but surprisingly they were not completely abolished, and survived the suppression of the monasteries and the increased severity of the criminal law under Henry VIII. A series of statutes abolished the privileges in the case of the more serious offences. In Henry VII's reign, Perkin Warbeck was able on two occasions to escape being executed as a traitor by taking sanctuary; but by the end of the Tudor Age, sanctuary and benefit of clergy had been abolished in cases of high treason and all the more serious crimes, and in most of the new felonies created by Acts of Parliament. An Act of 1489 enacted that a layman who claimed benefit of clergy should be branded on the thumb with the letter M in cases of murder and the letter T in cases of theft and other cases, and that he could not claim the privilege for a second offence. This was extended to priests by a statute of 1576.

The law about sanctuary was extensively altered by an Act of 1540, which was passed after the final suppression of the greater, as well as the lesser, monasteries; but it shows the popularity of the sanctuary system that Henry VIII did not take this opportunity of abolishing sanctuary altogether. Every fugitive in sanctuary was required at the end of forty days to go to the nearest of the eight sanctuary towns which were established in Westminster, Wells, Manchester, Northampton, Norwich, York, Derby and Launceston; but there were never to be more than twenty criminals in any sanctuary town, and if the nearest one was full, the criminal was to be sent on to the next one. If he refused to go there, he was to lose the right to sanctuary. There was to be no sanctuary for anyone accused of murder, rape, burglary, robbery in any house in circumstances which put an inmate of the house in fear of his life; of arson of houses or of barns filled with corn; or of robberies of churches or any hallowed place; and it had already been abolished for high and petty treason.

A sanctuary man was to lose the right to sanctuary if he committed any felony while residing in the sanctuary, of if he failed to report within three days of being summoned to do so by the Governor of the Sanctuary. He was only allowed to leave the sanctuary during daylight hours with a written licence from the Governor; he was not to wear a sword, knife or any other weapon; and he was to wear on his upper garment a badge, designed by the Governor of the Sanctuary, which was to be ten inches long and ten inches wide. If he left the sanctuary at night, or without complying with these conditions, he was to be imprisoned in the sanctuary prison for two days for the first offence, and for six days for the second, and for the third offence he was to lose the right of sanctuary.

The people of the eight sanctuary towns did not relish having these criminals living amongst them. The two thousand inhabitants of Manchester were sufficiently influential to protest effectively, because they were already beginning to develop a cloth industry and to produce linen and woollen goods which were valued for their quality. They persuaded Parliament that Manchester was a thriving and growing town, to which many people were coming from Ireland and elsewhere to work in the cloth industry, and that the manufacturing process required their linen and wools to be out of doors, night and day, for six months before the linen was 'whited' and the wools 'dressed up'. It was therefore essential that all the inhabitants of Manchester should be honest people, who would resist the temptation to steal the linen and wool. Parliament passed an Act in 1542 which enacted that Manchester should no longer be a sanctuary town, and that Chester should replace it as the nearest sanctuary.

The right of sanctuary and benefit of clergy survived the Tudor Age. In one respect benefit of clergy was extended, for an Act of Edward VI's Parliament in 1547 granted it automatically to all peers. Sanctuary was virtually abolished in 1623, but was not finally eliminated until 1697; and benefit of clergy, after being extended to women in the seventeenth century, was removed from more and more crimes, but survived in theory until 1841.

THE HOUSES

HOUSES and buildings are one of the greatest glories of the Tudor Age. Many Tudor houses, unlike those of earlier periods, still stand today, although very few buildings erected before 1450 still survive, apart from the stone castles, cathedrals and churches. Most of the houses built before the middle of the fifteenth century were of wood. Many of them were burned down after being set alight by an unattended candle or a burning faggot which had fallen out of the fireplace. Many more were not sufficiently sturdy to survive for more than a hundred years, even if they had lasted so long without catching fire. Many others were demolished in the Tudor Age to make room for new Tudor houses; for the idea of preserving old buildings of historical interest had not occurred to anyone before the nineteenth century.

By the reign of Henry VII, even some of the houses of the middle and lower classes were being built of stone or red brick. Stone was most usual in the north and west of England; but in the south-east, which in building as in all other respects was historically in advance of the rest of England, red brick became increasingly common.

In earlier periods, the cottages of the common people often consisted of only one room, on the ground floor, open to the rafters with a hole in the roof for the smoke from the fire to escape, and an attic under the roof which could only be reached by a ladder. There were holes or slits in the walls to let in the light, but no glass windows, and if the shutters over the windows were closed to keep the house warm, this involved sacrificing the light. At the end of the fifteenth century, any prosperous tradesman, craftsman or farmer who valued his social position wished to live in a house which had a 'solar', and perhaps also a parlour. The solar was the private room of the master of the house, where he lived, at least in the summer, though in winter he might move into the communal room in order to keep warm. The solar and the other rooms often had a small glass window.

While the ambition of the rising craftsman and yeoman was to have a house with a solar, the great nobleman was eager to build a magnificent mansion which was bigger, more modern, and more impressive than the mansions of other noblemen. Some of the most powerful lords did not wish to have a new house, but preferred to continue living in the medieval castles of their ancestors or predecessors. In this case, the old castle was usually modernized. Henry VII, Henry VIII and Elizabeth I were often in residence at Windsor Castle, which had been built for Edward III in the fourteenth century; and in the city of London, Baynards Castle and the palace of Bridewell, as well as the Tower, were medieval buildings. But Henry VII made important additions at Windsor, and completely rebuilt Baynards Castle. Henry VIII restored the White Tower at the Tower of London, and he also rebuilt Bridewell Palace in 1515.

The royal palace at Greenwich had also been a royal residence in the fourteenth century, but it had been greatly enlarged, and very largely rebuilt, by Edward IV. It was enlarged still further by Henry VIII, who was born there and resided there more often than at any of his other palaces. His daughters Mary and Elizabeth were also born at Greenwich, and Edward VI died there. Greenwich Palace continued to be a royal residence until it was pulled down by Charles II, and the royal hospital was built on the site.

In the North, there was a royal residence at Sheriffhutton, twelve miles north of York. Richard III had lived there as Duke of Gloucester when he governed the North of England for his brother Edward IV; and when he was King, he imprisoned Elizabeth of York there, where she remained until Henry VII freed her and married her. In 1525 Henry VIII appointed his six-year-old illegitimate son by Elizabeth Blount, Henry Duke of Richmond, to be the nominal President of the Council of the North which governed the North of England, and sent him to reside at Sheriffhutton. But he did not modernize the building, which remained a medieval castle. One corner of the castle wall still stands today in a farmyard in the village of Sheriffhutton.

The thirteenth-century palace of Sheen in Surrey was rebuilt by Edward III, and rebuilt again by Henry V. It was one of Henry VII's residences until it was burned down in an accidental fire in 1498. Henry VII then built a new and larger palace on the same site in a modern Italian style. He named it Richmond Palace, after his father's title of Earl of Richmond which he himself had borne before he became King and which referred to the village of Richmond in Yorkshire; and the name of the Surrey village around the palace was changed from Sheen to Richmond. Richmond Palace was much used as a royal residence by all the Tudor sovereigns, and Henry VII in 1509, and Elizabeth I nearly a hundred years later, both died there.

Henry VII had other modern residences. The royal palace at Eltham near

Blackheath had been built for Edward IV in 1479, and Henry VII often stayed there. Henry VIII spent much of his childhood at Eltham, but rarely visited it as King, though he carried out building works at the palace. There had been a royal residence at Woodstock in Oxfordshire since the twelfth century or earlier, but the palace was rebuilt between 1495 and 1501. Henry VIII often went there on his summer progresses. Elizabeth I was imprisoned there for a year in Mary's reign after her release from the Tower, and also occasionally went there on her progresses as Queen. The palace was badly damaged during the Civil War in the seventeenth century, and the ruins were finally demolished at the beginning of the eighteenth century when Vanbrugh built Blenheim Palace on the site for the Duke of Marlborough.

The palace of Oatlands near Weybridge in Surrey was rebuilt and greatly enlarged for Henry VIII on the site of an older house, but like Woodstock was destroyed during the Civil War. Nothing remains today of Henry's manor house at Newhall in Essex, where he carried out many modern improvements; of his house at Easthampstead in Berkshire; or of the royal manor house at Ampthill in Bedfordshire, where Catherine of Aragon lived for a time after her separation from Henry. Only the outer wall still stands today of the manor house at Grafton in Northamptonshire – now called Grafton Regis – where Henry VIII stayed regularly on his progresses, and where he had his last meeting with Wolsey a few weeks before the Cardinal's fall.

When Henry VIII became King, the first nobleman in his kingdom was Edward Stafford, Duke of Buckingham, the High Constable of England. He owned land in twenty-four counties, a house in London, another in Calais, and a fourteenth-century house at Penshurst in Kent, which he modernized; but his principal residence was at Thornbury in Gloucestershire. He built a great stone castle there in the medieval style but with sixteenth-century embellishments and decorations. It was unwise to build a great medieval castle which was obviously capable of being defended as a fortress against an enemy and against the King, and may well have been one of the factors which caused Henry VIII and Wolsey to have him arrested and executed as a traitor in 1521, though the building of Thornbury Castle was not referred to at his trial for high treason. The Duke of Suffolk was satisfied to live in more modest manor houses at Westhorp in Suffolk and at Grimsthorp in Lincolnshire; and though the Duke of Norfolk lived in a medieval castle at Framlingham in Suffolk, he could not be accused of building or enlarging it.

Thomas Wolsey, the son of an Ipswich butcher, was the most striking example of how building was used as a status symbol in the sixteenth century. After becoming a priest and entering the service of Henry VII, he had risen by 1514 to be Archbishop of York and Henry VIII's chief minister. It was in 1514 – the year before he became a Cardinal and Lord Chancellor of England – that he took a long lease of land on the

The south-west tower of Thornbury Castle, in Gloucestershire, built between 1511 and 1521 by Edward Stafford, Duke of Buckingham, in the medieval style but with sixteenth-century embellishments. After the execution of Buckingham in 1521 it remained uninhabited for two hundred years. Above is a detail from an engraving by J. Le Keux, after a drawing by G. Shepherd, 1813.

north bank of the Thames in the parish of Hampton, and began to build the palace of Hampton Court, having first ensured that the house would have an adequate water supply by bringing the water from Coombe Hill in Surrey, three miles away, in lead pipes through the village of Surbiton and under the Hagsmill river and the Thames.

Only a very small part of Wolsey's palace at Hampton Court still exists today, for it was rebuilt by Henry VIII, William III and George II. When the French ambassador visited Wolsey there in 1527 he was enormously impressed by the size and grandeur of Hampton Court, and wrote that there were two hundred and eighty rooms in the house; so it is clear that by far the greater part of Wolsey's palace must have been demolished to make way for the later buildings which were added in the sixteenth, seventeenth and eighteenth centuries.

At the same time that Hampton Court was being built, Wolsey was enlarging another house in Westminster on the banks of the Thames between Charing Cross and the palace and abbey of Westminster. It was known in Wolsey's time as York Place, but the name was changed to Whitehall after his downfall. Wolsey had two large mansions in Hertfordshire – his house of The Moor near Rickmansworth and another house at Tyttenhanger. He also had his houses as Archbishop of York in his diocese at Cawood near York and at Scrooby and Southwell in Nottinghamshire; but he never went there for sixteen years after he became Archbishop, until he visited his diocese for the first time after his fall from power in 1530.

In 1525 Wolsey gave Hampton Court to the King. On many occasions, particularly in later years, Henry VIII virtually forced his nobles, counsellors and bishops to make an exchange of houses with him which was greatly to his advantage and to their disadvantage. But Wolsey's transaction with Henry about Hampton Court was quite favourable from his point of view, for in exchange for giving Henry Hampton Court, Henry granted Wolsey the occupation of part of Richmond Palace as well as a suite of rooms in Hampton Court and in all the other royal palaces. It was another matter with York Place. When Wolsey was dismissed from his office of Lord Chancellor in 1529 he was forced to give York Place, The Moor and Tyttenhanger to Henry in return for a pardon for the offences that he was alleged to have committed against the King; and after being allowed to spend the winter in houses at Esher and at Richmond, he was ordered to reside in his diocese of York.

Wolsey travelled north and, crossing the Trent, entered his province and diocese; but having travelled three miles further to his house at Southwell, he remained there and went no further. It was the nearest he could be to London and the King's court while complying with the order to live in his diocese. While he was at Southwell in the summer of 1530 he carried out repairs and improvements to the house to turn it into a magnificent mansion. This created a bad impression at court, for Wolsey's enemies interpreted it as a sign that he was as ambitious as ever and would soon be plotting a return to power.

Wolsey's agent, Thomas Cromwell, who had served him for some years and had remained loyal to him, was lobbying influential people at court in Wolsey's favour, and he warned Wolsey of the effect at court of the building projects at Southwell. He wrote to Wolsey,

Sir, some there be that doth allege that Your Grace doth keep too great a house and family, and that ye are continually building. For the love of God therefore, I . . . most heartily beseech Your Grace to have respect to everything, and considering the time, to refrain yourself, for a season, from all manner buildings, more than mere necessity requireth, which I assure Your Grace shall cease and put to silence some persons that much speaketh of the same.

The building work at Southwell may have been one of the reasons why Henry became convinced that Wolsey was a menace to his royal authority and had better be finally got rid of. In the autumn of 1530 Wolsey travelled to York for his belated enthronement as Archbishop; but before he got there he was arrested at Cawood on a charge of high treason. His health gave way, and he died at Leicester Abbey while he was being taken south as a prisoner.

When Wolsey was at the height of his power and wealth – Lord Chancellor, Papal Legate, Archbishop of York, Bishop of Durham and Abbot of St Albans – he decided to found a new college in his old university of Oxford and a school in his native town of Ipswich. It was a period of great expansion in the university. Wolsey's own college of Magdalen had been founded in 1458, but the buildings were not finished until thirty years later, at the beginning of the Tudor Age. The great bell tower, which was added immediately afterwards, was being built when Wolsey was Bursar of the college in 1498 and 1499, and it was finished in 1505. In 1500, extensive work was being carried out at Bernard College, the residence of the Cistercian monks who were scholars at the university, which was afterwards converted into St John's College. During the next twenty years Corpus Christi College and Brasenose College were founded and built. In Cambridge, Jesus College, where Cranmer was a student and teacher, Christ's College, St John's College and Buckingham College were built between 1496 and 1519. The name of Buckingham College was changed to Magdalene College after Buckingham's execution for high treason. At King's Hall, the great gate was built, and other work carried out, between 1518 and 1535; the college was later incorporated into Trinity College.

Wolsey amassed the money which he needed to found his college at Oxford by obtaining a Papal Bull under which he suppressed twenty-two monasteries and seized their assets, and by asking, cajoling, and in some cases bullying and threatening, many noblemen and wealthy persons and institutions into contributing donations towards the cost of the work. The future of his colleges was threatened when he was dismissed as Lord Chancellor and disgraced in 1529. Henry VIII seized part of the revenues of Cardinal's College at Oxford, and ordered the removal of Wolsey's coat-of-arms which had been placed in every window; but he allowed the college to continue after changing the name to 'King Henry VIII's College'. It is now

PALATIVM REGIVM IN ANGLIÆ REGNO APPELLATVM NONCIVTZ,
Hæc eſt nuſquam ſimile.

Nonesuch Palace: detail from an engraving by Franz Hogenberg after a drawing by Joris Hoefnagel, 1582, which seems to be the earliest known picture of Henry VIII's 'folly'. The Palace was still incomplete when Henry died. A seventeenth-century painting is reproduced on pages 150 and 151.

known as Christ Church. But to Wolsey's great grief, his college at Ipswich was suppressed on a legal technicality; the teachers and students were ejected, and the property was seized by the King.

After Wolsey's fall, Henry VIII had four residences in the immediate vicinity of London – Whitehall, Greenwich, Richmond and Hampton Court – as well as his palace of The Moor, his manor house at Enfield, and his houses at Newhall, Hunsdon, Oatlands and Hatfield House in Hertfordshire, where his daughter Elizabeth lived. He frequently stayed at Hampton Court, and built additions to the palace, with an inner courtyard which was adorned by a great clock which Nicholas Oursian made for him in 1540; it showed the days of the week, and of the months, as well as the hours, the time of high water at London Bridge, the phases of the moon,

Barham Manor, in Suffolk, is on the site of an ancient moated manor house which belonged to the Church. On the dissolution of the monasteries it was acquired by Sir Richard Southwell, who rebuilt it in Tudor bricks, with eight octagonal chimneys having star tops, rising from crow-stepped gable-ends. The original windows are low-mullioned and transomed, formed from moulded bricks rendered not in cement, as commonly supposed, but in *septaria*, a smooth grey 'clay' dredged from nearby river estuaries. The three windows in the front roof were inserted later, probably in the eighteenth century. Small brick-built houses of this type are found almost exclusively in East Anglia.
Photograph by Lance Cooper.

Fleming's Hall, Bedingfield, Suffolk, is a typical example of a small manor house which later became a farmhouse. It is a combination of brick and half-timbering, and was built c.1550. The gable-ends, which give it a touch of style, carry two groups of four polygonal chimneys. The two-storeyed brick porch contains a four-centred entrance arch, with pediment and three-light transom window over it.
Photograph by Lance Cooper.

the signs of the zodiac, and the sun moving round the stationary earth. But Henry was not satisfied with these residences. He built himself a new palace of St James's in the fields to the north-west of Westminster, less than a mile from Whitehall; and he had a more ambitious project in mind. He wished to build a palace which would not only be bigger and better than any of his existing houses, but which would outshine the palaces of any other Prince in Europe. It was to be built near Ewell in Surrey and called Nonesuch.

The building work began in 1538. Henry demolished the whole village of Cuddington, which ceased to exist, enclosed and compulsorily acquired more than a thousand acres of agricultural land, and diverted several highways. He employed not only his usual English builders, but invited the famous Italian artists Antonio Toto dell'Nunziata of Florence and John of Padua to do the elaborate decorations on the gateways and façade of the palace. The result was a building rather different from the Gothic style of Hampton Court, St James's and the other buildings which had been erected since the days of Edward IV; it was a mixture of Gothic with the more ornate style of the Italian Renaissance.

Nonesuch Palace had not been completed when Henry VIII died in 1547, and he only spent four days there. The work was finished after his death, but Mary sold it to the Earl of Arundel. Elizabeth I often stayed there as Arundel's guest. It was at Nonesuch in August 1585 that the treaty was negotiated, after so much hard bargaining, between Elizabeth's counsellors and the Dutch delegates, by which she eventually agreed, reluctantly, to send military assistance to the States of the Netherlands in their fight against the rule of Philip II of Spain. In 1592, Arundel's heir sold Nonesuch to Elizabeth. After her death, the palace became a favourite residence of James I's Queen, Anne of Denmark, but it was pulled down by Charles II in 1670. The ruins were excavated by archaeologists and historians in 1959–60.

After Henry VIII dissolved the monasteries, he granted many of their lands as gifts to his counsellors and courtiers. Some of these counsellors and courtiers had served him for many years, often incurring personal expense in his service, and they expected and received these gifts as a suitable reward. Others obtained their share of the loot by luck. In the seventeenth century, the grandchildren of these fortunate people, and of their envious rivals, told stories of how their grandfathers had acquired their properties. They told how Sir Nicholas Partridge had won the Jesus bells at St Paul's Cathedral from Henry VIII one night at dice, and how a Devon gentleman, John Champernown, on a visit to the court, seeing a number of courtiers kneeling to the King as he passed by, knelt beside them, and to his surprise was granted the priory of St Germans in Cornwall as a gift because some officials had made a mistake. But in most cases the monastic lands were sold by the King to gentlemen and other private individuals. Some of the purchasers were speculators who bought the lands in order to resell them at a profit; but one way or another, the lands were ultimately acquired in most cases by the local country gentlemen.

Many of the monasteries owned property in different parts of England, often far away from the monastery building; but the building itself was one of the valuable assets of the monastery, especially the lead on the roof. The commissioners who were sent to suppress the monasteries were ordered to make sure that the lead was not stripped from the roof, and stolen, by the local inhabitants during the time that the house was empty after the monks had left. In order to prevent these thefts, the commissioners themselves stripped the roofs and sent the lead to the King's officials in London; it was usually shipped by sea from the nearest port. The result was that the buildings fell rapidly into decay, and as the gentlemen who bought the monastic lands did not wish to live in the monasteries, they demolished them and built new houses on the site, or nearby.

In the case of the great magnates, the new house was often a splendid mansion erected by one of the famous builders in their usual style. Lord Russell, who served on Henry VIII's Privy Council, first as Lord Admiral and then as Lord Privy Seal, was granted Woburn Abbey in Bedfordshire; and Sir William Herbert, who married Queen Katherine Parr's sister, obtained Wilton Abbey near Salisbury. In the reign of Edward VI, Russell and Herbert commanded the troops who suppressed the Catholic rising in Cornwall, and they supported Northumberland's *coup d'état* which overthrew Somerset. Russell was rewarded by being created Earl of Bedford, and Herbert was made Earl of Pembroke. They both built impressive houses at Woburn and Wilton; but Wilton was enlarged and altered by Inigo Jones in the middle of the seventeenth century, and Woburn was completely rebuilt in 1747.

William Fitzwilliam, Earl of Southampton, the Lord Admiral of England, built himself a splendid house at Cowdray on the outskirts of Midhurst in Sussex; the work, which was begun in about 1535, was carried out by the famous builders who had built Hampton Court and the other palaces for Wolsey and Henry VIII. It was there that he brought Margaret, Countess of Salisbury, the daughter of Edward IV's brother, the Duke of Clarence, as a prisoner. Her son, Reginald Pole, had gone to Italy, where he was created a cardinal by the Pope, and had written from Venice to Henry VIII denouncing him for repudiating Papal supremacy and putting to death Bishop Fisher, Sir Thomas More and the Carthusian monks who refused to acknowledge Henry as head of the Church of England. Pole told Henry, in his letter, that he was worse than Domitian, the Caesar who had persecuted the Christians in the first century after Christ.

The Countess of Salisbury and her son, Lord Montagu, wrote to Pole denouncing him as an abominable traitor, and sent a copy of their letters to the King; but this did not save them for long.

In 1538 Montagu was arrested. The evidence showed that he had said in a private conversation: 'I like well the doings of my brother the Cardinal [Pole] and I would we were both over the sea'; and he had also once said, again in a private conversation, that when Henry VIII was a little boy, his father Henry VII did not like him. On this evidence, Montagu was convicted of high treason, and beheaded. Someone testified that Montagu's friend, Sir Edward Neville, had once said, when he was a guest at Cowdray, that 'the King is a beast and worse than a beast', which was enough for him to be convicted as a traitor and beheaded together with Montagu.

Southampton and other members of the Privy Council arrived at the Countess of Salisbury's house at Warbledon in Hampshire, to interrogate her servants and search the house. They found no evidence against her except that she had forbidden her servants to read the Bible in English and had once been seen burning a letter – and why should she do this unless it was a letter from her son, the traitor Reginald Pole? The old Countess, who was nearly seventy, was taken to Cowdray and from there to the Tower, and as there was insufficient evidence to convict her of high treason she was condemned to death as a traitor by an Act of Parliament.

Henry kept her in the Tower for two years after the Act of Attainder had been passed, and then suddenly ordered her to be beheaded within the Tower, in the privacy of Tower Green, in May 1541. The old lady did not realize what was happening to her, and when she was told to lay her head on the block, she began wandering slowly and aimlessly around Tower Green. When they had managed to get her to the block, the inexperienced and nervous young headsman botched the execution, and only succeeded in killing her at the third or fourth stroke of the axe.

Wolsey was not the only great ecclesiastical dignitary to indulge in splendid building projects, though none of the others could compete with him. In Edward IV's reign, Cardinal Bourchier, the Archbishop of Canterbury, built a very impressive manor house at Knole on the outskirts of Sevenoaks in Kent. Bourchier's Lancastrian successor as Archbishop, Cardinal Morton, modernized his London residence at Lambeth on the south bank of the Thames by adding a gateway in the Gothic style of the period; he also rebuilt the tower of Canterbury Cathedral, replacing the old structure with the tower which still dominates the cathedral today. The work was finished in 1497, three years before Morton's death. William Warham, who succeeded Morton as Archbishop after a short interval, built a very large palace at Otford, though it was only three miles north of his smaller, but impressive, house at Knole.

Warham was always eclipsed by Wolsey, but he survived him, and did not die until 1532, when Henry was on the point of repudiating his allegiance to Rome. Henry's appointment of Thomas Cranmer as Warham's successor was seen on all sides as a step towards breaking with Rome and moving in a Protestant direction. When

Cranmer became Archbishop, he had eleven impressive residences – Lambeth, Croydon and Mortlake in Surrey, and Canterbury, Knole, Otford, Maidstone, Charing, Ford, Wingham and Aldington in Kent; but Henry VIII forced him to get rid of Knole, Otford, Maidstone, Charing, Wingham and Aldington in a number of exchanges by which he acquired a new palace at Beakesbourn near Herne, but which worked out very much to the disadvantage of the see of Canterbury. The Archbishop's palace at Canterbury was burned down in an accidental fire in 1543, leaving him with his four palaces at Lambeth, Croydon, Beakesbourn and Ford.

Cranmer's secretary, Ralph Morice, wrote a short biography of Cranmer for his friend John Foxe, when he was an old man, in about 1565. He described how on one occasion, thirty years before, Henry VIII asked Cranmer, in Morice's presence, to agree to an exchange by which Henry would acquire Knole for himself. Cranmer, who was very fond of Knole, was reluctant to agree, and suggested to Henry that it would be better if he gave him Otford instead, as it was larger and would be better able to accommodate all the gentlemen and servants who escorted Henry when he travelled to his houses in the country. Henry said that he did not like Otford as much as Knole, because Otford was in low-lying country, and Knole was on higher ground, and he always felt unwell when he was at Otford. This may have been imagination on Henry's part, because it was a widespread belief in the Tudor Age that people who lived in houses on high ground were less likely to catch the plague and fevers than those who lived in houses in low-lying districts. As Cranmer continued to stress the advantages of Otford, Henry said that he would have both Otford and Knole, so that his retinue could stay in the larger and less healthy house at Otford while he himself and a small number of attendants stayed three miles away at the pleasanter and healthier house at Knole. So Cranmer was forced to surrender both Otford and Knole to Henry, in exchange for far less valuable property, in 1537. Morice was anxious to defend Cranmer from the critics who condemned him for agreeing to these exchanges which so impoverished his see for his successors. 'For as touching his exchanges men ought to consider with whom he had to do, specially with such a Prince as would not be bridled nor be against said in any of his requests.'

Abbots and priors built, as well as bishops, not foreseeing that their monasteries would soon be dissolved. Improvements were carried out to the abbey churches at Westminster, Peterborough and Sherborne Abbeys. Splendid new apartments were built for the private residences of the abbots and priors at Mulcheney Abbey and Montacute Priory in Somerset, at Forde Abbey in Dorset, and at Thame Abbey in Oxfordshire. In all these cases the work was not finished until less than ten years before the dissolution of the monasteries.

No cathedrals were built during the Tudor Age. All the old dioceses already had cathedrals which had been erected before the end of the fourteenth century; and when Henry VIII created six new dioceses in 1540 the abbey churches of some of the dissolved monasteries were converted into the cathedrals of the new dioceses. But a number of new parish churches were built, at the expense of wealthy merchants and manufacturers. The thriving woollen clothiers built splendid churches at Lavenham and Long Melford in Suffolk and at Taunton in Somerset; and the equally prosperous ironmasters of the Weald of Kent built a spacious church in the village of Cranbrook which was much larger than the ordinary parish church.

The prestige building during the years between 1475 and 1550 could not have been carried out on such an extensive scale by the old building methods of the local independent masons and carpenters who had so slowly and patiently built the simple houses and cottages, and also the castles and cathedrals, of the Middle Ages. The new builders were big businessmen; they employed many workmen, used large cranes for work on high buildings, and worked far afield, beyond the districts where they lived and had their business offices. When building in brick developed on a large scale in England, the Dutchman, Baldwin, opened a brickworks at Tattershall in Lincoln-shire, where he made bricks for buildings all over south-east England. There was another large brickworks at Eton. These and other brickworks were able to supply Edward IV with over two million bricks for the additional fortifications which were erected at Dover Castle in 1480. The new type of builder, with his large labour force and modern methods, could complete his work much faster than the builders in earlier times. It had taken more than fifty years to build most of the medieval cathedrals; but the great edifices erected under Henry VII and the later Tudors were usually finished within fifteen years. As usual, the increased efficiency, and the splendid products which resulted from the improved working methods, were achieved at a cost in human terms. The masons and carpenters who worked for the new builders were still skilled craftsmen, but they could no longer exercise their personal judgment and taste. They had now to work according to the plan of the master-builder who employed them.

The size of the operations and the reputation of the new type of builders gave their names a snob value. Noblemen and bishops who emulated the building projects of the King and Wolsey wished not only to build better and bigger houses than their rivals, but liked to boast that they had engaged Wastell, Vertue, Redman or Needham to carry out the work. In some areas, a local man was able to develop a large building firm and acquire a reputation which ensured him a monopoly of the important building projects in the neighbourhood. William Orchard of Headington, on the outskirts of Oxford, built the tower and other buildings at Magdalen College, the Divinity School, and Bernard College (later St John's College) in the university, and the ante-chapel at Eton, between 1480 and 1504, and after his death Brasenose College at Oxford was built in 1519 by one of his pupils. In the west country, Hart

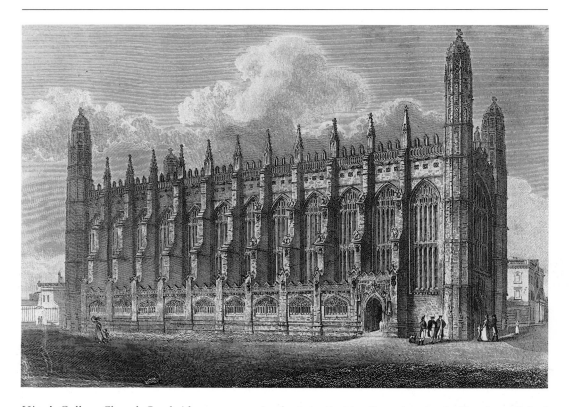

King's College Chapel, Cambridge: an engraving by John Smith, after a drawing by Bond, published in 1802. This shows the building virtually unchanged from that depicted in 1531 in an ink-and-wash drawing by its architect, John Wastell. He was probably the greatest of his day, but Henry VII and Henry VIII must share much of the credit for the completion of this superb building by a team of master craftsmen.

built the great church towers at Bristol, Cardiff and Wrexham; and in the North, Christopher Scoyne carried out the work at Ripon Minster, at St Mary's, Beverley, and at Fountains Abbey in Yorkshire, and on the spire of Louth church in Lincolnshire, between 1505 and 1525. He was also responsible for the upkeep of Durham Cathedral.

But the other famous builders were not limited to any particular area. Wastell built the tower of Canterbury Cathedral, Henry VII's chapel in Westminster Abbey, and the chapels in Peterborough Cathedral and King's College, Cambridge. William Vertue worked at St George's Chapel and the Lady Chapel at Windsor, at King's College, Cambridge, at Corpus Christi College, Oxford, and on the chapel of St Peter ad Vincula in the Tower of London and St Stephen's Cloisters in the palace of Westminster. Henry Redman, from Ramsey in Huntingdonshire, succeeded his father Thomas at Westminster Abbey and carried out the work on the tower of St Margaret's, Westminster, at Eton, at Greenwich, and at Windsor Castle, and built

The façade of Longleat House, near Warminster in Wiltshire, is one of the masterpieces of Tudor Renaissance architecture, and was described by Olive Cook, in *The English House Through Seven Centuries*, as 'the most classical looking of the great Elizabethan mansions'. It was built by Sir John Thynne, ancestor of its present owner, the Marquess of Bath. Surprisingly, no contemporary painting or engraving of it has survived, but the detail reproduced above of an etching by Sparrow, based on a seventeenth-century engraving by Knyff and Kip, shows much the same view of the façade as visitors saw in 1568 – and still see today.

Hampton Court, York Place, and Cardinal's College at Oxford for Wolsey.

The roods and timber work at all these buildings for Wolsey were done by the famous master-carpenter, Humphrey Coke. Another famous carpenter, James Needham, designed the roof of the great hall at Hampton Court, and was responsible for the work at the Tower, at Rochester, at Greenwich, at Eltham, at Petworth and at

Knole. Most of these eminent builders held for a time official positions in the King's service. Needham worked for some years for the garrisons at Berwick and Calais, and accompanied the army which invaded France in 1523. They were masters of their city livery companies and mayors of their home towns, though none of them followed the example of the builder, William Veysey, in the reign of Henry VI and became a member of Parliament. Needham, who began working at a master-carpenter's wage of tenpence a day, was able to buy extensive properties in Hertfordshire and Kent.

In building, as in so many other aspects of Tudor life, a great change took place after 1550. Neither Edward VI, Mary nor Elizabeth I engaged in building as Henry VII and Henry VIII had done. With Whitehall, Greenwich, Richmond, St James's and Nonesuch in the neighbourhood of London, apart from their manors further away, they did not need another palace, and all of them for different reasons, were much more economical than Henry VIII. The building of new towers and chapels in abbeys and cathedrals, and of new parish churches, also virtually stopped. But the nobility still built mansions, and so did some of the wealthier and more important knights and gentlemen.

These mansions were built in a new style. The palaces which Wolsey and his contemporaries erected had Gothic gateways and façades; inside the house, there was a big banqueting hall with large windows, but the other rooms were small, with small windows, though all the windows were of glass, unlike the apertures with shutters of the houses of earlier generations. On the first floor there was a long gallery on all four sides of the building, with bay windows at regular intervals in which there were fixed window seats. When public receptions took place at court, the King would often withdraw with one of his counsellors, or with a foreign ambassador, 'into a window' and sit and talk to him there in privacy, as no one else would venture to approach.

After 1550, the great houses built by the nobility were usually in stone, not brick, and the Gothic façade was replaced by simpler perpendicular frontages. They were built on four sides of a central courtyard, which was far larger than the courtyards of the first half of the century, so the sides of the building were much longer. Many of the rooms were large, with very large glass windows; the people who saw them were amazed, and had the impression that the house was made of glass. The lay-out and appearance of the houses resembled the palaces that had been built thirty years earlier on the Loire in France, but the size and features were exaggerated in the great houses of later Tudor England.

Many of these houses were wholly or partly demolished, and converted into even larger houses, in the late seventeenth and in the eighteenth centuries; but Longleat House, which the courtier and soldier, Sir John Thynne, built near Warminster in Wiltshire, still stands today, unaltered externally, just as it looked when it was completed in 1585. Kirby Hall in Northamptonshire, which was built for Sir

Sir William Cecill knight, Baron of Burghley Lord high Treaforer of England, knight of the moft noble order of the Garter and Mafter of her Ma:ᵗⁱᵉˢ court of wardes and Lyueries.

COR VNV VIA VNA

William Cecil, who was created Baron Burghley in 1571, was not merely the outstanding statesman of Queen Elizabeth's reign but also one of its greatest builders. He enlarged and modernized his family home at Burghley near Stamford. He also built a house at Theobalds, near Cheshunt.

149

The most frequently illustrated view of Henry VIII's dream palace, Nonesuch, is the drawing by Joris Hoefnagel, 1582, of which a detail is reproduced on page 138 of this book. Much less well-known is the large landscape oil-painting, which was bequeathed by the Founder in 1816 to the Fitzwilliam Museum, Cambridge. It is reproduced above. The artist is unknown, though it has been attributed to the Flemish painter Keirincz, and also to Vinkebooms.

This is almost certainly a companion painting to that of the Thames at Richmond, of which a detail is reproduced overleaf. There is no certainty about the date of either painting, but the clothes of the figures in the Richmond painting appear to date from about 1620. The painting reproduced above shows the north and west sides of Nonesuch Palace, with the avenue leading to the gatehouse, in front of which was a bowling green.

The Thames at Richmond, with a view of Richmond Palace (detail). A large oil painting of the Flemish School, artist not known, this is a companion picture to the painting of Nonesuch Palace reproduced on the two preceding pages. The left-hand half of the painting is reproduced here. Richmond Palace was rebuilt in 1501 by Henry VII, after having been destroyed by fire in 1497. It had previously been known as the Palace of Sheen, but was renamed Richmond after the title of Earl of Richmond which Henry VII had held before he won the crown. It ceased to be a royal residence in the time of Charles I, and only a fragment of the original building now remains.

Humphrey Stafford in 1575, and Wollaton near Nottingham, built for Sir Francis Willoughby in 1588, are other examples of the very large mansions in the modern style which knights, not noblemen, were erecting for themselves in the reign of Elizabeth I. Willoughby was a local landowner, but he built Wollaton with the money that he made in his ironworks, his glass manufacturing works, from selling woad to dyers, and above all from the profits of his coal mines.

In the year in which Wollaton was finished – the year of the Armada – Edward Phelips began building Montacute House near Yeovil in Somerset. At Montacute, money came first, then the house, and rank came last. When the Cluniac priory of Montacute was dissolved, Henry VIII granted the site and manor to his secretary, William Petre, who sold it to his fellow courtier, Sir Thomas Wyatt. It was forfeited to the crown when Wyatt's son was executed as a traitor after his revolt against Mary in 1554. She granted it to Petre again, whose son sold it to Robert Dudley, Earl of Leicester, who immediately resold it at a profit to Robert Freke, a gentleman from Dorset. But it was a young man from an unimportant local family, Edward Phelips, who, after he had become a successful barrister of the Middle Temple, built Montacute House; and it was after the house was completed in 1601 that he became Speaker of the House of Commons, was knighted, and last of all bought the manor of Montacute and the former monastic lands from the impoverished Freke. Montacute House is smaller than Longleat and Wollaton, but considerably larger than the gentlemen's manor houses which were built, in much the same style, in the second half of the sixteenth century.

William Cecil was brought up in his mother's house at Burghley in Northamptonshire, on the south-eastern outskirts of Stamford. As it was ninety miles from London, it could hardly be reached in two days' travel from the court, and when Cecil became Secretary of State under Edward VI he bought a house at Wimbledon; but he continued to spend much time at Burghley, even after he was again appointed Secretary of State by Elizabeth I on her accession, and in 1555 he began building a much larger house there.

In the summer of 1559, Cecil decided to use his house at Burghley for an important diplomatic meeting. In May John Knox returned to Scotland from his exile in Geneva, and his sermon in Perth sparked off a popular revolution all over the Scottish Lowlands, led by the Protestant lords of the Congregation. Within seven weeks the Congregation had entered Edinburgh in triumph, and the French government was preparing to send troops to suppress the revolt against Mary Queen of Scots and her husband, King Francis II of France. Cecil was convinced that England must intervene to support the Congregation in Scotland; but Elizabeth was very reluctant to help rebels, and was particularly hostile to Knox, who only a year before had written his book against 'the Monstrous Regiment of Women' in which he argued that for a woman to rule was against God's law.

Cecil, who had known Knox when they were both at Edward VI's court, was eager to meet him to discuss the best way in which English aid could be given to the Scottish Protestants; but he realized that it was important that it should not be generally known that Elizabeth's Secretary of State was meeting this notorious revolutionary leader, and he may not even have told Elizabeth about it. He therefore planned to meet Knox at Burghley, and wrote to Sir Henry Percy, the Deputy Warden of the East and Middle Marches, to give Knox instructions as to what he should do. Knox was to come incognito to Holy Island near Berwick, and then travel south along the Great North Road towards Stamford; but he was to leave the highway a few miles north of Stamford and ride across the fields to Burghley, entering the house by the back gate. He was to remain there, taking care not to leave the house, until Cecil arrived a few days later. Cecil assured Percy that he had given orders to his household to make sure that Knox would be well supplied with food and drink at Burghley. He probably remembered that Knox always appreciated good ale and wines.

Cecil's plans went wrong. Knox had been a preacher at Berwick for some years in the reign of Edward VI, and when he arrived by sea from Scotland at Holy Island he was recognized by some of his old parishioners. In view of this, Percy thought that it would be wiser if Knox did not go on to Burghley, and when Cecil heard what had happened he agreed that it would be too risky for the meeting to take place. Knox returned to Scotland, and Cecil conducted his negotiations with the Congregation through the Scottish Protestant lords who were less hateful to Elizabeth than Knox.

When Elizabeth created Cecil a peer in 1571, he took the title of Lord Burghley after the name of his house, and soon afterwards again began enlarging Burghley. The work was eventually finished in 1587. The exterior remains almost unaltered today, though the interior was much changed in later times. Cecil took the greatest interest in the building work, and himself suggested many of the details to his English and Dutch master-masons. The house contained many features of the architecture which was beginning to appear in Italy by the end of the sixteenth century and which resembled the elaborate Baroque mansions of a hundred years later.

Cecil also built himself another large house at Theobalds near Cheshunt in Hertfordshire, only just off the Great North Road. The building work began in 1563, when he had almost finished the first stage of the work at Burghley, and was largely completed by 1575. Unlike his urban residence of Cecil House in Drury Lane, Theobalds had the advantage of country air, but was much nearer to London than Burghley House. Elizabeth I stayed with him at Theobalds on ten occasions, the last time in 1597, less than a year before his death. The German traveller, Paul Hentzner,

William Cecil, 1st Baron Burghley, was an architectural enthusiast, and his chief interest was the expansion of his father's manor house in Northamptonshire, with the aid of a mason named John Symondes, who also worked at Kyre Park in Worcestershire. Burghley House was expanded in later years, when it was surrounded by a landscape setting by Capability Brown; but the view above shows the Tudor west front, dated 1577. *Photograph by Edwin Smith.*

155

visited Theobalds a few days after Burghley died; and though he could not go into the house, as all the family were in London for the funeral, the gardener showed him around the grounds. He was very impressed by their size, by the large lake with the rowing boats provided for the use of the guests, by the complicated labyrinths, the white marble fountain, and the summer-house containing marble statues of twelve Roman Emperors. In 1607 Burghley's son Robert gave Theobalds to James I in exchange for Hatfield House; but Theobalds was another of the royal residences pulled down by Charles II.

Thomas Howard, who loyally served Elizabeth I after his father, the Duke of Norfolk, was beheaded as a traitor, became an influential courtier and was created Earl of Suffolk by James I. In 1603 he began building his great mansion at Audley End, near Saffron Walden in Essex. Lord Cobham began rebuilding Cobham Hall in Kent in 1584.

As far as building was concerned, no on eclipsed Elizabeth Hardwick towards the end of the Tudor Age. Having inherited money, and acquired more by marriage, she married as her fourth husband George Talbot, Earl of Shrewsbury. Mary Queen of Scots was imprisoned for a time in the custody of Lord and Lady Shrewsbury at Chatsworth and at their other residences in Derbyshire. In 1585 Elizabeth Hardwick began rebuilding one of her houses, Hardwick Hall, and at the same time she started building another house less than a hundred yards to the north-east of Hardwick Hall. The new house was finished in 1597. It had more windows and glass than any of the other great Elizabethan mansions, though it was nearly equalled in this respect by Wollaton. It still stands unchanged today, though Hardwick Old Hall nearby is a ruin.

Many smaller manor houses for country gentlemen were also built during the Tudor Age. Compton Wynyates in Warwickshire, Hengrave Hall in Suffolk, Birtsmorton Court in Worcestershire, Brenchley Manor in Kent, and Little Moreton Hall in Cheshire, had been completed by 1560. Speke Hall in Lancashire and Barlborough Hall in Derbyshire, were built during Elizabeth's reign.

But the great majority of Englismen and women lived in much smaller and humbler houses. When Hentzner visited England in 1598 most of them were still made of wood. In London they usually had three storeys, and occasionally four; nearly all the houses outside London had only two storeys. These houses were not built by the famous builders but by local men who in many cases did very shoddy work. Occasionally some very good houses were built for the labouring classes. John Vesey was born in Sutton Coldfield in Warwickshire, and after he was appointed Bishop of Exeter in 1519 he spent a substantial part of his revenues on charitable work in his native town. He built fifty-one cottages for working people in Sutton Coldfield between 1530 and 1540, all of them in solid stone. Like nearly all the clergy under Henry VIII, he accepted the break with Rome and the royal supremacy over the Church; but his views were considered to be too conservative in Edward VI's reign, and he was deprived of his bishopric, which was given to Miles Coverdale, the veteran Protestant who had helped Tyndale translate the Bible into English. Coverdale was not burned as a heretic, like the other Protestant bishops, when Mary became Queen, because his brother-in-law John McAlpine, who was an eminent theologian in Copenhagen, persuaded the Protestant King of Denmark to intervene with Mary on his behalf; he was allowed to go to Denmark, but he was deprived of his bishopric, and Vesey was reinstated as Bishop of Exeter. Vesey died a few months later.

Very few artisans and labourers lived in houses which were as well constructed as those which Vesey built, and the authorities were worried by the failure to keep cottages in good repair. The attention of Parliament was first drawn in 1489 to the harm that was being caused to agriculture through the failure of landowners to repair the cottages of their agricultural labourers – the husbandmen – on whom the cultivation of the land depended. The Act of 1489 also deplored the decay of houses in towns and villages where formerly two hundred persons had lived and worked, and now there were only two or three inhabitants, so that there were 'churches destroyed, the service of God withdrawn, the bodies there buried not prayed for, the patron and curates wronged, the defence of this land against our enemies outward feebled and impaired, to the great displeasure of God, to the subversion of the policy and good rule of this land, and remedy be not thereby hastily purveyed'; but Parliament only took action about houses which were let with 'twenty acres of land or more lying in tillage or husbandry', or any such land in the possession of owner-occupiers. If the landowner failed to maintain these houses in a good state of repair, he was to forfeit half his annual rent, or profits from the land, to the King.

It was not until 1536 that Parliament legislated to remedy the failure to repair houses in towns. The fact that the good master-builders were all so busy building palaces and great houses for the King and the nobility may perhaps have been responsible for the poor construction of the houses of the common people; for to judge from the statements in the Acts of Parliament, the standard of housebuilding had fallen in recent years. Many houses in Nottingham, Shrewsbury, Ludlow, Bridgnorth, Queenborough in the Isle of Sheppey, Northampton and Gloucester 'now and of long time hath been in great ruin and decay, and specially in the principal and chief streets there being, in the which chief streets in times past have been beautiful dwelling houses there well inhabited, which at this day most part thereof is desolate and void grounds, with pits, cellars and vaults lying open and uncovered, very perilous for people to go by in the night without jeopardy of life'. Parliament was also worried that these ruined houses were causing evil smells which would damage health. Four years later, two more statutes were passed which were to apply to fifty-seven other towns; another six towns, and the Cinque Ports, were affected by an Act of 1542; and the last statute on the subject, in 1544, added another twenty-one towns, so that eventually the Acts applied to ninety-one towns in England and Wales, as well as the whole area of the Cinque Ports from Seaford to Margate.*

No attempt was made to save the older houses; but the Act required every occupier to maintain in repair any house which had been built during the twenty-five years before the Acts came into force, and which had not already completely fallen down. Every occupier must carry out the repairs within three years; if not, his landlord could reoccupy the property, and the tenant's interest in the house would be forfeited. If the landlord did not carry out the repairs within another two years, anyone who held a rentcharge on the land could move in and eject the landlord; but if the rentchargee did not do the repairs within one year, the mayor and corporation could enter into the property and become the owners of it. If the mayor and corporation did not repair the house within three years, it reverted to the original occupier who was apparently under no further obligation to repair the house which neither his landlord, the owner of the rentcharge, nor the local council had been willing to acquire at the cost of having to repair it. Any tenant who did carry out the repairs could deduct the cost from his landlord's rent.

This legislation seems to have dealt with the evil, at least to some extent, for no further statutes on the matter were passed during the Tudor Age; but fifty years later the government was concerned with another problem. Many husbandmen were leaving their work on the land, and their native villages, and were flocking to the towns, especially to London, where they lived in rooms in tenements in overcrowded conditions, or in hastily and shoddily-built houses which would soon become dilapidated structures. The authorities also feared that crime would increase if the towns were filled with unemployed persons, and the overcrowding led to the spread of disease, and to a shortage of fuel in London and Westminster.

Elizabeth I issued a proclamation on the subject in 1580, but as this had little effect, Parliament passed two Acts in 1589 and 1593.* They forbade anyone to build a new cottage in the countryside unless he gave the inhabitant of the cottage four acres of his own freehold land. The provisions were not to apply to houses for necessary workmen in coal or tin mining or slate quarrying, if the house was within one mile of their place of work; to any cottage within one mile of the sea or of any navigable river for habitation by sailors or by persons engaged in shipbuilding or in victualling or

---

* There were small differences in the various Acts as to the length of time during which the repairs had to be carried out, which probably explains why a few of the towns were included in more than one statute.

Hardwick Hall, 'more glass than wall'. Built by the Countess of Shrewsbury between 1590 and 1597, within yards of an older building. Perhaps the most splendid and least altered of the great Elizabethan houses, it was almost certainly designed by the great Elizabethan architect, Robert Smythson. After the death of 'Bess of Hardwick' in 1608 her descendants, the Earls and Dukes of Devonshire, chose to make Chatsworth their principal seat, but Hardwick remained in the Devonshire family until it was given to the National Trust in 1959. *Photograph by Edwin Smith.*

supplying ships; or to a gamekeeper's cottage in a park or forest. Contraventions of the Act were to be punished by a fine of ten shillings for every day that these cottages were inhabited.

No one of any rank was to build any house in London or Westminster or within three miles of the gates of London, unless it was in his own garden for the use of himself or his household, or was a house which, in the opinion of the local justices of the peace, was suitable for habitation by a person worth £3 in freehold land or £5 in goods. The Act did not apply to houses along the banks of the Thames which were inhabited by sailors or shipwrights, provided that the house was thirty feet from the wharf or bank, so that passers-by could walk between the house and the river, and was twenty feet from any other house, so as to reduce the risk of fire. No one was to divide his house into separate living accommodation unless each separate part of the house was considered by the JPs to be a suitable habitation for a person owning land worth £3 or goods worth £5.

The Tudor Parliaments made at least some attempt to deal with the problem of slum property and overcrowded tenements. They may not have done very much to relieve the conditions in which the great majority of the common people lived; but four hundred years later the descendants of these people, who for the most part are blissfully unaware of their ancestors' housing problems, can enjoy and appreciate the beauties of the magnificent palaces and houses which were built for the privileged few in the Tudor Age.

'Bess of Hardwick': Elizabeth Talbot, Countess of Shrewsbury (1518–1608)

Apart from portraits of notabilities painted by accomplished artists, few paintings survive from the sixteenth century illustrating the costumes of the period. Tapestries and embroidered pictures, however, are often more illuminating. So, too, are such primitive mural paintings as survive. Although these usually depict biblical scenes, the figures are mostly painted in costumes of the artists' own times. The mural reproduced above, which can still be seen in the Oak Lounge of the White Swan Hotel in Stratford-upon-Avon, dates back to 1555, and illustrates the apocryphal story of *Tobit and the Angel*. It was painted on the wall of what must have been in Tudor times the bar parlour of the inn, and it was probably familiar to Shakespeare as a young man.

COSTUME AND FASHION

IN the Tudor Age, as in all other periods of history, it was possible to tell a man's class and occupation by his clothes, although basically men of all classes wore the same type of dress. All men wore a shirt, the only garment which has remained almost unchanged, apart from the collar, for the last thousand years or more. The shirts of the common people were made of wool or linen; the nobility and wealthy classes sometimes wore shirts made of silk.

Above the shirt, men wore a doublet on the upper part of the body. The doublet was sometimes sleeveless, like a modern waistcoat, and sometimes had tight-fitting, or detachable, sleeves, according to variations in fashion and taste. The doublets of the common people were made either of wool or of the rough canvas material, mixed with wool, which was called 'kersey'. The wealthy classes often wore doublets of expensive materials, with elaborate patterns.

Until 1540, all men wore hose on the lower part of their bodies, as they had done for more than three hundred years. These were tights, stretching from the waist to the feet; they showed the outline of the thighs and legs, but the genitals were obscured by a triangular piece of material called the codpiece. Unlike modern tights, hose were not held up by elastic, which was not invented until the nineteenth century, but were laced to the doublet through holes in the doublet and hose, and tied.

The shoes worn by wealthy men changed with the fashion, becoming wider and less pointed at the beginning of the Tudor Age. In the first half of the sixteenth century they never had heels. Sometimes they were fastened by a strap across the instep; sometimes they were tight-fitting like a slipper. Labourers often wore boots for working in the fields, particularly in the winter, and noblemen and gentlemen wore boots for riding and walking out-of-doors.

It was in men's outer garments that the distinctions of class and occupation were most clearly shown. The labourer wore a woollen jerkin, or jacket, which was a coat with sleeves reaching from the shoulder to the knee, and fastened at the waist with a belt. It was a very good protection against the wind and rain for the husbandman when he worked in the fields in winter; on warm summer days, he removed it and worked in his doublet, in his shirt, or naked above the waist.

Middle-class men wore that emblem of respectability, the robe, or gown, reaching from the shoulder to well below the knee, often nearly to the ankles, open at the front, with short sleeves reaching to the elbow. The gown, like the white collar and tie in the middle of the twentieth century, was the badge which distinguished the middle-class man who had a sedentary occupation and a superior position from the husbandman or artisan who wore a shorter jerkin which did not impede him in performing physical labour. The gown was worn by priests, lawyers, schoolmasters and university lecturers, and merchants; it survives today in the vestments of the clergy, the barrister's and solicitor's robe, the academic gown, and the robes worn on official occasions by mayors of cities and boroughs and by the masters and wardens of the city livery companies. The gown was also worn by physicians and by the barber-surgeons, who, though they were regarded as socially inferior to the physicians, were very eager to show that they were superior to the lower classes.

The master-masons and master-carpenters, whose skill in building the great houses of the King, the nobility and the gentry was so highly valued, also insisted on wearing a gown, though master-carpenters usually distinguished themselves from members of other professions and crafts by wearing a carpenter's apron above their gowns. Master-butchers wore gowns, which they covered with an apron when they engaged in messy work in their slaughterhouses and shops; but their butchers' livery company issued ordinances in 1607, officially enforcing the practice which had become well-established by custom before the end of the Tudor Age, forbidding any butcher from wearing his apron, but only his gown, if he walked or stood on Sunday or on a holy day in any street in the city of London or within a mile from the city limits. Master-cooks wore gowns, covered with an apron, when they supervised the work in the kitchen or served a picnic for Elizabeth I on a hunting expedition; and by the end of the century the head gardener of a great lord was wearing fashionable dress as he walked through the garden, pausing to prune the occasional shrub, amid the under-gardeners digging and working in their jerkins or doublets.

Noblemen and gentlemen did not usually spend much time sitting in churches, schools, and counting-houses, but, like the husbandmen, were often out-of-doors, and took a good deal of physical exercise in hunting or riding. They did not wish to be encumbered with long robes, and tended to wear rather shorter gowns than those worn by the sedentary middle classes, though their upper garment was different from the rough jerkin of the labourer. At the beginning of the Tudor Age, noblemen and gentlemen wore gowns reaching to the knee when they were not in their riding coats.

Gowns were longer, reaching to the ankles, in 1500, but became shorter after 1520. It now became fashionable for noblemen and gentlemen to wear a short dagger hanging from the belt at the front of the body.

Men of all classes wore caps, bonnets and hats at all times, for they were hardly ever bareheaded. The husbandmen and artisans wore small round woollen bonnets; fashionable noblemen and gentlemen wore felt hats of various shapes, and occasionally adorned with a high crest of feathers. All men wore their caps and hats indoors and at meals. They only removed them when they retired alone or with their family in the privacy of their houses. Then they removed their gowns or jerkins and their doublets, and put on what they called their nightgown, which was very like a modern dressing gown. But even when wearing their nightgowns Tudor men were not bareheaded, for having removed their hats they immediately put on their nightcaps, which were fairly tight-fitting bonnets, and often elaborately embroidered. They wore their nightcaps all the evening, but removed them and replaced them with simple linen caps when they went to bed. When Henry VIII said: 'Three may keep counsel if two be away; and if I thought that my cap knew my counsel I would cast it into the fire and burn it', this was because his cap was nearly always on his head, even when he was alone, working in his closet.

Men only removed their hats in the presence of a superior, or otherwise as a sign of respect. Nobles and all other men removed their hats in the King's presence, though the King very often gave them permission to replace them on their heads. Servants and labourers removed their hats in the presence of their masters or of any gentleman; and nobles and gentlemen did the same in the presence of a nobleman or gentleman of superior rank to their own. An etiquette book of the middle of the fifteenth century, which was widely read and followed during the Tudor Age, insisted that servants must always be bareheaded when serving at table, and that this rule must be followed by the chief butler and steward of a gentleman or nobleman's household, and by nobles and gentlemen, however high their rank might be, when ceremoniously serving the King at his dinner table. They also usually removed their hats at the mention of the King's name. When anyone received a letter from the King which was delivered to him by a messenger, it was the practice for him to remove his cap and kneel as he took the letter.

Thomas Cromwell, the son of a blacksmith in Putney, who rose to be a solicitor, the confidential agent of Cardinal Wolsey, Henry VIII's Secretary of State, the King's Vicegerent in ecclesiastical affairs, Lord Cromwell of Oakham, Lord Privy Seal, and Earl of Essex, expected everyone to treat him with the respect due to his rank; but during the spring and summer of 1540 he was engaged in a desperate power struggle with the Catholic faction of Gardiner and the Duke of Norfolk, in which first one side and then the other seemed to be coming out on top. Henry finally authorized Norfolk to arrest Cromwell on a charge of high treason at a meeting of the Privy Council on the morning of 10 June and send him as a prisoner to the Tower. When Cromwell arrived for the meeting, he and the other Privy Councillors, who for so long had treated him with the greatest respect, stood outside in the courtyard waiting to go into the Council chamber. A gust of wind blew off Cromwell's cap. He expected all the other councillors to take off their own caps as long as he was bareheaded; but none of them did so. Cromwell said: 'A strong wind, my lords, to take off my cap and not take off yours.' He must have been expecting the worst as he went to take his place at the Council table. Then Norfolk called out: 'Cromwell, do not sit there; a traitor does not sit with gentlemen.' Norfolk arrested him on a charge of high treason and tore the collar of St George from his neck; and all the other councillors insulted and buffeted him as he was dragged to the barge which was to take him to the Tower. He was beheaded seven weeks later.

Men removed their hats to salute a lady, and often did so even to a lady of inferior rank. When Shakespeare wrote his play *Richard II*, he was thinking of the customs of 1595, not of 1399, when he made Richard II sneer at Bolingbroke, the future King Henry IV, who was trying to curry favour with the common people: 'Off goes his bonnet to an oyster-wench.' In Henry VIII's reign, contemporary observers considered it to be a sign of the King's great courtesy to ladies that he always removed his cap when he addressed them.

After Henry had divorced Catherine of Aragon and married Anne Boleyn, he was very angry that his daughter Mary refused to acknowledge that his marriage to her mother was void and that she herself was illegitimate. He forced Mary to serve as a lady-in-waiting to her baby sister, Elizabeth, the daughter of Anne Boleyn. In January 1534, when Elizabeth was four months old, Henry visited her at Hatfield in Hertfordshire. He played with her, but did not visit Mary, who was confined to her room at the top of the house. Mary had always been fond of her father, who had loved her when she was a child, and as Henry was leaving she looked out of her window in order to see him as he was mounting his horse in the courtyard. Several of the courtiers who were escorting the King noticed her at her window, but thought it would be wise not to salute her. Then Henry looked up and saw her. He coolly but courteously raised his cap to salute her before he rode away; and all the courtiers then followed his example, and took off their caps to her.

Women of all classes wore long dresses reaching to their ankles or trailing on the ground, as they did in every period of history before 1920; but lower-class women, when working in the fields or doing the housework, sometimes wore their dresses just a little shorter, an inch or two above their ankles, or kilted them up a little to be able to walk more freely. These women often rolled up their sleeves to the elbows when they were working; but no noble lady or gentlewoman, or merchant's wife or

Thomas Cromwell, 1st Earl of Essex (?1485–1540), Secretary of State to Henry VIII and Lord Privy Seal, a portrait after Hans Holbein the Younger.

daughter, wore short sleeves, for throughout the whole of the Tudor Age women's sleeves, whether loose or tight-fitting, always reached to the wrist.

At the beginning of the Tudor Age women wore under their gowns a dress which comprised the bodice and skirt called the 'kirtle'. The neckline was low and square-cut, and became lower and wider between 1500 and 1530. On their heads women wore a tight-fitting undercap, and over it the gable hood, which by 1500 had replaced the butterfly headdress of Edward IV's reign. The gable hood reached to the shoulders, and went half-way down the back, behind. It completely covered the hair.

Fashions in women's dress changed very little during the first forty years of the sixteenth century, except that Anne Boleyn, who had been educated at the French court, replaced the gable hood by the French hood after 1525. The French hood was worn at the back of the head, and stretched down the back like the gable hood; but the

167

OBIIT · ANNO   1509
3 · KAL· IVLII

Margaret Beaufort, Countess of Richmond and Derby, mother of Henry VII, painted in 1509 by Maynard Waynwyck. She wears a gable hood and conventional widow's dress, with a 'barbe' or white muffler under the chin. She was the founder of St John's and Christ's Colleges, Cambridge, and was noted for her interest in scholarship and the arts.

front of the head was uncovered, and revealed the hair of upper-class ladies for the first time for three hundred years. After the execution of Anne Boleyn, the French hood went out of fashion at court, where Jane Seymour reintroduced the gable hood; but it was now worn with the lappets turned up instead of hanging down on the shoulders. This new variety of the gable hood, like the French hood, was always worn over the undercap.

The fall of Anne Boleyn did not exclude the French hood for long. It was back at court soon after 1540, and was being worn by the King's daughters, the Lady Mary and the Lady Elizabeth.

Unmarried women sometimes wore their hair loose and flowing, which normally married women never did, though Cranmer wrote that Anne Boleyn came 'in her hair' to her coronation. Unmarried working-class women wore their hair flowing over their shoulders and fastened only by a ribbon; but married working-class women covered their hair with a simple linen headdress, and continued to do so

Catherine of Aragon, painted here by an unknown artist, married Henry VIII in 1509. Her dress is very much in the Spanish taste, with an emphasis on rich brocades and elaborate jewellery. Here she is wearing the early type of black velvet gable hood, faced with a band of gold and jewels. The square neckline of the brown bodice is edged with pearls and jewels. The undersleeves are of gold brocade. Apart from the Spanish touches the style is very typical of married women in the 1520s and 1530s.

while upper-class married ladies were allowing their hair to be seen under the French hood.

At the beginning of the Tudor Age, men wore their hair shoulder-length, usually parted in the middle. They were clean-shaven, as they had been for the previous seventy-five years since beards went out of fashion in about 1410. In 1510 all the Kings in Western Europe were clean-shaven – the Holy Roman Emperor Maximilian, King Ferdinand of Spain, King Louis XII of France and young King Henry VIII of England, as his father Henry VII had been. Hair was a little shorter than in 1485; it still covered the ears and reached to the collar, but did not flow on to the shoulders.

When Louis XII died on New Year's Day 1515, his young cousin Francis, Duke of Angoulême, became King Francis I at the age of twenty. He set out to dazzle Christendom by establishing a brilliant court as well as by a victorious campaign in

A clean-shaven view of Henry VIII, in a miniature painted by Lucas Hornebolte, dated 1525–26, now in the Fitzwilliam Museum, Cambridge.

Italy, and he grew a beard. Henry VIII was impressed by Francis I, and was eager to outshine him. When he spoke to the Venetian ambassador on May Day 1515 at an outdoor party in the woods near Blackheath, he asked him about the new French King: 'Is he as tall as I am? Is he as stout? What sort of legs has he?' Then, opening the front of his doublet, he showed the calf of his leg to the ambassador and said: 'Look here, and I have also a good calf to my leg.' He was interested to hear that Francis had grown a beard, but did not immediately follow his example.

In 1517 he decided to improve his relations with France, and entertained Francis's envoys at some outstandingly lavish banquets at Greenwich. A treaty of friendship was signed in October 1518, and it was agreed that Henry and Francis should meet. During the discussions about the plans for the meeting, Henry told the French ambassador that he would grow a beard, so that he and Francis could compare their beards when they met. Francis expressed his pleasure about this, and proposed to Henry that they should both promise not to shave off their beards until they met at 'the interview'.

Henry grew a beard; it was gold in colour, less red than the hair on his head. But Catherine of Aragon did not like him with a beard, and persuaded him to shave it off. When Francis heard that Henry had shaved off his beard, he was disappointed, and reminded him of his promise; but he understood when Henry explained that he had shaved it off to please his Queen. He agreed with Henry that in matters of this kind, the wishes of the ladies must always prevail.

During the next seven years, Henry grew a beard on more than one occasion, but always shaved it off soon afterwards, perhaps to please Catherine. According to John Stow, who wrote his *Annals* thirty years later, Henry ordered all his courtiers, on 8 May 1535, to cut their hair short, and set the example by having his own hair cut short

This detail of a painting of
Francis I by Joos van Cleve,
c.1530, shows a bearded
King of France.

and growing a beard; but in fact many courtiers were still clean-shaven and wearing
their hair covering their ears for some time after this. Henry himself has a beard, and
very short hair, fully revealing the ears, in the portrait of him which was probably
painted by Joos van Cleve in 1536, when he was forty-five, and in the well-known
portrait by Holbein a few years later. Edward VI already had very short hair when he
was Prince of Wales. Henry's brother-in-law, the Duke of Suffolk, and Sir Thomas
Wyatt, the poet and ambassador, both grew long beards before they died in 1545 and
1542; and the Earl of Surrey, who was beheaded on Henry's orders at the age of thirty
in 1547, wore a beard. But Suffolk, Wyatt and Surrey all had hair covering their ears.
William Fitzwilliam, Earl of Southampton, had long hair and was clean-shaven in
1542. Sir John Russell, who was created a peer in 1539 and Earl of Bedford in 1550,
wore a long beard, and had short hair with the ears visible, as did several other
courtiers and gentlemen when they were painted by Holbein before he died in
November 1543; but the Duke of Norfolk, Thomas Cromwell and Sir Thomas Elyot
are clean-shaven in Holbein's portraits, and the bottoms of their ears are hardly
visible beneath their hair, though the hair barely reaches the collar.

Cromwell did not approve of any unconventional man who grew his hair longer
than this accepted length. John Foxe, who greatly admired him, recorded an incident
in his *Book of Martyrs*, not to show how arbitrarily Cromwell exercised his power, but
in praise of his sense of propriety. Once when he was walking in the street he met a
servingman who had hair hanging over his shoulders. Cromwell asked him whether
his master had ordered him to wear his hair so long, or what other reason he had for
doing this. When the man replied that he had made a vow not to cut his hair,
Cromwell said that he would not force him to break his vow, but that he would stay in
prison until he decided to do so. The man was imprisoned in the Marshalsea and not

171

Sir Philip Sidney was still clean-shaven when he died of wounds incurred at the Siege of Zutphen in 1586. In this portrait, painted about 1577 by an unknown artist, his ruff is worn above a gilt-engraved metal gorget, with cuffs that match the ruff. His white leather doublet descends to a peascod belly. The trunk hose is heavily padded and is embroidered with gold braid.

released until his master had persuaded him to cut his hair to the conventional length.

The clergy and men of letters remained clean-shaven; but Sir Thomas More seems to have grown a beard in the Tower in the last months of his life before his execution in 1535, though the story that he asked the executioner not to cut off his beard, as the beard had not committed high treason, is almost certainly fictitious. In Europe priests had begun to wear beards by this time. Pope Julius II was wearing a beard as early as 1512, though this was most unusual at the period. Clement VII, who had earlier been clean-shaven, wore one in 1532, as did his successor, Paul III. Cardinal Pole had a long beard.

In England, the most authentic portrait of Gardiner shows him clean-shaven. Cranmer was still clean-shaven when Flicke painted his portrait in July 1545; but when Henry VIII died, he decided to grow a beard to show his grief at the King's

'A Gentleman in a Slashed Doublet', a painting c.1590 attributed to Sir William Segar. The term 'slashing' indicates slits of differing length cut and arranged in a particular pattern.

death. A portrait of Cranmer painted during the reign of Edward VI shows him with a long white beard, and he has a beard in the contemporary pictures of his martyrdom at the stake in 1556. His colleagues, the Protestant bishops and martyrs Nicholas Ridley and Hugh Latimer, had beards; and the picture of the martyrdom of another leading Protestant bishop, John Hooper, in 1555 shows him with a closely-cut beard.

After 1550, beards were worn by most noblemen and gentlemen for the next hundred years. Under Mary and Elizabeth they were usually worn from the ears, and cut short and to a point; but older men sometimes wore their beards long, like Lord Burghley. A few noblemen and gentlemen, like Philip Howard, Earl of Arundel and Sir Philip Sidney, were clean-shaven as late as 1580. By 1550, most noblemen and gentlemen had cut their hair shorter, revealing the ears. Hair then remained very short for forty years; but by 1590, a few fashionable young men had again begun to grow it long, sometimes reaching to the shoulders.

The 'Young Man in Red', by G. Stretes, c.1548, comes from Hampton Court, and is a handsomely dressed young gentleman of his time, his doublet opened to reveal the black embroidery on his shirt, which is repeated on the sleeves at the wrists. He wears a short gown and a codpiece, and a narrow belt for a sword. His shoes have rounded toes, and are closed up to the ankles. He has a flat cap, shortly to go out of fashion, with a feather at its side.

The fashion in dress as well as in beards and hair changed after 1540. Noblemen and gentlemen abandoned the gown and wore a shorter sleeveless cloak, sometimes with a high collar, fastened at the neck and hanging down the back. After 1580 men

It is interesting to see the similarity of the young Prince Edward's costume, c.1545, to that of the 'Young Man in Red,' though his doublet is buttoned down, not revealing his shirt except for the hanging sleeves. He, too, wears a flat cap with a feather, but his gown is handsomely trimmed with fur. His shoes are slashed, covering his feet up to the ankles, a new fashion developing in the fifteen-forties.

began wearing the cloak 'Collywestonwise', no longer covering the back, but over the left shoulder only. The flat cap of Henry VIII's reign was replaced after 1560 by a high bonnet, sometimes rising as high as six inches above the top of the head, with a

Sir John Petre, of Ingatestone Hall, shows the development of male costume in the fifteen-nineties. He wears a doublet with narrow-tabbed skirt, and close sleeves with wings. His trunk-hose is without a codpiece, which had been discarded by this date. He wears a ruff and falling band together, a fashion which continued into the seventeenth century.

feather, fastened vertically at the side of the bonnet, rising even higher. Instead of the short dagger, hanging in front of the body, men began after 1540 to wear a sword, or rapier, some three feet long, hanging behind the body, with the hilt near the left hip and the point behind the calf of the right leg.

Another development in men's dress after 1540 was one of those really fundamental changes in fashion which only occur once every century or even less frequently. The hose, which men had worn for the previous three hundred and fifty years, was replaced by breeches. There was an intermediary period between about 1540 and 1570 when men wore trunk hose, which were still tight below the knee, but from the thigh to the knee were loose and baggy, and often padded, and becoming increasingly elaborate and of more expensive material. By 1575 trunk hose had been largely replaced by Venetian breeches, which were often called 'Venetians'. When

The famous Hilliard miniature usually described as 'A Young Man among Roses', and sometimes claimed to be a portrait of Robert Devereux, 2nd Earl of Essex, c.1587. He wears a doublet with a 'peascod belly', very abbreviated trunk-hose and long nether stocks. He has a closed ruff and a cloak over one shoulder.

Knox and his collaborators translated the Bible into English and published it in Geneva in 1560, they wrote in the third chapter of the Book of Genesis that Adam and Eve, on discovering that they were naked, sewed fig leaves together and made themselves 'breeches', though the usual translation was 'aprons'. This was a successful attempt to be very up-to-date, for breeches, even in Central Europe, were only just beginning to be worn in 1560. Their opponents mockingly referred to the Geneva Bible as the 'breeches Bible'.

These breeches, which were even more elaborate than the upper part of trunk hose, reached to the knee, leaving the bottom part of the trunk hose as stockings. Breeches, in some form or other, remained for nearly three hundred years until they were replaced by trousers in the nineteenth century.

At the beginning of the Tudor Age the shirts of noblemen and gentlemen had a narrow band at the neck, no more than an inch wide, which was sometimes frilly and just visible above the doublet. After 1540 the neckband grew into a pleated collar which grew higher and more elaborate, until by 1570 it had given way to the ruff, a detachable collar, some three inches wide, fitting over the shirt and all around the neck. The ruff grew bigger, and by 1585 many fashionable noblemen and gentlemen were wearing very large ruffs. At its largest, the ruff, as worn in the last decade of the Tudor Age, covered the whole width of the shoulders, in a circle all around the neck, and had thirty-two pleats. This fashion lasted for about twenty-five years; but by 1610 the ruff was beginning to be replaced by the turn-down lace or linen collar lying on the shoulders.

The Protestant Reformation had its effect on costume at the court of Edward VI. With Latimer preaching to the King on the plight of the poor, and criticizing the greed and ostentation of the rich, and all the Protestant clergy denouncing the pomp and pride of Popish prelates, Edward's courtiers thought it best to avoid extravagance of dress, and black or dark garments tended to replace the brighter colours of Henry VIII's court. The Venetian ambassador, no friend to the Protestant Reformation, complained that Edward's court was dull and sombre. But some of the ladies at court seized any opportunity to be more elegant and frivolous. When the Queen of Scots, Mary of Guise, the mother of Mary Queen of Scots, who soon afterwards became Regent for her daughter, passed through London on her return to Scotland from a visit to France, Edward VI gave a great banquet for her at Whitehall in November 1551. Foxe, in his *Book of Martyrs* in 1563, praised Elizabeth I, then the Lady Elizabeth, for 'when all the other ladies of the court flourished in their bravery, with their hair frowsened, and curled, and double curled, yet she altered nothing, but, to the shame of them all, kept her old maidenly shamefacedness'. The ladies were

Opposite: the 'Ditchley Portrait' of Queen Elizabeth, by Marcus Gheeraerts, c.1592, painted for Sir Henry Lee (1533–1610) when she visited him at Ditchley, near Woodstock. He was her Champion, and had inaugurated the ceremonial tilts on the anniversaries of her accession to the throne. The portrait symbolizes her command of the map of England. She wears a gown with a trounced skirt over a French farthingale, cannon sleeves and large hanging sleeves.

Mary Fitton, Maid of Honour to Queen Elizabeth, was reputed to be the original of Shakespeare's 'Dark Lady of the Sonnets', and was a celebrated Tudor beauty, known to be the mistress of William Herbert, Earl of Pembroke, if not also of William Shakespeare. The painting, by an unknown artist, although exhibited in 1986–87 at the Royal Academy in a representative collection of English portraits, appears not to have been reproduced in colour before. It belongs to the Newdegate family at Arbury Hall in Warwickshire, into which Mary Fitton married.

now able to display their hair, for the gable hood had been generally replaced by the French hood, and more hair than ever was displayed. It was now often parted in the middle and lifted over pads at the side of the head, which gave the hair a wavy appearance. If Foxe's account is accurate, Elizabeth changed her attitude in later life.

When Mary Tudor became Queen and restored the Catholic religion, the Venetian ambassador was pleased to be able to report that pomp and dignity had returned to the English court, and that the Queen and her ladies wore richer garments than had been worn during her brother's reign. But Mary, with her religious piety and her strong aversion to sex, had no intention of encouraging frivolity of any kind, and though dress at her court was rich and stately, it was also matronly and unprovocative. The Venetian ambassador described the style of the ladies' garments as masculine; and the Spanish influence was noticeable, because of the frequent contact with King Philip and his courtiers. The low necklines were replaced by high collars which largely obscured the neck, and after 1560 women began wearing the same ruffs as the men. The ladies' necks were obscured for thirty years, but were once again visible after 1585, for when the gentlemen started to wear the largest kind of ruff, the ladies abandoned ruffs for the high collar behind the neck, open in the front and revealing the neck and throat. After 1560 women sometimes wore high bonnets with feathers, like the men's bonnets; but they often wore little jewelled caps on the back of their heads. Some older women continued to wear French hoods.

Their skirts also changed after 1540. The kirtle was divided into two parts, the bodice being separated from the skirt, which hung down over a support structure which was called the 'farthingale', jutting out from the waist. The farthingale, which originated in Spain, was being worn at Henry VIII's court in 1545, and generally by the time that Mary became Queen.

It was one of the duties of Mary's maids-of-honour to help her put on her farthingale, and on one occasion this caused some embarrassment to her maid-of-honour, Lady Frances Neville. One day Lady Frances's friend, Lord William Howard, the Lord Chamberlain, met Frances at court and tickled her under her chin, saying gaily to her: 'My pretty whore, how dost thou?' Lady Frances took the remark in good part, for neither of them realized that the Queen had overheard their conversation; but the Queen, in her innocence, did not know what the word 'whore' meant. A few minutes later, Mary summoned Frances to come and assist her with her farthingale; and as Frances knelt at her feet and arranged the farthingale, Mary said: 'God-a-mercy, my pretty whore'. Lady Frances told her how grieved she was that Her Majesty should think her to be such a woman. 'Have I said or done more than the Lord Chamberlain did?' asked the Queen. Lady Frances explained. 'My Lord Chamberlain is an idle gentleman, and we respect not what he saith or doth'; but she had not expected to be called this by the Queen. Mary then apologized. Another of

Lady Kytson, painted in 1573 by George Gower, was dressed obviously for a walk out-of-doors round her garden at Hengrave Hall in Suffolk (see page 156). Her high-crowned hat, with its ostrich feather and jewelled hatband, is presumably worn over an undercap. Her pleated ruff is worn over a transparent partlet. Her elaborate dress is surmounted by a red gown with a wide black fur collar running round her neck.

Mary's maids-of-honour, Jane Dormer, was present, and many years later, after she had married the Spanish ambassador and had become the Duchess of Feria, she told the story to one of the many English Catholic refugees who came to her house in Madrid, in order to show him how innocent and virtuous Queen Mary had been.

After 1580, the Spanish farthingale was replaced by the French farthingale, with hoops under the skirt which made the skirt protrude for about two feet on both sides of the waist, and then fall sharply, vertically to the ankles; but it did not quite reach to the ground as women's dresses had previously done. The French farthingale remained in fashion until about 1610. Brighter colours in women's dresses came in after 1570, replacing the black and white which had previously been worn. White continued to be the prescribed colour for the ladies of the court; but Lady Kytson was not the only lady of fashion to wear a red dress in 1573.

Jewellery, like buildings, was a status symbol in the Tudor Age. No one of lower

Margaret, Duchess of Norfolk, painted by Hans Eworth in 1562, in a very decorative close-bodied gown, with short over-sleeves and sham hanging-sleeves represented by pendant strips. She wears a tiny jewelled cap and high collar and ruff.

rank than a knight or the son of a lord was allowed by law to wear a gold ring or ornament, unless he owned land worth £200 a year in rent; but wealthy princes, nobles and merchants and their wives and daughters wore rings, gold chains, necklaces and brooches in order to display their wealth. The display was not wasted, for when men wore expensive jewellery, it always attracted attention. When Henry VIII in 1515 wore a gold collar with a diamond the size of a very large walnut, the Venetian ambassador duly reported it to the Doge and Senate, and added that Henry's 'fingers were a mass of jewelled rings'. It confirmed the general belief abroad that Henry VIII was very rich, and the English ambassador in Brussels wrote in 1522 that the great influence which Henry exercised in international affairs was very largely due to his great wealth. Elizabeth I followed her father's example in this respect. Though she was always reluctant to spend money on other things, she was willing enough to spend it on her jewels, and rightly believed that the costly rings on

An Elizabethan woman's bodice embroidered with figures of birds and flowers

her fingers and jewels on her breast and around her neck would raise her prestige with the foreign ambassadors and the distinguished visitors from overseas who came to her court to admire her.

Royal rings had another special function. When the King gave a ring as a gift to a counsellor or courtier, this was a sign that he did not wish this favoured person to be arrested except on his express orders. If, when a royal officer was arresting a suspect, the person whom he was arresting showed him the King's ring, he knew that he was not to proceed with the arrest until he had referred the matter to the King personally. There are several well-known instances of this. Cranmer's secretary, Morice, recorded the occasion when the Catholic faction in Henry VIII's Privy Council decided to arrest Cranmer on a charge of heresy. Henry got to hear of their plan, and summoned Cranmer to come to his apartment late on the previous evening. When he told Cranmer that his fellow-counsellors were planning to arrest him at the Council meeting the next day, Cranmer said that he was quite ready to be arrested as he was sure that he could prove his innocence at his trial. Henry replied:

O Lord God! What fond simplicity have you . . . Do not you think that if they have

184

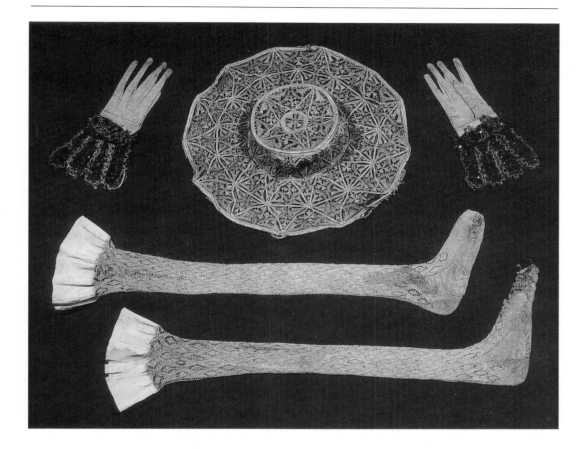

An openwork garden hat, silk stockings and gloves preserved in the Long Gallery at Hatfield House in Hertfordshire, and believed to have belonged to Queen Elizabeth I.

you once in prison, three or four false knaves will be soon procured to witness against you and to condemn you, which else now being at your liberty dare not once open their lips or appear before your face. No, not so, my lord, I have better regard unto you than to permit your enemies so to overthrow you.

He then gave Cranmer his ring and told him to show it to the counsellors when they arrested him next day. Cranmer did so, and as soon as the counsellors saw the ring, they realized that they had made a dreadful mistake. They went at once with Cranmer to the King, who upbraided them, and told them to have dinner with Cranmer and be reconciled to him.

An even better known story, though it depends on less reliable evidence than Morice's about Cranmer, is the tale of how Elizabeth I gave a ring to the Earl of Essex. When Essex was arrested and condemned to death as a traitor for his plot to arrest Elizabeth's counsellors in 1601, he sent the ring to Lady Nottingham, one of Elizabeth's ladies-in-waiting, and asked her to show it to the Queen. Lady Nottingham, whose husband was Essex's opponent in the Council, did not tell Elizabeth that Essex had sent the ring; and Elizabeth, who had been expecting Essex to send her the ring, interpreted his failure to do so as a sign of his pride and ambition and unwillingness to plead for her mercy. She therefore signed the warrant for his execution, and was greatly distressed when she discovered that he had in fact sent the ring to Lady Nottingham.

The subjects of the Tudor sovereigns were restricted in the display in which they could indulge, and the colours of their clothes, by the Sumptuary Laws, which had been in force since the fourteenth century but were strengthened during the Tudor Age. These statutes had two objects: to protect the English wool industry against foreign competition by restricting the wearing of imported foreign fabrics and furs; and to maintain the distinction in dress between the social classes. There was no need for legislation to prevent the husbandman from dressing like a gentleman, for the idea had never occurred to him; but domestic servants often dressed in the cast-off clothes that their masters had passed on to them; tailors who made clothes for gentlemen sometimes made the same clothes for themselves; and, at the top of the social ladder, earls sometimes dressed like dukes, and dukes sometimes dressed like members of the royal family. For a man to dress above his station in society seemed to people in the Tudor Age to be as wrong, and as much an offence punishable by law, as it would be today for an army corporal or second lieutenant, without authority, to sew an extra stripe on his arm, or to put a crown beside the pip on his shoulder. So the Tudor Parliaments dealt with the problem by a series of statutes which, for length, attention to detail, and complicated construction, can rival any twentieth-century legislation on town and country planning.

At the beginning of the Tudor Age, the restrictions on dress were governed by statutes of Edward IV's Parliaments of 1463 and 1483; but more extensive restrictions were imposed by four statutes passed in the reign of Henry VIII between 1510 and 1533. No one except the members of the royal family was to dress in cloth-of-gold or in any garment of purple colour, on pain of a fine of £20, which is about £10,000 in terms of 1988 prices; but dukes and marquesses were allowed to wear cloth-of-gold and purple in their doublets and sleeveless coats, provided that the material did not cost more than £5 a square yard. No one under the rank of an earl was to wear any sable fur; and no one under the rank of a baron could wear cloth-of-silver, satin, any garment with a gold or silver bordure, any woollen garment which was made 'out of this realm of England, Ireland, Wales, Calais or the Marches of the same, or Berwick', or any crimson or blue velvet. No one under the rank of a knight or a lord's son could wear a silk shirt, unless he owned land worth £20 a year in rents;

A working-man's habit.
Woodcut from *A Christall Glass of Christian Reformation* by Stephen Bateman, 1569.

and if the land was worth less than £5 a year, he could not wear any garment that was scarlet or violet in colour. Breaches of these provisions were punished by heavy fines, and forfeiture of the offending garment; but if any husbandman, shepherd or labourer, who did not own goods worth £10, wore hose which cost more than tenpence a yard, he was to be put in the stocks for three days. All these restrictions applied equally to the accoutrements in which the members of the various classes decked out their horses. The Acts did not apply to persons holding certain offices, to actors who wore the garments in plays, or to foreign ambassadors and to 'noblemen or other coming into the King's realm or other part of his obedience to visit or salute His Grace or to see the country, and not minded to make long or continual demeure in the same'.

The Acts contained a term which was found in nearly every Tudor statute which imposed fines and forfeiture as a penalty. Half the fine and half the value of the forfeited garment was to go to the King; the other half was to go to any informer who brought a private prosecution and sued for his share before the local JPs.

A more severe statute was passed by Philip and Mary's Parliament in 1554. No one under the rank of a knight's son, unless he owned land worth £20 a year or goods worth £200, was to wear any silk in his hat, bonnet, nightcap, girdle, hose, shoes, scabbard or spurs, on pain of three months' imprisonment and a fine of £10 for every day on which the garment was worn; and any master who found his servant wearing such a garment was to be fined £100 if he did not discharge the servant within fourteen days.

Servants were often dressed in livery, with their master's crest on their left sleeve. This was right and proper, but problems arose when a master gave a loyal servant his cast-off clothes. The Act of 1533 specified in precise detail how far this was permissible. The servant of a master who was a lord, knight, squire or gentleman and owned land worth £40 a year could wear any garment given him by his master, unless it was crimson, purple, scarlet or blue, and any fur of an animal which was to be found in the realm, except the fur of martens or black rabbits. Despite this ban on the colour blue for servants, it became the practice later in the sixteenth century for servants' livery to be blue; and blue became so well established in people's minds as the colour of servants' clothes that most gentlemen would not wear blue.

Although the Sumptuary Laws were so precise about the fabrics, colour and cost of the clothes of the various classes, they were rather ambiguous about their application to women. The Act of 1483 stated that it did not apply 'for any woman, excepted the wives and servants of labourers'; and the Act of 1510 exempted all women from the provisions of the Act. The Act of 1554 expressly referred to women, but enacted that it was not to apply to anyone over the rank of a knight's son or daughter 'or being wife to any of them', or to anything that 'women may wear on their caps, hats, girdles or heads'. A woman who dressed above her station might excite ridicule and disapproval; but it was only when a man did so that the social order was seriously threatened, and the Acts were aimed at men far more than at women.

Elizabeth's Parliament in 1563 dealt with the problem by prohibiting the sale of any clothes on credit. Nothing 'appertaining or tending to the apparelling, clothing, decking, garnishing or adorning of the body' was to be sold unless the whole of the purchase price was paid in money at the time of the sale or within twenty-eight days afterwards. The Act did not apply if the purchaser buying the garment had an income of £3,000 a year or more from land, fees or any other source.

If men and women in the Tudor Age had their choice of clothes restricted and prescribed in such detail by the State, they had the benefit of legislation for consumer protection which was not to be enjoyed by later generations until the twentieth century. Laws and regulations imposed price controls and ensured that minimum standards of quality were complied with. Some of the legislation was passed as a result of pressure by influential lobbies and counter-lobbies. The craft guilds in the cities and boroughs persuaded Parliament that the poor quality of clothes, of which the people complained, was caused by unskilled persons who were not members of their guild and made shoddy goods; while the independent producers outside the guilds argued that it was the monopoly enjoyed by the guilds which kept prices too high for the poorer people to afford.

Detail from *A Fête at Bermondsey*, c.1570, by Joris Hoefnagel (1542–1600), one of a group of Flemish refugees who settled in England and lived on the South Bank of the Thames, within sight of St Paul's. This painting has been at Hatfield House since some forty years after it was painted. It has always been described in inventories as 'A Marriage Fête at Bermondsey' or 'A Large Landscape of a Bridal'. The house depicted in the background is believed to have belonged to the Earl of Sussex, which was often visited by Queen Elizabeth. The wedding group, however, seems to represent people of various classes of English society.

Joseph, Mary and Jesus in the carpenter's shop. This unique archaeological relic in the heart of the City of London, which can be seen today in the entrance to the Livery Hall of the Carpenters Company, miraculously survived the Blitz of the Second World War, when the Carpenters Hall was

almost totally destroyed. It is characteristic of many sixteenth-century religious paintings in showing biblical figures wearing costume of the Elizabethan period. It is as accurate a documentation of a carpenter's working clothes in the mid-sixteenth century as one is likely to find in Britain.

The well-dressed gentleman of 1590: Lord William Russell in a doublet with peascod belly. He wears close-fitting venetians, with stockings drawn up over them. His costume is wholly appropriate to the environment of his home, Woburn Abbey. The painting is attributed to Marcus Gheeraerts the Younger.

In 1489 the MPs were persuaded that drapers, tailors, hatmakers and capmakers were charging 'excessive price having unreasonable lucre, to the great hurt and impoverishment of the King's liege people, buyers of the same'; they were selling hats and caps for three or four times what it had cost to make them. So Parliament fixed the maximum price for various kinds of cloth, and enacted that no hat could be sold for more than twenty pence or cap for more than 2s.8d. An Act of 1495 dealt with the problem of the poor quality of the cheaper fustian doublets that were worn by the common people. A good fustian doublet ought to have lasted for at least two years; but many people were finding that their doublets began to disintegrate after only four months. This was because they were not 'truly wrought and shorn with the broad shear' only, but were deceitfully made with iron instruments which ruined the material, by dishonest people, who made the doublets 'in the most highest and secret places of their houses'. These malefactors evidently did the work in their attics, where they would not be seen by their neighbours or by the passers-by in the street; and they did it so skilfully that the purchasers did not know whether the doublets which they bought were properly made or not. So the Act made it an offence, punishable on each occasion by a fine of twenty shillings, to make fustian doublets with irons or any instrument except a broad shear; and it authorized the Lord Mayor of London and the Wardens of the Shearmen's Company to search any premises where doublets were made to ensure that the Act was being complied with.

The consumer-protection legislation reached its height under Edward VI. An Act was passed in 1549 to protect consumers who suffered from woollen clothes which shrank in the wash. It specified the maximum amount by which any woollen garment which was offered for sale was allowed to shrink when wet. The sellers of cloth were required to state the length of the cloth sold, in a document which was to be sealed and attached to the cloth. The JPs in every town and village where cloth was made were to appoint overseers, who were granted powers to enter the house of any clothier to make sure that he was complying with the Act. Another Act in 1552 prescribed in greater detail the exact length and breadth of the various kinds of coloured and white cloths – of Long Worcesters and Short Worcesters made in Worcester and Coventry, of friezes made in Cardigan, Carmarthen and Pembroke, and of Manchester Cottons, which were not what we call cottons, but were a kind of woollen cloth. No one was to put any hair, flocks or yarn made of lamb's wool into any cloth; if he did, he was to repay to the buyer of the cloth twice the sum which the buyer had paid for it. An official 'Searcher of Cloth' was to be appointed in every district, and no cloth could be sold unless the seal of the Searcher of Cloth was attached to it; if the Searcher of Cloth found that the cloth was badly made, he was to mark the cloth with the letter F to show that it was faulty.

Parliament also tried to restrict the activities of persons who were called 'regrators' in the sixteenth century – those middlemen who bought goods to resell at a profit, thus raising the price which the consumer had ultimately to pay for them. An Act of 1552 enacted that no one was to buy wool unless he intended to use it to weave cloth, or for use in his own household, or to ship it to the Staple at Calais. If anyone who gathered wool from his own sheep did not sell it within a year, he could be compelled to sell it to any clothier who offered him the current market price in the neighbourhood. The Act caused hardship to the poor persons of Halifax; before the Act came into force, being too poor to own a horse, they walked three, four, five or six miles carrying wool on their heads and backs, in order to make a living by buying and reselling the wool. Parliament remedied their grievances by an Act of 1555. In view of the fact that the parish of Halifax was 'planted in the great wastes and moors where the fertility of ground is not apt to bring forth any corn nor good grass, but in rare places', and that the 'inhabitants altogether do live by clothmaking', they were permitted to buy and resell wool, as long as they resold it only in Halifax.

A series of statutes tried to restrict the persons who could become weavers and the places where weaving could be carried on. An Act of 1552 which prevented anyone from weaving cloth unless he had been apprenticed to a weaver for seven years was repealed two years later, because of the objections of weavers who had never been apprentices but had worked at the trade for five or six years or had married weavers' widows who had known how to make cloth for twenty years. The attempt to limit weaving to a few important towns in various parts of England was seriously weakened by a number of Acts which granted exemption from the provisions to Wales, the North of England, Cornwall, Suffolk and Kent, and the towns of Godalming in Surrey and of Bocking, West Bergholt, Dedham, Coggeshall, Boxstead and Leyton in Essex, and the villages along the River Stroud in Gloucestershire.

From time to time, the clothiers successfully complained to Parliament that the legal requirements as to the quality of their cloths were making it uneconomic for them to continue production, and were leading to closure of businesses and unemployment in certain districts; but though Parliament thereupon reduced the standards a little, the principle of consumer protection continued to be enforced. An exception was made in the case of garments which were manufactured only for export, because the MPs accepted the argument of the clothiers that there was nothing wrong in selling shoddy goods to foreigners. Edward VI's last Parliament in 1553 enacted that anyone who lived in Devon or Cornwall and made the cloths known as White Plain Straights and Pinned White Straights for export to Brittany might fill the cloths with hair, flocks, and yarn made of lamb's wool, which had been prohibited in the case of all other cloths by the Act of 1552, as these goods were 'but a base and coarse kind of clothes usually made for the use of poor people beyond the seas . . . for that in truth none of the same are worn or occupied within this realm'.

Freed from all restrictions, the weavers in Devon and Cornwall proceeded to make doublets for Brittany which were filled with flocks, chalk and flour; but some of them reached more influential customers than the Brittany peasants. Elizabeth's allies, the States of the Netherlands, complained, and so did some of her own subjects. So an Act was passed in 1601 which stated that as these doublets had been filled with 'deceitful things', and when put in water shrank 'to the great dislike of foreign Princes', the legal requirements as to quality were to apply to Plain White Straights and Pinned White Straights as well as to all other woollen garments.

The restrictions imposed by law on the making and purchase of hats were chiefly designed to help the manufacturers of the woollen caps which were worn by men of the lower classes. An Act of Mary's Parliament of 1553 enacted that any hat which was imported into the kingdom had to be sold at the port where it arrived, and made it an offence for anyone to buy more than twelve hats in any one transaction, thus discouraging foreign merchants from importing hats into England by forbidding sales in bulk. In 1556 an Act placed restrictions on the manufacture of felt hats in order to help the woollen capmakers; and no one under the rank of a knight or the son of a lord was allowed to wear a velvet hat or cap, or any hat or cap with a velvet covering.

In 1571 Parliament, on the petition of the Fellowship and Company of Cappers, passed an Act which went further in regulating dress than any other Tudor statute. After stating that the manufacture of woollen caps gave employment to eight thousand people in London alone and to many workmen in twenty-six other towns,* Parliament enacted that everyone over the age of six was to wear on their heads a woollen cap made in England with English wool, on every Sunday and holy day, except when they travelled out of the town or village where they lived, on pain of a fine of 3s.4d. for every Sunday or holy day on which they did not wear the cap. Masters, parents and guardians were liable to pay the fine if the cap was not worn by every servant and child who lived in their house. The Act did not apply to 'noble personages', to any lord, knight or gentleman who owned land worth twenty marks a year, and their heirs, to anyone who had held office as a warden of one of the livery companies of London, or to 'maidens, ladies and gentlewomen'.

It is unlikely that the average Englishman in the Tudor Age was either suprised or resentful at being compelled by law to wear a woollen cap on his head every Sunday.

* Exeter, Bristol, Monmouth, Hereford, Ross, Bridgnorth, Bewdley, Gloucester, Worcester, Chester, Nantwich, Newcastle, Ulcester, Stafford, Lichfield, Coventry, York, Beverley, Richmond, Derby, Leicester, Nottingham, Shrewsbury, Wellington, Southampton and Canterbury.

FURNITURE AND FOOD

T HE great advance in housebuilding in England at the end of the fifteenth century was not accompanied by any change in the furniture inside the houses. At the beginning of the Tudor Age Englishmen of all classes were still using the type of furniture which their ancestors had used throughout the Middle Ages. The poor man had a few simple wooden stools, perhaps one or two wooden chairs, a wooden table, a simple wooden bed, and perhaps a wooden chest; the chairs and tables often had three legs, as these were firmer on the uneven floors than those with four legs. The King, the nobility and the wealthy classes had many elaborately carved wooden chairs, tables, chests and beds, which were usually made of oak, but often of yew.

The Renaissance led to new developments in carving and design of furniture in Italy and Flanders at the beginning of the sixteenth century, and by 1550 many Flemish craftsmen had been invited to England to improve the furniture at court and in the houses of the nobility; but they merely elaborated the quality of the design of the wooden furniture. The carvings on the great oak chairs, tables and chests, and on the headboards of beds, became much more elaborate, and the wooden table-legs were carved into complicated shapes. But it was only in the very last years of the Tudor Age, about 1600, that the first upholstered furniture and the first chests-of-drawers appeared, very occasionally, in the house of a wealthy Englishman whose tastes were in advance of his contemporaries'; and they were not generally in use, even among the upper classes, until the reign of Charles II.

The oak armchairs were not as uncomfortable as might be imagined by later generations who are used to the luxury of upholstered furniture. The shape of the chair was designed to provide the maximum relaxation for the body, though people today, who are not accustomed to it, experience some discomfort from the solid oak front below the seat which makes it impossible for the sitter to put his legs back under the seat, even to the slightest extent. The wooden seat of the chair was made softer by a cushion placed on it; in wealthy households, this might be a velvet cushion.

The Great Bed of Ware

Wealthy families had large four-poster beds, surrounded by curtains which, like the linen caps worn by the sleepers in the bed, helped keep them warm in the cold bedroom after the fire had gone out, or had burned low during the night. They could display their wealth and taste by having bed-curtains of rich material, headboards with elaborate carvings, and by the size of the bed. But large beds were not the privilege of the nobility and the rich. In less prosperous households, there would often be one large bed in which all the members of the family slept together, while Henry VIII and Wolsey slept alone in a bed which was nearly as large. Gentlemen often provided a large bed in which their servants and labourers slept together, and this practice continued until the end of the nineteenth century.

One of these beds, 'the great bed of Ware', became famous because it was so much larger than any of the others. No one knows when it was made, though it has been dated as early as 1463 and as late as 1570. The later date is much more likely. It was for

A corner of Sizergh Castle, with its sixteenth-century panelling and leaded window panes. The oak buffet, the pewter dish, the candlesticks, and the earthenware jugs all belong to the same period.

many years in the inn, the Saracen's Head, at Ware, until it was moved to Rye House in the nineteenth century, and afterwards to the Victoria and Albert Museum in Kensington, where it can be seen today. It is 11 ft. 1 in. long, 10 ft. 8½in. wide, and 8 ft. high, and has ornate carvings on the headboard and legs. Some historians have suggested that so impressive and costly a bed could not originally have made for an inn, and must have been designed for one of the great houses in the vicinity, and later acquired by the inn. This may be so, but it was probably already in the Saracen's Head when Shakespeare wrote *Twelfth Night* in 1601, because Sir Toby Belch urges Sir Andrew Aguecheek to insert, in his challenge to Cesario, 'as many lies as will lie in thy sheet of paper, although the sheet were big enough for the bed of Ware in England'; and Ben Jonson referred to it in his *Silent Woman* eight years later. Shakespeare and Jonson and their audiences are much more likely to have heard of it if it was not in a private house but in an inn on the Great North Road where many people had seen it, and perhaps slept in it, sharing it with other travellers.

The walls of the rooms in poor men's houses were made of plaster; in the houses of the wealthy classes, they were finely carved oak panelling. There were no pictures on the walls. At the beginning of the Tudor Age, painting was almost unknown in England, and though portrait painting was introduced by Flemish artists in the reign of Henry VIII, the idea of landscape painting did not develop in England until the eighteenth century. Instead, the walls, in wealthy houses, were hung with tapestries. When the Venetian ambassador, Guistiniani, visited Wolsey at Hampton Court on diplomatic business soon after his arrival in England in 1515, he was led through eight anterooms before he reached Wolsey's presence, and saw in each of these rooms beautiful and expensive tapestries which were changed once a week and replaced by others equally magnificent. They depicted scenes from the Bible, with Esther, David and Solomon; from classical mythology, with Jupiter and Diana, Paris and Achilles, Jason and Hercules, and Helen of Troy; from the lives of Hannibal, Pompey and Julius Caesar; and from the medieval stories, *The Romance of the Rose*, and *The Duke of Bry and the giant Orrible*. On the borders of the tapestries, Wolsey's coat-of-arms was much in evidence.

There were mattresses and pillows on the beds, as there had been in the days of the Romans and at least in the houses of the wealthier classes throughout the Middle Ages. The inventories of Hampton Court show that Wolsey owned hundreds of mattresses and pillows; and humbler people usually had at least one mattress for their bed. These were often of very poor quality, and stuffed with material which was harmful to health; so in 1496 the Wardens of the Fellowship of the Craft of Upholsters within the City of London persuaded Parliament to stop the manufacture of featherbeds, bolsters and pillows made either of scalded feathers or dry puffed feathers, or of a mixture of flocks and feathers, 'which is contagious for man's body to be on'. They also wished to ban quilts, mattresses and cushions stuffed with horse hair, deer's hair or goat's hair, for 'by the heat of man's body the savours and taste is so abominable and contagious that many of the King's subjects have thereby been destroyed'. The practice had also impoverished many people and discredited the craft of upholstery. Parliament duly enacted that all featherbeds, bolsters and pillows must be stuffed with either dry pulled feathers or with clean down, and nothing else, and all quilts, mattresses and cushions only with clean flocks. The poorest families could not afford to buy mattresses, or pillows, and made their own. They were exempted from the provisions of the Acts, which did not apply to mattresses, bolsters, pillows or cushions which were made, not for sale, but for use in the manufacturer's own house.

The wealthier classes at least had ironware in their houses – iron chests, iron lampholders, and iron firedogs and firebacks, often engraved with the coat-of-arms of the owner of the house. In the greatest houses, there was an ostentatious display of silver and gold plate. Guistiniani was as impressed as he was meant to be with Wolsey's gold and silver at Hampton Court. Both he and the next Venetian ambassador estimated the value of all the plate in the house at 300,000 gold ducats, or £150,000 – which in terms of 1988 prices would be £75,000,000. Guistiniani wrote that the plate on view on the sideboard in the banqueting hall was alone worth £25,000, and that there was a cupboard in Wolsey's private chamber which contained gold and silver plate valued at £30,000.

The eating utensils of ordinary families were far simpler. The poorer classes ate off wooden plates; reasonably prosperous yeomen, like merchants and gentlemen, had pewter plates. The big demand for pewter dishes led to a surreptitious trade to which reputable pewterers and their guild objected. They complained to Henry VII that 'many simple and evil disposed persons . . . daily go about this your realm from village, from town and from house to house, as well in woods and forests', selling pewter and brass which had often been adulterated with other metals and had sometimes been stolen by thieves from their lawful owners. An Act of Parliament was therefore passed in 1504 which prohibited the sale of pewter anywhere except in fairs and markets; but it could take place at the buyer's house if the buyer had expressly requested the seller to come to his house to sell it to him there.

Every household in the country possessed at least one knife, which had nearly always been made in Sheffield in Yorkshire, where knives had been manufactured since the fourteenth century; but not even the greatest palaces had any eating forks, which were not known in England until a few years after the end of the Tudor Age. In every social class, meat was cut up with a knife and then placed in the mouth with the fingers. Spoons were used for soup and other dishes. The poorer families had wooden spoons, but for the rich, spoons gave another opportunity to display wealth and taste in silver. Silver spoons were made in various designs and fashions, which changed from one decade to another.

Water, beer, ale and wine were drunk from goblets made of wood, pewter, silver or gold. Only very rich households could afford to have gold or silver, though an Act of Elizabeth I's Parliament of 1576 fixed the maximum price of twenty-two carat gold at twelvepence per ounce, and of eleven ounce two pennyweight silver at twelvepence per pound. Drinking glasses were almost unknown in England before

Sir Henry Unton was a well-to-do Elizabethan gentleman, landowner, justice of the peace, soldier and diplomat, whose life was recorded at the request of his widow in a large memorial painting illustrating his varied interests. The detail reproduced above records a banquet, with Sir Henry at the centre of the table, with his wife on his right. Entertainment is provided by a chamber orchestra seated at the round table below and by masquers in classical garb progressing round the room.

Lord Cobham with his wife (on the left) and her sister Jane and their six children painted in 1567. The ages of the children are painted above their heads and are, reading from the left, two, one, twins of five, and four. They all wear their best clothes, with ruffs, padded sleeves and jewels, like those of their parents. The table is laid for dessert, with grapes, cherries, peaches, apples, pears and nuts. The plates are of silver and the wine goblet of gold. The painting is now believed to be by an artist known as the Master of the Countess of Warwick.

the fifteenth century, but by the beginning of the Tudor Age they were being manufactured in Venice on a large scale for export to the countries of Western Europe, including England. Henry VIII had a very large number of wineglasses which he had imported from Venice, and by his time it had become fashionable for the nobility and the wealthy to drink from Venetian glass.

The manufacture of 'Normandy glass' for window panes had been taking place, on a small scale, since the thirteenth century at Chiddingfold in Sussex; but it was not till the beginning of Elizabeth I's reign that a much finer glass of the Venetian type was made in England by Jean Carré, who had learned the art of glassmaking in Antwerp, but had come to England as a Protestant refugee from the persecution in the Netherlands. By 1567 he was operating two 'glasshouses' where he manufactured glass near Loxwood in Sussex, with a labour force composed of Huguenot refugees from Lorraine. Before he died in 1572 he had opened more glassworks near Alfold in Surrey. Enterprising Englishmen were soon following his example. By 1585 John Lennard, who was the Earl of Leicester's tenant at Knole, had opened a glassworks at Sevenoaks, and by this time glass was being made throughout the Weald, at Kirdford, Wisborough Green, Petworth and Northiam in Sussex, and at Penshurst in Kent, as well as at Ewhurst and in the Guildford area in Surrey.

But in this area the glassworks had to compete with the ironmasters of the Weald for the wood and other fuel which were rapidly becoming in short supply; and Edward Henraye, who owned the glassworks at Petworth, had opened two new glassworks near Uttoxeter in Staffordshire. Before the end of the Tudor Age, glass factories were opened in Hampshire, Wiltshire, Gloucestershire, Nottinghamshire and Northumberland. But the ordinary household used glass only for their window panes. Drinking glasses were still used only by rich and fashionable families, and even at the end of the Tudor Age most of the mirrors used by the common people were made of steel, not glass.

In the sixteenth century, people usually rose at 5 a.m. in the summer and at 6 a.m. in the winter. They sometimes attended prayers, or did a little work before breakfast, and after this first meal set about performing the main part of their daily duties. At about 11 a.m. they ate their main meal of the day, their dinner, a word which until the end of the nineteenth century always meant the midday meal. They then carried on with their work until they had supper at about 5 or 6 p.m., though artisans and labourers were required to work until after 7 p.m. When Parliament was in session, the lords and MPs began the day's proceedings at 8 a.m., and only occasionally met again after dinner for a second session in the afternoon. Most people went to bed at about 9 p.m.

The routine was different at Henry VIII's court. The King's pages rose before 7 a.m. to light his fire, but Henry normally did not rise and dress till about 7.30 a.m.,

Silver Apostle Spoons were only used by the well-to-do in the sixteenth century, and today they are extremely rare, though occasionally copied and faked. The spoon on the left is of St Peter, made in York by R. Gylmyn in 1572. It is seven inches long, and is the only known example showing St Peter with crossed keys rather than a single key. The spoon on the right, 7¾ inches long, was made in York in 1585, and is the only known example where St Matthew is shown with a carpenter's rule, on which the measures are clearly visible. *Photograph by courtesy of How of Edinburgh.*

though occasionally, when he wished to have a long day's hunting, he rose as early as 4 a.m. He sometimes ate a meal in his bedchamber for breakfast, but his first real meal was dinner, which began at 10 a.m., or a little earlier. On ordinary days he had supper when he returned from hunting at 4 p.m.; but on holy days the meal times were adapted to fit in with the times of Mass and other court ceremonies. After supper, Henry read the State papers, and then stayed up till after midnight, watching masques, dancing, and gambling at cards and dice.

In comparison with the lower classes in other European countries, ordinary Englishmen ate well during the Tudor Age. They lived on beef, mutton, capons and pigeons. They ate wheat bread and rye bread, butter, cheese, eggs and fish. When Hentzner visited England in 1598 he noticed that they ate more meat and less bread than the French, and had better table manners; that large quantities of oysters were

Silver communion cups of the Elizabethan period are relatively common, but secular wine cups are of extreme rarity. This superb example is not of the embossed type associated with church plate. It has a baluster stem, conical bowl, and concave spreading foot, the bowl and foot engraved with foliated scrolls and formalized fruit and flower devices. The maker's mark is I.G. in a monogram, and it was registered in London in 1591. The same craftsman made what is called the Vice-Chancellor's Cup at Cambridge University. *Photograph by courtesy of S. J. Phillips Ltd., of 139 New Bond Street.*

on sale in London; and that they put a great deal of sugar in their drinks, which he thought was the reason why so many Englishmen and women, including the Queen, had black teeth.

The English ate puddings, pastries and biscuits, and several kinds of fruit and vegetables – apples, pears, strawberries, cherries, damsons, peaches, oranges, figs, grapes, beans, peas, cabbages, leeks, carrots, turnips and parsnips; but potatoes were

Oak armchair with
geometrical pattern inlay.

not known until the Spaniards found them in Peru and John Hawkins brought them
back to England from the West Indies in 1563. When Sir Walter Raleigh sent an
expedition in 1585 to what is now Virginia and North Carolina, his sailors returned
with potatoes, and Raleigh then cultivated them on his estates at Youghal in Ireland.

A great deal of honey was eaten, and as English honey had a reputation for being
particularly good, it was exported in large quantities to France and other foreign
countries. But unscrupulous producers and sellers sometimes adulterated the honey
with other ingredients. It was partly in order to preserve the reputation of English
honey abroad, as well as to protect the home consumer, that Parliament passed an Act
in 1581 which also applied to the sale of bees' wax. Every barrel of honey sold was to
contain thirty-two wine gallons of honey, every kilderkin sixteen wine gallons, and
every firkin eight wine gallons. The seller of honey had to brand the head of every

barrel with the two letters of his Christian and surname,* in letters of at least $1\frac{1}{2}$ inches, so that he could be traced if the honey failed to comply with the requirements of the Act. If the filler of the barrel marked it with someone else's initials, he was to pay a fine of £5 for each offence, of which half was to be paid to the Queen and half to anyone who sued for the money before the local JPs.

The Englishman had a reputation throughout Europe for gluttony; it was said that overeating was the English vice, just as lust was the French vice and drunkenness the German vice. Some Englishmen became very fat, and were famous for it. Henry VIII ate enormous meals, but as a young man he was slim, perhaps because he always took a great deal of physical exercise. By the time that he was forty-five he was suffering from painful ulcers in his leg which prevented him from riding or walking without the greatest difficulty; but though he ceased to take exercise, he ate as much as ever. He then became very fat. We know from his suit of armour in the Tower of London that in later years he was fifty-four inches around the waist.

According to the story told by a seventeenth-century writer, a special machine was made, with pulleys, to lift Henry on to his horse and to carry him from room to room in his palaces. But he still liked the outdoor life which he had always enjoyed, and in the last winter before he died at the age of fifty-five he insisted on going out in the coldest weather, when most of his courtiers and servants would have preferred to stay indoors. Having been lifted on to his horse by the pulleys, he would sit there, wrapped up against the cold, watching his hawk pursue its prey, or a great killing of stags in an enclosure, though he had once chased stags for thirty miles a day.

Edmund Bonner, Bishop of London, was always portrayed by the illustrator of Foxe's *Book of Martyrs* as a fat man. He began his career as one of Wolsey's agents, and was with him at Cawood at the time of his arrest. He then entered the King's service, and was sent by Henry to confront the Pope at the time of the repudiation of Papal supremacy. He distinguished himself by insulting the Pope in a stormy interview at Marseilles; but he was appointed Bishop of London just at the time when Henry intensified the persecution of Protestants under the Act of the Six Articles, and it was his duty to preside at the heresy trials in London, where the Protestants were most numerous, in the years after 1540. Under the Protestant government of Edward VI, Bonner was deprived of his bishopric and imprisoned in the Marshalsea for four years for resisting the measures in favour of the Reformation; but when he was released and reinstated a Bishop of London in Mary's reign, he was once again in a position to persecute Protestants on an even greater scale than he had done under Henry VIII.

---

* It was almost unknown in the sixteenth century for any Englishman or woman to have more than one Christian name.

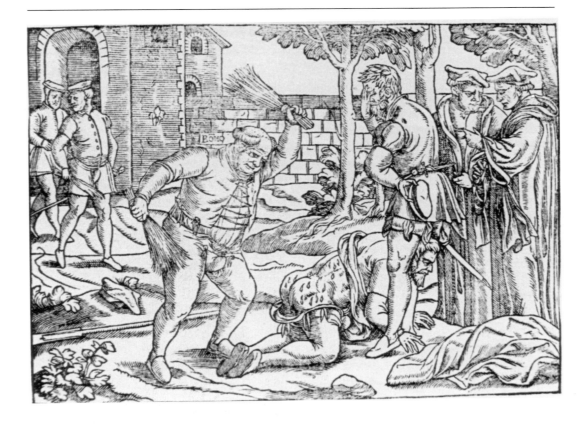

Bishop Bonner flogging a Protestant. From the original edition of Foxe's *Book of Martyrs*, 1563. Bonner was annoyed that the illustrator emphasized his fatness.

The Protestants hated him more than any of their other persecutors. Foxe, John Knox and the other Protestant propaganda writers denounced him as 'bloody Bonner', and their successors were still calling him this in the seventeenth century. Although this was probably due above all to his position as Bishop of London, it was also partly because of his personality. He was rude and brutal to the prisoners whom he interrogated at their trials; but what seems to have particularly angered his victims was his coarse and jovial humour, which they thought was particularly out of place when he was condemning men and women to be burned. They were also disgusted by his fatness.

When Elizabeth became Queen, Bonner went with the other bishops to greet her when she came from Hatfield to London; but she shrank from him in horror, and refused to allow him to kiss her hand. He opposed her decision to make England Protestant, and he was again deprived of his bishopric and imprisoned in the Marshalsea, where he died ten years later in 1569. He was so hated by the London

Henry VIII's suit of armour, c.1540, when he was forty-nine years old and in every sense a very substantial warrior.

Protestants that he had to be buried in secret to avoid a hostile demonstration during his funeral; and thirty years afterwards, when the Londoners saw an ugly, coarse and fat man in the street, they would say that he was Bonner.

He preserved his brutal sense of humour in adversity as he had in his hour of triumph. When someone showed him, in the Marshalsea, the picture in Foxe's *Book of Martyrs* of him torturing a Protestant martyr, he commented: 'A vengeance on the fool, how could he have got my picture drawn so right?'

It was on Sundays and the holy days that the Englishman most indulged in overeating. Nearly every day in the year was a saint's day, often named after obscure saints whose names are forgotten today. At the beginning of the Tudor Age people dated their letters, and kept a note of the days throughout the year, far more by the saints' days than by the days of the month. They would sometimes date their letters 'this third day of February', 'this ninth day of August', or 'this fifteenth day of November'; but until about 1550 they were more likely to date them 'St Blaise's Day', 'the eve of the feast of St Laurence', and 'the morrow after St Erkenwald's Day'.

Most of these saints' days were ordinary working days, but the more important ones were holy days. People did not work on Sundays and on holy days – which is the origin of the modern word 'holidays' – but, after going to Mass, spent the day chiefly in eating and drinking. There were several holy days in every month of the year, which from the thirteenth century to 1752 began in England on 25 March. Several of the most important were abolished during the reigns of Henry VIII and Edward VI. After Mary reunited England to Rome in 1554, Cardinal Pole proclaimed that 30 November, the day on which the reunification took place, should be the Feast of the Reconciliation, to be celebrated as a holy day to all eternity; but it was only celebrated for four years.

The Twelve Days of Christmas included Christmas Day, St Stephen's Day, St John the Apostle's Day, Childermas, and the lesser feast of St Thomas of Canterbury on 29 December, the day of his martyrdom in 1170; his greater feast was on 7 July, the anniversary of the erection of his tomb in 1220. The first of January was still called New Year's Day, in memory of the time in the twelfth century when the calendar year had started on 1 January, and not on 25 March. It was the day on which people gave each other gifts; at court, the courtiers gave the most expensive gifts which they could afford to the King and to their superior in the hierarchy of State and Church, and noted with interest which counsellors and courtiers received the most expensive gifts from the King. The Twelve Days of Christmas ended with Twelfth Day on 6 January.

There were fast days as well as holy days. The fast days, on which people had to eat fish and not meat, served three purposes: they fulfilled the religious duty of abstinence and self-abnegation; they conserved the supply of meat, which was particularly desirable during Lent in February and March, when stocks were low after the winter; and they helped the fishing industry, which the government wished to encourage. The fast days were every Friday and Saturday; every day throughout Lent and the four weeks of Advent before Christmas, except Sundays; and the eve of every holy day; but when the eve of a holy day fell on a Sunday, the fast was held on the Saturday.

Apart from certain categories who were excused from fasting, such as the sick, and pregnant women, it was not very difficult for any individual to obtain a dispensation from the diocesan bishop, allowing him to break the fasting laws. Erasmus regularly obtained a dispensation from fasting, on the grounds that eating fish upset his stomach, as well as the dispensation which he was regularly granted allowing him to live outside his monastery and not to wear monkish garb. Erasmus's statement about his stomach may or may not have been justified, but there is no doubt that many dispensations were improperly obtained by influence and by bribing officials.

The Protestants objected to holy days and fast days, because there was nothing in the Bible which suggested that any day of the year, apart from the Sabbath Day, was any holier than any other, or that men should fast on Fridays, Saturdays or in Lent. They ate meat on the fast days, and were duly punished by the bishops' courts for this defiance of the authority of the Church. The Catholics said that the Protestant arguments for refusing to fast were really an excuse for indulging in gluttony; the Protestants replied that they avoided gluttony on all the days of the year, as all good men ought to do, instead of making fast days an excuse for gluttony on the holy days.

Henry VIII and his government strictly enforced the fasting laws, which Henry himself always observed, and any breach of the laws continued to be punished after the repudiation of Papal supremacy; but in 1537 one of the greatest of the holy days in England, the feast of St Thomas of Canterbury on 7 July, was abolished, along with the lesser feast day on the anniversary of his martyrdom on 29 December. This was followed by a great propaganda campaign against Becket. Pilgrims had come from all over England and Western Europe to lay their gifts on St Thomas's tomb, in memory of his martyrdom at the hands of the impious King, Henry II, and celebrating the triumph of the Church in forcing Henry II to do penance at his tomb. But Henry VIII ordered the clergy to denounce Becket in the pulpits as a traitor who had defied the authority of his King at the instigation of a foreign Pope. After a commission of inquiry had officially condemned Becket as a traitor, his bones were dug up and burned, his shrine in Canterbury Cathedral closed, and the treasures at his tomb forfeited to the King under the usual treason laws. It took twenty carts to carry the treasures from Canterbury to London. Nothing that Henry had done had so outraged the Pope's supporters; it persuaded the Pope at last to pronounce the sentence of excommunication against Henry, which he had hitherto refrained from doing.

On 6 July 1537 Cranmer held a banquet in Canterbury at which he publicly ate meat, to show that it was no longer the eve of a holy day. His action attracted much attention and aroused great indignation in many quarters. His critics were particularly shocked that an Archbishop of Canterbury should so publicly repudiate his saintly predecessor in the see.

In ordinary circumstances, Cranmer believed in fasting and in ecclesiastical

It was said that over-eating was the English vice. Here a banquet is being prepared. An engraving by Justus Sadeler, after Antonio Tempesta.

abstinence. In 1542 he tried to restrain the gluttony of the clergy by issuing an order in the Convocation of Canterbury restricting the number of dishes which could be eaten at a meal. Archbishops were only to be served with six different dishes of meat or fish, and with four different dishes as a second course. Bishops were to have only five dishes of meat or fish, and three as a second course; archdeacons and deans, four of meat and fish, and two as a second course; and the lower clergy three of meat or fish, and two as a second course – that is to say, only two out of, for example, custard, tart, fritters, cheese, apples or pears. Archbishops were only to be allowed three partridges in one dish, and all lower ranks of the clergy, including bishops, only two; but archbishops were allowed to eat six blackbirds in one dish, bishops four blackbirds, and the clergy below the rank of bishop three blackbirds. The order aroused so much opposition, and was so widely ignored, that it proved impossible to enforce, and it was withdrawn after a few months.

Although Cranmer allowed Archbishop Edward Lee of York and himself the privilege of eating more than any of his bishops or lower clergy, he did not always take advantage of the order. In the evenings, he would often sit at the supper table wearing white gloves to show that he was fasting, and eating nothing.

During the drive against the Protestants which followed the Act of the Six Articles and the fall of Cromwell, orders were issued for a strict enforcement of the fasting laws. In London, Bonner and the Lord Mayor sentenced several Protestants to short terms of imprisonment for eating meat on fast days. When the persecution of the Protestants was intensified in 1543, the authorities in London sent officers to enter the people's houses at dinner time to see what they were eating.

In the reign of Edward VI, one of the first problems with which the government of Somerset and Cranmer had to deal when they introduced the Reformation was the Protestant demand for the abolition of fasting during Lent. Gardiner wrote to Somerset to protest. 'Every country hath his peculiar inclination to naughtiness,' he explained, 'England and Germany to the belly, the one in liquor, the other in meat; France a little beneath the belly; Italy to vanity and pleasures devised; and let an English belly have a further advancement, and nothing can stay it.'

Somerset and Cranmer decided to suppress fast days in theory but to continue them in practice. 'An Act for abstinence from flesh' was passed in 1549. It declared that although no day or food was holier than any other, nevertheless as 'due and godly abstinence is a mean to virtue and to subdue men's bodies to their soul and spirit, and considering also that fishers and men using the trade of living by fishing in the sea may thereby the rather be set on work, and that by eating of fish, much flesh shall be saved and increased', it was hereby enacted that no one should eat meat on any Friday or Saturday, in Lent, or on any day which had hitherto been a fast day, except on abrogated holy days. The Act did not apply to the sick, to pregnant women, to soldiers in any garrison whose commander had authorized them to eat meat, or to persons who obtained a licence from the King to do so. Anyone who broke this law was to be punished by a fine of ten shillings and ten days' imprisonment, during which time he was not to be given any meat. For the second and subsequent offences, the penalty was increased to a fine of twenty shillings and twenty days' imprisonment without meat. The Act then repealed all other laws enforcing fasting. This meant that the ban applied only to eating meat, and not the 'white meats' of butter, cheese and eggs. An Act of 1552 abolished a number of holy days, including Corpus Christi Day and All Souls' Day, but retained most of them; and though many fast days were abolished, the prohibition on the eating of meat was to continue on all the days on which it was formerly banned.

Under Mary, all the old holy days and fast days, and the fasting laws of the Catholic Church, were reintroduced; but the laws of Edward VI were re-enacted under Elizabeth I. In the statutes passed by her Parliaments, the days on which meat was prohibited were called 'fish days', not 'fast days'.

The fasting laws never applied to drink, and anyone who suggested that they did ran the risk of being regarded as a heretic; for Christ had shown his approval of wine by converting the water into wine at the wedding feast in Cana as the first miracle that He performed; and King Henry, the Supreme Head (next under Christ) of the Church of England, was in the habit of drinking wine.

The ordinary Englishman drank beer, or ale if he was a little wealthier, but a good deal of wine was imported from Bordeaux. Wine was too expensive for most people, though an Act of 1536 fixed the maximum price at which Gascon, Guion or any French wine could be sold at eightpence a gallon. Malmsey wine from Greece cost more, for the maximum price permitted was twelvepence a gallon; and 'sack' (sherry) from Xeres in Spain was even more expensive, and could be sold at any price up to 3s.4d. a gallon. Ale cost a good deal less, for the Act fixed the maximum price at fivepence for a firkin of nine gallons. Beer cost half the price of ale, with the maximum price fixed at fivepence for a kilderkin of eighteen gallons. The price was increased to sixpence a kilderkin in 1544, because the rise in the price of timber had made it more expensive for the brewers to obtain their beer barrels. Breaches of the Act were punished by a fine of 4s.4d. for every time that a seller charged more than the maximum price.

The most expensive drink of all was that very rare luxury, hypocras, a sweet liqueur imported from Smyrna and the Levant by Venetian merchants and brought by them to England. It was served at the end of banquets at Henry VIII's court; and at royal christenings and funerals, when no other refreshments were served, the proceedings always ended with wafers and hypocras.

It was not only because wines were more expensive that the ordinary Englishman drank beer. He preferred beer, and would drink nothing else. In the first military campaign of Henry VIII's reign, 7,000 English soldiers were sent to Fuenterrabia in northern Spain to help Henry's father-in-law, King Ferdinand, conquer the kingdom of Navarre from the French. When they found that they could not obtain any beer in Spain, but only wine or cider, they mutinied; and their commander, the Marquess of Dorset, was forced to bring them home. Henry VIII was very angry, but was persuaded by the Spanish ambassador that it would be politically expedient to pardon the mutineers. This was probably the last time during his life that Henry would have done such a thing.

Henry's generals and counsellors never forgot the mutiny at Fuenterrabia, and thirty years later, when the campaign against Scotland was being planned in 1542, it was considered to be of paramount importance that the army should not run short of beer. Orders had been issued to the sheriffs and gentlemen in the North of England to be at Newcastle with their tenants, ready to march into Scotland, on 2 October; but as the ships coming from London with the beer had not arrived, the date was put off to 7 October; and as there was still no news of the beer, the date was again put off till 11 October. The beer did arrive on 7 October, but there was not as much as had been expected. The Duke of Norfolk, who was to command the invasion of Scotland, wrote to Henry VIII, explaining that there would only be enough beer for a six-day campaign in Scotland, even if he rationed the men to two pots of beer a day, which he feared might cause trouble.

Norfolk had no alternative, in the circumstances, but to march with his men to Berwick, and he led them across the Border on 22 October. But either his quartermasters had made a mistake in their arithmetic about the beer, or the soldiers drank more than their allotted ration of two pots a day; for Norfolk soon realized that the beer would give out after only four days. He encountered virtually no opposition from the Scots, and duly devastated the Merse and the frontier districts of Scotland; but the shortage of beer forced him to retreat into England.

Henry was lucky. Norfolk's retreat so heartened the Scots that they launched an invasin of England before they were ready, and, crossing the Border in the Western Marches, marched straight into a bog at Solway Moss, where they suffered a humiliating defeat from which only a handful of Scots succeeded in escaping back across the Border into Scotland.

The war against the Scots continued with increasing savagery, and in the spring of 1544 Henry decided to send an army to destroy Edinburgh, 'putting man, woman and child to fire and sword without exception, where any resistance shall be made against you'. His general in the North was Edward Seymour, Earl of Hertford (later Duke of Somerset). Hertford assured Henry that he could march from Berwick to Edinburgh without meeting any serious resistance from the Scots; but there was one great difficulty. How would they be able to transport the beer for the army across the sodden roads and tracks of Berwickshire and Lothian over which carts could not move if they were heavily laden with beer barrels? The solution was found; an army of 16,000 men could be sent by sea from Tynemouth to Leith in 114 ships, and could march the few miles from Leith to Edinburgh and spend three days burning the city, while all the beer that was required could stay on board the ships at Leith. The plan was carried out successfully; every building in Edinburgh, except the castle, was burned, including the Palace of Holyroodhouse.

Even at court, more ale was drunk than wine. On ordinary days, when there was no special banquet, dukes and duchesses who were at court were provided with one gallon of ale for dinner and another gallon for supper, and with one pitcher of wine after supper. Earls, barons, knights and gentlemen were served with lesser quantities, according to their rank.

Apart from wine, ale and beer, the only other drinks were milk and water, for tea, coffee and cocoa only came to England in the seventeenth century, and there were no hot drinks except soup. It was risky to drink water, because of the filth that polluted the rivers and all stagnant water supplies; but many of the poor had to take the risk, and it was very usual for the rich to dilute wine with water. When Catherine of Aragon was being brought up as a child in Spain before 1501, at the court of her father and mother King Ferdinand and Queen Isabella, in preparation for her marriage to Arthur, Prince of Wales, she was taught to drink wine, so that she would get to like it before she went to England, as it would be unsafe to drink the water there. It was just the reverse four hundred years later, at the beginning of the twentieth century, when English children were taught to like wine before being taken on a holiday abroad, as it was unsafe to drink the water in France and Spain.

At court, particularly under Henry VIII, there was particularly heavy eating and drinking at all times, with lavish banquets on the holy days. There were also banquets on special occasions, to entertain a visiting diplomatic delegation which had been sent to Henry's court by a foreign sovereign. On the holy days the banquet was normally held at dinner, at 10 a.m., but the foreign ambassadors were often also entertained at great banquets in the evening. When the ambassador of the Holy Roman Emperor Maximilian visited Henry's court in July 1517, he was entertained at an evening banquet at Greenwich on St Thomas of Canterbury's day. The ambassador sat at the King's table with Henry, Wolsey, Queen Catherine, and Henry's sister Mary 'the French Queen', as she was still called though she was now the Duchess of Suffolk.

The guests were served with ten courses and sat at table for seven hours, for the banquet did not end till 2 a.m. Henry's musicians played throughout the meal. The Venetian ambassador, as usual, was impressed. 'Every imaginable sort of meat known in the kingdom was served', he wrote, 'and fish too, including prawn pasties of perhaps twenty different kinds, made in the shapes of castles, and of animals of various kinds, as beautiful as can be imagined. In short, the wealth and civilization of the world are here, and those who call the English barbarians seem to me to make themselves barbarians.'

In 1518 Henry decided to end the cold war with France, which had lasted for three years, and the Admiral of France was sent to England to sign a treaty of friendship with Henry and to solemnize the betrothal of Henry's two-year-old daughter, the Princess Mary, to Francis I's son. The Admiral was entertained at an evening banquet at Greenwich which again lasted till 2 a.m. There were eighty-two gold vases and fifty-two silver drinking cups on the table; and during the supper, servants entered, carrying a shaker six feet long in solid silver, which threw wafers into the air for the guests to catch and eat.

When Henry VIII created his illegitimate son Duke of Richmond, and appointed him Lord President of the Council of the North, Henry's counsellors drafted instructions to the Duke's officials as to what he and his household should eat for their dinner and supper at Sheriffhutton, on ordinary days and on fast days. The six-year-old Duke was to be served, for his dinner on ordinary days and holy days between Michaelmas and Shrovetide, a first course of soup, with two rounds of brawn, a helping of beef or mutton, with either swan or goose, a quarter (28 lbs.) of roast veal, three roast capons, and a 'baked meat', or biscuit. For his second course, he was to have another soup, four roast rabbits, fourteen pigeons, four partridges or pheasants, a wildfowl, fruit and biscuits, along with four gallons of ale and two pitchers of wine. For supper in the evening, he was to have a first course of soup, boiled meat, a quarter of roast mutton, three capons or hens, a wildfowl, and wafers; for his second course, five roast rabbits, fourteen pigeons, two wildfowl, two tarts, fruits and bread, with ale, wine, sauces and spices.

On the fast days, he was to have for dinner a first course of cod, half a salmon, two pikes, a sea-fish, a fresh-water fish, and biscuits, and a second course of turbot, a fresh salmon, two sea-fish, a fresh-water fish, shrimps, tarts and fruit; and at supper, a very similar diet with the addition of sturgeon as a second course. All this was supposed to be for the personal consumption of the little boy, for his Chancellor, his counsellors, his gentlemen and his grooms had a separate list of dishes allotted to them, each of them receiving less than the Duke and more than the official next below them in rank.

Of course the Duke could not eat all these dishes, and was not supposed to do so, for this was a display of ostentation and pride, not of gluttony. The food which he left over was taken by the servants and distributed to the villagers and the beggars who crowded into the courtyard of the castle at Sheriffhutton at dinner time and supper time to receive the uneaten portions of the Duke's dinner and supper and the dinners and suppers of the members of his household. The Duke was probably brought up to eat at the most a few mouthfuls from each of these dishes, and generously give the rest to the poor.

The purpose of it all, as with most of the things that Henry VIII did, was to impress. The Duke of Richmond's personal diet cost £1 18s.8d. a day in 1525, at a time when the husbandman was given an allowance of twopence a day for his food, and had to work six days a week for twenty weeks to earn £1 18s.8d. The cost of the dinners and suppers provided for the Duke and his whole household came to more than £66 a day, or £2,439 a year.

HUSBANDRY

IN Tudor society, although a minority of the population were noblemen, courtiers, gentlemen, priests and monks, lawyers, merchants and artisans, the great majority were husbandmen who worked as agricultural labourers on the land. But throughout the Tudor Age, husbandry was threatened by a series of problems which the government and Parliament were constantly trying to put right. The farmers suffered from a shortage of cheap labour, for some people did not wish to work on the land, and preferred to beg or steal; and others, who were willing to be husbandmen, pressed for higher wages and a shorter working day which threatened the farmers' profits. The situation was made worse by the middlemen and 'regrators' who bought up foodstuffs and resold them at a profit, thus raising the cost of the husbandman's food and increasing his need for higher wages; and the bad state of rural housing exacerbated the problem. While the farmer was facing these difficulties, the thriving wool trade in East Anglia and in south-west England meant that he could obtain good prices for his wool, and gave him every incentive to convert arable into pasture land and to keep sheep instead of tilling the soil.

By the beginning of the sixteenth century, the conversion of arable land into pasture was worrying statesmen and religious leaders. Sir Thomas More criticized the development in his book *Utopia* in 1516 as strongly as did his great religious opponent, Latimer, in his sermons thirty years later. But these economic and social anxieties did not concern the author of that very practical handbook for farmers, *The Book of Husbandry*. It was probably written by Sir Anthony Fitzherbert, a Judge of the Court of Common Pleas, who by a strange coincidence was one of the judges at the trial of Sir Thomas More who sentenced him to death; but Sir Anthony's brother, John Fitzherbert, may have been the author. Fitzherbert does not hesitate to advise his readers to enclose their land and to concentrate on sheepbreeding, and assures them 'that sheep, in mine opinion, is the most profitable cattle that any man can have'.

Like practical handbooks in the twentieth century, *The Book of Husbandry* was a best-seller. It was probably first published in 1523, and nine more editions appeared

Detail from *Summer*, one of a series of four Sheldon tapestries illustrating *The Seasons*, at Hatfield House in Hertfordshire. William Sheldon founded his tapestry factories in Warwickshire and Worcestershire shortly after 1560, and the work was carried on by his son and his grandson into the early seventeenth century. The last of *The Seasons* is dated 1611. This detail shows men reaping in the foreground and others shearing sheep beyond them.

The Month of September. One of a series of Flemish illuminated manuscripts known as *The Golf Book*, dating from c. 1500. It is evident that such activities as harvesting, ploughing and sowing spring corn occurred earlier in the year in the sixteenth and seventeenth centuries than they do today.

in the next forty-five years. Thirty years after the tenth edition of 1568, a new revised edition, 'now newly corrected, amended and reduced into a more pleasing form of English than before', was published in 1598. The book was evidently not written for the husbandman and labourer, most of whom were almost illiterate. From time to time, when Fitzherbert is digressing into moral exhortation, he quotes texts from the Bible and other maxims in Latin; but this does not mean that he was writing for Latin scholars, for the Latin texts are mostly those which any layman might have heard quoted in church on Sundays and holy days, and Fitzherbert usually translates them into English. No doubt many country gentlemen read the book, but there are passages in it which suggest that Fitzherbert was writing primarily for the yeoman farmer, who worked himself, with his wife, in the management of the farm, rather than for the gentleman.

Fitzherbert gave his readers useful advice about ploughing, suggesting that on balance it was better to plough with oxen than with horses, provided that the farmer had fields of pasture where the oxen could rest between the ploughing; for though horses were stronger than oxen, and could work for longer hours, it cost less to feed oxen; and when a horse became old, bruised or blind, he was useless. But if 'an ox wax old, bruised or blind, for two shillings he may be fed, and then he is man's meat and as good ox, better than ever he was'. He wrote about how to sow barley and oats, how to plough for peas and beans, how to make forks and rakes, how to fell and plant trees and make hedges, how to recognize and treat the various diseases which the animals might catch, and when to wash and shear sheep. He taught how to make a ewe love her lamb. If a ewe did not like one of her lambs, and was often striking it with her paw, Fitzherbert advised that the ewe should be tied by her paw to the side of the pen and that a dog should be placed near the lamb in a position where the ewe could see it. This would arouse the ewe's protective instincts towards her lamb.

The Book of Husbandry contained advice on how to repair a highway, for husbandmen were required to work for four days in the year repairing the highways, and this had been increased to six days in the year by the time that the tenth edition of the book was published, after Fitzherbert's death, in 1568. He had his own ideas about this, for he thought that the way in which highways were repaired, especially in the vicinity of London, was unsatisfactory. It was no use digging a trench on both sides of the road to drain the water, and then putting down gravel, because when the rains came, the soft earth beneath the gravel subsided, and the gravel went with it. Instead, Fitzherbert advised that, after brushing away all the surface water, earth should be put down in the spring; then, when it had become hardened during the dry weather by the pressure of cartwheels and the feet of pedestrians, the gravel should be placed on top of the dry earth.

The role of the farmer's wife is dealt with in *The Book of Husbandry*. Fitzherbert told

221

the farmer that she should 'first in a morning when thou art waked and proposeth to rise, take up thy hand and bless thee and make the sign of the holy cross. In nomine patris et filii et spiritus sancti Amen. In the name of the Father, the Son and the Holy Ghost. And if thou say a Pater Noster, an Ave and a Creed and remember thy Maker, thou shalt speed much the better'. This advice in the first edition of 1523 remained in all the editions in Henry VIII's reign, survived in two editions under Edward VI, and was of course in order in the 1556 edition under Philip and Mary. It still remained in the first edition under Elizabeth I in 1560. But it was changed in 1562. Instead of the wife being urged to make the sign of the cross and the husband to say a Pater Noster, an Ave and a Creed, the farmer and his wife were told to 'give thanks to God for thy night's rest and say the Lord's Prayer and other good prayers if thou canst'; and this Protestant version was reprinted in the editions of 1568 and 1598.

The rest of the wife's daily duties remained unchanged from the first edition of 1523. She must clean the house, feed the calves, prepare the milk, wake and dress the children, prepare her husband's breakfast, dinner and supper, and supervise the servants. She must make butter and cheese, feed the pigs morning and evening, and have a care for the hens, ducks, and geese, and collect their eggs. She should put her husband's sheep to good use by making clothes from their wool, and should know how to make hay, to minnow all kinds of corn, to make malt, and 'to help her husband to fill the muck wain or dung cart'. She should also be able to go to market if her husband is unable to go himself, and know how to buy and sell shrewdly at market. It was important that on these occasions she should give a true and full account to her husband of all the money she had spent and received at the market, and her husband should do the same to her; for many marriages had been wrecked because husband and wife concealed money matters from each other.

Although Fitzherbert and the farmers who read his book saw only the advantages of owning sheep, the government became increasingly worried, and in 1534 an Act was passed to restrict it. The statute declared that wealthy landowners had bought up arable land and converted it to pasture, and some had acquired as many as 24,000 sheep; this had doubled the price of corn, cattle, pigs, geese, chickens and eggs, and also of wool. So it was enacted that no landowner was to own more than 2,400 sheep,* excluding lambs aged less than one year, on pain of a fine of 3s.4d. for every sheep over 2,400 which he owned. No one was to take a tenancy of more than two farms unless he lived in the parish where the farm was situated.

Edward VI's Parliament passed a more drastic Act in 1552, which enacted that by 25 March 1553 every parish must have as much land in tillage as it had in any year since the beginning of Henry VIII's reign in 1509, and that such land must be kept in tillage for the next four years. But the Act proved to be unenforceable.

The legislation did not prevent the continued predominance of the sheep in agriculture. In 1555 Parliament tried to encourage dairy farming by enacting that any farmer who owned more than 120 sheep must keep one cow for every sixty sheep that he owned; but by the end of Elizabeth's reign the decline of tillage was alarming the

* The Act, after enacting that no landowner shall own more than 2,000 sheep, stated that whereas in some parts of England 'a hundred' means a greater hundred of six score, i.e. 120, and in other parts a lesser hundred of five score, this figure of 2,000 was to be interpreted as twenty of the greater hundred, with six score in each hundred.

government more than ever, and an Act was passed in 1597 which applied to the twenty-five counties where the situation was most serious. All land which had been converted to pasture since the Queen's accession on 17 November 1558, after having been in tillage for twelve years, was to be reconverted to tillage before 1 May 1599; and in future no land which had been in tillage for twelve years was ever to be converted to any other use.

From the beginning of the Tudor Age, the government was concerned about the shortage of the cheap labour which was needed in husbandry. Until the fourteenth century the land had been cultivated by serfs, or bondmen, but by the beginning of the Tudor Age serfdom had very largely disappeared in England. It lingered on in a few isolated pockets. Several monasteries owned bondmen, but they were manumitted and set free when the monasteries were dissolved, though as late as 1538 the Earl of Arundel refused to manumit a bondman at Cromwell's request, on the grounds that it would diminish the value of his lands for his heirs; and the man had to remain a serf. But by the beginning of the sixteenth century there were only a few thousand serfs remaining in England. All the other husbandmen worked for their employer, who was sometimes a country gentleman and sometimes a yeoman or man of lower rank, in return for wages paid either wholly in money, or partly in money and partly in clothing, food and drink.

After serfdom began to disappear in the fourteenth century, Parliament on several occasions passed a Statute of Labourers which fixed the maximum wage which could be paid to husbandmen and other workmen and artisans, and made it a criminal offence for any employer to pay, or for any employee to receive, a higher wage, though the employer was free to pay a lower wage and the employee to accept it, if they could agree to this by bargaining. At the beginning of the Tudor Age, the law was regulated by the Act of 1444, but a new statute was passed in 1496. It fixed the maximum annual wage that could be paid to a bailiff in charge of a farm at 26s.8d., with an additional five shillings per annum for his clothing, meat and drink if these were not supplied to him in addition to his wages. The maximum for a chief shepherd was twenty shillings per annum, with an extra five shillings for clothing, meat and drink. The ordinary husbandman was not to receive more than 16s.8d. per annum with 4s. for clothing, meat and drink; the woman servant no more than 10s. per annum with 4s. for clothing, meat and drink; and children under fourteen no more than 6s.8d. per annum and 3s. for clothing, meat and drink.

The wages of artisans were fixed on a daily basis, with a higher wage allowed in summer than in winter, as the workmen worked longer hours during the light summer evenings. The maximum wage of master carpenters, plumbers, bricklayers and joiners between Easter and Michaelmas was to be 6d. per day, or 4d. if meat and drink were provided for them, and 5d. per day, or 3d. per day with meat and drink, between Michaelmas and Easter. The summer and winter wages of many other categories of artisans were similarly fixed. The unskilled artisan and labourer was to receive, between Easter and Michaelmas, 4d. a day, or 2d. a day if meat and drink were supplied; between Michaelmas and Easter the wage was 3d. a day, or 1d. a day with meat and drink. Any employer who paid higher wages than these rates was to be fined 40s. for each offence, and every workman who accepted higher wages was to be fined 20s., eighty times his daily wage. If any artisan or labourer who was not in work was offered employment at these wages, and refused to accept it, the employer who had made the offer could ask the local JPs to imprison the artisan or labourer until he agreed to work for him.

The hours of work were also fixed, because 'divers artificers and labourers retained to work and serve waste much part of the day and deserve not their wages, sometime in late coming unto their work, early departing therefrom, long sitting at their breakfast, at their dinner and noonmeat,* and long time of sleeping at afternoon, to the loss and hurt of such persons as the said artificers and labourers be retained with in service'. So it was enacted that between the middle of March and the middle of September every artisan and labourer had to be at work before 5 a.m. and continue till between 7 and 8 p.m., with breaks of two hours for breakfast, dinner, sleep and noonmeat; and the workman was only to be allowed to sleep between the middle of May and the middle of August. In winter, the hours of work were to be from dawn to dusk, with the same breaks for meals. The Act also contained a provision that any workman who left his job without his master's consent, except to enter the King's service, was to be punished by one month's imprisonment and a fine of twenty shillings.

The legislation did not succeed in preventing artisans and labourers from obtaining an increase in wages, especially after the inflation began in about 1545. The influx of silver from the mines of Mexico to the money market at Antwerp, and Henry VIII's policy of debasing the currency as a way of raising money to pay for his war with France, nearly doubled prices in the next ten years; and by 1556 the husbandman's daily wage had risen to sevenpence.

John Ponet, the Protestant Bishop of Winchester, referred to this in a book against Queen Mary which he published in exile at Strasbourg in 1556 and which was smuggled into England. He tried to arouse the people's anger against the government by associating the inflation with the reintroduction of the Catholic religion, though in fact it had already been running at nine per cent a year under Edward VI.

* A light meal eaten during the afternoon.

When were ever things so dear in England as in this time of the Popish Mass and other idolatry restored? Whoever heard or read before that a pound of beef was at fourpence; a sheep twenty shillings; a pound of candles at fourpence; a pound of butter at fourpence; a pound of cheese at fourpence, two eggs a penny, a quarter of wheat sixty-four shillings, a quarter of malt at fifty shillings or above; the people driven of hunger to grind acorns for bread meal, and to drink water instead of ale?

The inflation ceased after 1560, and prices remained stable for about thirty years; but there was another sharp rise in prices at the end of the Tudor Age, when four bad harvests in succession between 1594 and 1597 caused an annual inflation of 10.4 per cent. The poorer classes suffered severely, because food prices, except for fish and ale, rose by 190 per cent in these four years, while wages hardly rose at all.

During the inflation of Edward VI's reign, Parliament tried to keep wages stable by passing an Act in 1549 to prevent combinations by workmen to obtain a rise in wages. It enacted that if any artificers or labourers conspired together to obtain higher wages or shorter working hours, 'or shall not enterprise or take upon them to finish that another hath begun', they were to be punished for the first offence by a fine of £10 or twenty days' imprisonment on bread and water; and for the third offence the offender was to pay a fine of £40, and if it was not paid within six days, he was to stand in the pillory, have one of his ears cut off, be forced to work as a labourer all his life, and be for ever incapable of giving evidence in a court of law.

The government tried to control the rise in prices as well as wages. In 1534 an Act was passed to reduce the excessive price of meat. If, in any district, farmers were refusing to sell their cattle to butchers at reasonable prices, the butchers could apply to the local JPs to fix a reasonable price for the cattle. More far-reaching measures against overcharging were taken in Edward VI's reign. It was forbidden to buy butter or cheese and resell it except in an open shop, fair or market, or to buy corn, wine, fish, butter, cheese, candles, farm animals or rabbits at any fair or market, and to resell them at any fair or market within four miles of where they were bought; and no one who bought oxen, cows, sheep or goats was to resell them unless he had kept the animals in his own house or farm for five weeks.

The Act did not apply to an innkeeper who resold them to customers in his inn; to anyone who had been licensed by the JPs as a common drover and who resold them more than forty miles from the place where he bought them; or to anyone living within one mile of the sea who bought and resold fish. But Parliament had dealt with profiteering in imported fish in another statute in 1542. Fishermen in the Cinque Ports, and in other places in Sussex and Kent, were in the habit of going to sea and meeting French and Flemish fishermen from Picardy, Normandy, Flanders or Zeeland in the Channel or the North Sea, buying their fish from them, and bringing it

Gardeners at work in a kitchen garden. A somewhat stylized woodcut in *The Gardener's Labyrinth*, published in 1572 under the name of Henry Dethicke, which disguises the identity of a prolific gardening writer called Thomas Hill.

back to England to resell at a profit. Parliament, believing that the fish would be sold at cheaper prices if the French and Flemish fishermen came to English ports and sold it there themselves, made it illegal for anyone to buy fish abroad, or at sea, and resell it in the King's realm; but this did not apply to fish that had been bought in Ireland, Scotland, the Orkneys and Shetlands, or in Iceland or Newfoundland.

In view of the law which prohibited artisans and labourers from leaving their employment without their masters' consent before the expiry of their term of service, many workmen refused to enter into the usual contract of employment for a year or three months. They became casual labourers, or 'journeymen', who agreed to serve a master only from day to day, and left, when they felt inclined, to take a better job elsewhere. This was prohibited by an Act of 1550, which declared that 'many young folk and servants of sundry occupations' would not take employment by the year, 'but at their liberty by the day, week or otherwise work . . . to the intent that they will live idly at their pleasure, and flee and resort from place to place, whereof ensueth more inconveniences than can be at this present expressed and declared'. So it was enacted that weavers, tailors, shoemakers and other craftsmen were not to employ any unmarried person for a term of service of less than three months, on pain of one month's imprisonment and a fine of 40s.

Every journeyman who worked at any trade was to be compelled to accept any employment which he was offered in his trade for three months, six months or a year at wages which, if the parties could not agree, should be assessed as reasonable by the Mayor or the local JPs. If he refused to take this employment, he was to be punished by one month's imprisonment and a fine of 20s. The statute also enacted that no unmarried person who had never been married – it did not apply to widowers – could be employed as a husbandman for a term of less than one year.

The laws regulating wages and hours of work continued to be widely avoided, and in 1563 Elizabeth I's Parliament tried again. It recognized that one reason why the law had not been enforced was because the rise in prices had made the wages too low; so the Act no longer fixed a maximum wage for the various classes of labourers, but, taking inflation into account, enacted that the wages should be fixed by the local JPs, who had to meet for this purpose every year within six weeks after Easter and send their order to be confirmed by the Privy Council before 12 July. Any employer who paid more than the maximum wage laid down by the JPs was to be punished by ten days' imprisonment and a fine of £5, and a servant who accepted a higher wage was to be sentenced to twenty-one days' imprisonment. The Act confirmed the working hours laid down in the earlier Acts. Between the middle of March and the middle of September the husbandmen and artisans were to be at work by 5 a.m. and not leave work till between 7 and 8 p.m., and their rest breaks during the day were not to exceed two and a half hours, including half an hour 'at the most' for a sleep between the middle of May and the middle of August. Between the middle of September and the middle of May they were to work from dawn to dusk, with one and a half hours for work breaks.

The Act of 1563 went further than any earlier legislation in conscripting labour for the farms. It drew up a comprehensive list of thirty-one trades, from clothworkers and tailors to arrowheadmakers and cooks, and enacted that any unmarried man, or married man under thirty, who had been trained in these trades could be ordered by the Mayor or local JPs to take employment in his trade on a yearly contract of service unless he was working in husbandry or in the household of a nobleman or gentleman.

A domestic garden scene, c.1600, embroidered in stumpwork with various coloured wools on a canvas background. The ladies' necks are decorated with strings of pearls, and some of the flowers have coloured buttons sewn on to them.

229

A detail from the Bradford
Table Carpet, acquired by
the Victorian and Albert
Museum from the Earl of
Bradford's collection at
Castle Bromwich Hall. It
shows a great variety of
English rural pursuits,
worked in silk on linen
canvas in tent stitch. The
borders of the 'carpet' are
designed to hang over the
edges of the table.

A cherry bush, a detail from one of the Oxburgh bed hangings, c.1570, embroidered by 'Bess of Hardwick', the Countess of Shrewsbury, when she was appointed custodian of Mary Queen of Scots. They largely occupied their enforced leisure with needlework. This hanging is signed with Bess's initials, and is embroidered in silks on linen canvas and applied to velvet. Other bed-hangings in the series are to be seen in Oxburgh Hall in Norfolk.

Any other man between the ages of twelve and sixty, unless he was a fisherman, a sailor, a university student, or if he or his father owned land worth 40s. a year or goods worth £10, could be compelled to work as a husbandman for any master who was willing to employ him. Any unmarried woman between the ages of twelve and forty could be ordered by the JPs to take service for a year, a quarter, a week or a day with any master whom they saw fit to appoint. If the man or woman refused to accept this employment, they were to be imprisoned until they agreed to take the job. The JPs were given power to order that at haymaking and harvest time any artisan 'and persons as be meet to labour' should work from day to day on the land for any farmer whom the JPs nominated; and if they refused to do so, they were to be placed in the stocks for two days and one night. No master could dismiss a servant, and no servant could leave his employment, without a quarter's notice on either side, except for a good reason which had been accepted by the local JPs; and any servant who did so was to be imprisoned. The Act also provided that any servant who assaulted his master, mistress or any person appointed to a position of authority over him was to be imprisoned for a year and suffer any further punishment that the JPs chose to inflict, provided that it did not entail the loss of his life or limb.

At the end of their terms of service, the husbandman and artisan were not permitted to leave the town or parish in which they had been employed, unless they had obtained a certificate from the local vicar, for which the vicar was entitled to charge them twopence. The certificate was to be signed and dated by the vicar, and to be in this form: 'Memorand, that AB late servant to CD of E, husbandman, in the county of − , is licensed to depart from his said master and is at his liberty to serve elsewhere, according to the statute in the case made'. No one was permitted to employ any person who did not produce such a certificate, and any workman who did not produce it within twenty-one days, when required to do so, was to be whipped as a vagabond.

The Act attempted to prevent husbandmen from leaving the land by enacting that craftsmen could only take a youth as an apprentice if he lived in a market town in the same county and was not the son of a husbandman or labourer.

It was the JPs themselves who came off best as a result of the statute. It provided that every JP who carried out his duties under the Act was entitled to five shillings a day for his expenses, to be paid to him from the parish rates.

If the MPs hoped that this long and complicated statute of 1563 would finally solve the problem of the labour shortage in husbandry, they were disappointed. There continued to be evasions of the law, and when Parliament passed another Act in 1597 to clarify some ambiguities, it complained that the Act of 1563 was not being properly enforced.

The government throughout the Tudor Age was also concerned with the problem

Another illustration from *The Gardener's Labyrinth*, 1572. The occupation appears to be training vines.

of housing for agricultural workers, for they knew that one of the factors which threatened to cause the decay of husbandry was that no houses were available for husbandmen. An Act of 1489 compelled landowners who let arable land to maintain in a good condition any houses on the land; but this Act was ineffective, and more far-reaching legislation was passed in the last years of the Tudor Age. A statute of 1597 enacted that any house which had been let with twenty acres of land for at least three years since the accession of Elizabeth I in 1558, except the dwelling house of a nobleman or gentleman, 'shall be adjudged a House of Husbandry for ever'; and any landowner who had allowed houses of husbandry to fall into disrepair since 1558 was to rebuild a specified number of new houses to replace them.

There was another great cause for concern, which was as serious as the decay of husbandry. The shortage of timber was already being felt at the end of the fifteenth century, and it became much worse during the Tudor Age. Wood was still very largely used in housebuilding, as well as in the building and repair of ships, and it was the most usual form of fuel, though peat was also burned, and by the middle of the sixteenth century coal was becoming more common, especially in the districts near the coal mines. The development of the iron industry in the Weald of Sussex, Surrey and Kent, and later the glassworks which opened in the area after 1560, greatly increased the demand for wood as a fuel for the furnaces, and led to tree-felling and deforestation on a scale which alarmed the government. When Edward VI's Parliament in 1553, pursuing its consumer-protection policy, enacted that every faggot of wood sold in London or Westminster must be at least 3 feet long and 20 inches in circumference, it complained about the poor quality of timber offered for sale 'these sixty years . . . by reason of the great scarcity of wood, that is happened since the time of the said King Edward IV'.

Parliament took action in 1544 to restrict the felling of trees. It enacted that anyone who felled a wood consisting of trees of less than twenty-four years' growth was to leave at least twelve oak, elm, ash or beech trees standing in every acre of woodland; and no one was permitted to convert woodlands of more than two acres into arable or pasture land unless the woodlands were within a quarter of a mile of his dwelling house. But there were many exceptions to the Act. It did not apply if trees were felled in order to provide timber for building or repairing houses, dams, bridges, or ships; and it did not extend to woods in the Weald of Kent, Surrey or Sussex, or within two miles of the sea in Cornwall, or to any trees that were felled by the King's command.

With such important exceptions, it is not suprising that the Act did not cure the evil, and further restrictions on tree-felling were introduced in the reign of Elizabeth I. No oak, beech or ash tree growing within fourteen miles of the sea or of any navigable river which was one foot or more wide at the stump was to be used as fuel; but again there was an important exception, for the Act was not to apply to Sussex, to the Weald of Kent, or to the parishes of Charlwood, Newdigate or Leigh in Surrey.

It was not until 1585 that Parliament at last dealt with the deforestation of the Weald. The MPs realized that because of the number of ironworks in Sussex, Surrey and Kent 'the great plenty of timber which hath grown in those parts have been greatly decayed and spoiled, and will in short time be utterly consumed and worked'. So it was enacted that no new ironworks could be started except on the site of an already existing one, or by an ironmaster who could provide the necessary fuel for the ironworks entirely from timber growing on his own land, on pain of a fine of £300; and no one was to burn as fuel in an ironworks any oak, ash or elm tree which was one foot square or more at the stub. But the shortage of timber continued to be a serious problem until the use of coal for fuel became more widespread in the seventeenth century.

SCHOLARS AND DOCTORS

A T the beginning of the Tudor Age, England had the benefit of the educational system which the Church had maintained throughout the Middle Ages. There were grammar schools all over the kingdom. Many of them were attached to cathedrals and monasteries, but some were independent new foundations; William of Wykeham, the Bishop of Winchester and Lord Chancellor, had founded the school at Winchester in 1387, and Henry VI had founded Eton College in 1440. Later, towards the end of the Tudor Age, the school at Harrow was founded in 1571 by a benefactor from a humbler station in society, the local yeoman, John Lyon.

The purpose of the grammar schools was to give a good education to the more intelligent boys of the locality, including a few exceptionally gifted boys of the lower classes. Cardinal Pole was expressing the traditional attitude of the Catholic Church when he wrote in 1556 that the chief purpose of the grammar schools was to educate poor children; but already by the beginning of the Tudor Age an increasing proportion of the pupils were gentlemen's sons, and the tendency increased after the Reformation. The sons of the nobility, and of course royal Princes, were educated at home by a tutor. Girls were taught at special girls' schools attached to monasteries and nunneries. The great majority of children – the sons and daughters of the husbandmen and artisans – did not go to a grammar school; but though some of them received no education, many, and probably most, of them were educated at the ABC school in their parish, where a schoolmaster taught them the alphabet, simple arithmetic, and just enough Latin for them to learn the Lord's Prayer, the Ave and the Creed. The teacher at the ABC school was often the parish priest; but sometimes it was a less educated man who had applied for the post, and sometimes it was a woman.

After the invention of printing, which had originated in Germany and the Netherlands in the 1450s and had been introduced into England by William Caxton in 1477, children were taught to read at the ABC schools. The proportion of the labouring classes in England during the Tudor Age who could read and write was higher than is sometimes realized, especially after the Convocation of Canterbury in 1529 ordered every parish priest to teach the children in his parish to read and write. This is clear, not only from the number of political and religious tracts which were circulated, legally and illegally, by the contending religious factions, and by the efforts of the government to suppress them, but also by the legislation requiring the people to fill in written forms on so many occasions. Written certificates as to the size and ingredients of the goods offered for sale had to be attached to casks of wine and honey, and to bales of cloth; watermen on the Thames were required to carry a written document from 'the Overseers and Rulers of all the Wherrymen and Watermen', certifying their competence; and the Act of 1589, which tried to restrict the very prevalent crime of horse-stealing, compelled the Tolltaker or chief officer of any fair where a horse was sold to enter in a book the Christian name, surname and place of residence of the seller.

Girls, as well as boys, were taught to read and write. When Sir Thomas More was educating his daughters in the years after 1510, it was very unusual for girls to learn to read and write, like royal princesses and More's daughters; but ninety years later, Shakespeare did not think it necessary to give any explanation to his audiences as to why Rosalind and Celia in *As you like it*, Lady Macbeth, and the merry wives of Windsor could read the letters that they found and received, and why Olivia and Maria in *Twelfth Night* could write, though Malvolio mentions that Maria's letter was in a 'Roman hand'. He meant that it was written in our modern handwriting, the 'Italian hand' which was beginning to replace the Gothic handwriting which everyone in England had used before the middle of the sixteenth century.

Boys usually started studying at the grammar school at the age of seven, though Erasmus and some other educationalists thought that this was too late. According to the educational system which the Christian Church had taken over from the theorists of ancient Rome, they were taught first the *trivium* – the three subjects, grammar, dialectic and rhetoric – and at a more advanced stage the *quadrivium* – the four subjects of geometry, arithmetic, music and astronomy; but these classifications were widely interpreted. The boys were taught English grammar, Latin, to write compositions in prose and verse, some elementary ancient history, geography, simple arithmetic – all done with Roman numerals – and the calculations by which the Church calendar was ascertained; the elements of the philosophy of Aristotle, St Augustine, Anselm, and Thomas Aquinas; the rules of the plainsong of Church music; the theory of the harmony of numbers; the current theories of the medicinal value of the various plants and foods; and the movements of the celestial bodies, in an inseparable mixture of what we now call astronomy and astrology. They were not taught any French, for although princes learned to speak perfect French so that they could talk and write to

Erasmus. Portrait by
Quentin Matsys (1464–1530),
painted in 1517 and now in
the Galleria Nazionale in
Rome.

foreign sovereigns, it was very unusual for gentlemen, or even noblemen, to
understand French.

Many of the teachers in the schools, whether they were priests, monks, laymen or
women, were of a low calibre. Erasmus, who had his own theories about education
which he put forward in his book *De Pueris Instituendis* (On the Teaching of Boys) in
1529, thought that it was wrong that boys should be taught by women teachers,
because women were too cruel, and women teachers were often drunk. But he was
not too enthusiastic about monks as teachers, because, although they were usually
kind, their views were too narrow.

Erasmus was living in Basle when he wrote his book, but he had spent many years
in England, as well as in his native land, the Netherlands, and he did not restrict his

criticism of schoolteachers to any particular country, though he says at one point that the teachers in France were the worst of all. Two years after he wrote the book, the English courtier and diplomat, Sir Thomas Elyot, wrote *The Boke named the Governour*, in which he made much the same criticism of schoolmasters and their educational methods as those made by Erasmus. Both Elyot and Erasmus believed that the reason for the low standard of education was that school teachers were underpaid, and that because of this they had a low status in society, and the profession attracted an undesirable type of person.

Erasmus and Elyot were not the only modern-minded intellectuals who condemned the brutality of schoolmasters, and their excessive use of flogging as a punishment. The schoolmasters' attitude was in line with the tradition of the Church, which taught that to suffer pain, particularly by flagellation, was good for a person's soul, and helped him to enter Heaven: 'thou shalt strike him with a rod, and shalt thereby deliver his soul from Hell'. When distinguished men of letters like Sir Thomas More, as well as some priests and monks, whipped themselves for their own good, it is not surprising that schoolmasters believed that it was good for boys to be repeatedly whipped. Erasmus described the case of a boy of ten, who had recently come from the care of a loving mother to a school where the master was a priest. The priest falsely accused the boy of having committed some offence, whipped him till the boy fainted, and then said: 'The lad, of course, has done nothing to deserve all this, but it is necessary to curb his spirit by wholesome discipline.' Erasmus considered that this kind of schoolmaster had a very bad effect on the boys. 'The school is in effect a torture chamber,' he wrote, perhaps with a little exaggeration. 'Blows and shouts, sobs and howls fill the air. Then it is wondered that the growing boy hates learning, and that in riper years he hates it still.' He added that no master would ever beat his horse or his slave as unmercifully as schoolmasters beat the boys in their charge.

Elyot used less vivid language than Erasmus, but reached the same conclusion. 'By a cruel and irous master the wits of children be dulled, and that thing for the which children be oftentimes beaten is to them ever after fastidious, whereof we need no better author for witness than daily experience.' Cranmer's secretary, Morice, expressed the same point of view in the account of Cranmer's life that he wrote for John Foxe. He wrote that Cranmer told him that his father 'did set him to school with a marvellous severe and cruel schoolmaster, whose tyranny toward youth was such that as he thought the said schoolmaster so appalled, dulled and daunted the tender and fine wits of his scholars that they [more] commonly hated and abhorred good literature than favoured or embraced the same.' These comments show that cruel schoolmasters were a common phenomenon in the Tudor Age, and that the more advanced intellectuals were agreed in condemning them.

Erasmus pointed out that royal children would never be ill-treated by their tutors as ordinary children were by their schoolmasters; but princes and princesses were subjected to reasonable chastisement when they were naughty. This created a problem when Edward VI became King at the age of nine. Somerset and Cranmer, who always knelt to the boy when they spoke to him, were constantly emphasizing that an infant King was as absolute a ruler as an adult King and extolling the sanctity of the person of King Edward, the English infant Josias; and they could not contemplate the possibility of whipping the King when he misbehaved. So they invented the idea of having a whipping boy, and punishing another boy, whom the King liked very much, whenever the King did something wrong. The King would thus be deterred from being naughty, and would behave himself in order to spare his playmate from punishment.

Edward VI's whipping boy was Barnaby Fitzpatrick, the son of an Irish chief who had been sent to the English court as a hostage for his father's loyalty. He was rewarded for his sufferings by Edward's friendship, and by the knighthood which Edward conferred on him, though unfortunately for Sir Barnaby the King did not live long enough for him to reap the full benefit of their childhood friendship in grants of land.

At the end of Elizabeth's reign, a play by Samuel Rowley about Henry VIII, *When you see me, you know me*, was acted on the London stage. Edward and his whipping boy appear in a scene which was certainly intended to be farce, not tragedy, with Cranmer insisting on whipping Barnaby for the King's offences, and Edward promising to give the whipping boy a knighthood. He tells the whipping boy that none of the gentlemen knighted by Henry VIII had shed as much blood for their King as the whipping boy had for him. But Rowley got Barnaby's name wrong, and was almost certainly mistaken in thinking that Edward VI already had a whipping boy when he was Prince of Wales.

The suppression of the monasteries was a blow to education, for many of the grammar schools disappeared with the monasteries which had supported them. The nobles, gentlemen and speculators who acquired the monastic lands were sometimes moved by their consciences and by the exhortations of the clergy to continue to maintain the grammar schools which the monks had run; but in many cases the new owners merely used the land where the school had stood for their own profit. No one was more shocked at this than the Protestant divines who had called most loudly for the suppression of the monasteries, for one of their objections to monasteries was that money was given to monks to pray uselessly for the souls of the dead, who had already been predestined for either Heaven or Hell, when the money could have been put to a much better use in providing for education and other charitable work.

Even when the local gentry decided to continue to maintain a grammar school,

Sir Thomas More and his family (detail), painted by Rowland Lockey in 1592, a copy of Holbein's painting of the same group. In the part reproduced here Sir Thomas More (who had died in 1535) is sitting on the left. On his left, standing, is his son, and beyond, seated, are his three daughters.

The Royal Touch. The disease now called scrofula – tuberculosis of the lymph nodes at the side of the neck – was known as 'the King's Evil', and it was believed that it could be cured by a royal touch because of the holy oil with which the monarch was anointed at his or her coronation. In this miniature in the Library of Westminster Cathedral Queen Mary is shown exercising this gift they often excluded poor children from the school. Morice described to Foxe how Cranmer managed with difficulty to preserve the grammar school at Canterbury as a place of education for the sons of the poor after the great priory of Christchurch was suppressed in 1540. When the archbishop and a number of other commissioners met to decide the future of the school, Sir Anthony St Leger, Sir Richard Rich and another commissioner suggested that only gentlemen's sons should be admitted to the school; they thought that a son should follow his father's vocation, and that only gentlemen's sons should learn the knowledge of government; for there was as much need of ploughmen as of any other class, and not every man could go to school. Cranmer admitted that there was much truth in this, and that if a gentleman's son and a poor man's son were of equal ability, the gentleman's son should be preferred; but he said that poor men's children were often more studious than gentlemen's sons, and to exclude them completely from grammar schools would be to deny God's right to bestow His gifts wherever He would, and as presumptuous as setting up a Tower of Babylon [sic]. He thought that if this were done, God would punish gentlemen by making their children dolts.

A small proportion of grammar school boys went on to receive higher education in one of the two universities which had been established at Oxford and Cambridge in the thirteenth century, about four hundred years after universities had first appeared in Italy. Women were not admitted to the university till more than two hundred and fifty years after the end of the Tudor Age. The boys normally went there after seven years at the grammar school at the age of fourteen, but exceptionally clever children sometimes started earlier, including Thomas Wolsey, the brilliant son of an Ipswich butcher, who in 1484 went to Magdalen College at Oxford at the age of eleven.

The discipline was not so excessive in the universities as in the grammar schools, but the fourteen-year-old undergraduates were sometimes whipped for misconduct, and were not exempt from the punishment until they graduated, which they usually did after four years' study. The graduates continued to be under some degree of discipline at the university, for like everyone else in Tudor society they were required to obey the orders of their superiors in the hierarchy maintained by State and Church. Fellows of the university colleges were not allowed to marry, and had to resign their fellowships if they did; and university and college life was so closely associated with the Church, and so many university graduates were in holy orders, that it continued, even after the Reformation, in Elizabeth's reign, to be run in many ways along the lines of a monastery or a cathedral establishment.

The Chancellor of the University, with the Vice-Chancellor, the Proctors and their subordinate officers, had legal authority not only over the graduates and undergraduates of the university, but over the citizens of the towns of Oxford and

243

Cambridge, the inhabitants of the neighbouring villages, and travellers who passed through the town and area, including the English and foreign merchants who came to the great Stourbridge Fair which was held just outside Cambridge every year during the three weeks beginning on 18 September. This sometimes led to conflicts between the Chancellor of the University and the Mayor and corporation of Oxford and Cambridge, and to the antagonism between town and gown on which so many writers have commented throughout the centuries. But this was an uneven conflict, for the University held the upper hand, and nearly always won. The University had far more influence at court than the Mayor and corporation, for most of the Privy Councillors and other important courtiers were themselves university graduates.

The universities usually took the precaution of electing as their Chancellor one of the most powerful men at court; but in view of the fact that, under Henry VIII, Edward VI and Mary, the most powerful man at court was often denounced as a traitor a few years later, this meant that a succession of University Chancellors and High Stewards were arrested and executed for high treason. Sir Thomas More was High Steward of Oxford University; and at Cambridge, during the forty years between 1513 and 1553, the University had as its Chancellor Fisher, Cromwell, Gardiner, Somerset and Northumberland. Gardiner was the only one of these to escape with nothing worse than five years in prison; all the rest lost their heads on the scaffold. Statesmen and courtiers were more secure under Elizabeth I, and no harm befell Robert Dudley, Earl of Leicester, the Chancellor of Oxford University, or William Cecil, Lord Burghley, the Chancellor of Cambridge University.

At the beginning of the Tudor Age the literary Renaissance, which had started in Italy nearly fifty years earlier, had not yet reached England. It had hitherto been accepted that the study of divinity was by far the most important function of a university, though the canon law of the Church, the Roman civil law, and medicine were also considered suitable subjects to be taught there. The arrival of Greek scholars in Italy in the middle of the fifteenth century, which increased after the Turks captured Constantinople in 1453, made the intellectuals aware of an ancient pagan culture which was much richer than the pagan culture of ancient Rome which they could read in Latin. This led to the growth of the humanist movement; for in the fifteenth and sixteenth centuries, humanists were not people who were atheists or agnostics and opposed to Christianity, but Christians who believed that it was permissible to study the literature of the pagans of the ancient world as well as Christian divinity. The more conservative and narrow-minded churchmen opposed the humanists; but from the beginning the humanists had the support of the Popes, the Cardinals, the Kings, and the higher ranks of the establishment in Church and State all over Western Europe. It became a mark of culture and progress to learn the Greek language and to admire everything that was Greek.

Before the end of the fifteenth century, a handful of intellectuals at Oxford were eager to learn Greek, though they had to go to Italy to do so, as there was no one in England who could teach it to them. William Tully of Selling, the Prior of Christchurch, Canterbury, had learned Greek before he died in 1494. By 1500 William Grocyn, Thomas Linacre, William Lilly and William Latimer were leading Greek scholars, and within a few years Thomas More had joined them, and had become a close friend of Erasmus, who was the most eminent Greek scholar in the Netherlands. Cardinal Morton, Archbishop Warham, Wolsey and Henry VIII gave official encouragement to the humanists, and Fisher, despite all his duties as Bishop of Rochester, Chancellor of Cambridge University, and a member of the Privy Council, started to learn Greek himself when he was more than fifty years old.

In 1511, Erasmus came to Cambridge to give unofficial lectures in Greek. Richard Croke was appointed as the first official lecturer in Greek at Cambridge University in 1519, and he was followed there by Sir Thomas Smith, who later became one of the leading diplomats of Edward VI and Elizabeth I. In 1540, when Henry VIII created the five Regius Professorships at Cambridge in Divinity, Civil Law, Physic, Hebrew and Greek, Sir John Cheke became the Professor of Greek; and Roger Ascham, who was tutor to Henry VIII's children, was another leading Greek scholar. Unlike Croke, who was conservative and Catholic in religion, Smith, Cheke and Ascham were Protestants, though Cheke distressed his Protestant friends by recanting and becoming a Catholic in order to avoid being burned after he had been extradited from the Netherlands to England in Mary's reign.

Smith and Cheke were strong supporters of Erasmus's views on Greek pronunciation, for Erasmus had pointed out that the Greeks in the sixteenth century ignored the diphthongs in the pronunciation of the vowels which the ancient Greeks had used, and also pronounced some consonants differently. Erasmus's views were opposed by the German scholar, Reuchlin, and the correct pronunciation of Greek became a very controversial issue. When Cheke used Erasmus's pronunciation in his lectures at Cambridge after 1540, he gained a great deal of support from the undergraduates; but that arch-conservative, Stephen Gardiner, had been elected Chancellor of the University after Cromwell's fall. He supported the traditional pronunciation, and in 1542 issued an order as Chancellor of the University, forbidding anyone from using Erasmus's pronunciation, and announcing that any undergraduate who did so was to be whipped. This made the pronunciation of Greek a religious and political issue; and after the triumph of Protestantism under Elizabeth I, Erasmus's pronunciation was restored at Cambridge.

The study of law at the universities was confined to the canon law and Roman civil law, for the common law of England was taught and learned in the four Inns of Court in London. Neither the canon, the civil nor the common law were affected by the

Renaissance and the study of Greek, because the textbooks of ancient Rome, and the Codes of the Emperor Justinian of Constantinople in the sixth century after Christ, were written in Latin and were already known to English lawyers in the twelfth century; and in law, unlike literature and the arts, the ancient Romans had made a much more important contribution than the ancient Greeks. The English common lawyers were in conflict with the Court of Chancery, where the Lord Chancellor, with his system of equity, interfered with the common law of the Court of King's Bench, the Court of Common Pleas, and the Court of Exchequer; while the international 'law merchant', with its bills of exchange and negotiable instruments, was applied in the courts merchant which the merchants had established in London, Bristol and the chief commercial cities and ports.

After the disappearance of feudalism, sales of land increased, and this strengthened the influence of the common lawyers. By 1500, the more successful barristers of the Inns of Court were earning very large fees; when Thomas More was still a young man, he was earning £400 a year from his legal practice, at a time when the husbandman's wage was fixed at 16s.8d. a year. But barristers and solicitors were required to provide their services free of charge to the poorer litigants under a system of free legal aid which had been instituted by Henry VII. An Act of 1495 provided that any poor person who could not afford the cost of litigation could apply to the Lord Chancellor who, at his discretion, could allow the applicant to dispense with the payment of court fees and could order an attorney to act for him, and counsel to appear for him in court, without charging any fees.

The common lawyers increased their influence as well as their wealth during the Tudor Age. By the second half of the sixteenth century, barristers were playing a leading part in the House of Commons, and some of them were filling important positions in the Queen's service.

The study of medicine, unlike the study of law, was greatly affected by the humanist studies in Greek. Medicine had always been admitted as a proper subject of study and practice by the Church, for though disease was a punishment sent by God for our sins, for which the only real cure was prayer and repentance, there was no objection to a Christian trying to alleviate the consequences of disease by applying medical remedies; there was Scriptural authority for this, because Isaiah cured Hezekiah's boil by placing a lump of figs on it. From the earliest times the Christians had impressed even their pagan enemies by the care with which they tended their sick; but this consisted largely of loving tenderness and faith-healing based on a trust in Christ. Christians were often ignorant and suspicious of the physical remedies which had been prescribed by the pagan physicians of ancient Greece and Rome. This medieval Christian attitude contributed very little to medical knowledge, though it agrees with one trend in twentieth-century thinking in rejecting pills in favour of spiritual, or psychological, contentment and in placing great emphasis on the importance of a healthy and moderate diet.

During the Middle Ages the chief centre for the study of medicine was the University of Salerno in Italy, the oldest university in Europe, which had been founded in the ninth century. At the beginning of the Tudor Age, nearly every physician in England knew the principles of medicine which were laid down in a long Latin poem written by Salerno University to the King of England. There is some dispute about the origin of the poem, but it was probably written towards the end of the eleventh century to William the Conqueror, whose son, Duke Robert of Normandy, had studied for a short time at Salerno University on his way to the Holy Land. After the invention of printing it was often published in the original Latin; and though an English translation was not printed until 1607, it had probably already been translated and learned by heart in English by many doctors during the Tudor Age.

> The Salerne School doth by these lines impart
> All health to England's King, and doth advise
> From care his head to keep, from wrath his heart;
> Drink not much wine, sup light, and soon arise . . .
> Rise early in the morn, and straight remember
> With water cold to wash your hands and eyes,
> In gentle fashion, reaching every member.
> And to refresh your brain when as you rise,
> In heat, in cold, in July and December,
> Both comb your head, and rub your teeth likewise.
> If bled you have, keep cool; if bath'd, keep warm;
> If dined, to stand or walk will do no harm . . .
> Long sleep at afternoons, by stirring fumes,
> Breeds Sloth and Agues, Aching heads and rheums.

The poem goes on to describe the beneficial effect of eating eggs and other foods, and the harm that can be done to the eyesight by anything that over-stimulates it, like baths, leeks, onions, garlic, pepper, beans, lentils, bright sunshine, wind, tears, wine and women.

By the beginning of the sixteenth century, while the ordinary English medical practitioner was reciting the appropriate parts of this poem to his patients, the leaders of the profession were enthusiastically studying the works of Galen, the brilliant Greek physician from Pergamum (Bergama) near Smyrna, who had moved to Rome in A.D. 163 to become the physician of the Emperor Marcus Aurelius and the most fashionable doctor in the city. He had been accepted as an authority on medicine throughout the Middle Ages, partly because he believed that there was only one God, and the Church overlooked the fact that his religion was much closer to Judaism than to Christianity; but it was only after the Renaissance that some of his four hundred books which had not been lost became available in Western Europe. They were translated into Latin and published in 1490 in Venice, and the original Greek text was published there in 1525. Galen was regarded as the leading medical authority in England throughout the Tudor Age, though in Basle that audacious and arrogant innovator, Paracelsus, was telling his students in 1527 that his shoelaces knew more about medicine than Galen ever did.

Thomas Linacre was a striking example of the intellectual all-rounder who did so much to promote the Renaissance in England. He was born at Canterbury in about 1460, studied at Oxford, and became a diplomat in Henry VII's service. He later became court physician to the young King Henry VIII, and also took holy orders so that he could enjoy the revenues of several ecclesiastical benefices which he had been granted. But his chief interest was always the study of Greek. As a physician and a Hellenist, he was particularly interested in Galen's works; although he was the most eminent physician in England, he never wrote any book himself, but translated many of Galen's books into English.

Another all-rounder, the diplomat Sir Thomas Elyot, decided to follow up his book about education by writing another book on medicine and diet in English for the general reader. In *The Castel of Helth*, which was published in London in 1541, he constantly quoted Galen as the authority for his advice. In view of the progress that was made in medicine during the next four hundred years, and which is being made in every decade in the twentieth century, it seems extraordinary that the physicians in the Tudor Age should have accepted, as their most authoritative textbooks, the works which Galen had written fourteen hundred years before. It shows not only the state of sixteenth-century medicine, but the excessive veneration which the sixteenth-century intellectuals in all fields paid to anything that was Greek.

The leading English physician in the reign of Elizabeth I was her court physician, John Kaye, who thought it appropriate to Latinize his name to Caius. He followed his predecessors in worshipping Galen. The authority of Galen was not discarded until the fact that blood circulates, which completely disproved him, was discovered by the English physician, William Harvey, who was born at Folkestone in 1578 but did not make his discoveries until twenty years after the end of the Tudor Age.

But the Tudor physicians were forced to admit that Galen's books did not provide any remedy for the new diseases which caused such havoc in the sixteenth century. When Henry VII's army reached London in September 1485 after their victory at Bosworth, a hitherto unknown illness appeared, which became known as 'the sweating sickness', or 'the sweat'. It forced Henry VII to postpone his coronation till 30 October. This outbreak passed away quite quickly, but the sweating sickness returned from time to time, and with particular virulence in 1517, 1528 and 1551. In July 1517, four hundred people died in Oxford in one week; in some towns, one-third or even half of the inhabitants died. In 1528, two thousand died in London; and in July 1551, eight hundred died in London in a week.

The disease came on very suddenly. People who were feeling perfectly well were suddenly affected as they lay in bed, sat at the dinner table, or walked in the street. They sweated profusely, and were dead, sometimes within ten or twelve hours, and sometimes within four hours; 'some merry at dinner, and dead at supper', wrote the Tudor historian, Edward Hall. If they survived for twenty-four hours they were saved, and recovered very quickly. It was important that the patient should be neither too hot nor too cold; he should lie quietly in bed, well wrapped in warm blankets but in a room which was only moderately warm, with his arms crossed on his breast, in order to prevent the air from reaching his armpits. Although his fever made him very thirsty, it was important that he should not be given a cold drink, for those who drank anything always died. Women were much less likely to catch the sweat than men, though Henry VIII was being over-confident when he believed, during the epidemic of 1528, that Anne Boleyn would escape the infection which had appeared in her household; she caught the sweat, but quickly recovered.

Henry, who was always afraid of catching infectious diseases, went to great trouble in 1528 to avoid the sweating sickness; leaving the immediate vicinity of London, he retreated to a tower at Hunsdon in Hertfordshire with only one servant in attendance. One of his secretaries, Brian Tuke, caught the sweat, but, unlike most of the other victims, he did not panic. He was convinced that psychological factors played an important part in catching the disease, for the sweating sickness was known throughout Europe as 'the King of England's disease', and only Englishmen caught it; while it was raging among the English population of Calais,* not a single case was reported a few miles away at Gravelines, although merchants were continually travelling between the two towns. But when someone with the sweat came from Sussex to London, and this became known, a thousand people in London fell ill that same night, though children never caught it, unless their parents had told them about it. Tuke duly recovered quickly from the sweat; and the French ambassador in London, Jean du Bellay, noticed that, despite all that people said about the sweating sickness, only two thousand people had died of it in London, although forty thousand people had caught it.

---

* After the conquest of Calais in 1347, most of the French population left, and by the sixteenth century nearly all the inhabitants of Calais were the descendants of English settlers.

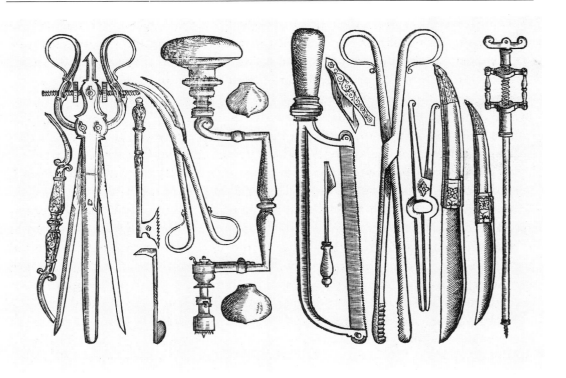

Surgical instruments of the sixteenth century, illustrated in *A Profitable and Necessarie Book of Observations* by William Clowes, 1585.

Although the English in the Tudor Age spoke so much about the sweating sickness, the plague claimed many more victims. There were several outbreaks of plague in Henry VIII's reign; but the worst visitation was in 1563, when it was brought back to England by the English troops who returned from the disastrous expedition to Le Havre in support of the French Protestants. Between June 1563 and June 1564, 17,046 people died in London, which was about one in six of the inhabitants, as the population was probably about 100,000. The plague returned on several occasions during Elizabeth's reign, though nothing on the same scale recurred until the summer of 1603, a few months after Elizabeth's death, when 38,000 people died in London – about the same proportion as in 1563–4, for by 1603 the population of London had increased to about 200,000.

There was no cure for the plague except to allow the people to die and to take strict measures to segregate those who had caught it or had come into contact with it. During the outbreak of 1563, the houses where cases occurred were required by law to be marked by blue crosses on white paper and the words 'Lord, have mercy upon us', and all the doors and windows of the house were to remain closed for forty days.

When Henry VIII visited Calais in 1532, orders were given that all sufferers were to be taken out of their houses and carried to a field outside the town and left to die there, so that there should be no risk of them infecting the King. This was sometimes done in other towns, even when the King was not coming.

There were other new diseases which suddenly appeared in Europe during the Tudor Age. The first cases of syphilis occurred when the French army occupied Naples in 1494, though there were national disagreements about its origin; the French called it 'the Italian disease', and the Italians called it 'the French disease'. It had become very prevalent in every country in Europe by the middle of the sixteenth century, particularly among the upper classes; many people at the French court were infected, including King Francis I. No one suggested until the nineteenth century that Henry VIII's ulcers were a symptom of syphilis. It is very unlikely that he caught it, because, apart from his wives, he had only two mistresses who could have infected him; if any of them did, it was probably Anne Boleyn's sister Mary, who, according to Francis I, had been the most immoral woman at his court when she spent some years there before she returned to England to become the mistress of Henry VIII.

Smallpox and measles were new diseases, and both were very serious. Elizabeth I nearly died of smallpox in 1562. Mary Queen of Scots' husband, Darnley, fell ill with measles in 1567; but he was well on his way to recovery when he was assassinated as he fled from his sick bed at Kirk-o'-Field after the house had been blown up by gunpowder.

The emphasis of the Tudor physicians was on diet. Elyot distinguished between persons with hot stomachs, who have little appetite and like warm food, and those with cold stomachs, who have big appetites and enjoy eating large quantities of cold foods. He prescribed the right sort of vegetables and other dishes which should be eaten during the four seasons of the year – in winter, which lasts from 8 November to 8 February; in spring, from 8 February to 8 May; in summer, from 8 May to 8 August; and in autumn, from 8 August to 8 November.* He advises his readers to avoid excessive eating and drinking at all times.

The disease of scrofula – tuberculosis of the lymph nodes at the side of the neck with ulceration of the overlying skin – was known as 'the King's evil', because both physicians and the people believed that it could be cured if the sufferer was touched by the King, who was supposed to have acquired this healing power through the holy oil with which he was anointed at his coronation. All the Tudor sovereigns

---

* Elyot was writing in 1541, when the Julian calendar was in force throughout Western and Central Europe. It was ten days behind our modern Gregorian calendar, which was adopted in the Catholic countries in 1582 but not in England till 1752. The dates which Elyot gives for the duration of the seasons are, in terms of our calendar, 18 November, 18 February, 18 May and 18 August.

touched thousands of people to cure them from scrofula, and the practice continued after the Reformation and throughout the seventeenth century until the days of Queen Anne.

The most common cure for many diseases was blood-letting, which was adopted on religious as well as on medical grounds. Not only did physicians believe that diseases could be cured by getting rid of bad blood – a doctrine which had been duly approved by Galen – but monks believed that a man could rid himself of his sins by ejecting the evil ingredients in his blood. This was probably the origin of the occupation of barber-surgeon. It seems strange in the twentieth century to combine the professions of a surgeon and a hairdresser; but barbers were regularly employed in monasteries to cut the hair and shave the heads of the monks in order to give them a clerical tonsure, and on these occasions the monks would often ask the barber to bleed them so as to get rid of their sins with the bad blood. Bleeding was carried out either by venupuncture, from a vein, or by placing leeches on the naked body of the patient.

The distinction between physicians and barber-surgeons, which in a very different form still exists today between physicians and surgeons, derived from the intellectual approach of the physicians of the Tudor Age. The physicians did, of course, take personal care of their patients; but as almost the only cures which they could suggest were virtuous living and good diet, their approach was largely theoretical. They therefore spent much more time writing books than attending to patients, when they were not studying Greek, or performing the ecclesiastical and diplomatic duties which they so often combined with their medical practice. The barber-surgeons were not intellectuals, but practical men, who, without knowing Greek, or ever writing, or even reading, a book, set fractures and healed wounds in the traditional way which they had been taught by their predecessors and had picked up by practical experience. Their services were higly valued, particularly by the army in wartime, but they were not considered to be the social equals of the physicians.

The barber-surgeons were forced to carry out their surgical operations with methods which horrify those of us who are fortunate enough to live in the twentieth century. They pulled out teeth with tongs, straightened fractures by sheer physical strength, and amputated legs and arms, in all cases without any kind of anaesthetic, while the patient was given a good dose of alcohol and was held down by the surgeon's assistants. Wounds were cauterized by applying a burning iron or boiling oil to the wound. English surgeons in the Tudor Age continued to apply this method to the wounds of soldiers, or to criminals who had had a hand or an ear cut off as a judicial punishment, for more than fifty years after the great French surgeon, Amboise Paré – who wrote his books on surgery in French because he could not speak Latin – had discovered, to his surprise, during the French campaign in Italy in

Unauthorized medical practitioners. A woodcut from *A Profitable and Necessarie Book of Observations* by William Clowes, 1585.

1536, that the wounded soldiers recovered more quickly when he had no instruments available with which to cauterize their wounds, and therefore merely washed and bandaged them.

Child delivery was carried out by midwives, who were trained and supervised by surgeons. Babies were sometimes delivered by Caesarean operations. This was widely believed to have occurred when Jane Seymour gave birth to Edward VI. The popular ballad *The Death of Queen Jane* was probably being sung very soon afterwards, though the earliest written record of it dates from the seventeenth century. In the song, Jane says to the surgeon: 'Rip open my two sides, and save my baby'; but in fact Edward VI was almost certainly born by natural process, and Jane died twelve days later from septicaemia, like so many other mothers during the Tudor Age.

In the reign of Henry VIII, steps were taken to control the practice of medicine by both physicians and surgeons. Thanks to Linacre's influence with the King, an Act of Parliament was passed in 1512 which forbade anyone to practise as either a physician or a surgeon within seven miles of the city of London without a licence from the Bishop of London or the Dean of St Paul's, which was only to be granted after the applicant had been examined by four doctors of physic. It was also forbidden to practise as a physician or surgeon outside the London area without a licence from the diocesan bishop, but this did not apply to graduates of Oxford or Cambridge

Universities. In 1540 the authority of the College of Physicians was extended over apothecaries; no apothecary was permitted to sell any drug which had not been approved by four members of the Fellowship of Physicians, on pain of a fine of a hundred shillings for each offence.

It was also in 1540 that an apparently contradictory statute was passed which on the one hand united the Company of Barbers and the Company of Surgeons in the Company of Barber-Surgeons, but also for the first time separated the two occupations. Parliament was worried because barber-surgeons sometimes caught 'pestilence, great pox [syphilis] and such other contagious infections' from their patients, and then passed on the infection to their customers when they shaved them and washed their hair. So the statute enacted that no barber could practise as a surgeon, and no surgeon could practise as a barber. All surgeons practising within a mile of the city of London were required to display a sign in the street outside their surgeries so that the public should know where to find them. Surgeons were to be exempt from the obligation to wear armour when serving in the army in wartime. The Company of Barber-Surgeons was to be allowed to have four bodies of executed criminals every year for them to dissect for the study of anatomy, which had been revived at the beginning of the sixteenth century under the inspiration of Leonardo da Vinci. The Act was to be enforced by four Masters or Governors of the Company of Barber-Surgeons, of whom two were to be surgeons and two were to be barbers.

But, as so often with Tudor legislation, there were lobbies and counter-lobbies at work to influence Parliament, and a statute which proclaimed the need to prevent unskilled practitioners from taking advantage of the public and lowering professional standards was often followed by another statute which denounced the governing body of a profession for furthering its professional interests to the detriment of the public welfare. The Acts of 1512 and 1540 were followed by a statute of 1545, which accused the Company of Barber-Surgeons of 'minding only their own lucres and not having the profit or ease of the diseased or patient' in mind. The surgeons had 'sued, troubled and vexed divers honest persons, as well men as women, whom God hath endued with the knowledge of the nature, kind and operation of certain herbs, roots and waters', and who had used these herbs to cure sore breasts in women, a pin or web in the eye, corns on the hands, burns, sore mouths, stone, or other ailments, although these herbalists had taken no remuneration for their efforts and had helped poor people 'only for neighbourhood and God's sake of pity and charity'. This was contrasted with the attitude of the surgeons, for 'it is now well known that surgeons admitted will do no cure to any person but where they shall know to be rewarded with a greater sum or reward than the cure extendeth unto; for in case they would minister their cunning to sore people unrewarded, there should not so many rot and perish to death for lack of help of surgery as daily do'.

After more denunciations of the iniquity and incompetence of surgeons, the Act authorized all persons with experience of herbal cures, or of drinks which would remedy the stone, to administer them to the poor without being harassed by the surgeons.

It was fortunate for the inhabitants of London that the Act of 1545 made it possible for these herbalists to help them, for they were indeed suffering and dying from neglect; but Parliament, in blaming the greed of the surgeons, had not dared to mention the true cause. The suppression of the monasteries and religious establishments had harmed hospitals as much as grammar schools. In 1545 Henry VIII suppressed chantries, hospitals and mental institutions which had been founded by charitable benefactors; he did this ostensibly for religious reasons, but really as an excuse to raise money to pay for his war against France. The sick and the mentally ill were turned out of the hospitals and left to roam the streets, unless they were conscripted into the army, or helped by the charity of philanthropists. As in the case of schools, the harm was slightly mitigated by the more public-spirited members of the Privy Council and the leading bishops, especially after Henry's death, though the seizure of religious property continued in the reign of Edward VI.

In November 1552 Nicholas Ridley, the Bishop of London, wrote to Sir William Cecil, the Secretary of State, about the plight of the homeless in London.

> Good Master Cecil, I must be a suitor to you, in our good Master Christ's cause; I beseech you be good to him. The matter is, Sir, alas, he hath lain too long abroad, as you know, without lodging, in the streets of London, both hungry, naked and cold. Now, thanks be to Almighty God, the citizens are willing to refresh him, and to give him both meat and drink, clothing and firing; but alas, Sir, they lack lodging for him. For in some one house I dare say they are fain to lodge three families under one roof.

Ridley and the Lord Mayor of London, Sir George Barnes, persuaded Edward VI to open two hospitals in London, St Thomas's in Southwark and St Bartholomew's in Smithfield; to give his empty palace of Bridewell as a house of correction for vagabonds and harlots; and to open Christ's Hospital as a grammar school. A number of grammar schools in other parts of England were founded in the reign of Edward VI, though there is some truth in Professor R.H. Tawney's statement that 'King Edward VI's Grammar Schools are the schools which King Edward VI did not destroy'; and the physician and historian, Sir Arthur MacNalty, has estimated that it took two hundred and fifty years before the hospital accommodation in London was restored to the position which existed before Henry VIII's expropriations in 1545.

SHIPS AND VOYAGES

IN the sixteenth century, the English were protected by their navy from the full impact of continental wars. The Tudor Age began with a successful foreign invasion of England, when Henry Tudor led his French, Breton and Scottish soldiers to victory at Bosworth; and England was threatened by invasion on several occasions during the next hundred years. Perkin Warbeck on two occasions landed in England with a foreign force. The Scots invaded the North of England in 1497, 1513 and 1542. The French burned Brighton in 1514 and Seaford in 1545. There was a false invasion scare in 1539, and two very real invasion threats in 1545 and 1588. But on every occasion the danger passed; the invaders were either defeated, or withdrew before they were driven out. The chain of fortresses which Henry VIII built along the south coast from Deal and Walmer to Hurst and Portland were never put to the test, because the English navy always held the mastery of the 'Narrow Seas' (the Straits of Dover) and the Channel, as it had done since the days of Edward III in the fourteenth century.

The English in the Tudor Age travelled a great deal by water, both on the rivers and at sea. There were obvious advantages in this, when the roads were so bad and slow. In London, people used the barges to cross the Thames, as there were no bridges between London Bridge and Kingston; and it was easier to go from Greenwich or Westminster to Richmond and Hampton Court by barge than by horse overland. The wealthier people had their private barges and their private stairs and landing places; the ordinary Londoner travelled by public barge. This was not always satisfactory. Barges were sometimes unsafe, and watermen inexperienced; and the authorities were a little suspicious of those individualists who did not wish to serve a master, but preferred to be self-employed as watermen, especially as they often went into hiding to avoid being pressed into service in the navy in wartime.

Philip and Mary's Parliament passed an Act in 1555 to control watermen. The Mayor and Aldermen of London, at their first meeting every year, were to appoint eight Overseers and Rulers of all the Wherrymen and Watermen who rowed on the

The Thames below Tower Bridge. Detail from Visscher's panorama of the River Thames, published in 1618 but probably engraved several years earlier.

River of Thames between Gravesend and Windsor. In any barge with two oarsmen, at least one of them had to have a certificate from the Overseers that he was 'a sufficient and able waterman'; and no unmarried man who was neither the master of a household nor employed by some master was to row for hire on this stretch of the river unless he had been apprenticed to a waterman for at least one year. Every barge carrying passengers for hire had to be at least twenty-two and a half feet long and four and a half feet broad in the midship, and be able to carry safely two passengers sitting on either side; and no barge could be used to carry passengers unless it had been inspected by the Overseers and Rulers, who were also required to fix the fares which the watermen were entitled to charge for the various stages between Gravesend and Windsor. A waterman who failed to comply with these requirements could be fined, imprisoned and have his barge forfeited.

Barges also operated on the other major rivers; and the government encouraged the development of new inland waterways. The most ambitious project, which was begun in 1571, was to build a new river so 'that the River of Lee otherwise called Ware River might be brought within the land to the north part of the said city of

London'. The Lord Mayor of London and the sheriffs and JPs of Middlesex, Essex and Hertfordshire were to have power to requisition land up to sixty feet on both sides of the new river, and were to appoint sixteen commissioners, four from London, four from Middlesex, four from Essex and four from Hertfordshire, to supervise the construction of the new river, along which all the Queen's subjects were to have the right to travel. But the commissioners could not raise the necessary money, and almost nothing was done for forty years, until they sold their rights in 1609 to an enterprising businessman in the City of London, Hugh Myddelton. He developed the new river, not for navigation, but to improve London's water supply. The New River, retaining its original name, continues to provide drinking water for Londoners in 1988.

The Tudor Parliaments planned other ventures to create new waterways and conduits, passing Acts to dredge, and keep clear for navigation, the Thames, the Severn, and the 'River of Exeter', and to bring water to Gloucester, Poole and Plymouth.* The efforts of Sir William Bowyer, the Lord Mayor of London, to bring water to the city from 'divers great and plentiful springs at Hampstead Heath, Marylebone, Hackney, Muswell Hill' and other places within five miles of London, culminated in an Act of Parliament of 1543; and a plan was sanctioned by Parliament in 1585 to build a harbour on the sea at Chichester and a canal one and a half miles long to link it to the city of Chichester. In all these cases, the authorities who were appointed to administer the projects were given power to acquire the necessary land by compulsory purchase, with reasonable compensation to be paid to the landowners.

Travel by sea was always uncertain and risky for, apart from the danger from pirates, the sailors and travellers were at the mercy of the winds until steamships replaced sailing ships in the nineteenth century. With a favourable wind, travel by sea could be faster than by road; but the sailing ships could be delayed for many days by contrary winds or by absence of wind. When Henry VIII and his army crossed the Narrow Seas to launch an invasion of France from Calais in 1513, the three hundred ships sailed from Dover at 4 p.m. on 30 June, on a cloudless summer day, and arrived at Calais at 7 p.m.; but Gardiner and Edward Fox had a very different experience when they made the same crossing in February 1528, having been sent by Wolsey on an important, urgent and arduous winter's journey to Orvieto in order to persuade the Pope to grant Henry VIII an annulment of his marriage to Catherine of Aragon.

Gardiner and Fox set out from Westminster and reached Dover late in the evening of Tuesday 11 February. They sailed for Calais next morning; but when they were

* See the statutes, respectively, of 1536, 1543, 1539, 1542, 1543 and 1585.

Henry VIII embarking at Dover in 1520 (detail) on his way to Calais for a meeting with Francis I of France on the Field of Cloth-of-Gold. Henry can be seen in the stern of the ship in the centre, which was presumably his flagship, the *Henry Grâce à Dieu*, popularly known as the *Great Harry*.

Sir Francis Drake (?1540–96), seafarer, explorer, and Vice-Admiral. Painting by Marcus Gheeraerts the Younger, 1591.

half way across, the wind turned against them, and they were forced to return to Dover. They sailed again on the Thursday morning, but were again blown back, and waited at Dover for another thirty-six hours until they seized their opportunity of a favourable wind and sailed at 2 a.m. on the Saturday morning. But when they were in mid-Channel, the wind dropped completely, and they stayed there becalmed, or drifting very slowly, all day Saturday and half of Saturday night, until at 2 a.m. on Sunday they found that they were within four miles of Calais. Then a tremendous tempest arose, the greatest that the mariners had ever seen. The ship's captain decided to anchor, but this proved to be impossible, and they were driven by the gale on to the coast of Flanders, though for a long time they were unable to land. Eventually Gardiner and Fox and two of their servants managed to land in the ship's boat, within a quarter of a mile of Gravelines, leaving their other servants and the ship's crew on board the ship, which was blown into Dunkirk harbour and badly damaged in entering the port. Gardiner and Fox had been for two days and two nights without food and had been very seasick; and their horses, when they were eventually landed from the ship at Dunkirk, were too ill to travel; but Gardiner and Fox managed to hire other horses in Gravelines and rode to Calais, where they arrived at 8 p.m. on Sunday, four and a half days after they had first sailed from Dover.

The winter gales caused the greatest difficulties, and changed the course of history in December 1559 and January 1560 when Elizabeth I sent a fleet to Scotland to help the Scottish Protestant revolutionaries, while the government of the Duke of Guise in France wished to send reinforcements for the French garrison that was holding Leith for Mary Queen of Scots and her mother, Mary of Guise. Elizabeth's sea-captain, William Winter, sailed with fourteen ships to the Forth, leaving Gillingham at 9 a.m. on 27 December. He arrived off Harwich at 3.30 that afternoon, and next morning sailed at 10 a.m. and anchored in Yarmouth Roads at 4 p.m.; but then the wind changed, and he waited off Yarmouth for a week, where his ships were badly battered by the gale. Winter decided to return to Harwich to have some of them repaired; but the winds made it impossible for them to get further south than Dunwich, and after staying at sea for two days and nights they were back at Yarmouth on 13 January. Next day they sailed north, but when they reached Flamborough Head after a nineteen-hour journey they were driven back to the Humber, and could not get north of Flamborough Head until 5 p.m. on 16 January. There they encountered a tempest. They lost all their boats and some of the ships were scattered; but the rest of the ships managed to continue their journey and reached Bamborough Castle at 4 p.m. on 18 January and Eyemouth at 11 a.m. on 20 January.

Winter finally entered the Forth with eleven of his fourteen ships on 23 January, twenty-seven days after leaving Gillingham; but the French had run into even greater difficulties than he had done. Sailing from Le Havre and Calais, they came within sight of Scotland, but were then driven back by the gales and had to return to France. The French garrison at Leith, deprived of reinforcements, was forced to surrender after a four-month siege to the troops that Elizabeth had sent by land from Berwick. By the Treaty of Edinburgh of 6 July 1560, the French agreed to withdraw from Scotland, which became a Protestant state and passed from the French into the English orbit of influence.

The great uncertainty about the duration of a sea-voyage made it difficult to calculate the amount of food which should be taken in the ship. The general rule adopted in the English navy was that if the carcass of one bullock was taken for every member of the crew for a four-month voyage, this was ordinarily enough to cover emergencies; but as the meat had to be salted, and it was impossible to preserve fruit or fresh vegetables for a long journey, the men fell ill from scurvy and other diseases, which were responsible for many of the deaths which occurred among the crews.

The ships which made these hazardous voyages in the sixteenth century seem very small to us, in the twentieth century, when there are battleships and aircraft carriers of more than 50,000 tons. When Henry VII became King, he decided to build the most powerful navy in Europe. He already had four excellent warships which had been built for Edward IV and Richard III, but in 1490 he built two ships which were larger than any which had previously been known, and which made a great impression on his contemporaries at home and abroad. The *Regent* was 1,000 tons, and carried 225 small guns, the serpentines, which were not capable of sinking an enemy ship, but could shatter her rigging and rake her decks. The *Sovereign* was only a little smaller than the *Regent*, and both were substantially bigger than the French ships, the *Grande Louise* and the *Cordelière*, of 790 and 700 tons, which had hitherto been the largest ships in Europe. The *Regent* and the *Sovereign*, like the two French ships, had three masts, instead of the one or two masts which had been usual until the end of the fifteenth century.

The *Regent* was sunk in the attack on Brest in 1512 at the outbreak of Henry VIII's first war against France; but Henry replaced it with an even larger ship which was launched his presence at Erith in 1514. It was officially named the *Henry Grâce à Dieu*, but was usually referred to as the *Great Harry*. It was 1,500 tons, with four masts, with topgallant sails on three of them, and carried 184 guns of varying calibres. A year later, Henry attended the launching of another warship at Woolwich, accompanied by Catherine of Aragon and his sister Mary the French Queen, who had just married the Duke of Suffolk. Mary named the ship the *Virgin Mary*, but soon everyone was calling her the *Mary Rose*. She was smaller than the *Great Harry*, being 400 tons, but had 120 oars and could carry 1,000 soldiers; and her 207 guns were so powerful that the Venetian ambassador believed that no town in the world could

The *Henry Grâce-à-Dieu*, generally known as the *Great Harry*, a watercolour drawing from the same series as that of the *Mary Rose* on pages 270–271.

withstand their fire-power. The ambassador described how Henry greatly enjoyed himself at the launching. He was dressed in a doublet of gold brocade, and in scarlet hose, and repeatedly blew on a captain's whistle a yard long which was hanging from a thick gold chain around his neck.

During his last war against France, Henry VIII bought three more warships, the *Jesus of Lubeck*, the *Murrian*, and the *Struse of Dawske* (Danzig), of 700, 500 and 450 tons. When the French were preparing to invade England with 40,000 men in the summer of 1545, Henry had a fleet of eighty ships at Portsmouth which were ready to meet the enemy. On 19 July he dined in the *Mary Rose*. Suddenly the French appeared off Portsmouth, and the *Mary Rose* went into action against them. The French had already retreated, and the *Mary Rose* was on the point of returning to harbour, when

Originally built for Sir Walter Raleigh and named the *Ark Raleigh*, this ship was sold for £5000 to the Queen's Navy and renamed the *Ark Royal*. It became the English flagship, which was commanded by Lord Howard of Effingham against the Armada in 1588.

she capsized and sank with the loss of all but thirty of her crew of five hundred. Henry was eager to raise the ship, so that he could use her guns again, and employed some Italian experts to do the work; but after three unsuccessful attempts, the project was abandoned, and the *Mary Rose* was not raised until 1982. The *Great Harry* survived for a few more years, but was accidentally burned in 1553.

Elizabeth I, who was more economical and less ostentatious than her father, never built a ship as large as the *Great Harry*. Her largest ship was the *Triumph* of 1,100 tons, which was built in 1561, when the *Jesus of Lubeck* was still in service. Twenty-six years later, Sir Walter Raleigh built a ship of 800 tons, which he intended to name the *Ark Raleigh*; but while she was still on the stocks he sold her in 1587 to Elizabeth I for £5,000, and the name was changed to the *Ark Royal*. She was Lord Howard of Effingham's flagship in the battle against the Armada.

But the sailors who travelled to unknown lands at the farthest ends of the earth sailed in much smaller ships. At the beginning of the Tudor Age, no one in Europe had been to the American continent or further south along the coast of Africa than the mouth of the Congo river. Then in 1488 the Portuguese captain, Bartolomé Diaz, sailed round the Cape of Good Hope. In February 1489 the Genoese seaman, Christopher Columbus, wrote to Henry VII and asked him to finance an expedition to find a western route across the Atlantic to Asia. But Henry refused, and it was from Spain that Columbus sailed in 1492 on the voyage that took him to Cuba and to discover the New World of the American continent. In 1497 the Portuguese Vasco da Gama sailed around the Cape of Good Hope to India.

The Venetian sailor, Giovanni Caboto, had for many years been trading with England, and had bought a house in Bristol, where he anglicized his name to John Cabot. In his youth he had been to Mecca and had seen the wares which Arab merchants had brought there from China and Eastern Asia; and he believed that it would be possible to sail west from England across the Atlantic and reach China that way. It would thus be possible to open up a profitable trade route between Western Europe and China, for goods could be carried more cheaply by sea than by the long land journey through Asia Minor and the Ottoman Empire; and he had been told by a Portuguese sailor that the coast of China was only a few hundred miles west of Ireland. He took some time to persuade Henry VII to authorize his expedition, but Henry eventually agreed, and granted letters patent to Cabot and his son Sebastian and his two other sons, after Cabot had promised to give him twenty per cent of all the profits that he made from his voyage.

Cabot sailed from Bristol on 2 May 1497 with a crew of eighteen sailors. At 5 a.m. on 24 June he sighted an island off the coast of Newfoundland and named it St John's Island because it was the Feast of St John the Baptist. He claimed the territory on behalf of Henry VII, and returned to Bristol convinced that he had reached China. He set off on another voyage next year with the intention of getting to Japan, and sailed north from Newfoundland, entering Baffin Bay and sailing along the coast of Greenland as far north as $67\frac{1}{2}°$. He died soon after his return to England, but his son Sebastian Cabot carried on, undertaking many voyages on behalf of the English, Spanish and Venetian governments, including a voyage to Brazil and the River Plate for Charles V in 1526. The English did not engage in any further discoveries in America during the reign of Henry VIII, but English fishermen went every year to Newfoundland to catch fish.

In 1521 a Portuguese expedition under Magellan sailed round the world, by South America through the Straits of Magellan, across the Pacific to the Philippines, and back to Lisbon by the Cape of Good Hope. This voyage fascinated explorers all over Europe, and stimulated speculation about the existence of a North-west Passage and a North-east Passage. The philosophical theory of 'harmony' made the men of the sixteenth century believe that if there was a South-west Passage from Europe to Asia by the Straits of Magellan and Cape Horn, and a South-east Passage by the Cape of

Good Hope, there must also be a North-west Passage to the west of Greenland and a North-east Passage to the north of Norway.

In 1576 a Yorkshire seaman, Martin Frobisher, persuaded the Earl of Warwick to finance his expedition to find the North-west Passage. He was encouraged by Elizabeth I, for it was believed that in the north-west regions there was a hitherto unknown substance, which they called 'black earth', which could be turned into gold by alchemists. He sailed from Blackwall in the Thames with a crew of thirty-five men in three ships, the largest of which was 25 tons. He reached the coast of Labrador, but did not get as far north as the Cabots had done seventy-eight years before; and the black earth which he brought back with him turned out to be merely iron-pyrites. He made two more expeditions in 1577 and 1578, but was equally unsuccessful. John Davis from Devon tried to find the North-west Passage in 1585, and again in the next two years. At his third attempt, in 1587, he reached 73°N in Baffin Bay, where he was stopped by ice; but he believed that he had found the North-west Passage to China. Both Frobisher and Davis served against the Armada. Frobisher died in 1594 from wounds received in fighting the Spaniards in Brittany. Davis was killed by Japanese pirates near Sumatra in 1605.

The attempt to find a North-east Passage led to more profitable results. In the reign of Edward VI, old Sebastian Cabot, who was nearly eighty, planned an expedition with the support of merchants of the City of London, though Cabot was too old to go on the voyage himself. Three ships under the command of Sir Hugh Willoughby and Richard Chancellor sailed from London, where their expedition had aroused great interest, in May 1553; but adverse winds prevented them from getting any further than Harwich. After a month the wind changed, and they sailed to the north of Norway, but off the Lofoten Islands they were separated by gales. One ship, under Willoughby, was wrecked on the coast of Lapland, where Willoughby and his men died, probably of cold, in January 1554. Chancellor and the other two ships entered the White Sea, and reached the harbour, near the monasteries of St Michael and St Nicholas, where the town of Archangel was built thirty years later. Chancellor travelled to Moscow, where he was received by the young Tsar, Ivan the Terrible, and friendly diplomatic relations were established between England and Russia. After returning safely to England, Chancellor made another voyage to St Nicholas and Moscow; but on the return journey, he was shipwrecked and drowned off the coast of Aberdeenshire in 1556.

His voyages and contacts in Moscow interested some English merchants, and a Muscovy Company was formed to develop trade with Russia. The Company sent to Russia an enterprising traveller, Anthony Jenkinson, who before he was twenty had been to North Africa, Aleppo, and many other places in the Eastern Mediterranean. In 1558 he sailed to St Nicholas and was granted permission by the Tsar to open an

English House, as a trading centre, in the town of Kholmogory on the River Dvina, about sixty miles from St Nicholas. From his base at Kholmogory he travelled up the Dvina to Vologda, which was a much longer distance than the overland route but easier and safer. From Vologda he proceeded overland to Moscow, where he established excellent relations with Ivan the Terrible. On one occasion he dined in private with the Tsar, sitting opposite him at a table which was only a little lower than Ivan's.

The Muscovy Company was interested in the possibility of developing trade, not only with Russia but also with Persia, hoping, with the Tsar's goodwill, to bring goods from Persia through Russia. After Jenkinson returned to England, the Company interested Elizabeth I in the idea, and Jenkinson set off again for Russia, carrying letters from Elizabeth to Ivan the Terrible and to 'the Sophy', as the English called the Shah of Persia. Under the Russian calendar the years were dated, not from the birth of Christ, but from the beginning of the world; and Elizabeth's letters to Ivan and the Shah were 'dated in our famous city of London the 25 day of the month of April in the year of the creation of the world 5523 and of our Lord Jesus Christ 1561 and of our reign the third'. Both the letters were written in Latin.

Jenkinson sailed from Gravesend with the letters on 14 May 1561. He reached St Nicholas on 14 July, Vologda on 8 August, and Moscow on 20 August. He stayed there for some months while Ivan and the Persian ambassador in Moscow made arrangements for his journey to Persia, and left Moscow with the Persian ambassador on 27 April 1562, travelling by water down the Volga to Astrakhan, where they arrived on 10 June. But Jenkinson then ran into difficulties. He went to Bokhara and established friendly relations with Abdullah Khan, the King of Khiva; but because of wars in the region he was unable to get to Persia, and had to return to Moscow. He made another attempt to reach Persia, and was eventually received in audience by the Shah at Kazvin in 1564; but the Shah and his ministers were unfriendly, and Jenkinson thought he had been lucky to leave Persia alive.

But thanks to Jenkinson's excellent relations with Ivan, the trading prospects for English merchants in Russia appeared to be very hopeful, and in 1568 Elizabeth decided to send one of her ablest and most experienced diplomats, Thomas Randolph, to Moscow. Randolph had spent several years as her ambassador in Edinburgh at the court of Mary Queen of Scots, and had played a very important part in the intrigues and revolutions which had overthrown Mary and established her son, the infant James VI, as King in her place. His selection for the mission to Russia shows the importance which Elizabeth attached to it.

Randolph sailed from Harwich on 22 June 1568, and reached St Nicholas on 23 July, where he noted, like a good Protestant, that 'the apparel of the monks is superstitious, as ours have been', and that 'their Church is fair, but full of painted images, tapers and candles'. Randolph followed the usual route which Jenkinson had taken, to Kholmogory, then by water up the Dvina to Vologda, and overland from there to Moscow. His seven-hundred-mile journey up the Dvina took five weeks, for his barge had to be pulled by hand for most of the way. He found excellent inns between Vologda and Moscow, and was impressed when he crossed the Volga at Yaroslavl to see that it was a mile wide.

When he reached Moscow at the end of September, he was annoyed and disturbed to find that he was confined in a house as a virtual prisoner for five months. During this time he and his retinue were lavishly supplied with food and drink, but they were not admitted to the Tsar's presence or allowed to see or communicate with either Ivan's ministers or with the English merchants in Moscow. When the Tsar at last agreed to see him in February 1569, he was very friendly. Randolph was very satisfied when he left for England at the end of April. Travelling again by Vologda, he embarked at St Nicholas at the end of July, and reached London in September.

But relations between England and Russia were sensitive. Ivan was very offended by Elizabeth's refusal of his offer of marriage to her lady-in-waiting, Lady Mary Hastings; the English diplomats resented the attitude of the Russians, who seemed to regard all foreign sovereigns, including Elizabeth, as being the Tsar's inferiors; and the representatives of the Hansa merchants in Russia tried to influence the Russian officials against their English commercial competitors. At one time Ivan turned against Jenkinson, who feared for his safety in Moscow; but he persuaded Ivan that the whole trouble had been caused by the tactlessness of the Russian ambassador in England and of some ignorant Englishmen in Moscow; and thanks entirely to Jenkinson's ability, good relations were re-established. Ivan came to trust the English in Moscow so much that he appointed their physician, Dr Mark Ridley, who was a cousin of the bishop and martyr, Nicholas Ridley, to be his own personal physician.

The English merchants of the Muscovy Company, with their English Houses in Moscow and Kholmogory, succeeded in establishing trade between Astrakhan and London along the Russian rivers and by sea from St Nicholas, though there were many cases of friction between the Russians and the English diplomats in Moscow during the following years. Relations worsened after Ivan the Terrible's death, but improved again when Boris Godunov became Tsar. As for Jenkinson, he returned to England, and lived quietly in Northamptonshire till he died, aged over eighty, in 1611.

The English people were very interested in the travels and adventures of their seamen and traders. Richard Hakluyt, an Oxford scholar, collected the reports which the travellers had written and in 1589 published them in his book *The Principall Navigations, Voyages, Traffiques and Discoveries of the English Nation Made by Sea or Over-*

ANN°. DÑI 1581.   ÆTATIS SVÆ 44.

Sr John Hawkins

Sir John Hawkins (1532–95), a kinsman of Drake, was a member of a family among the first to open an English trade with the Guinea Coast. He became Treasurer of the Navy and commanded *The Victory* against the Spanish Armada. This portrait by an unknown artist is dated 1581.

the ship

Gonnepowder Shotte of yzo

The *Mary Rose*, sister ship to Henry VIII's flag
Anthony Roll, a series of drawings of

hotte of Stey.
nd Leide

Bowes Bowestynge
Arrowes Morbys pycke
Byllys Daert for toppi

Great Harry, a watercolour drawing from the
eet made by a nautical draughtsman.

Sir Martin Frobisher (c.1537–94), painted by Cornelius Ketel in 1577 after Frobisher's return from the second of his three Arctic voyages. He is wearing a sailor's cord round his neck, with a whistle attached, which became known later as a boatswain's call. Frobisher was vice-admiral during Drake's expedition in 1585–6, and was captain of the *Triumph* in the Armada campaign, when he was knighted on board the flagship by the lord admiral.

land to the Remote and Farthest Distant Quarters of the Earth at any time within the compasse of these 1600 Yeeres. He included the accounts of the travellers in Muscovy; but the readers' chief interest was in the adventures of their seamen who had challenged the power of the Spaniards on the 'Spanish Main', the Western Atlantic and the Caribbean.

In 1562 the Plymouth sailor, John Hawkins, sailed to Guinea on the coast of West Africa to participate in the slave trade in competition with Spanish, Portuguese and French traders. The traders kidnapped young blacks in Guinea, but acquired most of their victims by buying from the native chiefs the prisoners whom the chiefs had captured in wars with other native tribes. They carried the prisoners across the Atlantic and sold them as slaves in the Spanish colonies in the West Indies, for the Spanish settlers there had discovered that blacks from Africa were physically stronger, and could work harder and longer, than the native inhabitants who had lived in the West Indies before the Spaniards arrived.

Hawkins and his kinsman, Francis Drake, and other seamen from Devon made several expeditions to Guinea to take slaves to the West Indies, although the Spanish slave-traders claimed to have a monopoly of the trade. The English slave-traders were no more inhibited by moral scruples from engaging in the trade than were their Spanish, Portuguese and French competitors. Slavery was a well-known feature in sixteenth-century Europe. Apart from the few cases of slavery in England, any Christian soldier or sailor who fell into the hands of the Turks or the Moors was likely to be kept as a slave if he was not killed by his captors; and the Spaniards enslaved the Moslem prisoners whom they captured in their wars in the Mediterranean and North Africa. They could justify their action in taking blacks from Africa to the West Indies as slaves on the grounds that the blacks were thus introduced to the doctrines of Christianity, which alone could save their immortal souls, apart from the fact that many of them would probably have been killed by their native captors if the European traders had not persuaded the captors to sell them as slaves. Hawkins was so far from having a guilty conscience about engaging in the slave trade that when he was granted a coat-of-arms, he chose as his crest the figure of a black man bound in chains.

The conflicts between Englishmen and Spaniards over the slave trade led to friction in the Caribbean, and this became worse as the relations between Elizabeth I and Phillip II deteriorated after 1568. When English volunteers were fighting for the Dutch against the Spaniards in the Netherlands, and Spanish volunteers were fighting for the Irish against the English in Ireland, Elizabeth agreed to allow English sailors to wage their private war against the Spaniards on the Spanish Main, where Drake and his colleagues seized Spanish ships at sea and sometimes raided Spanish towns on the mainland of Central America.

In 1577 Drake set out on his voyage around the world, a journey which no one had accomplished except Magellan nearly sixty years before. As with all the expeditions by Elizabethan seamen, a consortium of influential courtiers put up the money and obtained letters of marque from the Queen in return for her receiving a share in the spoils of their voyage. These letters of marque made the seamen, in international law, privateers and not pirates, which was of very little use to them if they fell into enemy hands, but at least protected them against lawsuits in the English courts.

After going to some lengths to deceive the Spaniards into thinking that he was intending to go to Guinea or the Mediterranean, Drake sailed from Plymouth on 13 December 1577 with 164 men in five ships; the largest of them, his flagship the *Golden Hind*, was 100 tons. He went to Brazil, and south along the east coast of South America, and through the Straits of Magellan into the Pacific. He was then able to sail north, raiding the Spanish towns on the west coast, for as the Spaniards did not expect the English to enter the Pacific, all their warships were in the Atlantic, and could not reach Drake without sailing through the Straits of Magellan or around Cape Horn, for there was no other way to go by sea from the Atlantic to the Pacific until the Panama Canal was built in 1902.

Drake sailed up the west coast at least as far north as what is now San Fransisco and perhaps beyond Vancouver to some point on the coast of the modern British Columbia in Canada. He then crossed the Pacific, sailing for sixty-eight days without sight of land, and returned by the Cape of Good Hope to England, landing at Plymouth on 26 September 1580 after a voyage of nearly three years. Only fifty-seven of his crew of 164 survived the journey; but he had brought back gold and jewels worth £600,000 from an expedition which had cost £5,000, and gave every member of the syndicate which financed it a profit of £47 for every £1 which he had invested. The Queen's share of the proceeds persuaded her to ignore the protests of the Spanish ambassador about Drake's acts of piracy during the voyage.

Drake's example was followed six years later by another English sailor, Thomas Cavendish, who between 1586 and 1588 led the third expedition, and the second English expedition, to sail round the world. Drake himself continued his raids on Spanish shipping; in 1586 he looted and burned Cartagena, in the Gulf of Darien in South America, which was the richest city in the New World. His exploit made him a hero to the Protestants and a devil to the Catholics throughout Europe; when his portrait was displayed in a shop window in Ferrara, crowds gathered in the street to gaze at the features of 'the great English corsair'. Every enterprising young Englishman longed to follow his example and win riches and glory on the Spanish Main. The courtier, sailor, soldier, poet and historian Sir Walter Raleigh decided to lead a voyage of exploration himself, and in 1595 sailed to South America and up the River Orinoco.

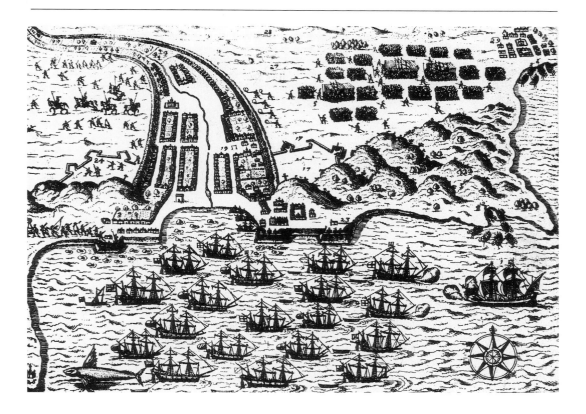

Santiago, chief port of the Cape Verde Islands, was captured by Drake almost without a shot being fired. For ten days the town was scoured for provisions and finally it was burnt and left desolate.

Drake's successes were the decisive factor which finally persuaded Philip II to send an expedition to conquer England, in response to the appeals from the English Catholic refugees that he should liberate their native country from the tyranny of the heretic Queen. His nephew, the Duke of Parma, who commanded the Spanish forces in the Netherlands, was to cross the sea with his army and land near Margate, from where he could march on London. But Parma had only galleys, and no larger warships, in the ports of the Netherlands. When Philip informed him of his plan, Parma offered to take his army across to Margate in the galleys, as there were no English warships in the North Sea; but by January 1588 the English and their Dutch allies had stationed a fleet off the coast of the Netherlands; and Parma told Philip that it would no longer be possible for his galleys to cross to Margate, or even to leave port, except under the protection of a powerful Spanish fleet. So Philip decided to send a large Armada, under the command of the Duke of Medina Sidonia, to sail from Spain up the Channel to the Netherlands to escort Parma's 18,000 soldiers to Margate.

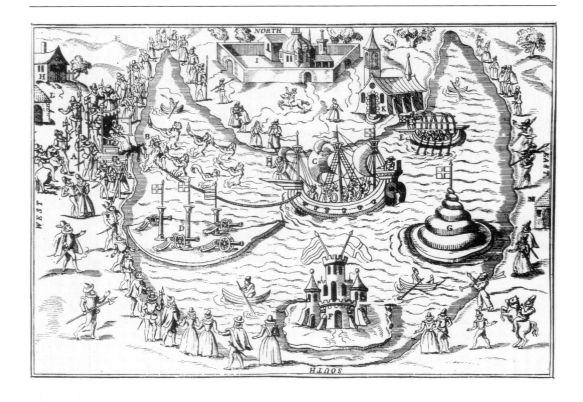

The defences of London were improved in 1588 by an Italian engineer, Giambelli, who also invented the fireships which were used so successfully off Calais.

But Philip committed an extraordinary lapse, which certainly contributed, at least to some extent, to the defeat of the Armada. Although Parma repeatedly wrote to him that it would be impossible for his galleys to leave port except under the protection of the Armada, Philip either did not appreciate this, or for some reason did not clearly explain it to Sidonia. His instructions to Sidonia were to sail to Margate and meet Parma at a place to be agreed between them. Sidonia did not realize that Parma's troops and galleys would not leave Dunkirk and Sluys unless he went there to fetch them and escort them to Margate.

On 30 May 1588 (20 May by the English Old Style calendar) the Armada sailed from Lisbon, which had been an important Spanish port since Philip II's conquest of Portugal in 1580; but the fleet was scattered by storms, and forced to take shelter at Corunna, and it was not until 22 July that the Armada left Corunna, heading for Margate and the link-up with Parma. There were 130 ships in the Armada, carrying 19,000 soldiers and 8,000 sailors; the total number on board, including the

276

Charles Howard, Lord
Effingham and Earl of
Nottingham (1536–1624).
Painting by Daniel Mytens,
c.1620.

administrative and medical staff and the priests, was 30,693. Most of the English
ships were at Plymouth, though some of them were helping the Dutch navy to
blockade Parma in the ports of the Netherlands. The total English force consisted of
197 ships. Most of them were smaller than the Spanish ships, though no ship in the
Armada was as large as Frobisher's ship, the *Triumph*, of 1,100 tons. Some of the
English ships were only 35 tons. The English had better manoeuvrability and

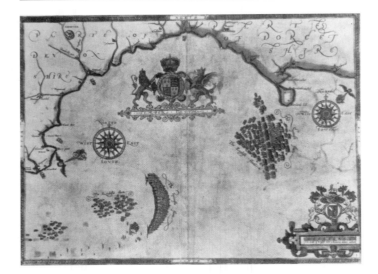

This is one of a series of charts of the First Armada engagement, engraved by Augustine Ryther after plates drawn by Robert Adams to illustrate Ubaldino's *Expeditionis Hispanorum*, 1588. This chart shows the arrival of the Spanish fleet off the Lizard at 4 p.m. on Friday 19 July (29 July, New Style).

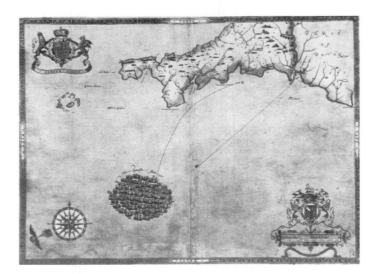

The English fleet engages the Spanish fleet off Dodman Point, Cornwall, having left Plymouth, tacked along the coast, and got to windward.

superior fire-power, for Sir John Hawkins, at the Admiralty, had overhauled and modernized the navy in recent years. The English cannon had longer range, and prevented the Spaniards from pursuing their usual tactic of coming alongside the enemy ships, throwing grappling hooks to hold them, and boarding them in order to fight hand-to-hand on the decks; and events proved that the English guns were also superior in close-range bombardment.

The Commander-in-Chief of the English navy was Lord Howard of Effingham in

The English squadrons harrying the crescent of the Spanish fleet passing the Isle of Wight on Thursday 25 July (4 August, New Style).

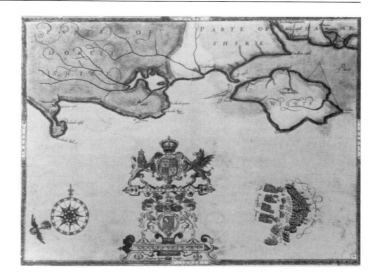

The defeat of the Armada off Gravelines, Flanders, on Monday 29 July (8 August, New Style).

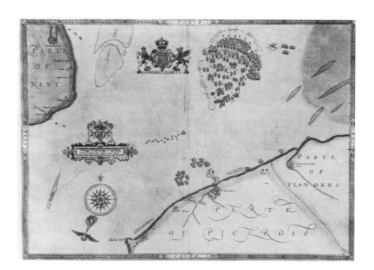

his ship the *Ark Royal*. Drake had become a national hero after his expedition to the West Indies in 1585–6, but only a nobleman could hold the office of Lord Admiral and command the navy, and there would have been endless friction with the other naval commanders if Drake had been appointed as supreme commander. Drake, in the *Revenge*, was a Vice-Admiral under Lord Howard.

The Armada was sighted off The Lizard on the afternoon of 29 July (19 July Old Style), and the first engagement with the English fleet took place off Plymouth on 31

July. As there was hardly any wind in the fine summer weather, the Spanish ships sailed very slowly eastwards up the Channel, pursued by the English and fighting a running battle with them during the next five days. At this time an incident took place which shows the nature of naval warfare in the Tudor Age. Lord Howard ordered Drake to lead the English fleet in pursuit of the Armada during the night of 31 July, and to place a lantern at the poop of the *Revenge* to show the other ships where to go. But Drake saw some ships on the starboard side which he thought might be some Spanish ships trying to turn behind the English fleet; so he extinguished the lantern and went to investigate. He discovered that the ships were German merchantmen which had nothing to do with the Armada; but he then encountered one of the most valuable ships in the Armada, the *Rosario*, and captured her and her booty. Modern historians have condemned Drake for disobeying the orders of his Commander-in-Chief, which in later centuries would probably have resulted in Drake being court-martialled; but neither Howard nor any of the other officers complained of his conduct, except that Frobisher was annoyed that Drake had taken more than his fair share of the prize money.

After five days' fighting, the Spaniards had lost only three ships, and the English had been unable to prevent the others from proceeding as far as Calais. But Sidonia did not know where he was to meet Parma, though he had sent several messengers by sea to Bruges in an attempt to contact Parma and find out about the meeting place. He therefore decided to anchor in Calais Roads, and to wait there till he heard from Parma.

On 7 August (28 July Old Style) Lord Howard, Drake, Winter and the other English naval commanders held a Council of War and decided to attack the Armada that night with fireships. Eight burning ships were sent to be driven by the wind into the Spanish fleet as it lay at anchor in Calais Roads. The Spaniards had been afraid of fireships ever since Drake had used them in his attack on Cadiz fifteen months before, and many of the sailors panicked, and weighed anchor. Seeing this, Sidonia ordered the whole fleet to weigh anchor, and a gale arose and scattered the Spanish ships. They fought a battle off Gravelines with the English fleet, in which the English had much the better of the exchange of cannon fire, chiefly because the Spaniards were short of ammunition; and the gale drove the Armada north, up the east coast of England. Many ships were lost, and many Spaniards were drowned off the coasts of Zeeland and Friesland. The English pursued the Spaniards as far north as Newcastle, but by that time, like the Spaniards, they had used up their ammunition, and turned back. After the remaining Spanish ships had rounded the north of Scotland, more of them were wrecked on the Irish coast, and the survivors who landed were massacred by the English garrisons, in one case after they had surrendered on a promise that their lives would be spared. Only sixty-seven of the 130 ships returned to Spain.

Robert Dudley, Earl of Leicester, a painting attributed to Sir William Segar, c. 1585, three years before Leicester's death at the age of fifty-six.

Sir Richard Grenville (1541–91) commanded *The Revenge* off the Azores in 1591.

While the Armada was sailing up the Channel, the English government was making preparations to defend the Queen and realm if Parma landed. An army of 22,000 men was assembled at Tilbury, under Leicester's command, ready to meet Parma if he arrived, as the English expected, on the Essex coast; and a bridge of boats was built across the Thames between Tilbury and Gravesend across which the army could march if Parma landed in Kent. Leicester persuaded Elizabeth to visit the troops, and she spent two days at Tilbury on 8 and 9 August (Old Style). By this time, the danger was past, as the shattered remnants of the Armada were already north of the Forth; but the English could not be sure of this.

On the second day, Elizabeth addressed the army, and probably made the speech which has come down to us as her 'Tilbury speech'. A poet who was present, and said that he heard her words, included a different version of them, in verse, in a poem about the Armada which he published a few weeks later; but thirty-five years afterwards the Earl of Essex's chaplain, who had been at Tilbury with the Queen, sent a copy of her speech to the Duke of Buckingham. It seems to have been either the draft of the speech written by a speech-writer, or a note taken down immediately after the speech with a view to publishing it as an official report, although in fact this was never done. It probably approximates very closely to the words which she spoke that day.

For Elizabeth, the defeat of the Armada was marred by a personal tragedy. Leicester, whom she would have married twenty-eight years earlier if this had been politically possible, died of a disease at the age of fifty-six, only twenty-seven days after she had been with him at Tilbury. A few days before, he had written to her asking a favour for an old servant. She wrote on the letter 'His last letter', and kept it in a chest in her bedchamber till the day of her death.

The victory over the Armada saved England from invasion, but it did not end the war, which continued with varying success for the remaining fifteen years of the Tudor Age. The English expedition to Portugal in 1589, which was largely financed by a private consortium, was a disaster; for too few of the Portuguese rose in revolt against the Spaniards, and Drake, because of faulty intelligence, missed the opportunity of destroying the Spanish fleet at Santander. The battle at the Azores in 1591 was also unsuccessful, though the heroism of Sir Richard Grenville, and his fight in the *Revenge* against fifty-three Spanish ships, won the admiration of the people of England. These defeats were more than avenged by the burning of Cadiz in 1596 and the victory at Kinsale in 1602 over the Spanish forces in Ireland; but the war dragged on until James I, to the disgust of many of his English subjects, made peace with Spain in 1604.

LAW-ENFORCEMENT AND WAR

FROM a twentieth-century point of view, one of the contradictions of Tudor society is that laws were constantly being made and directives issued by the government which interfered with every aspect of the lives of English men and women to an extent which even a modern totalitarian state has never attempted, while at the same time there was hardly a trace of the bureaucracy, of the hordes of civil servants, secret policemen and army officers and soldiers who have been a feature of nearly every state in the nineteenth and twentieth centuries. The Tudor monarchy was a despotism, but it was a despotism run very much on the cheap, and largely by unpaid but enthusiastic amateurs.

There were a small number of secretaries and clerks who accompanied the King as he moved from Greenwich to Westminster and from Richmond to Hampton Court, and when he went further afield to Windsor and Grafton during his summer progress; and there were other secretaries and clerks who stayed and worked in Westminster. Under Henry VII and Henry VIII, many of the leading members of the secretariat and government were churchmen, like Wolsey, Gardiner, Ruthall, Pace, Vannes and Edward Fox; but from the beginning of the Tudor Age, some of the most influential of them were common lawyers and other laymen of comparatively low rank, like Henry VII's ministers, Edmund Dudley, who was a simple Sussex gentleman, and his colleague, Richard Empson, a Northamptonshire man of lower rank. After 1530, an increasing number of these higher government officials were laymen, and under Elizabeth I there were hardly any churchmen left. Many of the secretaries in the last years of Henry VIII and under Edward VI were prominent intellectuals, like the poet Thomas Wyatt, the Regius Professors of Civil Law and Greek, Thomas Smith and John Cheke, and the authors Thomas Elyot and William Thomas.

These secretaries and courtiers usually attached themselves to some influential nobleman at court, under the system which was known as 'faction'. There is nothing

284

Sir Thomas Wyatt (1503–42), diplomat, courtier and poet, was believed to have been Anne Boleyn's lover before her marriage to Henry VIII. He was for a time imprisoned in the Tower on charges of treason. A drawing by Hans Holbein the Younger in the Royal Library at Windsor.

Tho: Wiatt Knight.

mysterious or particularly Tudor about faction, which has existed, and still exists today, in civil service departments, in large commercial organizations, and in many office buildings. It is the system by which the most powerful men in an organization engage in a struggle for power and position with each other, while their subordinates tend, for reasons of personal affection, loyalty and self-interest, to attach themselves to one or other of these leaders, and rise and fall with him. The sixteenth-century preachers and writers, including Shakespeare, were always condemning faction, and glorifying the ideal courtier and royal servant who thought of nothing except rendering loyal service to his master, the King; but that shrewd and experienced politician, William Cecil, Lord Burghley, advised his son that if he wished to advance at court, it was essential that he should attach himself to some powerful nobleman and win his patronage; and Shakespeare and everyone else knew that in practice most people at court supported some faction.

If an official in the King's service found that the leader of his faction had been arrested as a traitor, he tried to join the faction of the man who had supplanted his former leader. Under Henry VIII, whenever a leading courtier was arrested as a traitor, the other courtiers wrote to the King and the new favourite, denouncing the fallen minister in the most violent language and asking to be rewarded for their services by a grant of part of the traitor's lands when they were forfeited to the King after his trial and conviction. There was no time to lose, for there were always plenty of other courtiers hoping to get their share of the traitor's lands; so people wrote, staking their claims, as soon as they heard of the arrest, and long before the fallen minister had been convicted, or even charged, with high treason. Often the traitor's son and other members of the family joined in these denunciations in the hopes that the King would remit the forfeiture and restore the traitor's lands to his family. The traitor himself probably approved of his family's attitude, hoping that something would be saved by their action.

Local government was administered by the sheriff of the county, by the mayors in the cities and boroughs, by the JPs in the shires, and by the parish bailiffs and constables and the officers of the watch. The sheriff was appointed by the King. He was always one of the most prominent gentlemen of the county. There was a sheriff in most of the counties of England, but there were a few counties which had to share a sheriff with a neighbouring county. Surrey and Sussex shared a sheriff; so did Essex and Hertfordshire, Somerset and Dorset, Warwickshire and Leicestershire, Nottinghamshire and Derbyshire, and Oxfordshire and Berkshire. In 1566 a statute was passed which explained that this was because, in the past, these counties 'were not then so well inhabited with gentlemen of good ability to serve in the said office as (thanks be to God) they be at this present'. The Act enacted that henceforth each of these counties should have its own sheriff; but this had to be modified by a new Act in 1571 which provided that Surrey and Sussex should once again share a sheriff. By this time another officer had been appointed to increase the control of the central government in the counties. After 1550 it became the practice to appoint a Lord Lieutenant in every county, with precedence over the sheriff, for the Lord Lieutenant was a nobleman and the sheriff a knight or a gentleman.

The sheriff was responsible for arresting criminals and holding them in custody in the county jail; and an Act of 1504 enacted that the sheriff should pay a fine if a prisoner escaped because of his negligence. The fine was to be at least £40 if the prisoner who escaped was accused of high treason, £20 if he was accused of petty treason or murder, and £10 if he was accused of any other felony; but the JPs could impose a higher fine if they thought fit.

The general public were required to help in catching fugitives from justice; whenever the JPs proclaimed the hue and cry, every inhabitant in the parish was expected to turn out to find the criminal. If a felony was committed in any parish and the perpetrator was not found, all the householders in the parish were liable to a fine. This was a great hardship to the people of Burnham in Berkshire, for the roads from London to Henley-on-Thames and from London to Reading ran for three miles through the parish, and through the woodland that was called 'The Thicket'. Thieves often hid in the Thicket and attacked and robbed the travellers as they passed along these two busy highways; but how could the poor husbandmen of the villages and hamlets in Burnham, who were working in the fields, prevent these robberies? especially as the travellers who were robbed did not usually report the thefts until they reached the town of Maidenhead, and the authorities at Maidenhead often forgot to pass on the information to the bailiffs and constables of Burnham. After the inhabitants of Burnham had had to pay fines for not catching the thieves, amounting to £255 in the course of a single year, a statute of 1597 relieved them from their liability to pay the fine if the theft had not been immediately reported to them. Parliament also modified the rigour of the law for all parishes in England by enacting in 1585 that if several criminals were involved in a crime, the parish where it was committed could avoid being fined even if only one of the criminals was arrested.

From time to time, the government adopted another method of inducing large numbers of the population to participate in upholding the law. When Henry VIII divorced Catherine of Aragon and married Anne Boleyn, an Act of Parliament was passed in 1534 which obliged everyone, when asked, to take an oath that he believed that the children of the King's marriage to Anne Boleyn would be the lawful heirs to the throne. Anyone who refused to take the oath when required to do so could be sentenced to imprisonment for life. The oath was put to everyone in authority; the Privy Councillors, after taking the oath themselves, administered it to the sheriffs; the sheriffs administered it to the JPs; and the JPs to the masters of households in their district, who were supposed to administer it to all their family and servants who were over fourteen years of age. There are no surviving records of exactly how many people took the oath, but we know that it was administered to 7,342 people in the first three months alone, and a substantial proportion of the population must have taken it.

Next year, another Act required everyone, if asked, to swear an oath that he believed that the King was Supreme Head on earth of the Church of England; and as another Act made it high treason to deny the King's right to any of his titles, anyone who refused to take the oath could be executed as a traitor. The Oath of Supremacy was not administered to the general public, but only to holders of offices. A handful of people, like Fisher, More and the Carthusian monks, refused to take the oath, and were executed as traitors; but nearly everyone to whom it was administered agreed to take it.

In Elizabeth I's reign, everyone in a position of authority was required to take a new Oath of Supremacy, by which he swore that he believed the Queen to be the Supreme Governor of the Church of England. No one could hold any official position, or any ecclesiastical benefice, sit in Parliament, or practise as a lawyer, unless he was prepared to take the oath; and a refusal to swear, when asked to do so, was punishable by death as high treason for the second offence. This practice of making the people swear an oath was an effective way of enforcing compliance with government policy, because the people were taught, and believed, that a man committed a mortal sin and endangered his soul if he swore a false oath, although the Pope was prepared to grant a dispensation allowing people to swear a false oath which they were forced to take under duress, if, before they took it, they made a secret protestation that they did not intend to be bound by the oath that they were about to take.

Despite the lack of an effective system of law enforcement, the law-abiding majority of the English people ensured that order was maintained in general in nearly all the shires in the realm. At the beginning of the Tudor Age, there were two exceptions: in Wales and parts of Northumberland, the government was unable to enforce its authority. The Council of the Marches of Wales, which sat at Ludlow under the presidency of the Bishop of Coventry and Lichfield, was quite unsuccessful in suppressing crime in Wales; but the situation was largely remedied by the legislation of 1536. Wales was divided into counties on the English model which continued in existence until 1974, and a number of Welsh gentlemen were persuaded to act as local JPs, although the new laws abolished the Welsh law of inheritance and banned the use of the Welsh language in the law courts and on all official occasions. Measures were also taken to control the river traffic across the Severn in order to stop criminals from escaping into Wales and Welshmen from crossing into England to commit crimes in Gloucestershire and Somerset. By an Act of 1535 any ferryman at the passages of Aust, Framilode, Purton, Arlingham, Newnham or Portishead or at any other ferry across the Severn between England and South Wales, was prohibited from carrying any person, cattle or goods in his ferry at night, between the hours of sunset and sunrise; and he was not to carry any traveller at any time unless he knew who he was, and was able to tell the authorities his name and address if he were asked to do so.

The situation was not so easily remedied in Northumberland as in Wales. Along the northern and southern banks of the Tyne there was complete lawlessness, for Tynedale and Redesdale were what would today be called 'no-go' areas'. The family loyalties and feuds made it impossible to find local gentlemen who were prepared to act as JPs and administer the local government, as in the other counties of England; and although the English and Scottish robbers on both sides of the Border often raided and fought each other, they were also usually prepared to shelter the robbers of the other nation who escaped across the frontier whenever the English or Scottish authorities took action against them. The Lord Warden of the Eastern Marches at Berwick periodically sent men-at-arms into Tynedale and Redesdale to arrest notorious outlaws, and occasionally succeeded in catching them. But it was only once or twice in a decade that a leading criminal from these districts was brought to Newcastle, put on trial, and hanged.

Henry VII tried to remedy the situation by an Act of Parliament of 1495. The Act stated that the murders and felonies committed by the criminals in North and South Tynedale, and their collaboration with the Scots, were endangering the safety of the King's subjects in Northumberland, Cumberland, Westmorland, Hexhamshire, the bishopric of Durham, and parts of Yorkshire. It enacted that any landowner who let his land to a new tenant was to find two other landowners who owned land worth £20 a year, who would stand surety for the good behaviour of the new tenant; if the land was let without these sureties, the landlord was to be fined forty shillings per acre and the tenant was to be imprisoned for a month. But this Act proved quite ineffective, and lawlessness in Tynedale and Redesdale was worse in the sixteenth century than at any other time before or since.

The government of Elizabeth I made another attempt to deal with the lawlessness in Tynedale and Redesdale in an 'Act for the more peaceable government of the parts of Cumberland, Northumberland, Westmorland and Durham' in 1601, because many of the inhabitants of these counties had been kidnapped, sometimes from their homes and sometimes when they were travelling on the highway, and held as prisoners until a ransom had been paid for their release; and there were also many cases in which inhabitants of the Border region, 'being men of name', threatened to burn villages, houses, barns or corn unless they were paid money 'commonly there called by the name of blackmail'. Yet these criminals 'ordinarily resort and come to markets, fairs and other public assemblies and meetings and do there converse, traffic and trade with other Her Majesty's subjects'. So the statute enacted that these offences should be felonies punishable by death. Whenever one of these crimes was committed in these counties, the names of the criminals who had perpetrated them were to be proclaimed and read out once every six weeks in Carlisle, Penrith and Cockermouth in Cumberland, in Appleby and Kendal in Westmorland, in Newcastle-upon-Tyne in the county of Newcastle-upon-Tyne, in Morpeth, Alnwick and Hexham in Northumberland, in the city of Durham, in Darlington, Bishop Auckland and Barnard Castle in the bishopric of Durham, and in the town of Berwick-upon-Tweed. They were also to be proclaimed at every fair held in any of these places. Anyone who should 'relieve, entertain or confer' with a proclaimed outlaw, or who did not 'do his best endeavour to take and arrest' him, was to be imprisoned for six months, and not released until he had found two sureties who were prepared to be responsible for his good behaviour for a year.

But all the efforts of Wolsey, Henry VIII, and Elizabeth I and her ministers to enforce the royal authority were unsuccessful. Tynedale and Redesdale remained lawless throughout the Tudor Age until the union of the crowns of England and Scotland under a Stuart King made it possible at last for the royal authority to be enforced on both sides of the Border.

Although the rest of England was normally law-abiding, there were occasionally serious riots, like the attack on aliens in London during the 'Evil May Day' riots in 1517; and there were eight rebellions against the government during the Tudor Age. In 1497, at the time when Perkin Warbeck was periodically landing somewhere in England and trying unsuccessfully to persuade the people to rise in his support, the Cornishmen revolted against the taxes which Henry VII had imposed on them, and marched on London. They got as far as Blackheath before they were defeated and dispersed. Henry contented himself with executing three of the ringleaders, and did not punish the others.

In October 1536, a revolt broke out in Lincolnshire against the dissolution of the monasteries and against the lower-class politicians – the 'villein blood' – in the Privy Council, especially Thomas Cromwell, and the 'heretic bishops'. It had petered out within a few days, but not before it had spread to Yorkshire, where there was a far more serious insurrection under the leadership of the noblemen and gentlemen of the county. By the end of November, 40,000 rebels, armed with pikes, were at Doncaster, ready to cross the Trent and march south. Henry VIII's general, the Duke of Norfolk, had only 7,000 troops with which to oppose them; and the dry autumn had caused the water level in the Trent to fall so low that it would soon be possible to ford the river at many places. So Norfolk persuaded Henry VIII to grant nearly all the rebels' demands and to pardon them for having taken part in the rebellion.

Henry most graciously received the rebel leaders at Greenwich, and their followers dispersed and went home; but two months later, a very minor revolt broke out in the East Riding of Yorkshire. Henry used this as an excuse to arrest and execute nearly all the leaders of the earlier revolt and to hang some four hundred of their followers, not for their participation in the first rebellion, for which they had been pardoned, but on trumped-up charges of having taken part in the second abortive rising. Three of them were executed as traitors because they had called on the people to stay quietly in their houses and not help the rebels; for it was argued that this was treasonable, as they should have told them to leave their houses and help suppress the rebellion.

In the reign of Edward VI, two formidable revolts broke out almost simultaneously in the summer of 1549; and at the same time there were riots against enclosures of land in several counties in south-east England. The people of Devon and Cornwall were rebelling against the recent introduction of the Protestant Book of Common Prayer, and demanded the restoration of the old Catholic Mass and the burning of heretics. The people of Norfolk, most of whom were Protestants, demanded an end to enclosures of common land.

The rebels in the West murdered one prominent local Protestant, and several Protestant supporters fled from the district. One of these was a Protestant seaman, Edmund Drake, who later became a clergyman; he fled from Tavistock to Kent with his family, including his infant son, Francis Drake. Francis spent his adolescence learning seamanship on the Medway, and imbibing the Protestantism of his neighbours in Kent.

The government expected the Western rebels to march on London, and took the precaution of destroying the bridge at Staines to prevent them from crossing the Thames and reaching the northern bank; but the army that Somerset sent against them, under Lord Russell and Sir William Herbert, defeated the rebels at Clyst St Mary before they had left Devonshire. The government sent Sir Anthony Kingston and other officers to try the rebels by courts martial, and many were executed, including the Mayor of Bodmin. When Kingston arrived at Bodmin, the Mayor invited him to dinner. Kingston accepted the invitation, but told the Mayor to erect a scaffold in the courtyard of his house, as it would be necessary to hang some rebels. After dinner, the Mayor told Kingston that the scaffold had been erected. Kingston then ordered the Mayor to go up on to the scaffold, as it was he who was to be hanged on it.

The Protestants were convinced that the rebellion in the West had been instigated by a handful of Papist priests, particularly by the vicar of Poundstock, near Bude, in Cornwall.

> The vicar of Poundstock, with his congregation,
> Commanded them to stick to their idolatry.
> They made much provision and great preparation,
> Yet God hath given our King the victory.
> They did rob and spoil all the King's friends;
> They called them heretics with spite and disdain;
> They roffled a space like tyrants and fiends;
> They put some in prison and some to great pain;
> As was William Hilling, that martyr truly,
> Which they killed at Sampford Moor in the plain;
> Where yet God hath given our King the victory.

John Dudley, Earl of Warwick, defeated Kett's rebels on Mousehold Hill, a few miles north of Norwich, and suppressed the rebellion. Kett and several of the rebels were executed. Warwick returned to London to plot the *coup d'état* which overthrew Somerset, who was thought to have encouraged the rebellions by his liberal policies. Warwick became the ruler of England, and two years later was created Duke of Northumberland.

He persuaded Parliament in 1550 to pass an Act against unlawful assemblies. If twelve or more persons assembled with the object of removing a member of the Privy Council from office, or bringing about any change in the law, or burning houses or barns, or obtaining lower rents or a lower price of corn, they were to be executed as traitors or felons. If more than forty of them assembled, anyone, including their wives or servants, who brought them money, weapons, food or drink was also to be executed as a traitor. If two or more persons, but less than ten, assembled for any of these purposes, they were to be punished by a year's imprisonment and a fine. No mayor or JP who killed any of them in dispersing them was to be liable to punishment or damages; and tenants of a lord of a manor who were between the ages of eighteen and sixty were to forfeit their land if they refused to serve in the forces against them.

Northumberland was overthrown by another revolt, which broke out when Lady Jane Grey was proclaimed Queen after the death of Edward VI in July 1553. Mary called on the people to support her as the rightful Queen, and within a few days forty thousand people had assembled at Framlingham, ready to fight on her behalf. It shows the moral effect of the royal name, and the attachment of the people to the principle of hereditary monarchy, that this was the only revolt during the Tudor Age which was successful. Wyatt's Protestant rising in Kent next year, in protest against Mary's plan to marry Philip of Spain, was suppressed; and so was the Catholic rebellion in the North against Elizabeth I in 1569, when five thousand men rose under the Earls of Northumberland and Westmorland. They captured Durham, burning the Book of Common Prayer in the cathedral and celebrating Mass there; but the rising in the North was suppressed before Philip of Spain had time to send them any effective aid. More than six hundred of the rebels were executed after summary trials by courts martial.

In 1601, Elizabeth's former favourite, Robert Devereux, Earl of Essex, led a revolt in London, ostensibly to protect himself against the members of the Privy Council who were planning to arrest and assassinate him. It was easily suppressed, and Essex and five of his supporters were executed.

Whenever a rebellion broke out, the government was confronted with the same problem which it faced on the outbreak of war, because there was no standing army at the King's disposal, except for the garrisons in the two frontier outposts at Berwick and Calais. There was also a very small force of men-at-arms who resided at court to protect the King's person. Within a month of his victory at Bosworth, Henry VII had created a corps of fifty men-at-arms whom he named 'the Yeomen of the Guard'; and Henry VIII increased their number to six hundred in 1520.

In times of war and rebellion, the King relied on the old system which had existed in feudal times. He ordered his nobles to summon the gentlemen in their counties to come with their tenants, bringing a specified number of horsemen, infantrymen and bowmen, to muster at a certain place on a certain date. When there was a threat of invasion by the Scots, or an invasion of Scotland was being planned, the lords and gentlemen of the northern counties were ordered to assemble at Newcastle, usually in about three week's time.

When the Pilgrimage of Grace broke out, Henry VIII called on the nobles and gentlemen throughout the West Midlands to go with their tenants to join the Duke of Suffolk and the Earl of Shrewsbury at Nottingham and Mansfield for service against the rebels, while the gentlemen in the South of England were told to come to Ampthill to form a reserve army. He was able to assemble an army of seven thousand men within a fortnight.

When a French invasion was expected in the summer of 1545, Henry made preparations for armies totalling 90,000 men to be ready to assemble to repulse an invasion attempt at any point between Lincolnshire and Cornwall. Preparations were made to light beacons on the hills all the way between the South coast and the North of England, so that the people throughout the realm could be warned of the invasion far more quickly than any horseman could ride from the Channel to the Scottish Border. Three beacons were built on every hill; one fire was to be lit when the enemy fleet was spotted; a second fire when the enemy approached within four miles of the coast; and a third when they landed. When a French raiding party landed at Seaford and burned the town and Sir John Gage's house at Firle, all three beacons were lit, and the levies of Kent and Sussex were ordered to assemble at Uckfield; but by the time they arrived there, the French had already re-embarked.

When the Rising in the North broke out in November 1569, Elizabeth raised an army of 28,000 men in the traditional way by calling on the nobles and gentlemen of the whole realm to join the advance-guard under the Earl of Sussex and the reserve army under the Earl of Pembroke; and the army of 22,000 men which was assembled at Tilbury in 1588, when the Armada was sighted off the Lizard, was raised in the same way.

In London, all the citizens between the ages of eighteen and sixty were required to enrol in the city trainbands and to be ready, when summoned, to defend the King and the city against a foreign invader or English rebels. When there was a rumour in April 1539 that the armies of the Emperor Charles V in the Netherlands were about to launch an invasion of England – it was a false report – 16,500 men turned out in the

A battle with the Scots in 1545. An illustration from Holinshed's *Chronicles of England*, 1577.

trainbands and marched in armour from Mile End to St James's Park, and back by Holborn and Newgate through the city, while Henry VIII stood for five hours at the gatehouse at Whitehall to see them march past. The London trainbands came out in January 1554 to defend Queen Mary against Wyatt's rebels, and they suppressed Essex's rebellion against Elizabeth I in 1601.

The English continued to rely on this type of army long after foreign kings were enlisting mercenaries to fight their wars. By the end of the fifteenth century, mercenaries were being widely employed in Europe. The Emperor Maximilian fought his wars in Italy against Francis I in 1516 with Swiss mercenaries whom he paid with money lent to him by Henry VIII. A king who needed mercenaries made a contract with the captain of the mercenaries and paid him a lump sum, and the captain assembled a band of mercenaries and paid his men the wages for which they were prepared to serve. But it was not a wholly satisfactory arrangement, for mercenaries could not be relied upon to fight as bravely or loyally as native soldiers fighting for their own king. The English were proud of being able to dispense with mercenaries, and were envied for this in other countries.

Henry VIII fought his wars against France and Scotland in 1513 and 1522–3 using only his English soldiers; but he supplemented them during his last war with France by enlisting German and Spanish mercenaries for the first time in 1544 and 1545. He at once encountered the drawbacks of mercenaries. He became involved in arguments with the captain of the mercenaries as to whether their first month's pay should be reckoned from the day when they set out from their assembly point at Aachen or only when they reached the battle area at Boulogne, where they were to serve. On another occasion, a German mercenary captain seized the envoys whom Henry had sent to negotiate with him, and refused to release them until a ransom had been paid. Mutinies by mercenaries were common, for when mercenaries mutinied, the king who had hired them had only two choices: either to give in to their demands, or to hire other mercenaries to suppress them.

Henry had a more satisfactory experience with the 1,300 Spanish mercenaries whom he hired to fight against the Scots in 1545; but in their case, too, there were some minor difficulties, because the mercenaries, who were billeted in private houses in Newcastle, refused to eat English food, and their landladies complained about the smell of the Spanish food which they cooked for themselves in the landladies' kitchens.

In the reign of Edward VI, Somerset's government hired Spanish and German mercenaries to suppress the revolts in Devon and Norfolk. Mercenaries were usually prepared to fight for any king who hired them, and for or against either Protestants or Catholics, irrespective of what their own religion might be. But they were often reluctant to fight against their own sovereign, and though some mercenary captains were prepared to do so, a captain often inserted a clause in his contract by which he agreed to serve against any prince except his own sovereign, or against a sovereign whom he had served in the past and hoped to serve again in the future. The Catholic Spanish mercenaries who were hired to suppress the revolts of 1549 were quite happy to fight against Catholic rebels; but one of the reasons why Northumberland decided to submit to Mary in 1553 was that he feared that the Spanish mercenaries in his army would be reluctant to fight against a princess who was known to be the protégée of their own sovereign, Charles V.

Mary refused to hire Spanish mercenaries, or to accept the help of the Spanish troops whom Charles V offered to her, to suppress Wyatt's rebellion, because she thought it would be politically unwise to do so, as Wyatt was accusing her of betraying English interests to Spain; and she insisted on employing only the London trainbands to suppress the revolt. Elizabeth I reluctantly agreed to lend money to the Dutch Protestants and to Henry of Navarre to hire German mercenaries to fight against the Spaniards in the Netherlands and in France; but when she eventually agreed to send her own troops to help them, they were English soldiers enrolled in the traditional way; and she suppressed the long-drawn-out rebellion in Ireland between 1594 and 1603 with English soldiers.

During the first half of the sixteenth century, great advances were made in military

Siege warfare. An illustration from Holinshed's *Chronicles*, 1577. The town was first reduced by gunfire whilst cavalry in armour waited to attack.

weapons. Gunpowder and cannon had first been used by the English at Crécy in 1346, but it was only after the outbreak of the war between Charles V and Francis I in 1521 that they came into widespread use. During the next thirty years, they revolutionized military strategy. Cannons were made for use in sieges which were far more powerful than any earlier guns, and with a much longer range. By 1544, when Henry VIII's cannons at Boulogne fired 100,000 rounds into the town during the three months' siege, the heaviest guns, the culverins, had a range of one and a half miles and could fire sixty rounds a day; while the smallest siege-guns, the falcons, with a range of 1,920 yards, could fire 120 rounds a day. Guns with this range enabled the supporters of Mary Queen of Scots to prolong the civil war in Scotland, and to cause Elizabeth I many worries, merely by holding Dumbarton and Edinburgh Castles; for their guns at Dumbarton could control the estuary through which a French or Spanish army could enter the Clyde; and the cannon in Edinburgh Castle could hit every house in Edinburgh, though the Canongate was out of range. Elizabeth was greatly relieved when her Scottish supporters captured Dumbarton Castle in a daring night attack; but she could not feel safe from the danger of a foreign invasion of England through Scotland till Edinburgh Castle had surrendered, after she had sent an army to reduce it, equipped with siege-guns made in the Sussex iron

The arquebus, which was called by the English a 'hagbut'. It was gradually displaced by the handgun, which had greater range and accuracy, but was heavier. In the 1570s the Spaniards had only fifteen musketeers to a hundred arquebusiers, but by 1600 the proportion was about equal in all Western armies. A drawing by Jacob de Gheyn, after Heinrich Goltzius, 1587.

foundries, and accompanied with a unit of engineers who could mine the defences of the castle.

Mining was another new weapon which came into general use during the sixteenth century. A castle or fortified town could be captured if the walls were successfully mined, though mines, like cannon, sometimes exploded prematurely and killed the soldiers who were operating them. Elizabeth and her Scottish allies were lucky at Edinburgh, because the bombardment and the mining operations knocked down part of the castle wall, which happened to fall into the well and blocked it up with debris. The garrison were therefore deprived of their water supply, and forced to surrender.

Sieges sometimes ended when the defenders and the commander of the besieging army agreed that the castle or city should be surrendered and the garrison allowed to march out with honours of war, which meant that they could leave with their weapons and horses. Sometimes they were granted less favourable terms, and allowed to leave in safety on condition that they abandoned their weapons and horses. But the besieging general might insist that they should surrender 'at mercy', which meant that he was entitled, at his will, either to kill the defenders or allow them to go free. Whichever course he adopted, he was spared the trouble and expense of guarding prisoners-of-war, except for the higher-ranking officers and the wealthier soldiers, who were held for a good ransom. Sometimes all the garrison which had surrendered at mercy were allowed to go free; sometimes the victors killed as many of them as the number of their own soldiers who had fallen during the siege; sometimes all of them were butchered in cold blood a day or two after the surrender. The French killed their Spanish prisoners after the surrender of Hesdin in 1552; the Spaniards killed the defenders of Haarlem in 1573; and the English killed nearly all the Spanish and Italian soldiers who surrendered at mercy at Smerwick in Ireland in 1580. If the defenders refused all demands for their surrender, and decided to 'abide the cannon' and face the bombardment and storming of the fortress or town, they were normally all killed.

The English armies had won their great victories in the past, including their crowning glory of Agincourt in 1415, by the longbow which their archers used to such deadly effect. The English were very reluctant to abandon their traditional weapon which for three hundred years had spread such fear among their enemies, and they continued to rely on archers well into the sixteenth century when every other army in Western Europe was using the new small firearm, the arquebus, which the English called the 'hagbut'. The infantryman, who normally fought with the pike, or halberd, could carry the hagbut without being too heavily weighed down; and it could also be carried by the cavalry, though they had to dismount from their horses to fire it. The hagbut was erected on a stand, the fuse was lit, and the explosive was fired from the gun. The cavalry soon abandoned it for the pistol, which changed the nature of the cavalry charge. Instead of charging into the enemy with lances, as had been done in earlier times, the sixteenth-century cavalry halted their charge when they were at close range to the enemy and discharged their pistols at them. The older type of cavalry charge was reintroduced by Gustavus Adolphus and Prince Rupert in the seventeenth century, who trained their cavalrymen to charge into the enemy with drawn swords.

The respective merits of the hagbut and the longbow were constantly discussed by English commanders and military experts during the first half of the sixteenth century. The hagbut had a range of about 400 yards, while the longbow could not shoot an arrow much over a furlong of 220 yards; the hagbut was more destructive

Cavalry and pikemen assembled at Thérouanne in 1513 for the meeting between Henry VIII and the Emperor Maximilian I. Detail from a panoramic painting by an unknown artist.

Detail from a sixteenth-century Flemish tapestry showing how the handgun achieved a mastery over armoured cavalry in the battle of Pavia, 1525.

A musketeer, with his weapon over his shoulder and its rest in his other hand. A drawing by Jacob de Gheyn, after Heinrich Goltzius, 1587.

than the arrow, and the noise of the explosion and the novelty and reputation of the weapon had a demoralizing effect on the enemy. On the other hand, several arrows could be shot from a longbow in the same time which it took to fire one round from a hagbut; and the hagbut could not be used in the rain, as the gunpowder would not ignite if it was damp.

Henry VIII himself was in two minds about the merits of the hagbut and the longbow. He was himself an excellent archer, and his natural conservatism made him favour the traditional English weapon; but he was always fascinated by new weaponry. He was very interested in the reports which he received of a new kind of shell which was used by Charles V's army in France in 1543 which, after being fired

The arquebus in action. Engraving by Jacques Callot (1592–1635) for *La Vie de Ferdinand 1er de Medicis*, by Mateo Roselli.

into a town, bounced along the street and burst into flame every time it hit the ground; but this prototype of an incendiary bomb was not developed.

The bowmen of England won their last great victory when they defeated the Scots at Flodden in 1513; but by the time of Henry VIII's last war in 1544, hagbuts were being increasingly used in the English army, though the longbow was not abandoned till the 1590s. In skirmishes in which a small number of men were engaged, like those which took place in the civil wars in Scotland, the appearance of a unit of hagbutters could have a decisive influence; in pitched battles with large armies, they were less effective. Before the end of the sixteenth century, the musket had largely replaced both the hagbut and the longbow.

The new explosive weapons had made armour of little use; but the soldiers' fears of the dangerous and painful wounds caused by cannon shells, hagbuts and muskets made them demand that they be protected by armour, which continued to be worn in war, more perhaps for psychological reasons than as a real protection, until the middle of the seventeenth century, though it was lighter than the very heavy armour which had been worn by the cavalry in earlier times and was still worn in tournaments in the sixteenth century.

An Act passed by Philip and Mary's last Parliament in 1558, during the war against France, required landowners to provide weapons and equipment for the army according to their wealth. It listed bows and arrows, hagbuts and 'harness' (armour) among the things to be provided. Owners of land worth £1,000 a year or more had to supply six horses which could carry demilancers, with armour for at least three of these horses; ten light horses for the light cavalry; four corselets; forty Almayn rivets; thirty longbows, thirty sheaves of arrows, thirty steel caps, twenty halberds, twenty hagbuts and twenty morians (helmets without visors). Less was demanded from less wealthy landowners. At the bottom of the scale, the landowner whose rents were only £5 a year had to supply one coat of plate, one longbow, one sheaf of arrows and one steel cap.

The cavalry was considered in the Tudor Age to be the most aristocratic and glorious branch of the army, as it was in every period of history until the beginning of the twentieth century; but England suffered from a lack of large horses which were strong enough to bear riders clad in heavy armour. The shortage of suitable horses was a serious drawback in wartime, for the English had to import large horses from the Netherlands for use in the army, and they could only do so with the permission of the Habsburg rulers of the Netherlands. The traditional alliance with 'Burgundy', as the English in the Tudor Age still called this territory when speaking about the alliance, meant that in ordinary circumstances the Emperor Maximilian and Charles V would agree to allow the horses to be exported to England; and this was one of the factors, as well as the wool trade, which made all English statesmen reluctant to quarrel with the Emperor. But Henry VIII nevertheless did so on several occasions, particularly after he repudiated his marriage to Charles V's aunt, Catherine of Aragon, and furthered the Reformation, which Charles strongly opposed. Fortunately for Henry, Charles was always more eager to fight the French than to inconvenience Henry, and Henry was very successful in playing off Charles and Francis against each other; but occasionally, when Charles's relations with Henry were very bad, he refused for a short while to allow the horses to be exported to England.

The Tudor Kings tried to deal with the problem by severely restricting the export of horses and by encouraging the breeding of larger horses. An Act of 1495 made it an offence to export any horse from the kingdom, or any mare, unless the mare was more than three years old and not worth more than 6s.8d. By an Act of 1536, everyone who owned a park more than one mile in circumference was to keep two mares who were capable of breeding and were at least fourteen 'handfulls', high, a handfull being four inches; and everyone who owned a park more than four miles in circumference was to keep four such mares. The owners were not to allow these mares to be covered by any horse which was less than fourteen hands high. The Act was not to apply to parks in Westmorland, Cumberland, Northumberland or Durham.

But this statute did not prevent mares from breeding with small horses which they met in forests and on common land; so an Act of 1540 made it an offence to put out to pasture on any forest, chase, moor, heath or common land any horse which was less than fifteen hands high in twenty-five English counties and in Wales, or less than fourteen hands high in the other counties of England. Another Act of 1542 compelled every duke and archbishop to own at least seven horses which were more than three years old and were at least fourteen hands high; every marquess, and every bishop whose bishopric was worth £1,000 a year in revenues, was to have five such horses; every bishop, viscount or baron whose bishopric or lands were worth 1,000 marks a year was to have three; and every other bishop, viscount or baron, and any layman with lands worth 600 marks a year and every ecclesiastic with lands worth 500 marks a year was to have two. With men of lower rank, their duty to breed large horses was linked to their wives' extravagance; for if any man wore a silk gown after Michaelmas 1544, or if his wife wore a French hood or bonnet of velvet, or any pearl, stone or gold chain around her neck or on any part of her body, he was to keep one horse which was more than fourteen hands high; but this did not apply if he was divorced or separated from his wife.

The new developments in military weapons, and the employment of mercenaries, made war increasingly expensive. This raised a serious problem for every King, for his nobles and most of his people continued to expect that he would carry on the tradition of his ancestors and engage in war, even if he could not afford to do so, although they did not wish to pay taxes to provide the money for the war. Sixteenth-century rulers told their subjects exactly what they had to believe about religion, how many times they should cross themselves during the service of the Mass, what they should eat on Fridays and Saturdays, and the maximum value per square yard of the materials which they were permitted to wear in their hose; but the Kings always hesitated to make their peoples pay new taxes which were not sanctioned by tradition.

The King was able to raise revenue from customs duties paid on imported goods; he had certain rights over wards; when a bishop died he could wait for one year before appointing a new bishop and could take the revenues of the see for himself during this year; and he received the rents and other profits which were paid to him by the tenants of his own lands. From time to time, he succeeded in persuading his clergy in Convocation and the MPs in the House of Commons to vote him a 'tenth' or a 'fifteenth' – one-tenth or one-fifteenth of the revenues of ecclesiastical benefices and the lands of the laymen. Sometimes, especially in wartime, the clergy and people were called upon to make a voluntary loan to the King; and if any subject refused to pay the voluntary contribution, for which he was asked, he ran the risk of being treated like the London alderman who refused to contribute in 1542; he was conscripted into the army which was sent against the Scots, and the Privy Council ordered the army commanders to place him in the most dangerous places and to make him perform the most arduous fatigues.

The King's reluctance to impose new taxation was very wise, because the ordinary Englishman, though he did not complain that he was obliged to wear a woollen cap every Sunday, strongly resented having to pay an unusual tax, and was ready to join a rebellion to prevent it. So the Kings had no alternative but to borrow money from Italian or Flemish bankers, even if the banker asked them to pay a higher rate of interest than the maximum which was permitted under the laws against usury which were periodically enacted during the Tudor Age;* for they knew by experience and from a study of recent history that the surest way for a prince to become unpopular was to follow the advice of Colet, Erasmus and the small group of intellectuals and abandon the expensive path of military glory.

* An Act of 1495 made all usury illegal, and enacted that if anyone lent money at interest he was to forfeit the sum that he had lent. An Act of 1545 made it lawful to charge interest provided that the rate did not exceed ten per cent; if the moneylender asked for a higher rate of interest, he was to forfeit three times the sum lent and be imprisoned during the King's pleasure. The Act of 1545 was repealed in 1552 by a statute which again made all usury illegal; but the Act of 1545 was re-enacted in 1571.

SPORTS AND PASTIMES

T HE vigorous and brutal men of the Tudor Age engaged in vigorous and brutal sports; but sport, like everything else, was regulated by the government. People were expected to take part in those sports which were suitable for persons of their rank. It was right for noblemen and gentlemen to engage in activities which trained them in horsemanship and the art of war; but the labourers and artisans, who were required by law to be at work on six days in the week from 5 a.m. till after 7 p.m., did not have much time to play games, and were not encouraged to do so. On Sundays and holy days, when they were not at work they were to practise archery, which would be useful in wartime, and not take part in any game which competed with archery. Certain kinds of games were also condemned on moral and religious grounds, for long before the Puritan revolution in the seventeenth century the Church tried to prevent the people from indulging in frivolous and immoral sports.

For nobles and gentlemen, the greatest sport was still the tournament, as it had been for the last three hundred years. Knights jousted against each other, and displayed their prowess, while the admiring ladies watched them from the stands. The ladies had always been an important factor in the ritual of the tournament; they gave their scarves or handkerchiefs to the knight of their choice, and he wore it during the tournament; they cheered him on, and sometimes incited him to take additional risks to prove his courage and devotion to them; and they rewarded the victor with a garland and perhaps with a kiss. They also sometimes contributed to the cost of the tournament.

At the beginning of the Tudor Age, tournaments were more popular with the nobility than they had ever been; but they were becoming further and further removed from the reality of war. Steps were taken to minimize the risks to the participants by dressing them in a heavy suit of armour with a helmet with a visor covering all the face except for the slits for the nose and eyes. This was just at the time

This lively woodcut from Holinshed's *Chronicles of England*, 1577, was originally intended to illustrate one of Henry VIII's jousts, watched by Catherine of Aragon. But jousts were obviously such a social feature of the sixteenth century that the publisher of the book did not hesitate to reproduce this woodcut more than once, on appropriate occasions.

when the development of artillery in war made armour less of a protection in battle, and when the armour worn in war was becoming lighter.

In a tournament, the knights were separated from each other by a wooden barrier about four feet high. Each knight rode on the right-hand side of the barrier, carrying his lance in his right hand, and using it to strike at his opponent as they galloped past each other on opposite sides of the barrier. As the jouster struck with his lance across the barrier at the opponent on his left, the angle at which the lance struck the armour of the adversary lessened the force of the blow and reduced the risk of serious injury; and by the sixteenth century the lances used in tournaments were much more brittle than the lances of the cavalry charge of the Middle Ages. If a jouster dealt his opponent a hard enough blow with the lance, it would splinter and do no further damage; and if a knight splintered his lance when he jousted, this showed that he was skilful and vigorous.

Tournaments were held at court on the more important holy days, and on special occasions, such as the visit of an important foreign envoy, or the signature of a peace treaty. Henry VII did not personally take part in tournaments; like most of the other kings of the time, he watched from the place of honour in the stands. But Henry VIII

307

took part, incognito, in the first big tournament of his reign; and as this made a good impression, he continued to joust in tournaments for the next twenty-six years. He found a worthy jousting partner and opponent in his brother-in-law, the Duke of Suffolk. Sometimes they were the 'defenders' in the tournament, who challenged all-comers, and took it in turn to joust against all the other competitors. Sometimes Henry and Suffolk jousted against each other. They did so in the tournament at Greenwich on St Thomas of Canterbury's Day in July 1517, when they impressed the spectators by riding eight courses, and both of them splintering their lances every time.

Despite the precautions taken to prevent injury, a tournament was not free from risk. It took skill and good horsemanship to avoid being thrown by a blow on the breastplate from the opponent's lance, even if the blow was softened by the angle and the splintering of the lance. Henry VIII and Suffolk were usually quite capable of remaining in the saddle; but at the tournament at Greenwich on 24 January 1536 Henry was thrown from his horse, and was unconscious for two hours. He never jousted again. A worse disaster befell King Henry II of France, who received a fatal wound at a tournament in Paris in 1559, when a fragment of a splintered lance entered his eye through the slit in his visor. He died ten days later.

Edward VI was too young to take part in a tournament, and King Philip did not do so, either as King in England or in Spain; and as both Mary and Elizabeth were unable to joust because of their sex, royal participation in tournaments ended in England in 1536. But tournaments continued to be held at court during Elizabeth's reign, with Sir Henry Lee and the Earl of Cumberland playing the leading part as the Queen's Champion.

Another great sport held at court during the Tudor Age was riding at the ring. A ring only a few inches wide was suspended on a thread, and a rider, approaching at full gallop, had to put the point of his lance through the middle of the ring. If his eyesight, concentration and steadiness of hand were good enough to enable him to do this, the thread would snap and he would carry off the ring on his lance as he rode by.

On days when no tournament was held, the King and his courtiers usually hunted, and noblemen and gentlemen hunted regularly. The animal hunted was ordinarily the stag, which in the Tudor Age was usually called the hart. In Alsace, the Emperor Maximilian hunted the wild boar, and boars were hunted all over the Continent; but

Opposite: George Clifford, 3rd Earl of Cumberland, miniature painting on vellum by Nicholas Hilliard, c.1590. Apart from commanding the *Elizabeth Bonaventure* against the Armada, Cumberland was courtier, gambler, navigator, and mathematician. He is painted here as Queen's Champion and Knight of Pendragon Castle, at the Accession Day tournament in 1590. The Queen's bejewelled glove is sewn on to his hat. He wears Greenwich armour, patterned with stars, of which pieces still survive.

Henry VIII jousting before Catherine of Aragon and her ladies at the tournament on 12 February, 1511, to celebrate the birth of Henry, Prince of Wales, who lived for only three months. The initial 'K' embroidered on Henry's surcoat and on the trappings of his horse, stands for 'Catherine'. The illustration is a detail from the Westminster Tournament Roll, which belongs to the College of Arms. The Accession Day tilts marked the return of the Queen to London after her summer progress to

Windsor, Richmond or Hampton Court. In mid-November she would make a state entry into London, arriving at the palace of Whitehall in time for the tournament. The tiltyard in Whitehall occupied roughly the area now taken up by the Horseguards Parade. A detailed account of the proceedings, given in 1584 by a visiting German, Lupred von Wedel, is quoted extensively by Sir Roy Strong in his book on *The Cult of Elizabeth*, 1977.

Sir Anthony Mildmay, watercolour on vellum, by Nicholas Hilliard, c.1593. This is described by Sir Roy Strong, in *Artists of the Tudor Court*, 1983, as 'one of Hilliard's most ambitious miniatures, for which he draws on the conventions of large-scale formal portraiture'. Sir Anthony Mildmay, who died in 1617, was the son of Hilliard's patron, Sir Walter Mildmay, Chancellor of the Exchequer.

'Certaine observations for an ostreger in keeping of a Goshawke'. A woodcut from George Turbervile's *Booke of Faulconrie*, 1575. The word 'ostreger', a corruption of the late Latin word *austercarius*, means 'a keeper of goshawks'.

the English wild swine was not as fierce or fleet of foot as the boar in Europe, and was hardly worth hunting. Sometimes a buck was hunted instead of a hart. Yeomen farmers hunted foxes, but no gentleman did until the end of the seventeenth century. When a hart or buck was killed, it was eaten.

Harts could be hunted at most times of the year, but not in mid-winter, and the King and his nobles then engaged in hawking instead. Falcons were trained for this sport, and statutes were passed to punish any poacher who stole their eggs. Poaching by night was considered to be a much more serious offence than poaching by day. An Act of Henry VII's first Parliament in 1485 made unauthorized hunting in private forests a felony punishable by death if the offence was committed at night or if the

313

The caption for this whole-page illustration in Turbervile's *Noble Arte of Venerie or Hunting*, (which is, as it were, a second volume of his *Booke of Faulconrie*) is: 'Of the place where and howe an assembly should be made in the presence of a Prince, or some honourable person.' The 'assembly', in modern terms, is a picnic or barbecue.

poachers had disguised or obscured their faces to prevent themselves from being identified; but if it was done in the daytime and without a disguise, it was only a trespass punishable by fine or imprisonment.

There was one exception to the legislation which prohibited the destruction of game or the stealing of birds' eggs. The authorities were alarmed at the damage caused by rooks and crows, who not only did great harm to the husbandman's crops but also damaged the thatch on the roofs of cottages and barns. An Act of 1533 enacted that every parish must keep nets for catching rooks. Anyone was entitled to enter land without the landowner's permission in order to destroy rooks, if permission had been asked and refused, without being liable for damages for trespass.

The writer and poet George Turbervile, who had been Randolph's secretary and had accompanied him on his journey to Moscow, wrote two books on hunting and hawking. In *The Booke of Faulconrie*, which was published in 1575, he wrote about the breeding and training of hawks; and in his other book, *The Noble Arte of Venerie or Hunting*, which was probably written at about the same time, he explained the

This well-drawn woodcut illustrates a ritual that is by no means dissimilar to those which survive today in English hunts. The 'Prince . . . takes an assaye of the Deare with a sharpe knyfe' and presents it to his lady.

proper way of organizing a hunt, including those occasions when a prince was present. He followed closely an authoritative French book on the subject, but introduced changes to take into account the different customs which in some respects were followed in England. In France, after the hart was killed, the chief huntsman cut off one of its feet and handed it, on his knees, to the King; in England, the huntsman, also on his knees, handed the hunting knife to the King, who stabbed the hart's carcass as if he were killing the hart. This English practice was adopted whenever Elizabeth I hunted.

But Turbervile stressed the importance of not going through this ritual until the hart was safely dead; for if the prince really tried to kill the hart, he might be seriously hurt or even killed, for a hart at bay could inflict great damage on its pursuers. Turbervile mentioned that an Emperor named Basil, who had performed deeds of great valour and had conquered all his enemies in war, had been killed by a hart,* a

---

* This is a slightly inaccurate account of the death of the Eastern Roman Emperor, Basil the Macedonian, who was pulled off his horse by a stag that he was hunting, and died of the fall, in 886.

Turbervile's somewhat surprising comment on this illustration is one that would quite sincerely be echoed by most huntsmen of all ages: 'A good keeper of Houndes should be gratious, curteous and gentle.'

frightened beast which normally did not dare to look at the weakest man in his kingdom; and this inspired Turbervile to some philosophical reflections. It should be a warning to princes not to oppress a humble subject and goad him into standing in his own defence, and 'like the worm, turn again when it is trodden so'. But Turbervile hastened to add that his words must not be interpreted as condemning hunting, for that would be contrary to his whole purpose in writing the book; 'and again I should seem to argue against God's ordinances, since it seemeth that such beasts have been created to the use of man and for his recreation'. Turbervile inserted in the book a poem, *The Wofull wordes of the Hart to the Hunter*, in which he expresses the hart's point of view; the hart, after lamenting the cruelty of the hunter who pursues him and tears him with hounds, prays to God that men will exterminate each other in their wars, so that harts will then be able to live in peace.

The government thoroughly approved of the traditional English sport of archery, as it trained men to use the weapon which had won so many glorious victories in wars. Henry VIII was a very good archer, and regularly practised at the butts. When Wolsey's gentleman usher, George Cavendish, who had been at Wolsey's deathbed at Leicester, travelled to London to tell the King how the Cardinal had died, he found Henry shooting at the butts in the park at Hampton Court. Henry told Cavendish to wait until he had finished shooting, and then changed into his nightgown, and taking Cavendish into the palace through a private door, spoke with him alone about Wolsey's last hours. When Sir George Douglas, the leader of the pro-English party in Scotland, had a secret meeting with Henry to receive his instructions, their talk took place in a lodge in Windsor Great Park when Henry was about to go shooting at the butts.

But from the very beginning of the Tudor Age, Parliament was worried about the decay of archery. An Act of 1487 declared that 'the great and ancient defence of this realm hath stand by the archers and shooters in long bows', but that the art 'is now greatly left and fallen in decay'. The MPs thought that this was because of the excessive price of longbows, and enacted that no one should sell a longbow for more than 3s.4d. But by 1504 they had come to the conclusion that there was another reason why men were neglecting the art of shooting with the longbow; it was because of the popularity of the crossbow, which was being used by more and more people, and often in very improper ways, including the destruction of the King's deer. So an Act was passed which made it illegal for anyone under the rank of a lord to shoot with a crossbow unless he owned land which brought him rents of 200 marks a year. This was followed by other statutes in 1512, 1515, 1534 and 1542, which made it an offence for anyone who did not own land worth £100 a year to possess a crossbow in his house or to carry one on the King's highway; but this did not apply to anyone who lived within seven miles of the sea or the Scottish Border, or to any inhabitant of Northumberland, Durham, Westmorland or Cumberland, who were permitted to keep crossbows in their houses for defence 'against thieves, Scots or other the King's enemies'. Anyone who owned land worth over £100 a year was entitled to seize and confiscate a crossbow from those who were forbidden to have them.

But Parliament in 1512 believed that it was not only because of the crossbow that 'archery and shooting in longbows is right little used but daily minisheth, decayeth and abateth more and more'; it was because people were playing tennis, bowls, and closh (skittles), and other illegal games. The laws against these games were to be more strictly enforced, and the owners of any premises where they were played were to be punished. Every man over seventeen and under sixty, except priests and High Court Judges, was to keep a longbow and four arrows in his house at all times; and every boy between the ages of seven and seventeen was to be provided by his father or master with a bow and two arrows, so that he could learn to shoot. The Mayors and JPs were to provide butts for archery practice in every town and place where they had existed in the past; and in order to ensure that longbows were available for poor people at reasonable prices, every bowmaker was to have two bows of elm for sale for every one bow of yew.

In 1542 Parliament passed a more extensive Act against unlawful games. It declared that the Act of 1512 was being evaded by 'many subtle and inventative and crafty persons' who were inventing new games, like shuffleboard (shove-ha'penny), to replace those which had been banned by the Act of 1512, and that people were

The Tudor version of tennis bore little resemblance to the lawn tennis of the twentieth century. It was played indoors with hand-strung rackets and balls made of leather shells stuffed with hair.

playing these games instead of practising archery. The result was that the bowmakers, and the fletchers who made arrows, could not make a good living, and they were emigrating to Scotland and making bows and arrows there for the enemy. So it enacted that no one was permitted to allow these games to be played on his premises unless he obtained a licence from the JPs. No artisan, husbandman, labourer, fisherman, waterman or any servingman was to be allowed to play tennis, dice, cards, bowls, skittles, quoits or any other unlawful game, except at Christmas; and at Christmas they could only play them in their master's house or in his presence. More penalties were imposed by an Act of 1555 against the owner of any premises where bowls, tennis, dice or any other unlawful games were played.

Another illegal game played by the lower classes was football, which had first been banned by a statute in Edward II's reign in 1314. The object of the game was to put the ball through the opponents' goalposts, which were often as far as two or three miles apart. There were no other rules; the ball could be kicked or thrown, or the players could pick it up and run with it; and they could be stopped by any means, by holding, punching, tripping, or tackling in any way. There was no limit to the numbers who could take part on either side, and often all the young men of the village would join in their team; sometimes even women took part. In many towns, a game of football was played in the streets on Shrove Tuesday. The match that was played every year in Chester was very ferocious until the authorities banned it in 1540 and insisted that there should be a race though the streets on Shrove Tuesday instead.

The game was very rough, and almost all the references to it, in books, letters and plays, are to someone being injured. The players were considered by the upper classes to be men of the lowest type. In Shakespeare's *King Lear*, the Earl of Kent contemptuously calls Oswald a 'base football player'. Sir Thomas Elyot, in *The Boke named the Governour*, condemned 'football, wherein is nothing but beastly fury and extreme violence whereof proceedeth hurt, and consequently rancour and malice do remain with them that be wounded, wherefore it is to be put in perpetual silence'. In Robert Laneham's description of the festivities at Kenilworth, when Leicester entertained Elizabeth I there in 1575, he mentions that one of the actors who took part in a pageant walked with a limp, because when he was young he had broken his leg playing football. In 1576 some football players were prosecuted at Middlesex Quarter Sessions for having taken part in a riotous football match between the villages of Ruislip and Uxbridge; and in March 1581 a coroner's inquest at South Mimms in Middlesex returned a verdict of murder against two men who had killed a member of the opposite team by a blow on the chest when tackling him during a football match on Evan's Field at South Mimms.

But the other games which were forbidden to the common people were becoming very popular among noblemen and gentlemen. Many noblemen, like the King, had tennis courts and bowling alleys attached to their houses. Tennis became so associated with the King that when lawn tennis was invented in the nineteenth century, tennis became known as 'real tennis' or 'royal tennis'. Henry VII played tennis at Windsor. When Charles V visited England in 1522, he and Henry VIII played tennis at Henry's palace at Baynards Castle in London. They were partners in a doubles match against the Prince of Orange and the Marquis of Brandenburg, who had come to England with Charles, while the Earl of Devon and Lord Edmund Howard acted as ball boys. The game was abandoned as a draw after they had played eleven games. Henry VIII also played bowls, and on one occasion, at Abingdon, lost £100 in a game of bowls to his Scottish brother-in-law, the Earl of Angus.

Bowls was played by gentlemen, priests and university fellows. When Cranmer was in prison at Oxford in 1555, and the authorities were putting the greatest pressure on him to recant and repudiate his heresies before he was burned, they adopted the well-known technique of varying the hard and the soft approach. After he had been kept for many months in rigorous conditions in the common jail of Bocardo in Oxford, he was transferred to the custody of the Dean of the college of Christ Church. He was kindly treated, and allowed to mix with the fellows of the college and to play bowls on the college green. After a few weeks he was taken back to Bocardo and treated more harshly than before.

There is no reason to doubt the truth of the story that Drake was playing bowls on Plymouth Hoe on 19 July 1588 (Old Style) when he was told that the Armada had been sighted off the Lizard, and that he said that there was time to finish the game before fighting the Spaniards. He was quite right, for it was not until eight hours later that the tide was right for the English ships to be rowed out of the harbour in the face of an adverse wind. The story was first recorded in writing in the eighteenth century, but there is a reference in a publication of 1624 to the fact that the English captains were playing bowls when the Armada was sighted; and as this was only thirty-six years later, there were many people still alive who remembered 1588 and the story may have been told by someone who was present.

The upper classes also had their sedentary and indoor pastimes. Chess had been played throughout the Middle Ages, but important developments in the game took place in Spain at the end of the fifteenth century. New rules were introduced, which have lasted till the twentieth century; the queen, which hitherto had only been able to move one square diagonally, was given the much greater powers which she possesses today; the bishop's move was no longer limited to two squares diagonally, with no power over the intervening square; pawns were allowed to move two squares at the first move; and castling was introduced. New openings were developed by experts, especially the Spanish bishop, Ruy Lopez, whose opening is still called after him, at least in the English-speaking countries. The new rules had been adopted in England by the beginning of the sixteenth century. In England, as in Spain, the game seems to have been particularly popular with the higher clergy, for Foxe mentioned that both Cranmer and Nicholas Ridley played a game of chess after dinner every afternoon.

Many nobles and gentlemen, like Henry VIII, preferred the excitement of gambling at cards and dice. The most usual card game was cent, which was almost identical with the game which was afterwards called piquet. Men of letters also sometimes played cards.

In the evenings, after supper, dancing often took place at court, especially under Elizabeth I, who enjoyed dancing even more than Henry VIII had done. The Queen and courtiers often danced the pavane, which was so stately that lawyers, merchants and men of letters could dance it in their long gowns. The galliard was more energetic, and the volta, in which the gentleman clasped the lady round the waist and lifted her into the air, was the most energetic and daring of them all. Gentlemen were advised by their dancing-masters to remove their rapiers and hand them to their lackeys when they danced the volta, to avoid the risk of tripping over them, though rapiers could safely be worn while dancing a pavane. Elizabeth I, despite her strict sense of propriety, was prepared to allow the volta and to dance it herself.

This motley assembly of itinerant musicians playing an assortment of instruments is one of the illustrations in *Orchesographie*, a curious treatise on dancing by Thoinot Arbeau, published in 1588.

At the beginning of the Tudor Age, the only music that was known, at least at court and among the educated classes, was the Church music of the Middle Ages; and the same type of music was used for dancing and in songs for which it seems most inappropriate to us in the twentieth century. The drinking songs of the German mercenaries who served in England in the last years of Henry VIII and under Edward VI were sung to the doleful tunes of an ecclesiastical dirge, although the words were about the joys and excitements of a mercenary's life, with food, drink and gold. Henry VIII himself was very fond of music; he not only played the lute but also composed music, writing a Mass as well as several love songs. The tunes of the love songs, and of his cheerful *Pastime with good company*, sound to twentieth-century ears as lugubrious as the music of his Mass.

No other type of music was recorded until after 1550, when for the first time the kind of tunes which we know today were sung by the Protestant extremists who a few years later became known as Puritans. Their opponents referred to the doleful psalms which the Puritans sang, but to our ears they sound less doleful than the music to which Elizabeth I and Mary Queen of Scots danced the pavane. It is unlikely that the Puritans invented a completely new style of music, and probably the people had for many years been singing folk songs with this kind of simple tune, which was never heard at court or in church, and was therefore never recorded.

The Puritans, with their denigration of the role of the priest and their emphasis on the participation of the congregation in the church services, introduced the practice of singing hymns. The hymns were paraphrases of the psalms, put into English rhyming or blank verse, and slightly altered so as to give more emphasis to aspects of Puritan propaganda. The hymn-writer was William Kethe, who escaped from England in Mary's reign and lived as a refugee in Geneva with Knox, Goodman, Whittingham, Foxe and other extremists. When he returned to England after Elizabeth's accession, he was appointed rector of Okeford Superior in Dorset; and though he was always suspect in the eyes of the ecclesiastical hierarchy because of his connections with the Puritans, he retained his benefice until his death in 1608. His version of the hundredth psalm, *All people that one earth do dwell*, which was written when he heard of Mary's death and Elizabeth's accession, called on the people to sing to the Lord with cheerful voice, for the Lord our God is good and His mercy is for ever sure. At the same time he wrote:

> Now Israel may say, and that truly,
> If that the Lord had not our cause maintained . . .
> When all the world against us furiously
> Made their uproars and said we should all die,
> Now long ago they had devoured us all . . .
> God that made Heaven and earth is our help then,
> His name hath saved us from these wicked men.

Knox used Kethe's hymns in Scotland, and published several of them in the *Form of Prayers and Psalms* of the Church of Scotland which was published in 1565. Eighty years later, they became the battle songs of Cromwell and the Puritans during the English Civil War.

Until the end of the sixteenth century, serious composers wrote music almost entirely for religious purposes. John Marbeck was the organist of St George's Chapel, Windsor. He would have been burned as a heretic in 1543, along with his three friends at Windsor, for having a copy of the English Bible in his possession, if Gardiner had not persuaded Henry VIII to pardon him because of his music. He was composing Church music until his death in 1585. Thomas Tallis was writing Church music for Elizabeth I's chapel in 1560; but by 1579 his friend William Byrd, who succeeded him at the chapel royal, was writing the music for songs which had nothing to do with religion, but with the delights of the spring and of love. During that decade of change, the 1590s, the madrigals of Byrd, Morley, Dowland and Weelkes became very popular.

Music was also used at court in the masques which by the beginning of the sixteenth century were a regular feature of the evening entertainments. The masque was a short theatrical performance with music. The themes were usually stories from

A late sixteenth-century engraving by Crispin van de Passe for *Hortus Voluptatum*, illustrating a musical party led by a lady on the virginals, a keyboard instrument of the zither type, played in a box.

Greek mythology, or sometimes from the Bible, or incidents in which allegorical figures like Chastity and Virtue appeared. Masques continued to be a feature of evening entertainments at court throughout the Tudor Age and the seventeenth century.

Pageants, which were performed out of doors, in the streets of London and elsewhere, were similar to masques. They were a feature of the sovereign's procession through London on the day before the coronation; the pageants at Elizabeth I's coronation procession in January 1559 were propaganda for Protestantism and the English Bible. Soon afterwards Elizabeth banned the pageants that were being performed by the Protestants in London in which Philip II was attacked and ridiculed. After the revolt in the Netherlands began in 1566, the English Protestants were outraged by the severity of the persecution there, and some pageants were acted in London denouncing the persecution and attacking Philip II; but Elizabeth banned them at the request of the Spanish ambassador. Philip reciprocated, and banned pageants in Spain which attacked Elizabeth. Even when relations between England and Spain had become so bad that they were on the eve of open war, Philip and Elizabeth still prohibited personal attacks on each other by their subjects.

Chere begynneth a treatyse how the
hye fader of heuen sendeth dethe
to somon euery creature to
come and gyue a counte
of theyr lyues in this
worlde and is in ma-
ner of a morall
playe.

Everyman.

The title-page of the first
edition of the famous
morality play, *Everyman*,
published in black letter
c.1509. It almost certainly
derived from the Dutch
counterpart, *Elckerlije*.

Pageants and masques were a feature of Elizabeth's progresses through her
kingdom in the summer. At Oxford, Cambridge, Kenilworth and elsewhere, she was
received on her arrival by youths and maidens dressed in the part of various virtues
and reciting odes in honour of virgin queens.

There were also stage plays, but these were viewed with some suspicion by the
authorities, at least at the beginning of the Tudor Age. They were too closely
associated with the plays performed by strolling players in the market towns and
villages. They were often obscene, and some of them were on the theme of Robin
Hood, and incited the spectators to become outlaws and rob the rich, apart from the
fact that the authorities disapproved of anything which distracted artisans and
husbandmen from performing their work, going to Mass, and practising archery.

The Act of 1572 included among those who were to be punished as vagabonds 'common players in interludes and minstrels not belonging to any baron of this realm or to any other honourable personage of greater degree'; but actors in the companies of various noblemen, like Shakespeare's actors in the Lord Chamberlain's company, were allowed to perform not only to their patron but before audiences of artisans and other members of the lower classes in London.

The plays that were acted at the beginning of the Tudor Age, apart from the illegal Robin Hood interludes, were all on religious subjects – the 'morality plays', with the characters pointing out the virtues and vices which should be emulated or avoided. The plays *Noah's Flood*, *The Death of Pilate*, *The Fall of Lucifer*, and *The Incredulity of Thomas* were among those which were often acted. One of the last to be written and acted before the repudiation of Papal supremacy was *Everyman*. The character of Everyman represented all men, with their faults and temptations, and the play emphasizes that the only way to attain salvation is by good works, by penance, especially self-flagellation, and through the sacraments and doctrines of the Catholic Church. Everyman is reminded by the character Five Wits that no emperor, king, duke or baron had the power which the least priest has been granted by God, to bear the keys to the blessed sacraments:

> Here in this transitory life for thee and me,
> The blessed sacraments seven there be,
> Baptism, confirmation, with priesthood good,
> And the sacrament of God's precious flesh and blood,
> Marriage, the holy extreme unction, and penance;
> These seven be good to have in remembrance.

This was at the time when the Protestants were challenging the official doctrine that the seven sacraments were the means of salvation, and asserting that they were merely the channels through which salvation could be attained; and Luther had declared that there were only three sacraments, not seven. In 1552, the Protestant Second Book of Common Prayer declared that Baptism and the Lord's Supper were the only two sacraments, and this again became the official doctrine of the Church of England under Elizabeth I.

A very different line was put over by the Protestant propagandist, John Bale, in his play *King John*, which was probably first written in 1538, though in its final form it was only completed after the accession of Elizabeth I, shortly before Bale's death in 1563. The characters in the play, besides King John himself, include 'England, a widow', 'Sedition, the vice', 'Civil Order', 'the Pope', 'Treason', 'Verity', and the monk Simon of Swinefleet, who, according to a tradition which was constantly

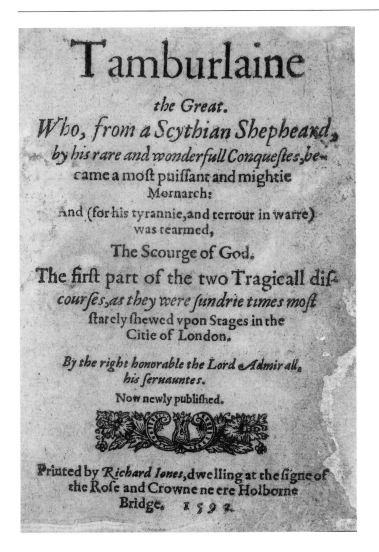

The title-page of the first printed edition of Christopher Marlowe's lurid tragedy, which had been produced in 1587.

referred to by the Protestants in the sixteenth century, had poisoned King John at Swinefleet on the Humber at the orders of the Pope by giving him a cup of poisoned wine, after the monk had sacrificed his own life by drinking first from the cup in order to persuade King John that it was not poisoned. The character Verity, who speaks the words of truth and wisdom throughout the play, declares that a king is, by God's Word, supreme in his kingdom and must never be criticized, even after he has been dead for three hundred years, like King John. In the final scene, a new character enters, 'Imperial Majesty', who is clearly meant to be Henry VIII, and Verity extols his absolute power. Imperial Majesty orders another wicked priest to be hanged, drawn and quartered, although he had induced him to confess by promising him his life, for Imperial Majesty is quite entitled to break his word if he chooses to do so; and the priest is taken away to Tyburn, protesting that he will be canonized by the Pope, like Thomas Becket.

In the reign of Henry VIII, a new type of play was being written; the light comedy, in which some philosophical truths emerge through the humour, reached England with other products of the Italian Renaissance. John Heywood wrote them for nearly seventy years, from his first plays in 1520, when he was a young protégé of Sir Thomas More, to his last works written very shortly before his death in 1587. Nicholas Udall, who was headmaster of Eton and a ferocious flogger until he was disgraced for homosexual offences against the boys, wrote the comedy *Ralph Roister Doister* in about 1535; it was an adaptation of Plautus's comedy of 206 B.C., *Miles Gloriosus*. *Gammer Gurton's Needle*, a very coarse farce by an unknown author, dealing with English village life, was first performed in 1552.

English dramatists also began to write tragedies, usually based on historical themes. Two young students of the Inner Temple, Thomas Sackville and Thomas Norton, wrote a play in blank verse, *Gorbaduc*, about a mythical early British King who was let down by his two sons when he divided his kingdom between them – a story which may have given Shakespeare the idea for his *King Lear*. It was first acted before Elizabeth I in January 1562. When Elizabeth visited Oxford in 1566, the scholars at Christ Church performed the play *Pelemon and Arcite*, based on the story from Greek mythology; but many tragedies were written about English Kings. The villainous Richard III was a favourite subject; eight plays were written about him in the years after 1565.

Sometimes the playwrights ventured to write plays about contemporary events, which had been expressly forbidden by Henry VIII's Privy Council in the period of repression in 1543, but was possible under the more tolerant régime of Elizabeth. *The King of Scots*, a tragedy about the assassination of Darnley, was performed in London within a few months of his death in 1567. The 'Spanish fury' at Antwerp in 1576, when Alva's soldiers killed, raped and looted, was the subject of a play, *Alarum for London*, performed a few months later in London, which warned the Londoners of what would be in store for them if Spanish soldiers were ever to capture the city. In one scene, two little boys plead for their lives with a Spanish soldier, who pitilessly kills them both.

These tragedies paved the way for the remarkable output of great dramatic plays which were produced, as well as the comedies, on the London stage in the last fifteen years of the Tudor Age. They began with Christopher Marlowe's *Tamburlaine* which was produced in 1587. Marlowe was a slightly suspect character in the eyes of the authorities. At Cambridge he was thought to have come under the influence of

A PLEASANT Conceited Comedie CALLED, Loues labors loft.

As it vvas prefented before her Highnes this laft Chriftmas.

Newly corrected and augmented
By W. Shakefpere.

Imprinted at London by W.W.
for Cutbert Burby,
1598.

The first edition of Shakespeare's *Love's Labour's Lost*, 1598, in the charming and appropriate typographical dress in which so many plays and books of verse appeared in the late Tudor period.

Francis Kett, an 'Arian' who followed the teaching of the fourth-century theologian, Arius, and denied the divinity of Christ. Kett was one of the few people to be burned as a heretic in Elizabeth's reign, suffering at the stake in Norwich in 1589. There was a passage in *Tamburlaine* which was interpreted by Marlowe's critics as suggesting that he did not believe in God. But Marlowe escaped from the persecution which he would almost certainly have suffered thirty years before; according to one theory, this was because he was protected by Walsingham in return for agreeing to act as an agent in the government's secret service.

328

Marlowe lived for six years after writing *Tamburlaine* before being killed in a brawl in 1593, when he was on the point of being arrested for atheism and sedition. During this time he wrote five more tragedies in blank verse – *Dr Faustus*, *The Jew of Malta*, *The Massacre at Paris* (the Massacre of St Bartholomew), *Edward II*, and *Dido, Queen of Carthage*. In 1589 Marlowe's friend, Thomas Kyd, wrote *The Spanish Tragedy containing the Lamentable End of Don Haratio and Bel-imperia, with the Pitiful Death of Old Hieronimo*, a very popular play about murder and revenge. Kyd was suspected of being involved with Marlowe in the circulation of atheist and seditious leaflets, and after being arrested and tortured, died in 1594 before he could write another tragedy, unless he was the author of the play *Titus Andronicus*, which is usually attributed to Shakespeare. In 1592 Shakespeare's first play was performed, *The Contention betwixt the Two Noble Houses of York and Lancaster*, which is now known as *Henry VI, Parts II and III*. His *Tragedy of King Richard III*, and his three comedies, *A Comedy of Errors*, *The Taming of the Shrew*, and *Love's Labour's Lost*, followed within a year. Before the end of the Tudor Age, in the eleven years between 1592 and 1602, twenty-four of his plays were performed in London, including *Romeo and Juliet*, *The Merchant of Venice*, *Henry V*, *Julius Caesar* and *Hamlet*.

Elizabeth I herself came to see several of Shakespeare's plays performed, and particularly enjoyed *The Merry Wives of Windsor*. Her approval enabled him to survive the difficulty in which he became involved when his play *Richard II* was revived, six years after it had first been performed, at the time of Essex's rebellion in 1601. Apparently Essex's supporters paid the actors to perform it, thinking that a play about a successful *coup d'état* and the deposition of a king would be good propaganda at the time of Essex's rising. Elizabeth was very upset, and complained that the play had been performed forty times in London and had led people to say that she was Richard II. The scene in the play in which Richard abdicates in Westminster Hall was cut out in the remaining performances that year; but Shakespeare escaped without any loss of the royal favour.

The advance in the quality and status of the theatre since the days when plays had been included among unlawful games and actors were regarded as vagabonds was due to the patronage of the nobility; for in view of the Act of Parliament which exempted actors from the whippings and ear-croppings which were the fate of vagabonds, only if they were attached to the household of a nobleman, this patronage alone made it possible for the theatre to survive. Much of the credit must go to the Earl of Leicester, who in 1574 was the first nobleman to arrange for his actors to perform to the general public in London. The stage was in the courtyard of an inn, the Bull in Bishopsgate, and for some years all plays were acted in the courtyards of inns. The parts were played by professional actors, but no women acted in plays until after 1660, and the women's parts were played by young boys.

The Swan Theatre, on Bankside, was out of range of London's city authorities, in a centre of entertainment including bull-baiting and bear-baiting rings and the archery butts in St George's Fields. The drawing reproduced here is reputed to have been made by the Dutch artist Johannes de Witt on a visit to London in 1596. The theatre had been built in 1595, and its interior closely resembled the structure of the yard of an inn.

Leicester's players played for some years at the Bull, and other companies acted at the Bell Savage inn in Ludgate, the Blackfriars inn, and the Red Bull in St John's Street. Then James Burbage, who was the manager of Leicester's players, decided to build a theatre which would be used for no other purpose except to perform plays to the public. In 1577 he opened the Theatre in Holywell Lane in Finsbury Fields, and the venture was a success. A few years later, a rival company opened a second theatre in London, the Curtain, not far from the Theatre. After these two theatres had survived and prospered for fifteen years, the great boom in stage plays in the 1590s led to three more theatres being opened between 1592 and 1598 – the Rose Theatre, the Swan Theatre in Paris Gardens, and the Globe Theatre, all of them close to each other on the river in Southwark. A sixth theatre, the Fortune Theatre, in Golden Lane, was opened in 1600, and three more theatres had been built by 1613.

Although the comedies of Ben Jonson and Shakespeare were popular, the

Richard Burbage, who was an artist as well as the outstanding actor of the Elizabethan stage, may quite possibly have painted this portrait of himself. It was for Burbage that Shakespeare wrote *Othello*, *King Lear* and *Hamlet*.

dramatic tragedies were appreciated even more. By far the most successful was *The Spanish Tragedy*. The great feature about all of them was the violence and cruelty in the stories, though unlike more modern examples of violence in the theatre they were dignified by the magnificent verse in which they were written. The violence in the plays matched the cruelty of the broadsheets which were sold in the streets of London, with the accounts of the tortures shamefully inflicted by Catholics on Protestant martyrs in France and the Netherlands, and those most justly inflicted by Protestants on Catholic traitors who attempted to assassinate the Queen and foreign Protestant leaders. These bloodthirsty accounts were often illustrated by horrific woodcuts showing tortures and mutilations in the most realistic and unpleasant detail. Often the imagination of the writers exceeded the worst malice of the torturers. Balthasar Gérard, who murdered William the Silent in the Netherlands in 1584, was horribly tortured before being executed; but the tortures which he suffered were not as appalling as those described in the fictitious account of his execution which was sold in London.

The dramatists likewise gave full scope to their imagination. The real Timur i Leng in the fourteenth century massacred whole populations in Asia, but the subtle cruelties which he inflicts on his prisoners in Marlowe's *Tamburlaine* were invented by Marlowe. The ancient Romans committed many cruelties, but the story of Titus Andronicus, with all its horrors, is pure fiction, which was first invented by an unknown author before 1592, and adapted for the London stage in 1594 by Shakespeare and by several other English dramatists.

Today, when there is so much discussion about the effect which violence on television has on the violence which is committed by criminals in real life, it is interesting to see how, at the end of the Tudor Age, violence in the theatre and in real life went hand in hand. There was more cruelty in the administration of justice, in the methods of waging war, and in life in general, in 1600 than in 1500 or 1700, and the theatre of 1600 was much more violent than a hundred years earlier and later. There were no eyes gouged out or hands or tongues cut off in the morality plays of Henry VII's reign; and by 1700, when burnings and hanging, drawing and quartering were almost, if not completely, obsolete, the worst thing that happened to the characters in the plays of Congreve, Farquhar and Vanbrugh was to be mocked and rebuffed by their mistresses or seduced and deceived by their lovers.

It is not surprising that the theatre of the 1590s was violent, because it had to compete with the counter-attraction of bear-baiting, which was often carried on at the same premises, for Paris Gardens was the most popular place for bear-baitings, as well as a popular theatre. Bear-baiting was already popular at the beginning of the sixteenth century; when Erasmus visited London in 1510, he commented on the number of bears that were kept there for baiting. Bears still roamed wild in English forests, and they were captured and placed in the charge of a bearward, who kept them available for baiting. Bear-baiting was popular with all classes. Kings and nobles kept their own bears and bearwards, and watched bear-baitings in the gardens of their palaces and houses; the ordinary people of all classes went to public bear-baitings.

The procedure was to fasten the bear's legs to a post by a chain, and then set fierce dogs on him. The dogs tried to tear out the bear's throat, and although the bear's movements were restricted by his chains, he had enough room for manoeuvre left to him to evade the dogs and defend himself, and even to kill the dogs with his paws.

Henry VIII sometimes watched a bear-baiting. According to the Catholic writers, he appointed Cranmer as Archbishop of Canterbury at a bear-baiting. Elizabeth I enjoyed the sport more than her father had done, and bear-baiting became more popular during her reign than in the earlier part of the century. Soon after she became Queen she attended a bear-baiting with the French ambassador and enjoyed it so much that she stood watching it for several hours until six o'clock in the evening.

When she visited Kenilworth in 1575, a particularly grand bear-baiting was arranged for her, with thirteen bears in action against the dogs. The courtier Robert Laneham, who was present, wrote that 'it was a sport very pleasant' to see the bear trying to free himself from the dogs, 'with biting, with clawing, with roaring, tossing and tumbling . . . with the blood and slaver about his physionomy, was a matter of a goodly relief'.

When the German traveller, Paul Hentzner, visited England in 1598, he attended a public bear-baiting in London. After the usual baiting by the dogs, there followed another sport, whipping a blind bear. The bear, having been blinded, was fastened to a post by a chain. Five or six men then stood round the bear in a semi-circle with whips, 'which they exercise upon him without mercy, as he cannot escape from them because of the chain; he defends himself with all his force and skill, throwing down all who come within his reach, and are not active enough to get out of it, and tearing the whips out of their hands, and breaking them'. The proceedings sometimes ended with the torture of a pony; a monkey was tied to the pony's back, and dogs bit the pony's legs, while he desperately tried to shake off the monkey and the dogs.

It seems extraordinary to the twentieth-century mind that the Tudor legislators, who passed statutes which made it illegal for the lower classes to play tennis, bowls or skittles, should have allowed bear-baiting as almost the only sport which the people were permitted to see. It was actually protected by legislation. Bear-baitings were usually held on Thursdays. In 1591 the organizers of bear-baitings complained to the Privy Council that attendances at the baitings were falling off, because stage plays were being performed on Thursdays and were a powerful counter-attraction. The Privy Council thereupon sent an order to the Lord Mayor, commanding him to ban all stage plays on Thursdays, because 'in divers places the players do use to recite their plays to the great hurt and destruction of the game of bear-baiting and like pastimes which are maintained for Her Majesty's pleasure'. The Puritans condemned bear-baiting, and thought it was a judgment of God when the stand collapsed at a bear-baiting at Paris Gardens in 1583 and killed and injured many of the spectators; but bear-baiting continued throughout the seventeenth century, and was not finally stopped until it was banned by an Act of Parliament, on humanitarian grounds, in 1835.

Hentzner wrote that at the bear-baitings and in the theatres in London there were people walking around with baskets selling apples, pears and nuts at the various seasons of the year, and that nearly all the spectators were smoking tobacco in long clay pipes, 'into the farther end of which they put the herb, so dry that it may be rubbed into powder, and putting fire to it, they draw the smoke into their mouths, which they puff out again through their nostrils like funnels; along with it plenty of phlegm and defluxion from the head'. Drake and his fellow-explorers had brought back tobacco, as well as gold and jewels, from the New World.

For many years after Columbus and the Spaniards first found the natives in America smoking tobacco, they had no wish to imitate them; but by 1550 tobacco was being imported from the West Indies to Spain on a considerable scale, and many Spaniards were smoking cigars. In 1559 the French ambassador in Spain, Jean Nicot, sent some cigars to the French court. They became popular there and elsewhere in France, and the substance in them was called 'nicotine' after Nicot. But tobacco was almost unknown in England before 1585, when Drake, after one of his expeditions to the Spanish Main, brought back some tobacco and sold it to Raleigh. Thanks to Raleigh, smoking became fashionable at court, as well as in the inns frequented by sailors; but the habit did not really catch on in England for some years.

The situation changed after 1595, when smoking suddenly became very popular. Tobacco was sold in shops, not only in London and the ports, but in towns all over England, and was smoked everywhere, even in polite society. The English always smoked tobacco in clay pipes, as many Frenchmen and Spaniards did; but the Spanish habit of smoking cigars was quite unknown in England. In the words of a popular song which was probably first sung in the last decade of the Tudor Age:

> If all the world were sack [sherry], O!
> O then what should we lack, O!
> If, as they say, there were no clay
> How should we take tobacco?

Perhaps because tobacco was a new commodity, and was only beginning to be imported on a large scale, its price varied considerably from year to year and from place to place. In 1597 a pound sold for 35s. in London; in 1598, prices varied between 12s. and £4 10s per pound. In 1600 it was at 16s. a pound, and in 1603 at 30s. a pound. At all times it was very expensive by modern standards, with an ounce of tobacco costing at the least nearly two days' wages, and often three days' wages, for husbandmen and artisans; but this did not prevent a very rapid increase in smoking among all classes. Many people disapproved of smoking as much as others enjoyed it. Some physicians claimed that it had beneficial effects on health, and others argued that it was very harmful; and many people pointed out that smoking increased the risks of fire in houses.

In Ireland, it was mentioned in 1598 as one of the vices of the army captains who had been sent to suppress Tyrone's rebellion. A report to the government accused some of them of embezzling their soldiers' pay in order 'to buy them rich apparel, to maintain their pride and lasciviousness, their drunkenness and quaffing carouses, their tobacco and tobacco pipes'.

The controversy between smokers and non-smokers had become a well-known feature of English life when Ben Jonson's comedy *Every Man in his Humour* was first performed at the Globe Theatre in September 1598, with Shakespeare acting the part of old Knowell, a country gentleman. Knowell's young cousin, Stephen, who is a silly young man, not only talks a great deal about hunting and hawking and soldiering, but extols the delights of 'divine tobacco', which he offers to his friends. The old water-carrier, Cob, does not agree.

> By God's me, I marvel what pleasure or felicity they have in taking this roguish tobacco; it's good for nothing but to choke a man, and fill him full of smoke and embers; there were four died out of one house last week with taking of it, and two more the bell went for yesternight. One of them, they say, will ne'er scape it; he voided a bushel of soot yesterday, upward and downward.

The arguments about smoking were conducted in a more serious vein in 1602, when a London physician, Dr Bushell, denounced it in a book *A Work for Chimney Sweeps, or a Warning to Tobacconists dealing the pernicious use of tobacco*. In the same year, his book was answered in another book, *A Defence of Tobacco*. In 1604 the new King, James I, himself wrote a book against smoking; but the English continued to smoke, undeterred by medical opinion, by royal disapproval, or by the high taxation and price of tobacco.

BEGGARS AND VAGABONDS

IN the Tudor Age, there was a fairly large group of people who were outside society and in perpetual conflict with it. The authorities were very concerned with the problem of beggars, rogues and vagabonds, who refused to work as husbandmen on the land or as artisans in the towns, and roamed the countryside or congregated in the city streets, begging, stealing, and defying all authority. They were the sixteenth-century equivalent of the outlaws of the Middle Ages and the hippies of the twentieth century.

Some of them were soldiers discharged from the army, or sailors who had returned to port after a sea voyage. Some were retainers who had been in the service of a nobleman and had been forced to leave after Henry VII persuaded his Parliament to prohibit the retention of more than a limited number of retainers by an Act of 1504. Another source of vagabonds was provided after the dissolution of the monasteries by Henry VIII. The problem was not confined to the labouring classes, for there are many references in the statutes to university students who became rogues and vagabonds.

In Shakespeare's *Twelfth Night*, which he wrote in 1601, the Clown refers to the problem in his final song.

> But when I came to man's estate
> With hey, ho, the wind and the rain;
> 'Gainst knaves and thieves men shut their gate,
> For the rain it raineth every day.

Shakespeare was thinking about the vagabonds and the attitude of the law-abiding subjects towards them, as well as of the four wet summers of the 1590s, when it had rained nearly every day.

The government were guided by three principles in dealing with beggars and vagabonds, which remained constant throughout the Tudor Age, though the means adopted to achieve the desired ends varied from time to time. The first was that law-abiding people ought to give charitable alms to maintain the aged and impotent poor, who were unable to earn their living because they were old, blind, crippled, sick or infirm. The second was that able-bodied men and women, who preferred to beg and live as vagabonds rather than work, should be severely punished. The third was that all beggars, both the deserving poor and the able-bodied vagabonds, should be confined to their native parishes and not allowed to leave them and roam about the country at large.

When Henry VII became King, the tradition of almsgiving and help for the aged and impotent poor was well-established, and was regarded by the Catholic Church as one of the 'good works' which were necessary for a man to obtain salvation. Charity was practised in the monasteries, chiefly in the form of hospitality to the beggars who passed by, along the highway, or who lived almost permanently in the monastery. The law about able-bodied vagabonds was governed by an Act of Richard II's Parliament of 1383, which had been passed during the period of fear and class hatred that had followed the suppression of the Peasants' Revolt of 1381. The Act directed judges to treat vagabonds as 'to them best shall seem by the law'; and though an Act of 1388 provided that beggars should merely be imprisoned for forty days, the earlier statute was sometimes interpreted as allowing judges to impose the death penalty on vagabonds.

Under Henry VII's lenient régime, the harshness of the law was modified. An Act of 1495 declared that the King wanted all his subjects 'to live quietly and surefully to the pleasure of God and according to his laws, willing and always of his pity intending to reduce them thereunto by softer means than by such extreme rigour therefor provided in a statute made in the time of King Richard II'. The Act of Richard II was repealed, and it was enacted that all 'vagabonds, idle and suspect persons living suspiciously' should be put in the stocks for three days and three nights and fed only on bread and water; anyone who gave them any other food during this time was to be fined twelvepence on every occasion that he did so. After being released from the stocks, the vagabond was to return to the parish where he was born or was best known; if he failed to do so, he was to be put in the stocks again, this time for six days and six nights. Old or impotent beggars who were unable to work were to be allowed to beg, but only in their own parishes; if they went outside them, they were to be punished as if they were able-bodied vagabonds. It was to be no defence for a vagabond to prove that he was a university scholar, a soldier or a sailor, unless he could produce a certificate from the Chancellor of his university, his commanding officer or the captain of his ship, authorizing him to beg and go around the countryside.

A second statute of Henry VII made the law against vagabonds still more lenient. By an Act of 1504 they were only to be put in the stocks for one day and one night for the first, and for three days and three nights for the second, offence. But it was different in the harsher times of Henry VIII. His Parliament in 1530 enacted that the local JPs were to draw up a list of all aged or impotent beggars in their districts and give them a licence to beg in their own parishes only; but anyone else who begged, and any man or woman who was fit to work, who owned no land, had no master, and practised no trade, and who was found roaming the country 'and can give no reckoning how he doth lawfully get his living', was to be taken by the constables to the nearest market town 'and there to be tied to the end of a cart naked and be beaten with whips throughout the same market town . . . till his body be bloody by reason of such whipping'. He was then to be sent home to the parish where he was born, or where he had lived for the last three years; if he did not go there by the shortest route, he was to be whipped again. Anyone who gave food, money or shelter to a vagabond was to be fined any sum which the JPs chose to fix.

The Act, like the statute of 1495, expressly referred to university scholars and discharged soldiers and sailors; and new provisions were inserted to punish unauthorized persons travelling through the country and acting as solicitors, physicians, pardoners who pardoned sinners, palm-readers, or players of unlawful games and actors in unlawful plays. This group were to be punished more severely than any other, for they were to be whipped twice on two consecutive days. For the second offence they were again to be whipped twice, and on the third day put in the pillory from 9 a.m. till 11 a.m. and lose one ear; for the third offence they were to be whipped twice and lose the other ear in the pillory.

In 1536 the smaller monasteries, whose annual income was less than £200 a year, were dissolved and all the greater houses had gone by 1540. The monks themselves were paid pensions by the royal treasury for the rest of their lives, varying from £100 a year for the abbot to £5 a year for most of the monks, and forty shillings a year for the gardeners and some of the servants of the monastery; but many of the servants received nothing, nor did the beggars and others who had been granted hospitality in the monasteries. They added to the numbers of vagabonds in the realm. In July 1536 the Emperor's ambassador, Chapuys, reported that twenty thousand former inmates of the monasteries were begging on the highways. His figure is almost certainly exaggerated, because he was strongly opposed to Henry VIII's religious policy and to the suppression of the monasteries, and received most of his information from the Papist enemies of the government; and he knew that Charles V would be delighted to read such reports.

The government responded by passing another and even more severe Act against vagabonds in 1536, though further provision was made for giving charitable relief to

A sixteenth-century woodcut of a beggar being whipped through the streets, to the obvious enjoyment of the spectators. The vista through the archway suggests gruesome possibilities.

the old and impotent. The mayors and JPs were to make sure that all able-bodied vagabonds who had been whipped and sent home to their native parishes were 'kept to continual labour' there; they were to organize house-to-house searches once a month to find any vagabonds in their parishes; and they were to take any child over five years of age who was found begging in the parish and assign him to employment with a master until he reached the age of sixteen. If any child over twelve refused to take such employment, or left it without permission, he was to be whipped, and any constable who refused to whip him was to be put in the stocks for two days with nothing but bread and water. If any vagabond who had been whipped was found idly wandering for the second time, he was to be whipped again and have the upper part of his right ear cut off as an identification mark; and any constable who refused to cut it off was to be fined five marks (£3 6s.8d.) on every occasion that he refused to do so. For the third offence the vagabond was to be hanged as a felon. The provisions for the punishment of constables who refused to whip beggar children or to cut off the ears of vagabonds, like the fines imposed on anyone who gave vagabonds food or shelter, suggest that there was quite widespread sympathy for vagabonds. Parliament never found it necessary to impose punishments on constables who refused to assist at the burning of heretics or at the execution of Papist traitors.

339

The law against vagabonds was apparently enforced very vigorously under Henry VIII, for according to the historian Raphael Holinshed, who published his book in 1578, 72,000 thieves and vagabonds were hanged in Henry's reign, though the great majority of these were undoubtedly hanged for stealing, and not for committing their third offence as vagabonds. The figure of 72,000 is very large, and as the total population of England at the time was under three million, it amounted to two and a half per cent of Henry's subjects, which is almost as high a percentage of the population as the number of victims of Hitler and Stalin and the twentieth-century dictators. It has sometimes been suggested that this figure of 72,000 was a misprint or clerical error, and that 7,200 was the correct figure; but this overlooks the fact that in the Tudor Age people nearly always wrote figures in Roman numerals, and that no confusion could arise between lxxii^m (72,000) and vii^{m}cc (7,200). Seventy-two thousand is not impossible. The surviving records of proceedings at assizes and quarter sessions show that at most sessions some ten, twelve or fourteen defendants were hanged, most of them for theft. If an average of twelve people were hanged four times a year in each of the forty counties of England, this would give a total of 1,920 a year, or nearly 73,000 in the thirty-eight years of Henry's reign.

The vagabonds may have been responsible for some of the assaults on members of the public, the maiming of farm animals, and other acts of wanton destruction which became frequent in the last years of Henry VIII's reign; but many of these offences were probably committed by husbandmen and persons in other employment who had a grudge against society or wished for some other reason to indulge in hooliganism. The Act of 1545, which dealt with these offences, did not specifically attribute them to vagabonds, but to 'men of evil and perverse dispositions and seduced by the instigations of the Devil'. These malefactors surreptitiously set fire to stocks of timber which had been assembled by householders in preparation for carrying out building work on their houses; they broke down the heads of dams and other waters, cut conduit pipes, burned carts laden with coal or wood, damaged apple trees and pear trees, cut out the tongues of cattle and other animals, and cut off the ears of some of the King's law-abiding subjects. In view of the timber shortage in the kingdom, there was no doubt which of these offences was regarded as the most serious; for the Act provided that anyone who set fire to timber stocks was to be punished by death, whereas the other crimes referred to in the Act, including cutting off the ears of the King's subjects, were punishable only by a £10 fine payable to the King and compensation to the victim of three times the estimated damage which he had suffered.

After Henry VIII's death, Parliament adopted a novel solution of the problem of vagabonds. In 1547 Edward VI's first Parliament, under Somerset's reforming government, repealed many of the Acts of Henry's reign which had created new capital offences of treasons and felonies; but the statute which it passed against beggars and vagabonds was the most severe yet. The Act complained that previous laws against vagabonds had not been effective because those officers who should have enforced them had felt 'foolish pity and mercy' for the vagabonds; and it enacted that if any man or woman who was 'lurking in any house or houses or loitering and idly wander by the highways side or in the streets in cities, towns or villages, not applying themself to some honest and allowed art, science, service or labour' continued to do so for three consecutive days, he was to offer himself as a servant to any master who would pay him wages; if no master was willing to do so, he was to offer to serve some master for his meat and drink only. If he did not do this, anyone who encountered him could ask the JPs to make him his slave for two years. After the vagabond had been branded on the chest with the letter V, his new master was to take him, 'and only giving the said slave bread and water or small drink, and such refuse of meat as he shall think mete, cause the said slave to work by beating, chaining or otherwise in such work and labour, how vile soever it be, as he shall put him unto'. If the slave ran away during his two years of service, he was to be branded, when recaptured, with the letter S and become his master's slave for life.

As beggars and vagabonds often carried their children around with them as they wandered through the country, their children over five years of age were to be taken from them and allotted as servants to masters chosen by the JPs, with whom the male children must remain till they were twenty-four and the female children till they were twenty; if they ran away, they were to become the master's slave. If their parents, or anyone else, stole them away from their master, both the parent and the child were to become the master's slave. Anyone who gave shelter to an escaping slave was to be fined £10. If a slave, during or after his term of slavery, assaulted his master or mistress, tried to burn their house or corn, or plotted with other persons to lie in wait for their master or mistress and attack them, they were to be hanged, unless their master or mistress was prepared to take them as their slave for ever. The reference to slaves and their friends lying in wait for their master in order to ambush him is reminiscent of the plan of Caliban, Stephano and Trinculo to launch a secret attack on Prospero in Shakespeare's play *The Tempest*. These assaults were perhaps not an unknown occurrence in the Tudor Age.

It is not surprising that this extraordinary statute, after having been largely forgotten by historians for three hundred years, was re-discovered by Karl Marx in the Reading Room of the British Museum and cited by him in his *Capital* in 1867 as an example of class oppression; but it was repealed after three years on the grounds that it had not been enforced. The ferocious language of the Act was probably intended to frighten potential vagabonds, and this, rather than the punishment of the vagabonds, may have been the chief purpose of the Act; for the Act provided that it was to be read out in every market town on market day and twice a year at every quarter sessions. Even this provision may not have been enforced in practice, for the Act was so long that it must have taken more than half an hour to read it aloud.

The Act of 1550, which repealed this statute, reinstated the Act of 1530, which punished vagabonds by the slightly more lenient punishments of whipping and loss of ears, but not by death or slavery. It also enacted that any husbandman who refused to work for reasonable wages was to be deemed a vagabond. Any vagabond's children between the ages of five and fourteen could be taken from the vagabond and put to labour without wages for a master chosen by the JPs till they reached the age of eighteen in the case of a boy or fifteen in the case of a girl; if the child ran away, the master could punish him by putting him in the stocks. But it was provided that if two witnesses persuaded the JPs that the master was being 'unreasonable in ordering and bringing up' the child, they were to remove him and send him as a servant to another master.

The Act of 1550 introduced for the first time the institution which in later centuries became known as 'the workhouse'. A house was to be set up in every parish where the aged and impotent poor were to be sheltered and cared for, and put to any work of which they were capable, which they were to perform without wages; if they refused to go to the house or to do the work, they were to be treated as vagabonds. Two years later, an Act made new provisions for the collecting of alms for the maintenance of the poor in these houses. Instead of merely requiring the vicars to urge the people to contribute, the Act of 1552 enacted that the vicar and churchwardens were to elect every year in Whitsun week two 'Gatherers and Collectors of the Charitable Alms', who were to attend church on the following Sunday and 'gently ask and demand of every man and woman what they of their charity will be contented to give weekly towards the relief of the poor'; and the Collectors were to call on these people every week to collect the sums that they had promised to give. But there was no kind of compulsion on anyone to pay.

The restoration of the Catholic religion under Mary did not lead to any change in the government policy about beggars and vagabonds. The only respect in which the clock was not put back to 1533 was in regard to the monasteries; for though Mary restored to the monks a few of the monastic lands which were still in the possession of the Crown, she agreed to allow the purchasers of the confiscated property of the monasteries to retain the lands, as part of an unofficial bargain by which the representatives of the gentry in Parliament agreed to re-enact the law for burning heretics. The Acts of 1550 and 1552 for the punishment of able-bodied vagabonds and the relief of the aged and impotent poor remained unaltered; but for the first time a slight element of compulsion was introduced into the collecting of alms. If anyone in the parish refused to contribute to the relief of the poor in the houses established

A suppliant for alms, in torn and tattered garments, outside his humble dwelling. A woodcut from *A Christall Glass of Christian Reformation* by Stephen Bateman, 1569.

for them, the Gatherers and Collectors of the Charitable Alms were to 'charitably exhort him to give, and if he is obstinate shall send him to the bishop' of the diocese, who was to induce him 'by charitable means and ways tested' to contribute; and if he still refused, the bishop was 'to take order for the charitable reformation of every such obstinate person'.

Under Elizabeth the law remained unchanged until the Act of 1572, which repealed the earlier statutes for the punishment of vagabonds. Henceforth a vagabond was 'to be grievously whipped and burned through the grissel of the right ear with a hot iron' an inch wide, unless some 'honest householder' owning land worth twenty shillings or goods worth £5 agreed to take him into his service. If the vagabond left his employer, or if he was convicted of being a vagabond for a second time, he was to be hanged as a felon unless someone else agreed to employ him; and for the third offence he was in any case to be hanged, without benefit of clergy. Thus capital punishment for vagabonds was reintroduced, twenty-two years after it had been abolished by the Act of 1550. The aged and impotent poor were to be sent to the houses for the poor, which were now called 'Abiding Places'; and no beggars were to be allowed to go to those Tudor health resorts, the baths at Bath or Buxton, without a licence from their local JPs.

It is difficult to know how far the Acts against vagabonds were actually enforced in practice. The surviving records of the courts of assizes and quarter sessions contain very few cases of proceedings against vagabonds; but these records are incomplete, and in any case do not prove that vagabonds were not dealt with in the courts. The records show that about three-quarters of all the crimes tried in the courts were some form of theft, which is almost exactly the same percentage as it is in the courts in the twentieth century; and the most likely explanation of the absence of references in the court records to vagabonds is that it was simpler to prosecute and hang vagabonds for stealing, a crime which they were almost forced by circumstances to commit, rather than to proceed against them as vagabonds, when they could only be hanged for the third offence. It has been estimated that about eight hundred thieves were hanged every year in the reign of Elizabeth I, and many of these were almost certainly vagabonds.

An Act of 1576 inaugurated yet another change in policy and began the practice, which was to last for the next 260 years, of giving work to the aged and impotent poor to perform in their own homes. In every borough, the mayor was to keep a store of 'wool, hemp, flax, iron or other stuff' and hand it out to the aged and impotent poor for them to do any work that they were able, and were ordered, to do with these materials. The authorities were to pay them what they considered to be a suitable wage for the work done. If any old or infirm person refused to do the work, or spoiled or embezzled the materials, the churchwardens and Collectors and Governors of the Poor could decide, by a majority vote, to send the offender to the House of Correction 'in convenient apparel mete for such a body to wear . . . there to be straitly kept, as well in diet as in work, and also punished from time to time' as the Governors of the House of Correction saw fit. Any old or infirm person who was given poor relief but nevertheless went begging was to be whipped and burned through the right ear, and hanged for the third offence, unless an honest householder with the necessary property qualification was prepared to take him into his service.

The Act of 1576 for the first time imposed a punishment on those parishoners who refused to contribute to the cost of providing relief for the deserving poor or for maintaining a House of Correction. Anyone who refused to respond to the

344

exhortations of the Collectors for the Poor was to be forced to pay twice the rate that he would otherwise have had to pay.

The problem of vagabonds had always been accentuated by the soldiers discharged from the army; and after the whole nation had celebrated and given thanks to God for the victory over the Spanish Armada, Parliament at long last made special provision for discharged and wounded soldiers. A statute of 1593 enacted that any soldiers who had 'adventured their lives and lost their limbs or disabled their bodies' by their service in the army since 25 March 1588 could apply to the county treasurers for a weekly sum of money for their relief, to which every parish was to contribute. Any wounded soldier who, despite receiving a pension, went around begging, was to be punished as a vagabond.

The Parliament of 1597 passed five statutes dealing with old and infirm beggars, with vagabonds, and with wounded and impotent soldiers. The death penalty for vagabonds was again abolished, and was never reintroduced in England; it was retained only for discharged soldiers who were wandering around the country, committing crimes and terrifying the population. Vagabonds were to be punished by whippings, and persistent offenders could be sentenced by the courts to confinement in a House of Correction or to be banished from the realm. It was only if they returned without permission from banishment that they were to suffer death. Parishioners who refused to contribute for the relief of the poor could now be punished by imprisonment; and the parents and children of old, blind and infirm paupers were required to pay such contributions for their maintenance as were fixed by the JPs. These provisions were re-enacted by two statutes in Elizabeth's last Parliament of 1601.

The law for the relief of the deserving poor and the punishment of vagabonds, which was enacted in 1597 and confirmed in 1601, continued to apply with very little change till the New Poor Law was introduced in 1834, when the granting of relief to the poor in their homes, which in some form or other had existed throughout the Tudor Age, was virtually abolished. After another hundred years, the Abiding Places and workhouses of 1550 were in their turn abolished, and the principle of paying for poor relief by compulsory insurance was instituted in the twentieth century. But the dual problem of giving charitable relief to the poor and discouraging idleness is still with us in 1988, though no one now suggests that able-bodied shirkers should be punished by whipping, mutilation, enslavement or death.

TUDOR MEN AND WOMEN

W HAT were men and women like in the Tudor Age? It is not easy to understand the outlook of our ancestors, who are separated from us by only thirteen or fourteen generations, by studying the contemporary chronicles, the State papers, the Acts of Parliament, the ecclesiastical registers and the law reports, though we can learn a little more from the few diaries which have survived and from the words and behaviour of the characters in the plays of Shakespeare and his fellow dramatists.

Half a dozen inhabitants of London kept diaries which can still be read today, covering the years between 1485 and 1563. They all have a good deal in common. Charles Wriothesley, the herald, wrote rather more than the others about political events; and Henry Machyn, the undertaker, was particularly interested in funerals, the lying-in-state of the Kings and Queens, and the Masses held at the deaths of foreign sovereigns. But together they tell us a great deal about the ordinary life of the Londoners. They refer to the weather, to the very cold Christmas of 1536, when the Thames was frozen over and it was impossible to travel by barge, and the very hot summer of 1540, when the cattle died because the ponds had dried up. They did not have any way of measuring heat, for the first thermometer was not invented by Galileo in Italy until 1597, and the improved thermometer which he developed in 1612 did not reach England until later in the seventeenth century; but the comments of the diarists about the great heat and the bitter cold in the various years are confirmed in nearly every case by the records of the harvests and the price of corn.

The diarists describe the days of national celebrations, when all the churches in London rang their bells for a day and a night, and the conduits in the streets ran with wine, like the capture of Francis I by Charles V's army at Pavia in 1525 and the proclamation of Queen Mary during the revolt against Jane Grey in 1553. The executions of traitors and the burnings of heretics are often mentioned, usually very briefly and without comment. The Franciscan monk who kept the chronicle of the

None but Chriſt, none but Chriſt.

A woodcut from Foxe's *Book of Martyrs*, 1570, illustrating 'the order and maner of the burnyng of the constant Martyr in Christ John Lambert'. A refinement of this punishment was the raising of the martyr's body on the points of pikes, so as to give the flames an extra draught.

Greyfriars of London, both before and after the dissolution of the monastery, recorded very succinctly the burnings of heretics in the autumn of 1538:

> xxx Anno.* This year the xxii day of November was one Lambert otherwise called Nicolas, was burned in Smithfield for great heresy. And the xxix of November was burned in Smithfield John Mattessey a Dutchman, Peter Finch and his wife, for heresy. And this year in December was beheaded at the Tower Hill Lord Henry Marquess of Exeter, Lord Henry Montagu and Sir Edward Neville. And this year was all the places of religion within the city of London suppressed in November. And this year the xxiii day of December was burned in Smithfield Richard Turner weaver and Peter Florence butcher.

* The thirtieth year of Henry VIII's reign, which began on 21 April 1538.

347

But Charles Wriothesley, who was never as concise as the Franciscan monk, wrote at greater length about the execution of Lady Bulmer for high treason because of the support which she and her husband had given to the rebels of the Pilgrimage of Grace. He recorded that on 25 May 1537, after Bulmer and four of his colleagues had been taken to execution, 'Margaret Cheyney, other wife to Bulmer called, was drawn after them from the Tower of London into Smithfield and there burned, according to her judgement, God pardon her soul, being the Friday in Whitsun week; she was a very fair creature and a beautiful.'

Natural disasters are recorded, like the thunderstorm of 4 June 1561, when the steeple of St Paul's Cathedral was set on fire by lightning and St Martin's Church in Ludgate was burned down. The diarists, like most of the population, showed great interest in monstrous births; if a child with two heads, or without arms and legs, was born in Oxfordshire or Warwickshire, this was widely accepted as a sign that God did not approve of the government's religious policy. When a calf was born at Highgate in December 1548 with two heads, four ears, four eyes, eight feet and two tails, it was led into London and exhibited to the Lord Mayor and aldermen and the public in Newgate before it was taken to the fields outside the city and killed and buried.

The people were fascinated by unusual murder cases, like the case of young Lord Dacre of Hurstmonceux, who was usually called Lord Dacre of the South, to distinguish him from Lord Dacre of Gisland in Cumberland, who was Lord Dacre of the North. On the night of 30 April 1541 Lord Dacre and thirteen young gentlemen and yeomen from London, Sussex and Kent met at Lord Dacre's house at Hurstmonceux in Sussex and decided to go poaching on the lands of a gentleman who lived nearby at Hellingly. The party split into two groups, and set out for the woods by different routes. One group, which consisted of Lord Dacre and seven of his friends, encountered three of the landowner's gamekeepers, and a fight ensued in which one gamekeeper was killed. Lord Dacre and the seven other poachers who had met the gamekeepers were put on trial for murder, and condemned to death. There was much sympathy for the good-looking young nobleman of twenty-four, but Henry VIII insisted that the death sentence be carried out, and Lord Dacre was duly hanged at Tyburn.

No murder case during the Tudor Age attracted as much attention as the murder of Thomas Arden in his house at Faversham in February 1551* by his wife and the servant who was her lover, with the help of her maidservant and other servants and their friends in the town. The case had all the necessary ingredients of violence, sex,

---

* The date 1550 given in the official records and contemporary diaries, and on the commemorative plaque on Arden's house at Faversham, is the date by the Old Style calendar, by which the year began on 25 March.

A crude illustration from a late sixteenth-century chapbook purporting to record in detail the celebrated murder of Thomas Arden of Faversham by his wife and her lover, Mosbie, aided and abetted by the servants of the household, Black Will and Shakbag.

and the social standing of the victim, to arouse public interest. Mrs Arden was burned at Canterbury, because she had committed petty treason by murdering her husband. So had the servants by murdering their master; and the maidservant was burned and the menservants hanged, drawn and quartered at Faversham. The criminals from the town were merely guilty of murder, and were hanged. People still remembered the murder forty years later, when the play *Arden of Faversham* was performed on the London stage.

It was an age of violence, though gentlemen did not kill each other in duels on anything like the scale on which this occurred in France in the sixteenth century. The common people killed each other in brawls in taverns, and in playing football. Men struck each other when angry, and to avenge an insult. Masters regularly beat their servants, and Foxe obviously considered that Cranmer deserved special praise because he never struck or reviled a servant. The Act of 1543, which enacted that if anyone shed blood within the curtilage of the court he was to have his right hand cut off, expressly exempted a master from punishment if he shed the blood of his servant while he was chastising him.

Men and women often spat as an expression of contempt. They spat at men in the stocks and in the pillory. Women spat at admirers who irritated them, and clergymen spat at other clergymen with whom they disagreed on questions of theology. When

349

the Protestant martyr, John Philpot, the former Archdeacon of Winchester, was imprisoned in the King's Bench prison in Southwark in Mary's reign, waiting to be burned as a heretic, he met a fellow prisoner who was also about to be burned for heresy. The man was an Arian who, like Arius, denied the divinity of Christ. Philpot spat in the man's face, and spent his last days before he and the Arian were burned in writing a tract with the makeshift writing materials which had been secretly smuggled into the prison. It had the splendid title *Apology of John Philpot written for spitting upon an Arian*. He enthusiastically vindicated his action, for the word 'apology' in the sixteenth century meant 'justification', not an expression of regret.

Violence was always ready to erupt, particularly against foreigners. The English were famous throughout Europe for their hatred of 'strangers'. Foreigners who came to England were always encountering this hatred, though sometimes the English would take a liking to one of them, and say: 'It is a pity he is not an Englishman.' The feeling against foreigners was especially strong in London. In 1517, a rumour that the Italian merchants there were seducing the wives and daughters of Englishmen started a riot against foreigners, which Henry VIII sternly suppressed; he insisted on hanging several of the rioters to show the foreign merchants that they could safely come to England to trade.

The hatred of foreigners certainly played a part in turning the Londoners against the Protestants in the reign of Edward VI, when it was estimated that 5,000 foreign Protestants had come to London as refugees from religious persecution in their own countries. They constituted a substantial proportion of the 90,000 inhabitants of London in 1553. The Londoners did not like this, and supported Mary against Jane Grey; but within a few months the hatred of foreigners was a factor working in the Protestants' favour, after Mary married Philip of Spain, and many Spaniards came to England. 'The English hate us Spaniards worse than they hate the Devil', wrote one of King Philip's gentlemen, 'they rob us in town and on the road....We Spaniards move among the English as if they were animals, trying not to notice them; and they do the same to us'. The English had better opportunities for displaying their hatred of Spaniards in the reign of Elizabeth I. For every Englishman who fought against Spain out of his devotion to the Protestant cause, there were probably ten who did so because they hated Spaniards and foreigners.

Women were clearly regarded by everyone as being subordinate to men; but they were accorded a place of some importance and honour in society. Their husbands were expected to treat them kindly, and with respect; and Fitzherbert, in *The Book of Husbandry*, urged husbands to keep their wives fully informed about money matters.

We can form some idea of the attitude of Tudor men towards women by the conduct of the characters in Shakespeare's plays, though this is not an entirely reliable guide. In every generation, the heroes and heroines on the stage sometimes behave in the way in which conventional society expects them to behave, not in the way that the majority of the people of their generation in fact behave. In Shakespeare's case, he took many of his plots from stories which had been published in Italy more than fifty years earlier, and therefore showed the attitude of Italians in 1540 more than of Englishmen in 1590. We cannot assume that Shakespeare himself necessarily agreed with the sentiments expressed by his characters, even by his heroes and heroines, for he had to bear in mind what his audiences wanted and what his patrons would tolerate. But Shakespeare could not present on the stage any character who was not at least understandable to his audiences, and to this extent, at least, the opinions and behaviour of his heroes and heroines show what was acceptable to Englishmen in the 1590s.

Shakespeare's women have strong personalities and great determination, whether they are playfully mischievous, like Mistress Page in *The Merry Wives of Windsor* or Maria in *Twelfth Night*; admirable and virtuous, like Desdemona in *Othello*, Imogen in *Cymbeline*, Cordelia in *King Lear*, Volumnia in *Coriolanus* and Portia in *Julius Caesar*; evil, like Goneril and Regan in *King Lear*, Margaret of Anjou in *Henry VI*, and Lady Macbeth; or women who show great professional expertise, like Portia the lawyer in *The Merchant of Venice*, Helena the physician in *All's Well that ends Well,* and Viola the diplomat in *Twelfth Night*. Lady Macbeth is wicked, but she shows greater resolve and strength of character than her husband.

The ballads which were sung, and sold in the shops and streets in London, told stories not only of the exploits of English soldiers and seamen who fought against the Spaniards in the Netherlands, at Cadiz, and on the Spanish Main, but also of a heroic woman warrior; for the idea of a woman disguising herself as a man and surpassing all the men on the battlefield has fascinated people in every age until, in the twentieth century, it became possible for women to serve as soldiers without disguising their sex. The ballad of *Mary Ambree*, in the 1580s, told the story of a young English woman who accompanied her sweetheart when he went to fight as a volunteer in the Netherlands and, after seeing him killed in action, disguised herself as a man and performed deeds of valour against the Spaniards. When she is finally taken prisoner by the Spaniards, who boast of having captured an English knight and captain, she reveals the truth:

> No captain of England; behold in your sight
> Two breasts in my bosom and therefore no knight,

and then proceeds to demonstrate the virtue as well as the courage of English women by refusing the invitation of the Duke of Parma to become his mistress. She explains to him that a maiden of England will never agree to become the harlot even of a monarch.

In Tudor England gluttony, not lust, was the national sin, and the courts of the Tudor sovereigns, and Tudor society, were largely free from the sexual immorality of the court of the French Kings. There is nothing in English drama or literature to compare with the stories of the love affairs of noble ladies and merchants' wives in Queen Margaret of Navarre's *Heptameron* of 1530 and the Abbé Brantôme's *Lives of Gallant Ladies* fifty years later. Shakespeare's unmarried young women sometimes flirt and tease, but the only married women in all his plays who are unfaithful to their husbands are the very villainous Goneril and Regan. His plays show the double standards which in every age, at least until the twentieth century, have always been applied to extra-marital relationships when indulged in by men and women. Desdemona is virtuous, and the admirable Cassio never attempts to seduce his general's wife; but no one thinks the worse of him because he has a whore, Bianca.

A visitor from Mantua, who came to England in 1557, suspected that English wives were not always as virtuous as they appeared to be. He thought that many of them had lovers, though they were very careful to keep this secret, for if they were found out, they might be treated as bawds, and either ducked in the pond or exposed in a cart to public ridicule and contempt. Like many other foreigners, he found English women very beautiful, and thoroughly approved of the custom in England that when a man met a woman acquaintance, he greeted her with a kiss. The visitor from Mantua also commented on the fact that when Englishmen met, they usually shook hands, like the Germans did. He noted that there were no brothels in London, for 'the stews' had been suppressed after a big round-up of prostitutes and vagabonds in 1519.

Although Shakespeare's married women are strong and determined, they do not defy their husbands' authority over them. The only two who attempt to do so, Katherine in *The Taming of the Shrew* and Titania in *A Midsummer Night's Dream*, are eventually reduced to submission by the punishments which their husbands most properly inflict upon them. But married women also have their rights, the chief of which is not to be wrongly suspected of having committed adultery. Several of Shakespeare's virtuous wives are accused of adultery by jealous husbands who have been persuaded to do so by some villain acting in his own interests. Othello reacts by murdering Desdemona. He is portrayed as a noble character, apart from his one fault of being too credulous and being deceived by Iago's lies; and it is clearly implied that if Desdemona had in fact been guilty, he would have been quite justified in smothering her. In this, Shakespeare is following the tradition of his Italian sources. There were several cases in Italy and France of cuckolded husbands taking the law into their own hands and killing their adulterous wives; but if any English nobleman had done this in the Tudor Age, he would have been prosecuted for murder.

The motives of Shakespeare's villains in slandering these virtuous women tell us a good deal about the Tudor Age. Iachimo slanders Imogen merely because she has rejected his advances; but lust plays only a very minor part in Iago's slanders against Desdemona. His principal motive is the hope of gaining more rapid promotion in the army by incriminating Cassio. Don John in *Much Ado About Nothing* is a character that Tudor audiences could well understand. He wrongly accuses the virtuous maiden, Hero, of unchastity in order to prevent her marriage to a 'young start up' who may rival his influence at court.

Shakespeare was a friend of Marlowe and Kyd, who were suspected of atheism and sedition. He moved in a circle of unorthodox intellectuals who held opinions on morals which they did not dare to express openly, but which sometimes emerge in the plays. Hamlet, who is certainly portrayed as a sympathetic character, behaves on several occasions in a way which was outrageous by orthodox standards of the period. He murders Polonius, thinking that he is killing the King and committing the supreme and unpardonable sin of regicide; and he then proceeds to treat Polonius's corpse with a shocking lack of respect. On his way to England with Rosencrantz and Guildenstern, he first breaks open a letter sealed with the King's seal, and then forges the seal, an offence which was high treason and punishable by death in Tudor England. By these means he contrives for Rosencrantz and Guildenstern to be put to death without giving them time to confess their sins to a priest. Finally, in the last dramatic scene, he actually commits regicide by killing the King, after fighting a duel with Laertes during which the Queen states that Hamlet 'is fat, and scant of breath'. This remark was sure to raise a laugh from the audience at the Globe Theatre, for Shakespeare's leading actor, Richard Burbage, who played Hamlet, was a fat man who puffed and panted when he had to fight an energetic duel on the stage.

The subordinate position of women in society was not affected by the fact that for fifty years between 1553 and 1603 England was ruled by two female sovereigns. For a thousand years it was accepted by public opinion that the only position in public life which a woman was allowed to hold was to be head of State; for royal privilege was powerful enough to override the general rule about the inferiority of women. Elizabeth I, who often referred to the fact that although she was a weak woman she had been chosen by God to be a queen, wished to uphold the conventions of society and to exalt the royal prerogative by stressing that it was only because she was a queen that she was entitled to meddle in public affairs, which no other woman ought to do. This was accepted by the great majority of her subjects, though Nicholas Heath, the Catholic Archbishop of York, when opposing the Act of Supremacy in the House of Lords in 1559, said that as a woman could not be a priest or hold any position in the Church, she could not be its Supreme Head.

Knox, who throughout his life worked closely with several devoted women collaborators in the Protestant movement, challenged the concept of the royal prerogative by asserting that queens were no exception to the general rule that a woman could not hold any position of authority in the State. It was because Knox attacked her position as a queen, not her rights as a woman, that Elizabeth considered him to be a dangerous revolutionary.

The Protestant movement was originally a revolutionary movement against Church and State, and when Mary became Queen its extremist wing became revolutionary again, after a twenty-year interlude during which the Protestants had been the most zealous upholders of absolute monarchy. This may have been the reason why women were attracted to Protestantism. Many women rebelled against their inferior status, as well as the heresy laws, by becoming active in the Protestant movement. Women normally played no part in politics. When, after the suppression of the Pilgrimage of Grace in 1537, some women took down the corpses of executed rebels which had been left to hang in chains in the villages in Cumberland, the authorities assumed that they had done so on the orders of their husbands. In view of this, it is very significant that of the 283 Protestant martyrs who were burned in Mary's reign, as many as fifty-six were women.

Their Catholic opponents wrote a great deal about the wicked and presumptuous Protestant women. One of the points at issue between Catholics and Protestants was that the Protestants believed that priests should be entitled to marry. The Catholics thought that the Protestant priests had only become Protestants in order to gratify their lust by marrying women. As the Catholics did not recognize the validity of a priest's marriage, they called the wives of the Protestant priests their 'harlots'. From here it was only a step to asserting that all Protestant women were immoral. This became one of the main themes of Catholic propaganda. Sir Thomas More, in one of his scurrilous books against the Lutherans, wrote that Protestant men and women copulated in their churches during their religious services. The London shoemaker, Miles Huggarde, who wrote poetry, and in Mary's reign was granted a licence by the authorities to write and publish vitriolic tracts against the Protestants, repeated all the old libels about the immorality of Protestant women, and thought out a new one of his own: Protestant women encouraged their husbands to become martyrs so that they could be free to fornicate with their lovers and marry again as soon as their husbands had been burned at the stake.

One of the most prominent Protestant women was the Lincolnshire gentle-woman, Anne Askew. She had married a gentleman named Kyme, but showed her rebellious disposition by leaving her husband and calling herself by her maiden name of Askew as she went around London distributing Protestant tracts. She was suspected of secretly giving the tracts to various ladies in the household of Queen

The spectacular burning of Anne Askew and her fellow Protestant rebels in July 1546. This woodcut from Foxe's *Book of Martyrs*, 1570, vividly illustrates the ceremony, with spectators forming a ring round the pyre before a specially built grandstand in front of the St Bartholomew gatehouse to Smithfield. The Lord Mayor and other dignitaries watched the show whilst a sermon was preached.

Katherine Parr, including Katherine's sister, Lady Herbert (afterwards the Countess of Pembroke), and the Queen herself; but she refused to incriminate them when she was tortured on the rack, though her legs were so badly injured that she had to be carried in a chair to her execution when she was burned at Smithfield in July 1546. The simple and moving account of her torture, which she wrote and smuggled out of the Tower, was published by John Bale when England became a Protestant state under Edward VI less than a year after her execution.

It was about this time, according to Foxe, that Katherine Parr defended some aspect of Protestant theology in an argument with Henry VIII, and so enraged Henry that he angrily left the room, lamenting the day when women had become clerks, and gave orders for Katherine to be arrested and sent to the Tower. But Katherine was warned about this by Henry's pro-Protestant physician, Dr Butts. She went to Henry, acknowledged her fault in presuming to argue with him, and obtained his forgiveness.

There were a few individuals in the Tudor Age who had ideas which were far in advance of their contemporaries'. In 1516 Sir Thomas More wrote a book in Latin, *The Best State of a Commonwealth and the Island of Utopia*; it was an account of an

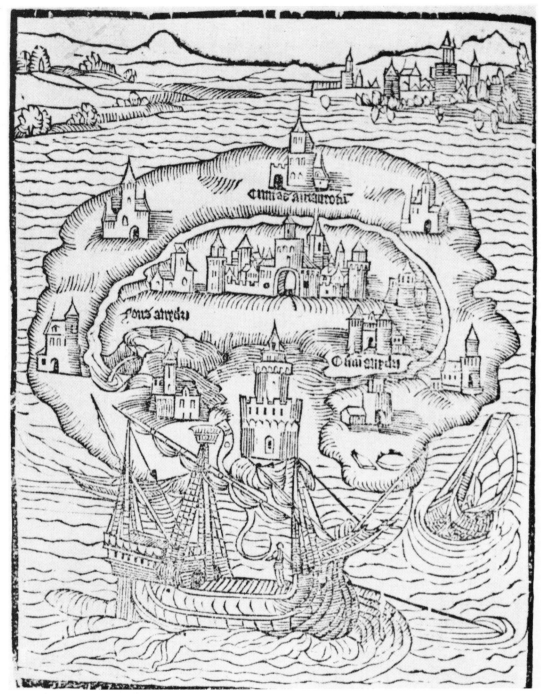

A map of Utopia, from the first edition of Sir Thomas More's famous book, which was printed in Louvain in 1516.

imaginary island off the coast of America which he called Utopia, a word derived from the Greek word meaning 'nowhere'. He thereby introduced a new word into every language in the world. The system of government which he described as existing in Utopia was even more regimented and authoritarian than life in Tudor England; but everything was based on strict logic and equality, and no one was exempted from the regimentation because he was above the rank of a lord or owned land which brought him rents of more than £100 a year.

In his book, More made some passing comments on the attitude of Englishmen at the time. He thought that the vice which most flourished in England in 1516 was pride.

> Pride measures prosperity not by her own advantages but by others' disadvantages. Pride would not consent to be made even a goddess if no poor wretches were left for her to domineer over and scoff at, if her good fortune might not dazzle by comparison with their miseries, if the display of her riches did not torment and intensify their poverty.

A few months after writing *Utopia*, More entered the service of Henry VIII, and soon he was being employed to write abusive books attacking Luther and the Protestants. He seems to have believed that the criticisms and witticisms, which he and his friend Erasmus had levelled at the corruptions of the established Church, had been responsible for the seditious doctrines and mob violence which had spread in Germany after Luther launched his attacks on the Papacy; and after he became Lord Chancellor he became a savage persecutor of heretics. It was at this time that he wrote, in one of his polemics against the Protestants, that he thought that some of his earlier books – he meant *Utopia* – should never be translated into English for the common people to read, and that if anyone translated them he would have the copies burned.

The humanitarian ideals, so far in advance of his time, in which More had believed in the days when he wrote *Utopia,* were being nurtured a few years after his death by a very small group of Protestants in London whom More would have burned if he had known about them. Richard Hilles was a London merchant who kept his opinions very secret in the years of the Catholic reaction which followed the Act of the Six Articles and the fall of Cromwell in 1540. His religious beliefs can roughly be called Zwinglian, probably because these were the most unorthodox and libertarian doctrines, apart from the extreme of Anabaptism, which it was possible to hold at the time. As a merchant, Hilles went every year to the Frankfurt fair, and from there he could safely write letters to the Zwinglian theologian, Bullinger, in Zürich, in which he told him what was happening in England. Hilles did not adopt the usual

Protestant line of blaming Gardiner for persuading the King to persecute Protestants; he placed the blame fairly and squarely on Henry himself. Although he was particularly indignant about the torturing and burning of the Protestants, he also disapproved of the cruelty with which Henry executed Papists whom he accused of high treason; and unlike the Scottish Protestants, he did not believe that Henry was advancing the Protestant cause when he sent his armies to burn Edinburgh and all the abbeys, houses and farms in the Border regions of Scotland.

It was one of Hilles's Protestant friends, Robert Brinkelow, who in 1545 published, anonymously and illegally, *The Complaint of Roderick Mors*. In his book, he refrained from attacking the King; instead, like other Protestants, he denounced the bishops, especially Gardiner, for allowing images in churches and burning Protestants, and accused Gardiner of having mistresses; but he also put forward some original ideas. He was opposed to burning any heretic, and approved of those cities in Germany where even Anabaptists were only banished and not put to death. He also condemned enclosures, and the new landlords who had taken the lands of the suppressed abbeys and had ejected their poor tenants 'to beg and steal and be hanged for it'; the judges, aldermen of London, and the rich who oppressed the poor; the injustice of the law by which the lands of convicted traitors were forfeited to the King, thus unfairly punishing the traitor's wife and children for his offence; and the system of making prisoners pay for their food and lodging in jail, where jailers sometimes charged four times the price that was paid for accommodation in the most expensive inns, and where poor prisoners could only obtain money to pay for their food by working as servants for the wealthier prisoners. But Brinkelow did not believe that these wrongs would ever be righted until there was a change in the manner of electing MPs, for under the existing system 'be he never so very a fool, drunkard, extortioner, adulterer, never so covetous and crafty a person, yet if he be rich, bear any office, if he be a jolly croaker and bragger in the county, he must be a burgess of the Parliament'.

John Foxe, though he believed that a man who swore blasphemously on a night ride in Cornwall was immediately struck dead by God when his horse plunged into a river, was in many ways in advance of his time. When he returned from exile in Switzerland after Elizabeth's accession, he published his *Book of Martyrs* in 1563, and followed it up with a second and much enlarged edition in 1570. It was a powerful piece of Protestant propaganda. Elizabeth's government ordered that copies of the book should be placed in every cathedral, and that sea-captains should take a copy in their ships and read it to their crews to teach them the nature of the Papist enemies against whom they were serving. In 1558, the Catholics were a majority of the population everywhere in England except in London and Kent; when Foxe died in 1587, a substantial majority of the people in nearly every county were probably

Protestants. This was at least partly due to Foxe's book.

Although nearly every Protestant who indignantly denounced the burning of Protestants by Catholics believed that it was right for Protestants to burn Anabaptists, Foxe had grave doubts about this. In 1575 a number of Anabaptists were arrested in London, and two of them were sentenced to be burned. Foxe unsuccessfully interceded with the Queen to spare their lives and subject them to some lesser punishment. He apologized for his attitude by explaining to Elizabeth that he was so soft-hearted that he could not bear to walk past a slaughter yard where animals were killed.

These views had made no impact on the population as a whole when the Tudor Age ended with Elizabeth's death at Richmond Palace at 2 a.m. on Thursday 24 March 1603; by the calendar then in force in England, it was the last day of the old year, 1602. The new year brought a new dynasty to the throne, and a new century and a new age had begun. It would be the century of John Elyot, John Hampden, Oliver Cromwell and the Levellers; of the revolution of 1688 and the introduction of the system of constitutional monarchy; of the last thirteen plays of Shakespeare, of the tragedies of Webster and Middleton, of Milton, Marvell, Dryden, Wycherley and Congreve, of the music of Purcell, the medical discoveries of William Harvey, the scientific work of Isaac Newton, the philosophy of Hobbes and Locke, and the beginning of modern England which emerged from the foundations laid during the Tudor Age.

SOURCES OF ILLUSTRATIONS

The references are the numbers of the pages on which the illustrations appear.

SOURCES

Chapter 1 – THE TUDOR FAMILY

AYLMER, J. – *An Harborrowe for Faithful & Trewe Subiectes agaynst the late blowne Blaste concerninge the Gouvernmēt of Women* (Strasbourg, 1559).

AUERBACH, ERNA, and ADAMS, C. KINGSLEY – *Paintings and Sculpture at Hatfield House* (London, 1971).

BACON, FRANCIS – *History of the Reign of King Henry VII* (ed. J.R. Lumby) (Cambridge, 1881 edn.).

BASKERVILLE, G. – *English Monks and the Suppression of the Monasteries* (London, 1937).

Calendar of Letters, Documents and State Papers relating to the Negotiations between England and Spain in Simancas and elsewhere (1485–1558) (ed. P. de Gayangos, G. Mattingly, R. Tyler, etc.) (London, 1862–1954) (*Spanish Calendar*), i.210, 239.

Calendar of State Papers and Manuscripts relating to English Affairs in the Archives of Venice and other Libraries in Northern Italy (ed. Rawdon Brown, Cavendish Bentinck, etc.) (London, 1864–1947) (*Venetian Calendar*), i.942.

CECIL, DAVID – *The Cecils of Hatfield House* (London, 1973).

CHRIMES, S.B. – *Henry VII* (London, 1972).

FULWELL, U. – *The Flower of Fame: containing the bright Renowne and moste fortunate Reigne of King Henry the VIII* (London, 1575).

GAUNT, W. – *Court Painting in England* (London, 1980).

HOOKHAM, MARY ANN – *The Life and Times of Margaret of Anjou* (London, 1872).

POLLARD, A.F. – *Henry VIII* (London, 1902).

REYNOLDS, GRAHAM – *Nicholas Hilliard and Isaac Oliver. An Exhibition. Victoria and Albert Museum* (London, 1947).

ROSS, C. – *Richard III* (London, 1981).

Statutes of the Realm (London, 1810–24): 1 Hen.VII, first statute (unnumbered).

STRONG, SIR ROY – *The English Renaissance Miniature* (London, 1983).

— *Gloriana: The Portraits of Queen Elizabeth* (London, 1987).

STRONG, SIR ROY, and MURRELL, V.J. – *Artists of the Tudor Court* (London, 1983).

Chapter 2 – LONDON

BARKER, FELIX, and JACKSON, PETER – *London: 2000 years of a City and its People* (London, 1974).

DAVEY, R. – *The Pageant of London* (London, 1906).

—— *The Tower of London* (London, 1910).

GLANVILLE, PHILLIPA – *Tudor London* (London, 1979).

GERARD, J. – *The Autobiography of an Elizabethan* (trans. by P. Caraman) (London, 1951).

HARPER, C.G. – *The Tower of London* (London, 1909).

HOME, G.C. – *Old London Bridge* (London, 1931).

HOSKINS, W.G. – *The Age of Plunder* (London, 1976).

HOWARD, P. – *London's River* (London, 1975).

KENT, WILLIAM (ed.) – *An Encyclopaedia of London* (London, 1937).

KNIGHT, C. – *London* (London, 1843).

LAMBERT, B. – *The History and Survey of London and its Environs* (London, 1806).

The Quenes Maiesties passage through the Citie of London to Westminster the day before her coronation (ed. J.M. Osborn and J.E. Neale) (facsimile reprint of 1559 London edn.)

STOW, J. – *A Survey of London* (Oxford, 1908) (reprint of 1603 edn.)

Valor Eccleiasticus temporis Regi Henrici Octavi (London, 1810–34).

WRIGLEY, E.A., and SCHOFIELD, R.S. – *The Population History of England 1541–1871* (London, 1981).

Chapter 3 – THE KING'S HIGHWAY

BUCHAN, J. – *A Book of Escapes and Hurried Journeys* (London, 1922).

Calendar of Scottish State Papers relating to Mary Queen of Scots 1547–1603 (ed. J. Bain, W.K. Boyd, etc.) (Edinburgh, 1898–1952).

CAVENDISH, G. – *Thomas Wolsey late Cardinall, his lyffe and deathe* (ed. R.S. Sylvester) (Early English Text Society edn.) (Oxford, 1959).

DONNE, W.D. – *Old Roads and New Roads* (London, 1852).

GREGORY, J.W. – *The Story of the Road* (London, 1931).

HARTMANN, C.H. – *The Story of the Roads* (London, 1927).

HOSKINS, W.G. – *The Making of the English Landscape* (London, 1955).

Letters and Papers (Foreign and Domestic) of the Reign of King Henry VIII (ed. J. Brewer and J. Gairdner) (London, 1862–1920) (L.P.) vol. xvi.

REID, R.R. – *The King's Council in the North* (London, 1921).

SAXTON, CHRISTOPHER – *An Atlas of England and Wales* (London, 1574–79).

SHAKESPEARE, W. – *The Works of William Shakespeare* (ed. W.A. Wright), (London, 1902–4).

State Papers . . . King Henry the Eighth (London, 1831–52), i.201.

Statutes of the Realm: 4 Hen.VII, c.3; 24 Hen.VIII, c.11, 16; 25 Hen.VIII, c.8; 26 Hen.VIII, c.7; 32 Hen.VIII, c.17; 34 & 35 Hen.VIII, c.12; 35 Hen.VIII, c.15; 37 Hen.VIII, c.3; 2 & 3 Edw.VI, c.38; 1 Mar., st.3, c.5, 6; 2 & 3 Ph. & M., c.8; 5 Eliz., c.13; 13 Eliz., c.23, 24; 18 Eliz., c.10, 17, 18, 19, 20; 23 Eliz., c.11, 12; 27 Eliz., c.19, 22; 39 Eliz., c.19, 23, 24; 43 Eliz., c.16.

Chapter 4 – THE ESTATES OF THE REALM

BASKERVILLE, op.cit.

DASENT, J.S. (ed.) – *Acts of the Privy Council of England* (London, 1890–1907).

FOXE, J. – *The Book of Martyrs.*

— *The Acts and Monuments of John Foxe* (ed. J. Pratt) (London, 1877, New York, 1965).

— First edition: *Actes and Monuments of these latter and perillous dayes touching matters of the Church* (London, 1563).

— Second edition: *The Ecclesiasticall History, conteyning the Actes and Monuments of thynges passed in every kynges tyme in this realm, especially in the Church of England* (London, 1570).

A History of St Paul's Cathedral and the men associated with it (London, 1957).

HOSKINS, – *The Age of Plunder*, op.cit.

House of Lords Journal, (vol. i, 1509–78).

HUGHES, P. – *The Reformation in England* (London, 1950–4).

L.P.

MACHYN, H. – *The Diary of Henry Machyn* (ed. J.G. Nichols) (London, 1848).

MACLURE, M. – *The Pauls's Cross Sermons 1534–1642* (Toronto, 1958).

MORICE, R. – 'A declaration concernyng . . . that most Reverent Father in God, Thomas Cranmer, late archbisshopp of Canterbury' in J.G. NICHOLS, *Narratives of the Days of the Reformation* (Camden Society), (London, 1859).

POWELL, ENOCH, and WALLIS, KEITH – *The House of Lords in the Middle Ages* (London, 1968).

Statutes of the Realm: 27 Hen.VIII, c.28; 31 Hen.VIII, c.13.

Valor Ecclesiasticus, op.cit.

WRIGHT, T. – *Three chapters of Letters relating to the Suppression of Monasteries* (London, 1843).

WRIOTHESLEY, C. – *A Chronicle of England during the reigns of the Tudors* (ed. W.D.

365

Hamilton) (London, 1875–7).

Zurich Letters (Cambridge, 1852–5).

Chapter 5 – HERETICS AND TRAITORS

The Bible and Holy Scriptures conteyned in the Olde and Newe Testament (Geneva, 1560).

DASENT, op.cit.

DIXON, R.W. – *History of the Church of England* (London, 1878–1902).

Encyclopaedia Britannica (11th edn.) (London, 1910).

FOXE, op.cit.

HERBERT OF CHERBURY, EDWARD, LORD – *The Life and Raigne of King Henry the Eighth* (London, 1649).

HOLDSWORTH, W. – *History of English Law* (London, 1903–9).

HUGHES, op.cit.

KNOX, J. – *The Works of John Knox* (ed. D. Laing) (Edinburgh, 1846–64).

Liturgies of Edward VI (ed. J. Ketley) (Cambridge, 1844).

L.P.

MORE, T. – *The Complete Works of St Thomas More* (ed. R.S. Sylvester, etc.) (New Haven and London, 1963–86).

READ, CONYERS – *Lord Burghley and Queen Elizabeth* (London, 1960).

– *Mr Secretary Cecil and Queen Elizabeth* (London, 1955).

Statutes of the Realm: 2 Hen.IV, c.15; 4 Hen.VII, c.13; 4 Hen.VIII, c.2; 22 Hen.VIII, c.14; 23 Hen.VIII, c.1; 25 Hen.VIII, c.14, 26; 26 Hen.VIII, c.13; 27 Hen.VIII, c.19; 31 Hen.VIII, c.14; 32 Hen.VIII, c.12, 26; 33 Hen.VIII, c.12, 15; 34 & 35 Hen.VIII, c.1; 2 & 3 Edw.VI, c.33; 5 & 6 Edw.VI, c.9, 10; 1 & 2 Ph. & M., c.3, 6; 4 & 5 Ph. & M., c.4; 1 Eliz., c.16; 18 Eliz., c.7; 39 Eliz., c.9, 19.

TYNDALE, W. – *Works* (Cambridge, 1848–9).

Chapter 6 – THE HOUSES

BRITTON, JOHN – *The Architectural Antiquities of Great Britain.* In five volumes (London, 1835).

COOK, G.H. – *The English Cathedral through the centuries* (London, 1960).

COOK, OLIVE, and SMITH, EDWIN – *The English Country House* (London, 1974).

DENT, J. – *The Quest for Nonsuch* (London, 1962).

DU BELLAY, M. and G. – *Mémoires de Martin et Guillaume Du Bellay* (ed. V.L. Bourrilly and F. Vindry) (Paris, 1908–19 edn.).

FULLER, T. – *Church History of Britain* (London, 1868 edn.).

GIROUARD, M. – *Hardwick Hall* (National Trust, 1976).

GIUSTINIANI, S. – *Four Years at the Court of Henry VIII: Selections of Despatches written by the Venetian Ambassador Sebastian Giustinian* (ed. Rawdon Brown) (London, 1854).

HARVEY, J. – *An Introduction to Tudor Architecture* (London, 1949).

HENTZNER, P. – *A Journey into England in the Year MDXCVIII* (ed. Horace Walpole) (Aungervyle Society Reprints) (Edinburgh, 1881–2).

JORDAN, R.F. – *A Picture History of the English House* (London, 1959).

KNOX, op.cit., vol. vi.

LAW, E. – *The History of Hampton Court Palace* (London, 1885–91).

LELAND, J. – *The Itinerary of John Leland in or about the years 1535–1543* (ed. Lucy Toulmin Smith) (London, 1964).

L.P.

MEE, A. – *Derbyshire* (London, 1949).

— *Wiltshire* (London, 1934).

MORICE, op.cit.

PEVSNER, N. – *Derbyshire* (London, 1963).

POLE, R. – *The Reform of England by the Decrees of Cardinal Pole* (ed. H. Raikes) (Chester, 1839).

READ, CONYERS op.cit.

Statutes of the Realm: 4 Hen.VII, c.19; 6 Hen.VIII, c.5; 7 Hen.VIII, c.6; 27 Hen.VIII, c.1, 22; 32 Hen.VIII, c.18, 19; 33 Hen.VIII, c.36; 35 Hen.VIII, c.4; 13 Eliz., c.10; 18 Eliz., c.11; 27 Eliz., c.29; 31 Eliz., c.7; 35 Eliz., c.6.

STRAUSS, SHEILA M. – *A Short History of Wollaton and Wollaton Hall* (Nottinghamshire County Council, 1978).

TIBBLES, A.J. – *Speke Hall* (Merseyside County Council, 1982).

TIPPING, H.A. – *The Story of Montacute and its house* (London, 1933).

Venetian Calendar

Victoria County History:

— *Bedfordshire.*

— *Derbyshire.*

— *Northamptonshire.*

— *Nottinghamshire.*

— *Somerset.*

— *Worcestershire.*

WOOD, A.C. – *A History of Nottinghamshire* (Nottingham, 1947).

Chapter 7 – COSTUME AND FASHION

ASHELFORD, JANE – *Dress in the Age of Elizabeth I* (London, 1988).

— *A Visual History of Costume: The Sixteenth Century* (London, 1983).

BORDE, A. – *The fyrst boke of the Introduction of knowledge* (no place, 1547?).

CUMMING, VALERIE – *Exploring Costume History 1500–1900* (London, 1981).

CUNNINGTON, C. WILLETT and PHILLIS – *A Handbook of English Costume in the 16th Century* (London, 1962).

—— *A Picture History of English Costume* (London, 1960).

CUNNINGTON, PHILLIS, and LUCAS, CATHERINE – *Occupational Costume in England* (London, 1967).

CRANMER, T. – *The Works of Thomas Cranmer* (ed. J.E. Cox) (Cambridge, 1844–6).

GIUSTINIANI, op.cit.

DIGBY, GEORGE WINGFIELD – *Elizabethan Embroidery* (London, 1963).

HEYWOOD, J. – *The Spider and the Flie* (London, 1556).

Holbein and the Court of Henry VIII (Buckingham Palace) (London, 1878–9).

KAULEK, J. – *Correspondance politique de MM. de Castillon et de Marillac 1537–1542* (Paris, 1885).

SPENSER, E. – *The Shepheardes Calender* (London, 1579).

Statutes of the Realm: 3 Edw.IV, c.5; 22 Edw.IV, c.1; 3 Hen.VII, c.13; 4 Hen.VII, c.8, 9; 11 Hen.VII, c.11, 19, 27; 12 Hen.VII, c.1, 4; 19 Hen.VII, c.17; 1 Hen.VIII, c.1, 14; 6 Hen.VIII, c.1, 6; 24 Hen.VIII, c.13; 25 Hen.VIII, c.18; 27 Hen.VIII, c.17; 33 Hen.VIII, c.3, 16, 19; 34 & 35 Hen.VIII, c.11; 37 Hen.VIII, c.15; 1 Edw.VI, c.6; 3 & 4 Edw.VI, c.2; 5 & 6 Edw.VI, c.6, 7, 8, 22, 24; 7 Edw.VI, c.8, 9; 1 Mar., st.2, c.11; 1 Mar., st.3, c.7; 1 & 2 Ph. & M., c.2, 7, 14; 2 & 3 Ph. & M., c.11, 12, 13; 4 & 5 Ph. & M., c.5; 1 Eliz., c.12, 14; 5 Eliz., c.6; 8 Eliz., c.11, 12; 13 Eliz., c.19; 14 Eliz., c.10; 18 Eliz., c.16, 21; 23 Eliz., c.9; 27 Eliz., c.17, 18, 23; 35 Eliz., c.9, 10; 39 Eliz., c.10, 13, 14, 20; 43 Eliz., c.10.

STRONG, R. – *The English Icon: Elizabethan & Jacobean Portraiture* (London, 1969).

VECELLIO, C. – *De gli habiti antichi et moderni di Diuerse Parti del Mondo* (Venice, 1590).

Venetian Calendar

Chapter 8 – FURNITURE AND FOOD

DAVIS, E. – *Furniture* (London, 1962).

DAVIS, FRANK – *A Picture History of Furniture* (London, 1958).

Encyclopaedia Britannica, op.cit.

FOXE, op.cit.

GIUSTINIANI, op.cit.

HENTZNER, op.cit.

JACKSON, SIR CHARLES – *An Illustrated History of English Plate* (London, 1911).

JACKSON, C.J. – 'The Spoon and its History' *Archaeologia*, vol. liii (London, 1892).

JONSON, BEN – *The Works of Ben Jonson* (London, 1875).

LAW, op.cit.

L.P., vols. iii, iv, xvii. xix.

MORICE, op.cit.

MULLER, J.A. – *The Letters of Stephen Gardiner* (Cambridge, 1933).

NICOLAS, H. – *Proceedings and Ordinances of the Privy Council of England* (London, 1834–7).

SHAKESPEARE, op.cit.

SMITH, P. – *Erasmus* (New York, 1923).

Spanish Calendar, vol. i.

Statutes of the Realm: 7 Hen.VII, c.7; 11 Hen.VII, c.19; 19 Hen.VII, c.6; 25 Hen.VIII, c.1; 27 Hen.VIII, c.9; 28 Hen.VIII, c.14; 33 Hen.VIII, c.4, 11; 34 & 35 Hen.VIII, c.7, 10; 35 Hen.VIII, c.8; 2 & 3 Edw.VI, c.19; 3 & 4 Edw.VI, c.21; 5 & 6 Edw.VI, c.3, 14, 27; 7 Edw.VI, c.5; 18 Eliz., c.15; 23 Eliz., c.8; 27 Eliz., c.11; 31 Eliz., c.8.

STRYPE, J. – *The Life and Acts of Matthew Parker* (Oxford, 1821 edn.)

Sussex Archaeological Collections (Lewes, 1955–61) (vols. 93, 96, 99, 152).

Sussex Notes and Queries (Lewes, 1939–50) (vols. 7, 13).

Venetian Calendar.

VICTORIA AND ALBERT MUSEUM – *Elizabethan Art* (London, 1948).

Victoria County History: *Hertfordshire* (London, 1902–14).

WINBOLT, S.E. – *Wealden Glass* (Hove, 1933).

Chapter 9 – HUSBANDRY

FITZHERBERT, (SIR A. ?). – *The Boke of Husbandry.*

— 1st edn. (London, 1523 ?).

— 2nd edn. (London, 1530 ?).

— 3rd edn. (London, 1533 ?).

— 4th edn. (London, 1534).

— 5th edn. (London, 1548).

— 6th edn. (London, 1552 ?).

— 7th edn. (London, 1556 ?).

— 8th edn. (London, 1560 ?).

— 9th edn. (London, 1562 ?).

— 10th edn. (London, 1568).

— 11th edn. (London, 1598).

LATIMER, H. – *The Works of Hugh Latimer* (Cambridge, 1844–5).

L.P., xiii (i). 304, 1263; (ii). 1263.

MORE, SIR T. – op.cit.

PONET, J. – *A shorte treatise of politike power* (Strasbourg, 1556) reprinted in W.S. Hudson, *John Ponet: Advocate of Limited Monarchy* (Chicago, 1942).

POWER, M.J. – 'London and the Control of the "Crisis" of the 1590s' (in *History*, N.S., lxx. 371–85) (Glasgow, 1985).

RAPPAPORT, S. – 'Social structure and mobility in sixteenth century London, Part I' (in *London Journal*, ix. 107–55) (London, 1983).

ROGERS, T. – *History of Agriculture and Prices* (Oxford, 1872).

Statutes of the Realm: 23 Hen.VI, c.12; 11 Hen.VII, c.22; 12 Hen.VII, c.3; 4 Hen.VIII, c.5; 6 Hen.VIII, c.3; 25 Hen.VIII, c.1, 13; 33 Hen.VIII, c.2; 35 Hen.VIII, c.17; 2 & 3 Edw.VI, c.15; 3 & 4 Edw.VI, c.19, 21, 22; 5 & 6 Edw.VI, c.5, 14; 7 Edw.VI, c.7; 2 & 3 Ph. & M., c.3; 1 Eliz., c.15; 5 Eliz., c.2, 4; 23 Eliz., c.5; 27 Eliz., c.19; 31 Eliz., c.7; 39 Eliz., c.1, 2, 12.

Chapter 10 – SCHOLARS AND DOCTORS

CASTIGLIONI, A. – *A History of Medicine* (New York, 1947).

CHILD, F.J. (ed.) – *The English and Scottish Popular Ballads* (New York, 1965 edn.).

COLLINSON, P. – *Archbishop Grindal* (London, 1980).

COOPER, C.H. – *Annals of Cambridge* (Cambridge, 1843).

ELYOT, T. – *The Boke named the Gouernour* (London, 1907 edn.).

—— *The Castel of Helth* (London, 1541).

ERASMUS, D. – *De Pueris Statim ac Liberaliter Instituendis Libellus* in W.H. Woodward, *Desiderius Erasmus concerning the Aim and Method of Education* (Cambridge, 1904).

FULLER, op.cit.

HALL, E. – *Chronicle* (London, 1809 edn.).

HAY, D. – 'Schools and Universities' in *The New Cambridge Modern History*, vol. 2 (Cambridge, 1958).

HENRY VIII – *The Love Letters of Henry VIII* (ed. H. Savage) (London, 1949).

HOLDSWORTH, op.cit.

L.P.

MACNALTY, A.S. – *Henry VIII, a difficult patient* (London, 1952).

MALLET, C.E. – *History of the University of Oxford* (London, 1924–7).

MORICE, op.cit.

MULLER, op.cit.

MULLINGER, J.B. – *The University of Cambridge* (Cambridge, 1873–1911).

RIDLEY, N. – *The Works of Bishop Ridley* (Cambridge, 1841).

ROPER, W. – *The Mirrour of Vertue in Worldly Greatnes* (London, 1903 edn.).

ROWLEY, S. – *When you see me you know me, Or, The famous Chronicle Historie of king Henry the eight* (Oxford, 1952 edn.).

SHAKESPEARE, op.cit.

Statutes of the Realm: 11 Hen.VII, c.12; 3 Hen.VIII, c.11; 28 Hen.VIII, c.14; 32 Hen.VIII, c.40, 42; 34 & 35 Hen.VIII, c.1, 7, 8; 37 Hen.VIII, c.10; 3 & 4 Edw.VI, c.2; 5 & 6 Edw.VI, c.6; 1 Mar., st.2, c.9; 2 & 3 Ph. & M., c.16; 23 Eliz., c.8; 31 Eliz., c.12.

TAWNEY, R.H. – *Religion and the Rise of Capitalism* (London, 1926).

Chapter 11 – SHIPS AND VOYAGES

Calendar of Scottish State Papers, i.620(3).

CHATTERTON, E.K. – *Sailing Ships* (London, 1909).

CHRISTY, M. – 'Queen Elizabeth's Visit to Tilbury in 1588' (*English Historical Review,* xxxiv. 45–61) (London, 1919).

CORBETT, J.S. – *Drake and the Tudor Navy* (London, 1898).

DELONEY, T. – *The Queen . . . at Tilbury* (London, 1588) in E. ARBER, *An English Garner* (London, 1877–96).

DURO, C.F. – *La Armada Invincible* (Madrid, 1885).

GRAHAM, WINSTON – *The Spanish Armadas* (London, 1972).

HAKLUYT, R. – *The Principal Navigations, Voyages, Traffiques & Discoveries of the English Nation* (Glasgow, 1903 edn.).

HOUSTON, A. – *The Romance of the New River: 20th Annual Report to the Metropolitan Water Board* (London, 1926).

HOWARD, op.cit.

LAUGHTON, J.K. – *State Papers relating to the Defeat of the Spanish Armada Anno 1588* (London, 1894).

L.P.

MATTINGLY, G. – *The Defeat of the Spanish Armada* (London, 1959).

MULLER, op.cit.

NEALE, J.E. – *Essays in Elizabethan History* (London, 1958).

RALEIGH, SIR W. – *The Discoverie of the large, rich and bewtifvl Empire of Gviana . . . performed in the yeare 1595 by Sir W. Ralegh, Knight* (London, 1596).

RODRIGUEZ-SALGADO, M.J., and the Staff of the National Maritime Museum – *Armada: An International Exhibition to commemorate the Spanish Armada* (London, 1988).

Statutes of the Realm: 27 Hen.VIII, c.18; 31 Hen.VIII, c.4; 33 Hen.VIII, c.35; 34 & 35 Hen.VIII, c.9, 25; 35 Hen.VIII, c.10; 2 & 3 Ph. & M., c.16; 13 Eliz., c.18; 27 Eliz., c.20.

THOMSON, G.M. – *Sir Francis Drake* (London, 1972).

UMBALDINO, P. – *Expeditionis Hisparorum* (1588).

Chapter 12 – LAW-ENFORCEMENT AND WAR

HALE, J.R. – 'Armies, Navies, and the Art of War' (in *The New Cambridge Modern History*, vol. ii (Cambridge, 1958).
—'Armies, Navies and the Art of War' (in *The New Cambridge Modern History*, vol. iii (Cambridge, 1968).
L.P.
MONTGOMERY OF ALAMEIN, Field-Marshal Viscount – *A History of Warfare* (London, 1968).
O'RAHILLY, A. – *The Massacre at Smerwick* (Cork, 1938).
ROSE-TROUP, FRANCES – *The Western Rebellion of 1549* (London, 1913).
ROSS, CHARLES – *The Wars of the Roses* (London, 1976).
Statutes of the Realm: 3 Hen.VII, c.5; 11 Hen.VII, c.8, 9, 13; 19 Hen.VII, c.10; 22 Hen.VIII, c.7; 23 Hen.VIII, c.16; 25 Hen.VIII, c.11, 22; 26 Hen.VIII, c.4, 5, 11, 12, 26; 27 Hen.VIII, c.5, 6, 26; 32 Hen.VIII, c.8, 13; 33 Hen.VIII, c.5; 34 & 35 Hen.VIII, c.26; 37 Hen.VIII, c.9; 1 Edw.VI, c.5; 3 & 4 Edw.VI, c.5; 5 & 6 Edw.VI, c.20; 1 Mar., st.2, c.12; 4 & 5 Ph. & M., c.2, 3; 1 Eliz., c.7; 5 Eliz., c.19, 22; 8 Eliz., c.16; 13 Eliz., c.8, 22; 27 Eliz., c.12, 13; 31 Eliz., c.12; 39 Eliz., c.25; 43 Eliz., c.13.

Chapter 13 – SPORTS AND PASTIMES

ANGLO, SYDNEY – *The Great Tournament Roll* (London, 1968).
ARBEAU, THOINOT – *Orchesographie* (London, 1588).
BALE, J. – *Kynge Johan: a play* (London, 1838).
BUTLER, S. – *Hudibras* (Cambridge, 1744 edn.).
Calendar of State Papers relating to Ireland during the reigns of Henry VIII, Edward VI, Mary and Elizabeth (ed. H.C. Hamilton, etc.) (London, 1860–1912), vii. 209.
CAVENDISH, op.cit.
CORBETT, op.cit.
ELYOT, – *The Boke named the Gouernour*, op.cit.
Everyman and Medieval Plays (ed. A.C. Cawley) (London, 1956).
HALE, in *The New Cambridge Modern History*, vol. iii.
HALL, op.cit.
HARPSFIELD, N. – *A Treatise on the Pretended Divorce between Henry VIII and Catherine of Aragon* (London, 1878 edn.).
HENTZNER, op.cit.
HUIZINGA, J. – *The Waning of the Middle Ages* (London, 1924).
JONSON, op.cit.

KNOX, op.cit, vol. vi.

LANEHAM, R. – *Robert Laneham's letter; Wherein, part of the entertainment untoo the Queenes Maiesty at Killingworth Castl, in Warwik Sheer in this Soomers Progress, 1575, is signified* (London, 1890).

MACINNES, C.M. – *The Early English Tobacco Trade* (London, 1926).

MARLOWE, C. – *The Plays and Poems of Christopher Marlowe* (London, 1905).

NICHOLS, J. – *The Progresses and Public Processions of Queen Elizabeth* (London, 1823).

SCHELLING, F. – *Elizabethan Drame 1558–1642* (London, 1908).

SHAKESPEARE, op.cit.

— *The Works of Mr William Shakespeare, in six volumes, adorn'd with cuts* (ed. N. Rowe) (London, 1709), Preface.

SHEARMAN, M. – 'Football: History' (in *Football*, ed. Duke of Bedford) (London, 1904).

Statutes of the Realm: 12 Ric.II, c.4; 1 Hen.VII, c.7; 3 Hen.VII, c.9, 14; 4 Hen.VII, c.12; 11 Hen.VII, c.3, 17; 19 Hen.VII, c.2, 4, 11; 3 Hen.VIII, c.3, 13; 6 Hen.VIII, c.2, 13; 24 Hen.VIII, c.10; 25 Hen.VIII, c.17; 31 Hen.VIII, c.2, 12; 32 Hen.VIII, c.8, 11; 33 Hen.VIII, c.6, 9; 2 & 3 Edw.VI, c.14; 3 & 4 Edw.VI, c.17; 5 & 6 Edw.VI, c.25; 2 & 3 Ph. & M., c.9; 8 Eliz., c.10, 15; 13 Eliz., c.14; 23 Eliz., c.10.

STRONG, SIR ROY – *The Cult of Elizabeth* (London, 1977).

TURBERVILE, G. – *The Booke of Faulconrie* (London, 1575).

— *The Noble Arte of Venerie or Hvnting* (no place or date).

YATES, F.A. – *The Valois Tapestries* (London, 1959).

Chapter 14 – BEGGARS AND VAGABONDS

HOLINSHED, R. – *Chronicles of England, Scotland and Ireland* (London, 1807–8 edn.).

L.P.

MARX, K. – *Capital* (London, 1930 edn.).

SHAKESPEARE, op.cit.

Statutes of the Realm: 7 Ric.II, c.5; 11 Hen.VII, c.2; 19 Hen.VII, c.14; 22 Hen.VIII, c.12; 27 Hen.VIII, c.25, 28; 31 Hen.VIII, c.7, 13; 37 Hen.VIII, c.6, 7; 1 Edw.VI, c.3; 3 & 4 Edw.VI, c.16; 5 & 6 Edw.VI, c.2; 2 & 3 Ph. & M., c.5; 5 Eliz., c.3, 20; 14 Eliz., c.5; 18 Eliz., c.3; 35 Eliz., c.4; 39 Eliz., c.3, 4, 5, 17, 21; 43 Eliz., c.2, 3, 7.

Chapter 15 – TUDOR MEN AND WOMEN

BALE, J. – *Select Works of John Bale* (Cambridge, 1849).

BRANTOME, P. DE B. – *Les Dames galantes* (Paris, 1947 edn.).

BRINKELOW, H. (pseud. RODERYCK MORS) – *The Lamētacyon of a Christen agaynst the Cytye of London* (no place, 1545).

BURGESS, ANTHONY – *Shakespeare* (London, 1970).

Chronicle of the Greyfriars of London (ed. J.G. Nichols) (London, 1852).

DEE, M.F. – *British Ballads* (London, 1926).

FOXE, op.cit.

GAYANGOS, P. DE. – *Viaje de Felipe Segundo a Inglaterra* (Madrid, 1877).

HUGGARDE, M. – *The Displaying of the Protestantes* (London, 1556).

London Chronicle in the times of Henry VII and Henry VIII (ed. C. Hopper) (Camden Miscellany No. iv) (London, 1859).

MACHYN, op.cit.

MARGARET OF ANGOULÊME, QUEEN OF NAVARRE – *L'Heptameron* (ed. M. François) (Paris, 1964 edn.).

MORE, SIR T., op.cit.

MOZLEY, J.F. – *John Foxe and his Book* (London, 1940).

Original Letters relative to the English Reformation (ed. H. Robinson) (Cambridge, 1846–7).

PHILPOT, J. – 'Apology of John Philpot written for spitting upon an Arian' (in Strype, Ecclesiastical Memorials, iii (ii) No. XLVIII).

SHAKESPEARE, op.cit.

Statutes of the Realm: 33 Hen.VIII, c.12.

Sussex Archaeological Collections, op.cit.

Venetian Calendar, vi (iii) App. No. 171.

THE EDITORS OF HORIZON MAGAZINE, in consultation with LOUIS B. WRIGHT, Director of the Folger Shakespeare Library – *Shakespeare's England* (London, 1964).

WRIOTHESLEY, op.cit.

Abbreviations

L.P. see *Letters and Papers* etc. in the sources for Chapter 3.

Spanish Calendar see *Calendar of Letters* etc. in the sources for Chapter 1.

Venetian Calendar see *Calendar of State Papers* etc. in the sources for Chapter 1.

INDEX